John Moen

Perspectives in Memory Research

Perspectives in Memory Research

edited by Michael S. Gazzaniga

A Bradford Book
The MIT Press
Cambridge, Massachusetts
London, England

© 1988 Massachusetts Institute of Technology

This book was set in Palatino by Achorn Graphic Services and printed and bound by Halliday Lithograph in the United States of America.

Library of Congress Cataloging-in-Publication Data

Perspectives in memory research.

"A Bradford book."
Bibliography: p.
Includes index.
1. Memory. 2. Neuropsychology. I. Gazzaniga,
Michael S.
BF371.P386 1988   153.1′2   88-8958
ISBN 0-262-07112-6

Contents

Preface

In 1985 I attended a conference at Xerox Park. Its sponsor, the Army Research Institute (ARI), wanted to know what important issues would be facing neurobiology in 2010. Dozens of scientists dealing with all kinds of issues showed up. At the registration table a framed sign in large type blared out, "Xerox Corporation, Think about the future, don't talk about it." After hearing several of the talks, including my own, I began to think that the conferees had engaged in the opposite enterprise. We were all talking about the future, but not many of us were truly thinking about it.

The army has a problem not much different from most organizations with a large work force. The volunteer army is not up to the same standards as the conscripted army. Those who sign up to work for Uncle Sam don't have quite as much going for them as they might. Yet modern weaponry is more complicated than ever. The army is faced with a large gap between the cognitive abilities of their recruits and the cognitive requirements of their equipment. In asking a group of scientists to consider the future, the army was really asking whether neurobiology and cognitive science could help fill this gap. Or to focus in on one aspect of their needs, could neurobiology and cognitive science offer any new tools for enhancing memory skills and thereby improve training?

I was intrigued by this question, and this book, funded by ARI, is to some extent the product of these musings. I asked scholars of the field of memory, with perspectives ranging from cellular analysis of synaptic change to functional analyses of everyday acts of memorizing and remembering, to state briefly where their particular subdiscipline currently stands and where they see it going. In particular, I was interested in any future research that would bear on issues of training. Not surprisingly references to training were few in the submitted chapters. All the contributors are in the forefront of their fields. Although their positions guarantee that their insights into the future of their fields are perceptive, it distances them from more practical concerns. What Bill Hirst and I thought was learned from these perspectives on memory research and how they might ultimately bear on the issues of training is summarized in the final chapter.

In August 1987 I tried to tell ARI what I learned from the assembly of the chapters in this book. Preparing for that talk was not easy. As the discussions in this volume settled into my consciousness, it became clear to me that the problem of memory is going to become a lot more complicated before it becomes clear. Neurobiologists are fascinated by the synapse. Thus, when a synaptic mechanism is unearthed that looks like a potential candidate for "memory," the mechanism is quickly acclaimed by the field as the "key to memory"—almost overnight. Yet, as some neurobiologists realize, the synapse is not the only potential source for permanent change. One could look not at the synapse but at the neuron itself as a key to memory, inasmuch as the mutability of a single neuron is staggering. One could also take a larger perspective and focus not on an individual synapse or neuron but on the circuitry formed by a collection of neurons and synapses. The pattern of the circuit, it is claimed, not the action of individual neurons and synapses, holds the key to memory. Computer scientists nicely underline this claim in their work with connectionist models. They can build a circuit, teach it something, and then look at the circuit to see how each individual node on the circuit has changed. The remarkable thing is that, each time the circuit is turned off and then on again, to restart the learning process, new changes in each node are made. The commonality between the new training trials is not at the level of the individual nodes but in the higher-order organization among nodes.

Problems arise not only in deciding the appropriate level of analysis for the physiological study of memory but also when discussing the psychology of memory. The once simple view that variations in memory capacity can be traced to differences in ease of consolidation is being challenged. There may not be just one form of memory, one form of consolidation. Moreover, variations in memory capacity might reflect individual skills of encoding and retrieval rather than simple differences in consolidation. We do know that memory capacity varies with intelligence. The higher the IQ, the better the memory. What is not known is why. Does the brain that supports a higher IQ have different capacities for memory? Or does the person with a higher IQ naturally acquire more information, and this rich database drives the superior memory? It is surprising that we do not have a definitive answer to these questions, for they seem quite basic.

The rather slim pickings this volume ultimately provides for those concerned with application and training should not be cavalierly dismissed as merely the nature of groundbreaking theoretical research. If I had to assign the blame for the present state of affairs, I would trace it to the limited resources assigned to the study of memory. Only a relatively few scientists are working on the problem. If issues of training are ever to be fully tackled, a major effort must be made to understand memory. The problems of training and, to take a larger perspective, the memory problems associated with aging are national concerns and as such should be tackled at the national level. With sufficient resources the story of memory will finally find itself addressing practical problems.

I
Neurobiologic Considerations in Memory Function

1

Experience and the Biochemistry of Information Storage in the Nervous System

Ira B. Black, Joshua E. Adler, Cheryl F. Dreyfus, Wilma F. Friedman, Edmund F. LaGamma, Arthur H. Roach

The recent application of molecular approaches to the study of neural function has yielded a number of notable advances. For example, contrary to traditional views it is now apparent that single neurons use multiple transmitter signals, that different transmitters are independently expressed and regulated in the same neuron, and that experience alters gene expression in the nervous system. These and related insights are prompting alteration of long-held concepts of brain function. The new approaches are also encouraging a reformulation of some classic problems in the study of cognition. One particularly active area concerns the molecular basis of memory mechanisms.

The theoretical work of Hebb (1949), nearly half a century ago, focused attention on the synapse, the communicative junction between neurons, as the physical locus of learning and memory. Subsequently animal psychology has provided a behavioral framework, defining stimulus-response relationships, the nature and importance of timing in learning, and critical insights concerning the meaning of experimental paradigms themselves (Rescorla and Holland 1982). Another school has provided seminal discoveries by using relatively simple model systems to analyze process and mechanism. Elegant work in the invertebrates *Aplysia* and *Hermissenda* has elucidated cellular mechanisms involved in habituation and memory (Kandel and Schwartz 1982; Farley and Alkon 1985).

Complementary studies in mammals, defining the mechanisms associated with long-term potentiation in the hippocampus, a brain area long associated with mnemonic function (Lynch and Baudry 1984; Lynch 1986), and examining the pathways underlying conditioning of simple reflexes (Thompson 1986), have broadened concepts of learning and memory. Simultaneously the study of human memory in patients with different brain lesions has led to the formulation of new taxonomies of mnemonic function (Squire 1986). Finally, the recent use of computer simulation to analyze the processes of learning and memory has refocused attention on "connectionist" issues, the centrality of functional connections among neuronal arrays in the genesis of information storage (Sejnowski 1986; Sejnowski and Rosenberg 1986).

However, heretofore, the reigning model of memory and the nervous system has been based on a static conception of individual neurons, small neuronal populations, and molecules within neurons. In contrast, current work focusing on molecular transformations within neurons is providing a different, dynamic picture. Critical molecular processes appear to be in constant flux, influenced by environmental stimuli and conditions. Indeed, environmentally induced molecular change appears to constitute one mechanism by which external information is translated into neural language. This plasticity occurs at a fundamental level of neuronal function, alteration of gene expression.

Definition of information storage at the molecular level is yielding new insights about the nature of information processing itself; the new approaches are not simply sketching the characteristics of psychologic memory at another level of function in the nervous system. For example, functionally critical molecules in the peripheral and central nervous systems encode and store environmental information over time, indicating that the potential for mnemonic function is widespread. Consequently the notion that memory is localized exclusively to restricted populations in the brain appears to be ill-framed. Rather, information storage occurs in diverse neural subsystems that subserve entirely different neurophysiological roles. For example, storage over time occurs in the peripheral sympathetic system, which governs cardiovascular function, and in the brain locus ceruleus system, which appears to play a key role in arousal and attention.

In this chapter we examine a number of practical questions of critical importance. What relevant biochemical processes actually do transpire in the nervous system? Can molecular biochemistry contribute to the understanding of information storage in a dynamically organized nerve network? Specifically, can we detect biochemical processes that receive, transduce, encode, store, and transmit environmental information? In turn, how might such biochemical changes translate into long-lasting, altered function of the synapse?

Although a variety of modifications may potentially alter synaptic function, we focus on a single specific category, transmitter plasticity. Emerging evidence indicates that neurotransmitters, the prime agents of synaptic communication, also store information. Simply stated, in this instance the same molecules that govern millisecond-to-millisecond physiological neural function also represent environmental information over time. The molecules that mediate physiological actions such as motor control and coordination simultaneously encode and store environmental information. Normal physiology and "higher functions," such as memory, are inseparable. The mechanisms underlying this unity comprise the subject of this chapter.

Initially we focus on studies performed in the relatively simple and well-defined peripheral nervous system of the rat in vivo and in vitro. We then extend our discussion to the central nervous system to determine whether similar mechanisms regulate brain function. Throughout our inquiry we focus on the mechanisms that translate brief stimuli into relatively long-lasting molecular changes of high specificity and precision.

1.1   Transmitter Plasticity and Information Storage in the Sympathetic System

The peripheral sympathetic nervous system is a relatively well-defined accessible model long used for the study of neural function. In particular, the sympathetic transmitter, norepinephrine (NE), which mediates many of the physiologic consequences of discharge involved in the "fight-or-flight" reaction, has been the focus of intense interest. Classical work characterized the actions of NE and fostered a rather static view of sympathetic function in which impulse activity simply led to well-delineated physiological effects. Current studies now indicate, however, that impulse activity has far-reaching effects of direct relevance to information storage.

Transsynaptic impulse activity elicits long-term changes in the metabolism of NE in postsynaptic sympathetic neurons. Specifically, stressful stimuli, including drugs such as reserpine, or environmental stress that reflexively increases sympathetic discharge biochemically induces tyrosine hydroxylase (TH), the rate-limiting enzyme in NE biosynthesis (figure 1.1) (Kvetnansky 1973; Kvetnansky et al. 1971; Levitt et al. 1965; Mueller et al. 1969). The number of TH molecules actually increases in response to these environmental stimuli (Mueller et al. 1969). Moreover, the increase in TH protein is relatively long-lasting with respect to the inciting stimuli.

In fact, the kinetics of TH induction have been defined in detail and illustrate one molecular basis for information storage. Environmental stress and activation of the sympathoadrenal axis result in a two- to threefold increase in TH in sympathetic neurons within two days,

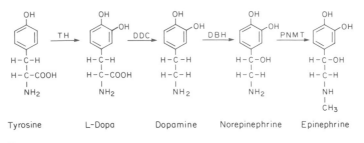

Figure 1.1
Catecholamine biosynthetic pathway. The relevant biosynthetic enzymes are indicated for each reaction. TH, tyrosine hydroxylase; DDC, L-aromatic amino acid decarboxylase (DOPA decarboxylase); DBH, dopamine-β-hydroxylase; PNMT, phenylethanolamine-N-methyltransferase.

and enzyme activity remains elevated for at least three days after increased impulse activity has ceased. In related experiments direct electrical nerve stimulation for thirty to ninety minutes increases TH activity for at least three days (Chalazonitis and Zigmond 1980; Zigmond and Chalazonitis 1979). Thus direct nerve electrical stimulation reproduced the effects of environmental stress and reserpine treatment, supporting the contention that these latter manipulations result in increased impulse flow. In summary, a brief stimulus evokes a long-term neural molecular change, constituting the temporal amplification that must transpire for memory to occur. Moreover, this biochemical alteration is physiologically significant, because the rise in TH catalytic activity results in an increase in NE synthesis. We now have the opportunity to relate environmental stress, altered TH activity, and the sympathetic fight-or-flight behavioral repertoire.

What molecular mechanisms are responsible for this information-storing process? Early work indicated that the transsynaptic induction of TH is inhibited by treatment with cycloheximide or actinomycin D, suggesting that ongoing protein and RNA synthesis are necessary (Mueller et al. 1969). Indeed, immunotitration with a specific antiserum directed against TH indicated that an increase in enzyme molecule number does accompany the transsynaptic increase in catalytic activity (Zigmond et al. 1980). Consequently indirect evidence suggested that increased impulse activity elicited a rise in RNA synthesis and increased TH synthesis with a resultant elevation of NE biosynthesis that persists long after the exciting stimulus has been removed.

The availability of a complementary DNA (cDNA) probe complementary to TH messenger RNA (mRNA) allowed us to test these

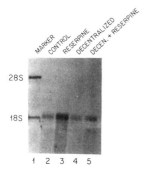

Figure 1.2
Northern blot analysis of TH mRNA in ganglia. Five micrograms of total RNA was denatured and separated by electrophoresis in 1.1% agarose gels containing formaldehyde. RNA was transferred to nitrocellulose, probed with pTH 0.4 and exposed to X-ray film for 2 days. Marker lane, 18S and 28S rRNA; control, vehicle treated, intact; reserpine, reserpine treatment, intact; decentralized, vehicle treated; decentralized + reserpine, denervated and reserpine treated. Data derived from Black et al. (1985).

conjectures experimentally (Black et al. 1985). Our goal was to determine whether transsynaptic impulse activity actually did increase the steady-state levels of mRNA encoding TH. Rats were subjected to unilateral denervation (decentralization) of the sympathetic superior cervical ganglion, and the contralateral ganglion served as a control. The rats were then divided into control and experimental groups. The control group was treated with vehicle, and the experimental group received reserpine, an agent that causes a reflex increase in sympathetic impulse activity. We examined TH mRNA and enzyme activity in the four groups of ganglia: (1) control (intact, vehicle); (2) intact, reserpine; (3) denervated, vehicle; and (4) denervated, reserpine. As expected, reserpine elicited a marked increase in TH enzyme activity, and denervation blocked this risk (Black et al. 1985). In addition, Northern blot analysis indicated that TH mRNA increased markedly in response to reserpine (figure 1.2). Moreover, decentralization prevented this increase, indicating that transsynaptic impulse activity does elicit a specific rise in TH mRNA (figure 1.2). Finally, inspection of the gel indicated that the cDNA probe hybridized to a single band of approximately 1,900 nt in all groups, corresponding to previous results obtained in adrenal medulla (Lewis et al. 1983).

A number of conclusions are warranted. The long-term induction of TH by relatively brief stimuli appears to be mediated by a rise in TH mRNA and increased biosynthesis of TH molecules. In turn, the rise in TH mRNA does not appear to be attributable to altered mRNA processing or to readout of alternative genes, as TH mRNA size is identical in all ganglia. However, because only steady-state levels of mRNA were examined, we cannot yet determine whether the increase was attributable to increased mRNA synthesis (increased gene readout) or to mRNA stabilization. (The issue of stabilization versus synthesis is examined later.) Nevertheless, it is apparent that one form of information storage in sympathetic neurons is dependent on altered expression of specific mRNA coding for transmitter-regulatory molecules. It is now important to determine whether environmental stress and direct nerve stimulation reproduce the effects of pharmacologically induced increases in impulse activity.

1.2 Multiple Transmitters and the Potential for Information Storage

The foregoing experiments indicate that transmitter mutability confers one form of information-storing capacity on the individual neuron. Recent studies, however, indicate that individual neurons are capable of expressing and releasing multiple transmitters simultaneously [for a review see Hokfelt et al. (1986)], vastly augmenting the potential for information storage in the single neuron. Do other transmitter species vary with alteration in impulse activity? If so, do different colocalized transmitters vary independently with environmental stimuli, leading to a variety of potential states representing external reality? These rather complex questions may be approached in the sympathetic system as well.

In addition to the classical transmitters, NE and acetylcholine (ACh), sympathetic neurons also contain neuropeptide transmitters such as substance P (SP) and somatostatin (Kessler et al. 1981, 1983). Moreover, the peptides also respond to transsynaptic activity. Denervation of sympathetic ganglia in vivo or treatment of rats with pharmacological agents that block ganglionic transmission results in a marked increase in SP (Kessler and Black 1982). Conversely activation of sympathetic impulse flow depresses SP (Kessler and Black 1982). In this instance, then, it appears that transsynaptic stimulation decreases the putative postsynaptic transmitter SP.

To analyze underlying molecular mechanisms, ganglia were explanted to the well-controlled culture environment. Explantation and consequent denervation resulted in a fiftyfold rise in SP within four days, and the peptide was localized exclusively to ganglionic neurons (Kessler et al. 1981). SP remained elevated for at least three weeks, the longest time examined. Further, somatostatin, an entirely different peptide, derived from a different precursor molecule, also increased in the denervated explanted ganglia (Kessler et al. 1981). Finally, veratridine, which elicits depolarization by inducing Na^+ influx, completely prevented the rise in SP; tetrodotoxin, which prevents transmembrane Na^+ influx, blocked the veratridine effect (Kessler et al. 1981). Thus depolarizing stimuli suppress SP in culture as in the live animal.

In sum, denervated cultured ganglia exhibit an increase in SP neuropeptide, mimicking the effects of surgical or pharmacological denervation in vivo. Moreover, depolarizing influences prevent the rise in SP. Notably, then, transsynaptic impulse activity apparently affects sympathetic catecholamines and peptides differently. As discussed earlier, we have already begun to analyze mechanisms governing the regulation of catecholaminergic traits.

What molecular mechanisms translate environmental events and membrane depolarization into altered neuropeptide metabolism? To begin approaching this issue, we used a cDNA probe complementary to mRNA coding for the SP precursor protein preprotachykinin (PPT). Initial experiments revealed that PPT mRNA was detectable in the ganglion in vivo, indicating that the low basal levels of SP peptide present in normal ganglia are synthesized endogenously and not transported from an external source (Roach et al. 1985, 1986). We turned our attention to the mechanisms mediating the rise of SP in culture. In fact, PPT mRNA increased before the rise in SP peptide. Specific message increased by 6 hours in culture, reached a plateau by 24 hours, and maintained high levels for at least 1 week, the longest time examined (Roach et al. 1985, 1986, unpublished). Moreover, an identical single band on Northern blot analysis was observed in all groups in which the PPT mRNA was detectable, suggesting that the same species of message was synthesized in basal and explanted denervated ganglia. Consequently the increase in SP peptide after denervation and explantation may well have been mediated by a rise in specific precursor message.

Does membrane depolarization regulate the steady-state levels of PPT mRNA? In fact, veratridine depolarization prevented the rise in PPT mRNA, in a tetrodotoxin-sensitive fashion (figure 1.3). Viewed in conjunction with the in vivo studies, these results suggest that impulse activity with attendant membrane depolarization depresses PPT mRNA, leading to a decrease in PPT precursor peptide synthesis, and a decrease in SP peptide itself. Conversely, decreased impulse activity results in an increase in specific message, precursor peptide, and SP. Note, however, that these sequelae are precisely opposite to effects on TH mRNA, TH enzyme, and NE synthesis. Stated another

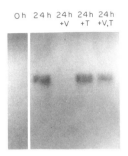

Figure 1.3
Northern blot analysis of PPT mRNA. RNA was extracted from uncultured zero-time ganglia (0 h) or from control ganglia cultured for 24 h with no drug (24 h), $5 \times 10^{-5} M$ veratridine (24 h + V), $10^{-7} M$ tetrodotoxin (24 h + T) or with both veratridine and tetrodotoxin (24 h + V, T). 5 µg of total RNA was used in each sample.

way, the individual sympathetic neuron encodes and stores the same or similar sequences of environmental events differently in different colocalized molecular species.

Consequently multiple molecular species are available in the neuron to code for environmental events over time. Furthermore, at least some of these different transmitter molecules are differentially regulated by external stimuli. In brief, the neuron may employ a combinatorial strategy in which a limited set of elements is used in multiple combinations to generate specificity and diversity in the representation of external influences.

Moreover, these molecules are not simply indifferent repositories of environmental information. Rather, the molecules are central to neural function, regulating communication among neurons in synaptic systems. Stated differently, impulse activity and neuronal depolarization, the very processes that mediate millisecond-to-millisecond function in the nervous system, apparently alter gene expression and the storage of neural information. Although the foregoing experiments suggest that impulse activity and depolarization may directly alter gene expression, indirect mechanisms remain to be examined. For example, even in the relatively simple sympathetic ganglion, impulse activity may affect multiple populations, leading to indirect effects on specific neurons.

Although it appears that impulse activity alters the expression of transmitter-specific genes, the precise intracellular mediating mechanisms remain to be elucidated. It is not yet clear, for example, whether impulse activity primarily affects gene readout itself or regulates message stability in sympathetic neurons. We have been able to approach this issue in the closely related adrenomedullary cell.

1.4   Depolarizing Influences and Gene Readout in the Adrenal Medulla

Parallel studies were undertaken in the adrenal medulla because this tissue is available in quantities adequate to examine gene readout in response to depolarizing influences. Previous experiments had indicated that the opiate peptide enkephalins and catecholamines were colocalized to adrenomedullary cells in a number of species (Schultzberg et al. 1978; Viveros 1979; Lewis et al. 1979; Hexum et al. 1980). A considerable body of evidence already indicates that impulse activity decreases enkephalin synthesis in the rat medulla in vivo (Schultzberg et al. 1978; Lewis et al. 1981; Bohn et al. 1983). We found that surgical denervation of the rat medulla or pharmacological blockade of impulse activity, depriving medullary cells of depolarizing influences in vivo, increased leucine-enkephalin (leu-enk) levels (LaGamma et al. 1984). Following the protocols outlined, we explanted medulla (now denervated) to culture and observed a fiftyfold rise in leu-enk with a concomitant increase in the mRNA encoding the enkephalin precursor [preproenkephalin (PPE) mRNA] (LaGamma et al. 1984, 1985). As expected, depolarizing influences blocked the increases in leu-enk peptide and in PPE mRNA (LaGamma et al. 1984, 1985). None of these regimens altered the activity of colocalized TH.

Thus depolarizing influences prevented the rises in mRNA coding for precursor and in the enkephalin peptide, mimicking mechanisms regulating sympathetic neuropeptides. In both instances steady-state levels of transmitter mRNA were decreased by depolarizing influences. However, in the case of the medulla, we had tissue sufficient to examine gene transcription itself.

To determine whether depolarizing influences alter readout of the PPE gene, nuclear runoff assays were performed (Clayton and Darnell 1983), and nucleotides incorporated into PPE messages were measured (figure 1.4). In fact, depolarization profoundly inhibited transcription of the PPE gene: Incorporation was virtually undetectable, compared to that in baseline denervated controls (figure 1.4). This effect was highly specific, for transcription of the actin gene was unchanged by exposure to depolarizing stimuli. Of even greater interest, transcription of the TH gene was also unaffected, indicating that expression of different neurohumoral genes is differentially regulated by depolarization at the level of gene readout.

Clearly we are just beginning to understand the neural genomic mechanisms that participate in the storage of information in the nervous system, and a multitude of questions remain. It is not even known, for example, whether the phenomenon of depolarization-

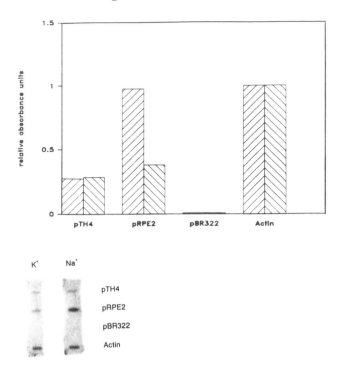

Figure 1.4

Transcription "runoff" assay in adrenal medullas. The rate of transmitter gene transcription was compared in medullas grown for 48 h in standard culture medium (RPMI 1640 supplemented with fetal horse serum and calf serum) plus 50 mM NaCl (Na$^+$) or 50 mM KCl (K$^+$), with minor modifications of published runoff protocols. Briefly, nuclei from ten explanted rat adrenal medullas dissected from the adrenal cortex were obtained by Dounce homogenization (pestle "A") in 0.3 M sucrose plus 0.1% Triton X-100 in 5 mM Hepes (pH 7.4, 1 mM MgCl$_2$), and 1 mM dithiothreitol. Nuclei were pelleted by gentle centrifugation (2,500 g) and washed twice with reaction buffer: 20 mM tris (pH 7.9), 20% glycerol, 140 mM KCl, 10 mM MgCl$_2$, 1 mM MnCl$_2$, and 14.3 mM 2-mercaptoethanol. Nascent RNA chains were labeled in situ with [^{32}P] UTP (3000 mCi/mmol) in reaction buffer plus 20 μg/ml creatine phosphokinase and 10 mM phosphocreatine, 0.5 mM ATP/CTP/GTP for 15 min at 30°C. The reaction was terminated by lysis of nuclei, treatment with ribonuclease-free deoxyribonuclease, proteinase-K, and separation from unincorporated label with a Sephadex G50 column. Labeled RNA chains were randomly cleaved with alkali (1 M NaOH) before hybridization to cloned DNA (pTH 4: tyrosine hydroxylase, pRPE 2: preproenkephalin; pBR 322 vector, or actin immobilized on a nitrocellulose filter) (bottom). Autoradiographs were analyzed by densitometry and recorded in relative absorbance units normalized to actin (top). Left hatched bars represent results from the Na$^+$ treated explants and right hatched bars from K$^+$ treated explants.

regulated gene readout occurs throughout the nervous system. Emerging data suggest, however, that this process is generalized. For example, recent studies indicate that cholinergic stimulation of neuronally differentiated pheochromocytoma PC12 cells rapidly induces transcription of the c-fos proto-oncogene (Greenberg et al. 1986). This observation is of particular interest because c-fos protein appears to regulate nuclear events occurring in response to environmental stimuli that could result in long-term neuronal change (Curran and Morgan 1985; Greenberg et al. 1985; Kruijer et al. 1985).

To summarize, study of the peripheral neurohumoral system is beginning to define molecular mechanisms that mediate the long-term storage of functionally important neural information in response to external stimuli. Depolarization induced by presynaptic signals regulates the steady-state levels of postsynaptic transmitter mRNA, probably by altering gene readout. Brief external events elicit long-term changes in neuronal function. Information about the external world is thereby stored through the very mechanism that serves neuronal intercommunication. Do related processes occur in brain neurons?

1.5 Molecular Plasticity and Information Storage in the Brain

In fact, extensive emerging evidence indicates that brain neurons transduce environmental stimuli into relatively long-lasting transmitter changes. It may be helpful to focus on central catecholaminergic systems, thereby building on our knowledge of peripheral neurons. The locus ceruleus (LC) has been a particularly intensively studied system. These remarkable, bilateral brain stem nuclei innervate structures throughout the neuraxis, projecting rostrally to the cerebral cortex, superiorly to the cerebellar cortex, and inferiorly to multiple segments of the spinal cord [for a review, see Moore and Bloom (1979)]. These neuroanatomical relations allow locus neurons to influence widespread centers in the central nervous system and are integral to information storage, as described in what follows.

The locus has been implicated in setting levels of arousal, attention, and vigilance throughout the nervous system (Aston-Jones and Bloom 1987). According to this view, the tonic release of NE, which occurs during such activities as grooming, sleeping, and eating, conditions the animal to internal vegetative demands. In contrast, phasic release of NE evoked by environmental stimulation prepares the nervous system for attention to external demands. The locus thus globally biases the nervous system toward internal or environmental

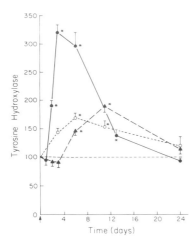

Figure 1.5
Time course of the increases in TH activity in locus ceruleus, cerebellum, and frontal cortex after reserpine treatment. Rats were treated with reserpine (10 mg per kilogram of body weight, subcutaneously) at time zero (arrow) or with saline. At varying times after injection, groups of six control and six reserpine-treated animals were killed, and enzyme activity was assayed in the indicated areas. Results are expressed as percent of respective controls ± SEM (vertical bars). Thus "100" represents enzyme activity in controls, which was 692.5 ± 52.56 pmol L-DOPA/pair · h for the locus ceruleus, 80 ± 6.7 fmol/μg protein · h for the frontal cortex, and 25 ± 1.2 fmol/μg protein · h for the cerebellum. *Differs from respective control at $p < 0.001$. Reprinted with permission from Black (1975).

demands and activities and thereby participates in transitions among behavioral states.

TH occupies a position in LC function that is entirely analogous to that already described in the sympathetic system. As the rate-limiting enzyme, TH determines flux across the NE biosynthetic pathway and consequently the amount of transmitter available for release. The TH enzyme and gene appear to be the same in the brain and the periphery, suggesting that some regulatory molecular mechanisms are common to the periphery and the brain. Indeed, such is the case.

Treatment of rats with reserpine, which is known to induce peripheral sympathetic TH, also induces the enzyme in the LC (Reis et al. 1974; Zigmond et al. 1974) (figure 1.5). After a single dose of reserpine, which is known to act immediately, TH increases 3.5-fold, reaching a peak in the nucleus at approximately 4 days but remaining significantly elevated for at least 2 weeks (Black 1975). Although these

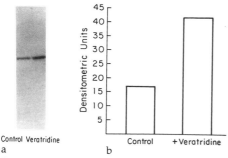

Control Veratridine
a

b

Figure 1.6
(a) Visualization of immunoreactive TH protein extracted from locus ceruleus cultures grown for 1 week and then exposed to control nutrient medium (control) or veratridine supplemented nutrient medium (veratridine) for an additional week. The TH was visualized with a specific antiserum and ^{125}I-labeled protein A. (b) Densitometric analysis. The density of the bands is expressed in arbitrary densitometric units. Reprinted with permission from Dreyfus et al. (1986).

results are provocative, interpretation of the in vivo experiments is difficult; for example, there is no simple, direct way to denervate selectively the locus in the brain stem to determine whether the effect is transsynaptic. In fact, any approach to the brain stem is hazardous, for this area is the crossroad of multiple life-support faculties.

We decided to approach the mechanisms by culturing the LC. The nucleus was grown in explant culture, and the effects of depolarizing agents were examined. Exposure of the explant to veratridine resulted in a significant increase in TH activity, and this rise was blocked by tetrodotoxin (Dreyfus et al. 1986), suggesting that depolarization with attendant Na^+ influx mediated the enzyme increase. Moreover, exposure to elevated K^+ also increased TH activity, suggesting that the effect was attributable to depolarization per se and not to nonspecific effects of a single pharmacological agent (Dreyfus et al. 1986). Was the increase in catalytic activity associated with true enzyme induction, an increase in molecule number, or with activation of preexistent enzyme? To approach this question, we performed immunoblot analysis with a specific antiserum against TH to quantitate enzyme protein after depolarization. TH molecule number was increased by depolarization (figure 1.6), suggesting that impulse activity may increase enzyme molecules in brain neurons, as in the periphery (Dreyfus et al. 1986).

Is the induction of brain TH by depolarizing stimuli dependent on altered gene expression as in the periphery? Indirect evidence suggests that this is the case. Treatment of rats with reserpine elicited over a fourfold increase in the steady-state levels of TH mRNA in the brain nucleus (Biguet et al. 1986). Viewed in conjunction with work already discussed, these observations suggest that depolarization of LC neurons increases TH mRNA with a resultant rise in TH protein synthesis, leading to elevated NE synthesis. Similar or even common molecular events in the brain and periphery may transduce environmental stimuli into neural information. The neural molecular information persists over time, forming the rudiments of a storage system.

1.6 Molecular Information in Other Brain Systems

Is the locus ceruleus peculiar among brain neurons, or do other functionally dissimilar populations alter transmitter metabolism or expression in response to external stimuli? One additional system that we have been studying is the dopaminergic substantia nigra (SN). The SN, which is located in the midbrain, plays a critical role in coordinated movement, and its degeneration leads to Parkinson's disease. Consequently, although catecholaminergic (dopaminergic), the SN serves a neurophysiological role that is entirely different from that of the LC. Yet the SN too exhibits transmitter plasticity in response to external events.

It had been known for some time that increased impulse activity increased nigral TH catalytic activity in vivo. We examined the SN in culture and found that depolarizing stimuli increased TH activity and that this rise could be attributed to an increase in TH enzyme protein, true enzyme induction (Friedman et al. 1985, 1986). Moreover, for the SN we were able to examine the effects of the physiologic presynaptic transmitters because these had been identified: The SN appears to receive an excitatory SP-containing pathway from the striatum (Cuello and Kanazawa 1978). In fact, exposure to a stable analogue of SP, or to substance K (NKA), another active peptide derived from the SP precursor, elevated TH activity and TH molecule number (Friedman et al. 1985, 1986).

We are presently attempting to determine whether the induction of nigral TH is also dependent on increased TH mRNA and whether increased gene readout is involved. Regardless of the underlying mechanisms, it is apparent that diverse central systems exhibit plastic responses to external stimuli, mimicking responses in the periphery. Both the central and the peripheral system are equipped with the molecular machinery to receive, transduce, encode, store, and transmit environmental information.

1.7   Spatial Organization and Information Processing

Thus far we have considered molecular mechanism while largely ignoring the geometry of neurons and their connections. Yet the spatial, neuroanatomical dimension confers special characteristics on the processes under discussion. The peptide transmitters and transmitter enzymes are synthesized within the perikaryon (cell body) and transported through the axon to terminals in different regions. Because axonal transport requires a finite period of time and because different terminals are located at varying distances from the cell body, the temporal profile of transmitter change differs at different synapses even in the same neuron. Synaptic specificity of altered metabolism derives in part from unique neuronal geometry.

The LC serves as a good example because the nucleus innervates widespread populations. After exposure to an external stimulus, TH increases in different LC terminals with different temporal profiles (figure 1.5). In the brain stem perikarya, TH peaks at four days; in the proximate cerebellum it peaks at eight days, and in the distant frontal cortex only after twelve days. Consequently, from a single stimulus leading to a common series of molecular and presumably genomic events in the nucleus, information is related to different terminal fields in distinct fashions. In the present example the cerebellum experiences peak elevation of TH four days before the frontal cortex, potentially leading to entirely different behavioral consequences and profiles in these functionally diverse regions.

It follows that the decay of information will vary with distance from the cell body as well. This contention is supported by comparing the decay of TH in the cerebellum and the frontal cortex (figure 1.5), although a finer-grained analysis is necessary to elucidate this point. Although sequelae must be documented in detail, it is clear that the temporal characteristics of functional neuronal change elicited by the environment are determined by the geometry of the nervous system and by the rules governing molecular interactions.

1.8   Some Implications for Memory Mechanisms

Simply stated, the single neuron is apparently endowed with enough complexity to exhibit the rudiments of mnemonic mechanisms. The cellular processes that sense environmental change, transsynaptic communication, and membrane depolarization set in motion a series of cellular and nuclear mechanisms that constitute information storage. Different patterns of impulse activity presumably will be found to activate and repress different families of genes, leading to different patterns of long-term information storage. Different patterns of activity have already been shown to alter the ratio of colocalized transmitters that are released by neurons (Stjarne and Lundberg 1986; Bartfai et al. 1986).

Although differential kinetics of molecular turnover may lead to differences in information storage by molecules in the same or different neurons, an entirely novel specificity is conferred by neuronal geometry. The topological characteristics of neurons as highly branched structures projecting for vast distances in three-dimensional space transform a neuron-wide event, such as altered gene expression, into multiple events with differing synaptic specificities. Because axonal transport of any molecular species is constant, whereas terminal fields lie at varying distances from the perikaryon, the temporal pattern of molecular changes will differ in different synapses of the same neuron. That is, synaptically selective alteration of function is generated both by the kinetics of molecular processing and by the structure of the neuron and nervous system. Thus a neuronal change may be translated into changes that are specific for individual synapses and reverberating synaptic arrays, as suggested by Hebb (1949).

Our observations indicate that diverse peripheral and central neuronal populations exhibit a biochemistry of information storage. Indeed, persistence of biochemical change may be a general property of neurons and their aggregates. Consequently the potential for mnemonic function may be widely distributed in the nervous system and not restricted to a small number of populations. The particular physiological, behavioral, or cognitive manifestations of information storage may simply reflect the specific neural populations involved.

It should be stressed that the narrow focus on the genome, mRNA, and the transmitter does not necessarily explain how multimodal memories become associated or how some memories persist for decades. However, molecular approaches in conjunction with the elegant molar approaches that are defining information processing at the neural systems level (Mishkin 1982; Mishkin et al., in press; Aggleton and Mishkin 1984) may begin defining higher-order problems in molecular terms. A clearer understanding of molecular plasticity of synapses that connect neurons and their arrays may help integrate mnemonic function in the molecular, cellular, and systems domains.

Acknowledgments

This chapter first appeared in an article in *Science* ["Experience and the biochemistry of information storage in the nervous system" by I. B. Black, J. E. Adler, C. F. Dreyfus, W. F. Friedman, E. F. LaGamma, and A. H. Roach, *Science* (1987), 236:1263–1268].

This work was supported by the National Institutes of Health under grants NS 10259, HD 21208, and NS 20788 and aided by grants from the American Parkinson Disease Foundation, the March of Dimes Birth Defects Foundation, the Dysautonomia Foundation, and the Alzheimer's Disease and Related Disorders Association. Arthur H. Roach is the recipient of a postdoctoral fellowship from the MRC of Canada. Ira B. Black is the recipient of a McKnight Research Project Award. We thank Michael Gazzaniga and L. Festinger for helpful discussions.

References

Aggleton, J. P., and M. Mishkin. 1984. "Projections of the amygdala to the thalamus in the cynomolgus monkey." *Journal of Comparative Neurology* 222:56–68.

Aston-Jones, G., and F. E. Bloom. 1981. "Activity of norepinephrine-containing locus coeruleus neurons in behaving rats anticipates fluctuations in the sleep-waking cycle." *Journal of Neuroscience* 1:876–886.

Bartfai, T., K. Iverfeldt, E. Brodin, and S.-O Ogren. 1986. "Functional consequences of coexistence of classical and peptide neurotransmitters," in *Progress in Brain Research. Vol. 68, Coexistence of Neuronal Messengers: A New Principle in Chemical Transmission*, T. Hokfelt, K. Fux, and B. Pernod, eds. Amsterdam: Elsevier, 321–330.

Biguet, N. F., M. Buda, A. Lamouroux, D. Samolyk, and J. Mallet. 1986. "Time course of the changes of TH mRNA in rat brain and adrenal medulla after a single injection of reserpine." *EMBO*, 5:287–291.

Black, I. B. 1975. "Increased tyrosine hydroxylase activity in frontal cortex and cerebellum after reserpine." *Brain Research* 95:170–176.

Black, I. B., D. M. Chikaraishi, and E. J. Lewis. 1985. "Trans-synaptic increase in RNA coding for tyrosine hydroxylase in a rat sympathetic ganglion." *Brain Research* 339:151–153.

Bohn, M. C., J. A. Kessler, L. Glightly, and I. B. Black. 1983. Appearance of enkephalin-immunoreactivity in rat adrenal medulla following treatment with nicotinic antagonists or reserpine." *Cell Tissue Research* 231:469–479.

Chalazonitis, A., and R. E. Zigmond. 1980. "Effects of synaptic and antidromic stimulation on tyrosine hydroxylase activity in the rat superior cervical ganglion." *Journal of Physiology* 300:525–538.

Clayton, D. F., and J. E. Darnell, Jr. 1983. "Changes in liver specific compared to common gene transcription during primary culture of mouse hepatocytes." *Molecular and Cell Biology* 3:1552–1561.

Cuello, A. C., and I. Kanazawa. 1985. "The distribution of substance P immunoreactive fibers in the rat central nervous system." *Journal of Comparative Neurology* 178:129–135.

Curran, T., and J. I. Morgan. 1985. "Superinduction of c-fos by nerve growth factor in the presence of peripherally active benzadiazepines." *Science* 229:1265–1268.

Dreyfus, C. F., W. J. Friedman, K. A. Markey, and I. B. Black. 1986. "Depolarizing stimuli increase tyrosine hydroxylase in the mouse locus coeruleus in culture." *Brain Research* 379:216–222.

Farley, J., and D. L. Alkon. 1985. "Cellular mechanisms of learning, memory, and information storage." *Annual Review of Psychology* 36:419–494.

Friedman, W. J., C. F. Dreyfus, B. S. McEwen, and I. B. Black. 1985. "Depolarizing signals increase tyrosine hydroxylase development in cultured mouse substantia nigra." *Society for Neuroscience Abstracts* 11:1141.

Friedman, W. J., C. F. Dreyfus, B. S. McEwen, and I. B. Black. 1986. "Substance regulates tyrosine hydroxylase in cultured embryonic mouse substantia nigra." *Society for Neuroscience Abstracts* 12(1):378.

Greenberg, M. E., L. A. Greene, and E. B. Ziff. 1985. "Nerve growth factor and epidermal growth factor induce rapid transient changes in proto-oncogene transcription in PC 12 cells." *Journal of Biological Chemistry* 260:14101–14110.

Greenberg, M. E., E. B. Ziff, and L. A. Greene. 1986. "Stimulation of neuronal acetylcholine receptors induces rapid gene transcription." *Science* 234:80–83.

Hebb, D. O. 1949. *The Organization of Behavior.* New York: Wiley.

Hexum, T. D., H.-Y. T. Yang, and E. Costa. 1980. "Biochemical characterization of enkephalin-like immunoreactive peptides of adrenal glands." *Life Science* 27:1211–1216.

Hokfelt, T., K. Fux, and B. Pernow, eds. 1986. *Progress in Brain Research. Vol. 68, Coexistence of Neuronal Messengers: A New Principle in Chemical Transmission.* Amsterdam: Elsevier.

Kandel, E. R., and J. H. Schwartz. 1982. "Molecular biology of learning modulation of transmitter release." *Science* 218:433–443.

Kessler, J. A., and I. B. Black. 1982. "Regulation of substance P in adult rat sympathetic ganglia." *Brain Research* 234:182–187.

Kessler, J. A., J. E. Adler, W. O. Bell, and I. B. Black. 1983. "Substance P and somatostatin metabolism in sympathetic and special sensory ganglia *in vitro.*" *Neuroscience* 9:309–318.

Kessler, J. A., J. E. Adler, M. C. Bohn, and I. B. Black. 1981. "Substance P in principal sympathetic neurons: Regulation by impulse activity." *Science* 214:335–336.

Kruijer, W., D. Schubert, and I. M. Verma. 1985. "Induction of the proto-oncogene fas by nerve growth factor." *Proceedings of the National Academy of Sciences USA* 82:7330–7334.

Kvetnansky, R. 1973. "Trans-synaptic and humoral regulation of adrenal catecholamine synthesis in stress," in *Frontiers in Catecholamine Research,* E. Usdin and S. Snyder, eds. New York: Pergamon Press, 223–229.

Kvetnansky, R., G. P. Gewirtz, V. K. Weise, and I. J. Kopin. 1971. "Catecholamine-synthesizing enzymes in the rat adrenal gland during exposure to cold." *American Journal of Physiology* 220:928–931.

LaGamma, E. F., J. E. Adler, and I. B. Black. 1984. "Impulse activity differentially regulates leu-enkephalin and catecholamine characters in the adrenal medulla." *Science* 224:1102–1104.

LaGamma, E. F., J. E. White, J. E. Adler, J. E. Krause, J. F. McKelvy, and I. B. Black. 1985. "Depolarization regulates adrenal preproenkephalin mRNA." *Proceedings of the National Academy of Sciences USA* 82:8252–8255.

Levitt, M., S. Spector, A. Sjoerdsma, and S. Udenfriend. 1965. "Elucidation of the rate-limiting step in norepinephrine biosynthesis in the perfused guinea-pig heart." *Journal of Pharmacology and Experimental Therapeutics* 148:1–8.

Lewis, E. J., A. W. Tank, N. Weiner, and D. M. Chikaraishi. 1983. "Regulation of tyrosine hydroxylase mRNA by glucocorticoid and cyclic AMP in a rat pheochromocytoma cell line: Isolation of a cDNA clone for tyrosine hydroxylase mRNA." *Journal of Biological Chemistry* 258:14632–14637.

Lewis, R. V., A. S. Stern, J. Rossier, S. Stein, and S. Udenfriend. 1979. "Putative enkephalin precursors in bovine adrenal medulla." *Biochemistry, Biophysics and Research Communications* 89:822–829.

Lewis, R. V., A. S. Stern, D. L. Kilpatrick, L. D. Gerber, J. Rossier, S. Stein, and S. Udenfriend. 1981. "Marked increases in large enkephalin-containing polypeptides in the rat adrenal gland following denervation." *Journal of Neuroscience* 1:80–82.

Lynch, G. 1986. *Synapses, Circuits and the Beginnings of Memory.* Cambridge, Mass.: MIT Press.

Lynch, G., and M. Baudry. 1984. "The biochemistry of memory: A new and specific hypothesis." *Science* 224:1057–1063.

Mishkin, M. 1982. "A memory system in the monkey." *Philosophical Transcriptions of the Royal Society of London,* sec. B, 298:85–95.

Mishkin, M., B. Malamut, and J. Bachevalier. In press. "Memories and habits: Two neural systems," in *The Neurobiology of Learning and Memory,* J. L. McGaugh, G. Lynch, and N. M. Weinberg, eds. New York: Guildford Press.

Moore, R. Y., and F. E. Bloom. 1979. "Central catecholamine neuron systems: Anatomy and physiology of the norepinephrine and epinephrine systems." *Annual Reviews of Neuroscience* 2:113–168.

Mueller, R. A., H. Thoenen, and J. Axelrod. 1969a. "Compensatory increase in adrenal tyrosine hydroxylase activity after chemical sympathectomy." *Science* 162:468–469.

Mueller, R. A., H. Thoenen, and J. Axelrod. 1969b. "Inhibition of trans-synaptically increased tyrosine hydroxylase activity by cycloheximide and actinomycin D." *Molecular Pharmacology* 5:463–469.

Reis, D. J., T. H. Joh, R. A. Ross, and V. M. Pickel. 1974. "Reserpine selectively increases tyrosine hydroxylase and dopamine-β-hydroxylase enzyme protein in central noradrenergic neurons." *Brain Resesarch* 81:380–386.

Rescorla, R. A., and P. C. Holland. 1982. "Behavioral studies of associative learning in animals." *Annual Reviews of Psychology* 33:265–308.

Roach, A. H., J. E. Adler, and I. B. Black. 1986. "Pattern of expression of the preprotachykinin gene in the rat superior cervical ganglion." *Society for Neuroscience Abstracts* 12(1):278.

Roach, A., J. E. Adler, and I. B. Black. 1987. "Depolarizing influences regulate preprotachykinin mRNA in sympathetic neurons." *Proceedings of the National Academy of Sciences USA* 84:5078–5081.

Roach, A., J. E. Adler, J. Krause, and I. B. Black. 1985. "Depolarization regulates the level of preprotachykinin messenger RNA in the cultured superior cervical ganglion." *Society for Neuroscience Abstracts* 11(1):669.

Schultzberg, M., J. M. Lundberg, T. Hokfelt, L. Terenius, J. Brandt, R. P. Elde, and M. Goldstein. 1978. "Enkephalin-like immunoactivity in gland cells and nerve terminals of the adrenal medulla." *Neuroscience* 3:1169–1186.

Sejnowski, T. J. 1986. "Open questions about computation in cerebral cortex," in *Parallel Distributed Processing: Explorations in the Microstructure of Cognition. Vol. 2, Applications,* J. L. McClelland and D. E. Rumelhart, eds. Cambridge, Mass.: MIT Press, A Bradford Book.

Sejnowski, T. J., and C. R. Rosenberg. 1986. *NETalk: A Parallel Network That Learns to Read Aloud.* Technical Report JHU/EECS-86-01. Baltimore, Md.: Johns Hopkins University, Electrical Engineering and Computer Science Department.

Squire, L. R. 1986. "Mechanisms of memory." *Science* 232:1612–1619.

Stjarne, L., and J. M. Lundberg. 1986. "On the possible roles of noradrenaline, adenosine 5'-tuphosphate, and neuropeptide Y as sympathetic co-transmitters in the mouse vas deferens," in *Progress in Brain Research. Vol. 68, Coexistence of Neuronal Messengers: A New Principle in Chemical Transmission,* T. Hokfelt, K. Fux, and B. Pernow, eds. Amsterdam: Elsevier, 263–278.

Thompson, R. F. 1986. "The neurobiology of learning and memory." *Science* 233:941–948.

Viveros, O. H., E. J. Diliberto, E. Hazum, and K.-J. Change. 1979. "Opiate-like materials in the adrenal medulla: Evidence for storage and secretion with catecholamines." *Molecular Pharmacology* 16:1101–1108.

Zigmond, R. E., and A. Chalazonitis. 1979. "Long-term effects of preganglionic nerve stimulation on tyrosine hydroxylase activity in the rat superior cervical ganglion." *Brain Research* 164:137–152.

Zigmond, R. E., A. Chalazonitis, and T. Joh. 1980. "Pre-ganglionic nerve stimulation increases the amount of tyrosine hydroxylase in the rat superior cervical ganglion." *Neuroscience Letters* 20:61–65.

Zigmond, R. E., F. Schon, and L. L. Iversen. 1974. "Increased tyrosine hydroxylase activity in the locus coeruleus of rat brain stem after reserpine treatment and cold stress." *Brain Research* 70:547–552.

2

Structure-Function Relationships in the Organization of Memory

Gary Lynch and Michel Baudry

Historically the neurobiological study of memory has been concerned with two topics: the mechanisms of storage and the sites at which storage occurs. Work in the first area typically deals with various types of synaptic changes that might account for the persistence of memory and the chemical mechanisms responsible for these changes. Increasingly specific hypotheses about the substrates and causes of memory are being developed from experiments with invertebrates and, more recently, from analyses of hippocampal long-term potentiation.

Work on the sites of storage in the brain falls into two categories. In the first, physiological techniques are used to follow the flow of activity through neuronal pathways with the goal of localizing sites at which learning modifies communication between cells. Progress has been made in this area, again most notably in studies using invertebrates (Kandel and Schwartz 1982; Alkon 1984; Gelperin et al. 1986) but also in recent and elegant work on lower brain regions of mammals (Thompson 1986). As expected, progress in "higher" brain regions (teleodiencephalon) has proven more difficult: Systems likely to be involved in learning have been identified (Cohen 1980; Weinberger 1982; Woody 1982), but linkages between particular groups of synapses and specific encoding episodes remain to be established.

The other approach to the "where" of memory uses lesions in laboratory animals or brain damage in humans as a starting point and asks whether individual brain regions are especially critical to the encoding, storage, and retrieval aspects of memory (Mishkin et al. 1984; Squire 1986). Experiments of these types have resulted in the increasingly popular idea that the hippocampus and the midline thalamus [and especially the dorsomedial nucleus (DMN)] play critical roles in the formation if not the storage of memory. This work has also served to reinforce a major conclusion drawn from cognitive psychology, namely, that the brain supports distinctly different types of memory systems, a vital point for the entire endeavor to analyze memory in terms of its neurobiological underpinnings.

There is a third level intermediate between the mechanistic and regional analyses at which memory might be explored. This involves studies of the neuronal circuitries lying within and between brain regions with the goal of identifying network characteristics (physiological properties, density of interconnections, types of cells, etc.) responsible for the phenomenology of memory. The network approach has been used little, at least in studies of mammals, probably because brain circuitries, particularly in the cortex where much of memory, at least in humans, is thought to lie, are complex and often poorly defined. But as advances continue in the understanding of the cellular neurobiology and regional dependencies of memory in the mammalian brain, the need for circuit-level analyses becomes ever more acute, especially if an integrative theory is to be achieved. An additional reason for beginning discussions of circuitries with memory capacities is the rapid progress being made by researchers using computer simulations of theoretical neuronal networks [see McClelland and Rumelhart (1986) for reviews by several workers]. The hypotheses and conclusions emerging from this field add an important and fascinating dimension to discussions of actual brain networks.

In an earlier paper a tentative effort was made to evaluate a series of forebrain projections in terms of their memory-related network properties (Lynch 1986). The argument was made that of the sensory modalities only olfaction possesses the simplicity required for circuit analyses while retaining the essential linkages (for example, with the hippocampus and the DMN) and features (cortical dependency) that characterize mammalian memory systems. Several conclusions were drawn from that discussion, among the most important of which was that the olfactory projections pass through a series of quite different circuitries and that these produce different types of memory. Here we extend the earlier speculations on olfactory networks and focus on the hippocampal formation. Our goals are (1) to illustrate the point that enough is known about the anatomy, physiology, and connections of this structure to begin developing hypotheses about how network features dictate memorial properties and (2) to identify missing information needed for developing formal theories. We use preliminary hypotheses to emphasize these points and (hopefully) to demonstrate the potential utility of a network approach to memory. The discussion will move from "macro" considerations, suggesting links between particular brain regions and various aspects of olfactory memory, to an analysis of specific networks in the hippocampus.

2.1   Olfaction as a Model for Studying Memory in Cortical-Subcortical Networks

Advantages of the Olfactory System

It is generally held that systems responsible for encoding and processing of certain types of memory in mammals are found in the forebrain, most notably in the cortex, the subcortical telencephalon, and certain areas of the diencephalon. Damage to particular areas in these regions can produce severe deficits in learning and memory that occur without gross changes in sensory and motor processes (Squire 1986).

The argument for using olfaction as a model for the study of memory in mammals is straightforward. Olfactory networks are centered in the forebrain, possess intimate connections with regions thought to be critical to memory processing, and are far simpler in design than the systems subserving other sensory modalities. Simplicity is meant here in both the "macro" sense of the number of anatomical stages involved in processing environmental events and storing representations of them and in the "micro" sense of the anatomical circuitries within each of those stages. Given this simplicity, it is possible to develop ideas about the relationship of particular structures to particular aspects or types of memory, ideas that are, at least to a degree, testable using conventional lesion and recording technologies.

Related to the simplicity point, the olfactory system is unique in the directness of its connections with the hippocampus and certain other structures thought to be crucial to memory processing. The primary olfactory cortex is only two synapses removed from the physical stimulus for smell and projects directly (monosynaptically) into the hippocampus, midline thalamus, and frontal cortex. Olfaction is the only sensory modality that provides anything like direct access to these structures and therefore should be especially useful in dissecting their roles in memory storage and retrieval. The internal anatomy of the various links in the chain of olfactory structures is also somewhat simpler than is the case of the other sensory systems. The primary cortex contains fewer layers than does the neocortex and is not the target of major inputs from subcortical and cortical regions. In part because of this it has been possible for neuroanatomists to provide quite detailed descriptions of the afferents, efferents, and associational projections of the first stage of cortex processing olfactory information [see Lynch (1986) and references therein]. This simplicity is needed for application of neurobiological methods and for the testing of cellular hypotheses about memory storage; it also allows for the development of realistic computer simulations required for network theories of memory.

Another advantage of olfaction for studies of memory is that its basic anatomy is quite conservative. The same fundamental organization has been reported for a variety of species from several orders of mammals. It is thus reasonable to assume that recognition and simple associative olfactory memory in humans involve much of the same circuitry as they do in other mammals, something that is more problematic in the other sensory modalities.

To elaborate this point, there is reason to suspect that the tremendous expansion and elaboration of the neocortex in mammals with large brains is accompanied by changes in the way even simple visual and auditory information is processed. Rats with massive damage to the visual cortex are capable of solving simple visual problems, whereas humans cannot even detect the sensory cues; a similar disjunction between common laboratory animals and humans occurs in auditory, tactile, and motor systems. The simple and evolutionarily conserved anatomy of the olfactory system suggests that this would not hold for olfaction, and rats with massive damage to the olfactory cortex exhibit profound deficits in all aspects of olfactory behavior. Using a system in which we can assume a considerable degree of commonality between rats and humans should simplify the task of applying the rich literature on memory found in cognitive psychology to neurobiological studies of memory.

The major reservation to using olfaction to study a ubiquitous phenomenon such as memory is that so much about smell is atypical. However, although the sensory transducers for all senses are highly specialized, the organization and function of the olfactory cortex itself may reflect general principles present in the neocortex. In fact, an argument can be made that evolutionary pressures related to olfaction were in part responsible for the enormous expansion of the cortex that is the hallmark of mammalian brain evolution (Jerison 1973; Lynch 1986; and references therein).

Aspects of Olfactory Memory

To establish the point that the olfactory system can be used as a model to study general features of mammalian (including human) memory, it is necessary to show that memories for odors exhibit properties common to all systems. In this section we briefly summarize evidence pertinent to this point. In addition, we attempt to identify aspects of olfactory memory that might reflect the operation of different brain regions and networks.

Contemporary psychologists hold that qualitatively different types of memory are operative in human and perhaps animal behavior. It is common to distinguish memories for facts or data (names, faces) from memories for procedures or rules (sequences of acts) (Anderson 1976; Tulving 1983; Rolls 1984; Mishkin et al. 1984; Schacter 1985; Squire 1986). Among many other differences, memory of the first type is rapidly acquired, whereas memory of the second type requires considerable training.

The idea that multiple stages are involved in learning, with the interaction of different memory systems, is also a theme that runs through much of modern animal psychology (for example, learning set formation in primates). The relationship between the fact/procedure dichotomy of the cognitive psychologists and the different stages involved in forming and using learning sets in animals has not been made explicit by theorists but seems inevitable.

Multiple stages are evident in olfactory learning, a point first made by Slotnick and his colleagues (Slotnick and Katz 1974). Multiple stages were also apparent in behavioral experiments conducted in our laboratory. In those studies rats were trained on series of odor pairs in a radial maze composed of eight alleys pointing outward from a central area. An animal would be placed in one arm and allowed to enter a central position. It then had to choose between two arms from which different odors originated; the position of the odors varied randomly from trial to trial. The reward for transversing the correct arm was water; a flashing light signaled an incorrect response. The rats were first familiarized with the maze and taught that water rewards were to be found at the ends of the alley arms. Acquisition of the first odor pair required as much as two hours of training and thirty to fifty trials. Over successive days, with different odor pairs used on different days, the rats became expert at the task and learned to distinguish the odors in about five trials (Staubli et al. 1986). This type of learning resembles primate learning set formation. That is, on the first several days of testing the rats appeared to acquire information about how to solve the problem (that odors are the pertinent cues, as opposed to spatial or intramaze information, that one of two odors is correct, that rapid decisions and responses are necessary, and so forth) and then used this information to learn discriminations rapidly on subsequent days.

Further studies of this simple problem provided considerable information about what was being learned and remembered and added support to the idea that primatelike learning sets were involved. Note that the rats could have mastered the problem in several ways, some of which do not require long-term memory. For example, they could simply learn the correct odor on the first one or two trials and then respond to it on successive trials on a given day; in essence, they did not need to "know" the incorrect odor to perform perfectly well. Moreover, the task did not require the rats to remember individual odors or their valence from one day to the next, and thus short-term memory (the memory lasting from trial to trial) was sufficient for solving the discrimination. In all, a short-lasting memory system for one odor would have been the most economical procedure for dealing with the problem. But in fact the rats learned both correct and incorrect odors and stored stable memories of them. This was made clear when the animals were tested after delays of at least twenty-four hours and then confronted with either the previously positive or negative odor paired with a novel cue. To test the strength of the memories, the significance of the previously learned odor was reversed relative to the new cue ("hemireversal"). Under these conditions the animals would, on retesting, continue to approach formerly positive and avoid formerly negative odors for five to ten trials (Staubli et al. 1986).

The memory of specific odors as studied in the experiments bears a number of resemblances to the fact memory category of cognitive psychologists. It is rapidly acquired (as noted) but is retained for long periods, as evidenced by the observation that rats retain excellent memory of individual odors for at least one month. The capacity of the data memory system, at least in humans (Standing 1973) and monkeys (Overman and Doty 1980) is enormous. This also appears to be true for olfactory memory in rats because they were able to learn thirty pairs of odors with no evidence of confusion (Staubli, Fraser et al. 1987). Finally, Tulving (1983) makes the important point that fact memory (or "semantic" memory in his classification scheme) possesses a gestaltlike property such that the psychological representation of a complex cue has a unitary property to it. To test if this is true for olfactory memory, rats were required to discriminate between complex odors that shared two of three components. It was reasoned that, if the animals stored unitary representations of these, they would not learn the single component that distinguished the two odors. This prediction was confirmed (Staubli, Fraser et al. 1986).

In the following sections we propose that olfactory memory includes the following components: (1) a neural representation of the stimulus, (2) linkages of this with motoric response patterns, (3) association of odor representations with objects and environments, and (4) linkages between environmental context and odors. The discussion will attempt to show that these components of memory are mediated by different links in the chain of olfactory connections running through the teleodiencephalon and reflect the connections and organization of those links.

It will be noted that one evident element of olfactory memory has not been included in our list: the association of olfaction with emotional and visceral responses. One might expect this component to involve the amygdala and hypothalamus, but the anatomy of the pertinent connections is, we suspect, too poorly understood to conduct even the qualitative analysis we are pursuing here.

2.2   Linking Brain Regions to Aspects of Olfactory Memory

Overview of Olfactory Projections through the Forebrain

The pathways by which olfactory information travels through the teleodiencephalon have been reviewed at length elsewhere [see Shepherd (1979) for an excellent summary; also Lynch (1986)] and is only briefly summarized here; later sections provide additional detail. The odor receptors in the nasal epithelium are simply modified dendrites of adjacent neurons, the axons of which collect together and enter the brain as the first cranial nerve. These primary fibers terminate in the olfactory bulb, a brain structure lying beneath the frontal lobes, where they synapse on the mitral cells. These neurons form a layer that encircles the bulb and projects into the lateral olfactory tract (LOT), the output pathway of the bulb. There are subtypes of mitral cells, and recent studies indicate the presence of regional interrelationships between certain groups of these (Shepherd, this volume). There is considerable evidence for the existence of a crude topography between the receptor sheet and the bulb, and specific odors do produce metabolic responses in the bulb that are restricted to patches (Jourdan 1982; Lancet et al. 1982). Thus it is widely thought that odors are, to some degree at least, initially coded in a spatial dimension in the bulb.

The mitral cells sit atop a dense layer of inhibitory granule cells, and a variety of other interneuron types are found in the various layers of the bulb. These are matters that cannot be discussed here, but there is every possibility for complex processing in the bulb [see Freeman (1981, 1987) for some intriguing ideas]. We should also note that the bulb receives inputs from several brain regions and that its operations are undoubtedly regulated by activities in forebrain areas, including some of those to be discussed later.

The fibers of the LOT travel on the ventral and ventrolateral (in small brains) surfaces of the brain and emit collaterals over a wide area that collectively can be considered the olfactory cortex. This in-

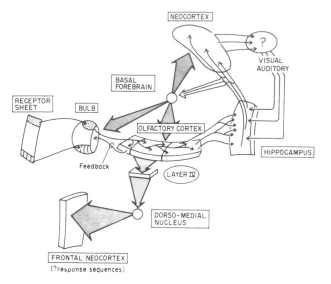

Figure 2.1
Schematic relationships between olfactory structures and cortical and subcortical structures. Solid arrows relate to the flow of information from the olfactory receptors to the bulb to the olfactory cortex and the hippocampus. Shaded arrows indicate either the convergence or divergence of the pathways.

cludes five regions: the anterior olfactory "nucleus," the periamygdaloid cortex, the olfactory peduncle, the pyriform cortex, and the entorhinal cortex (figure 2.1). The last two, which in many respects form a unit, are of primary interest here.

Both cortices possess a superficial layer of cells (layer II) that is monosynaptically innervated by the LOT. A broad layer of heterogeneous cells (layer IV) is also present in both the pyriform and entorhinal cortices. In the pyriform cortex these receive what appears to be a dense projection from layer II and III cells and in turn project to the medial segment of the DMN of the thalamus. The DMN then sends a projection to a segment of frontal cortex lying alongside the rhinal sulcus (hence "sulcal" cortex), the boundary between the neocortex and the paleocortex. The olfactory pathway thus enters the pyriform cortex and, through the deep layer cells, enters into a thalamocortical network. Layer II pyriform cells also generate a commissural-associational system that terminates on the dendrites of layer II cells in the pyriform and entorhinal cortex as well as the sulcal frontal cortex.

The entorhinal cortex is somewhat different. The layer II cells there, as in the pyriform cortex, generate a commissural-associational system but also send a massive projection known as the lateral perforant path into the dentate gyrus of the hippocampal formation (Raisman et al. 1965; Zimmer 1971; Steward 1976; Steward and Scoville 1976; Wyss 1981; Schwartz and Coleman 1981). These fibers together with a comparable projection from the adjacent, nonolfactory medial entorhinal cortex constitute the great majority (>90%) of all extrinsic afferents of the hippocampal formation. The deep layers of the entorhinal cortex do not appear to receive a large input from the superficial layer II cells but instead are innervated by the hippocampus; they project to the neocortex, particularly to zones neighboring the entorhinal cortex, and to the medial frontal areas (Swanson and Kohler 1986).

The hippocampal formation can be broken into four successive segments: the dentate gyrus, field CA3, field CA1, and the subiculum. The granule cells of the dentate gyrus innervate the field CA3 as well as a scattered group of polymorph cells in the hilus (the area contained within the C formed by the dentate gyrus) by means of the peculiar mossy fiber system. The polymorph neurons project back bilaterally to the granule cells.

Field CA3 is composed of giant pyramidal cells that emit axons that repeatedly collateralize. Some of these collaterals leave the hippocampus in an anterior direction to innervate the lateral septum and the basal forebrain; others ramify extensively within CA3 to form a dense commissural-associational plexus that extends into field CA1 as the Schaffer-commissural system. The Schaffer-commissural projections provide the only major input to the small pyramidal cells that form the field CA1. Recent studies have shown that the Schaffer axons also continue into the subiculum and the deep layers of the entorhinal cortex, thereby linking CA3 with the retrohippocampal cortex (Swanson et al. 1981).

Field CA1 is unique in that it does not possess a commissural-associational feedback system of its own—in every sense CA1 appears as a relay dominated by the field CA3. The majority of its axons terminate in the subiculum and deep layers of the entorhinal cortex; CA1 also sends a small projection anteriorly into the lateral septum and basal forebrain.

The subiculum generates a massive projection that travels in the fornix to the anterior thalamic nuclei and the mammillary bodies lying at the posterior edge of the hypothalamus (Swanson and Cowan 1975, 1977; Chronister et al. 1975; Meiback and Seigel 1975, 1977).

The hippocampal formation also receives a collection of sparse cholinergic inputs from the medial septal nucleus and catecholaminergic (Loy et al. 1980) and serotoninergic (Moore and Halaris 1975) fibers from the brain stem; small projections also arrive from under the hypothalamus and thalamus. Some of these connections, notably those from the septum and the brain stem are concentrated in the hilar region of the dentate gyrus with smaller projections elsewhere. There is reason to believe that these inputs, at least in the dentate gyrus, are to a considerable degree targeted for interneurons and possibly polymorph cells (Lynch et al. 1978).

To summarize, the olfactory projections from the bulb enter the pyriform-entorhinal cortex from which two large-scale systems emerge, one centered on the thalamus and cortex and the other running through the hippocampus to the basal forebrain and cortex. In the following sections we consider the possible roles of those subsystems in olfactory memory.

The Pyriform Cortex

We assume that the pyriform cortex assembles a unitary representation from the patches of bulbar cells activated by particular odors and thereby serves as the substrate of recognition memory for the olfactory system. The enormous capacity of recognition memory implies that its storage sites contain a large number of cells, a requirement that favors cortex or possibly hippocampal links in the olfactory circuitry. The hippocampus seems to be ruled out as the primary site of recognition memory because lesions that separate it from olfactory inputs do not interfere with the ability of rats to recognize odors learned before surgery. Moreover, physiological experiments have shown that electrical stimulation of the lateral olfactory tract when used as an odor cue produces changes in the responses generated by LOT synapses in the layer II cells in the pyriform cortex (Roman et al. 1987).

Functional changes thus can occur in the pyriform cortex as part of the learning process. There is no a priori reason to reject the idea that modifications in the olfactory bulb play a role in recognition memory, and it is perhaps reasonable to assume that these occur. In this section, however, we focus on the pyriform cortex and attempt to use information about its internal anatomy to derive more specific ideas about the relationships between circuit characteristics and this form of memory.

The pyriform cortex is composed of a superficial dendritic layer (layer I), a layer of cell bodies (layers II and III), a deep layer composed of a variety of neuron types (layer IV, or endopyriform layer), and a fiber plexus zone between layers II/III and layer IV. The LOT axons and collaterals travel and form synapses in the outermost portion of layer I (layer Ia). The LOT is the only major afferent found in this zone. Thus layer II and III neurons are disynaptically connected

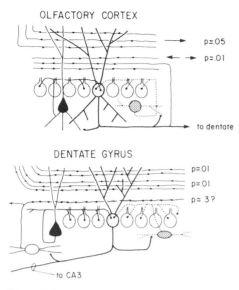

Figure 2.2
The organization of the olfactory cortex (top) and the dentate gyrus (bottom). In the olfactory cortex representation layer II neurons are shown receiving the LOT inputs in the distal dendrites and the commissural-associational inputs in proximal dendrites. Also represented are examples of feed-forward (solid neurons) and feedback (hatched neurons) inhibitory interneurons. The approximate respective densities of interconnections (*p*) are also given. In the dentate gyrus representation, note that collaterals from granule cells project to a polymorph neuron, making a dense feedback innervation of the granule cells.

to the nasal receptors, thereby representing the most direct connection between the periphery and any aspect of the cortex (figure 2.2).

It is crucial to note that, although some topography is found in the bulb, the LOT projections are exceedingly diffuse such that a small portion of the bulb contacts all parts of the pyriform cortex and each small region of the cortex receives input from all areas in the bulb. The system is divergent-convergent and possesses little organization. It is unlikely that neurobiological systems, constrained as they are by developmental rules, can be truly random, but it does appear that the LOT–pyriform-entorhinal system sacrifices much if not all of the topography found in the bulb.

There are approximately 50,000 mitral cells in the bulb; the number of cells in layer II of the pyriform cortex is not known, but it is probably somewhat greater than this. Similarly the number of LOT synapses formed per dendrite in layer Ia is unknown but is not likely to be more than a few thousand. If we assume 5,000 contacts, then the probability of a connection between a mitral cell and a layer II cell is about 10%, or somewhat lower if the collaterals have a tendency to multiply innervate their dendritic targets. In all, the LOT–pyriform cortex system constitutes a quasi-random matrix of low density (Lynch 1986).

The inner zone of layer I (layer Ib) is occupied by a massive commissural-associational system generated by the layer II neurons. In essence, this is a positive feedback system. This system, like the LOT projections, is extremely diffuse with relatively small regions of the cortex projecting to much of the remainder. The associational system does have a tendency to project in a caudal direction, causing it to generate an ever larger terminal field along the anterior-posterior axis of the pyriform-entorhinal cortex. If layer Ib contains the same number of synapses as we assumed for layer Ia ($\sim$5,000 per dendrite), then the commissural-associational system forms an even sparser matrix ($p < 0.01$) with the layer II and III cells than does the LOT projection to these neurons and again one with little evidence of organization.

Physiological studies have established that the LOT and commissural-associational synapses are excitatory [see Shepherd (1979) for a review]. The layer II system also contains a full complement of interneurons and seems to have both feed-forward and feedback forms of inhibition [see Haberly (1985) for a summary of recent work].

Besides projecting back onto themselves, layer II neurons also send projections into the pyriform fiber plexus, where they undoubtedly contact cells in layer IV; the associational system also continues caudally and merges with and adds to the commissural-associational system of the lateral entorhinal cortex. As noted, it also spills over into a zone of frontal cortex that lies opposite it on the upper side of the rhinal sulcus. This area proves to be the target of the DMN of the thalamus (and hence its designation as the frontal cortex), itself a target of the pyriform cortex.

The organization (or lack thereof) of the LOT–pyriform layer II system strongly suggests that this circuitry provides for the assembly of a unitary response to activation of disparate portions of the bulb. That is, a low-order massively divergent-convergent system ensures that any possible combination of bulbar cells will find a collection of layer II cells on which to converge. If the number of cells in the bulb is sufficiently large, then convergence on some cells will be adequate to depolarize them past their spike thresholds. These neurons will be scattered randomly throughout the cortex, but as a population they will constitute a response or representation that is essentially unique to their input signal. Note that this means that any particular neuron may participate in the representation of several odors—specificity exists in a random combinatorial network at the population level. A system such as this is required when confronting a world in which sensory stimuli can be composed of virtually any imaginable combination of primary elements, something that indeed is probably true of olfaction. That is, odors in nature are often composites of several primary odorants of different concentrations [see Lynch (1986) for a further discussion].

The idea that the pyriform cortex assembles representations of complex stimuli has received experimental support from the recent studies of Mouly et al. (1985); these workers found that electrical stimulation of disparate sites on the bulb was perceived by rats as an odor cue as readily as was stimulation at a single site.

Understanding the role of the feedback system will require physiological studies of how these afferents and the LOT interact with individual layer II neurons. In a low-density matrix cells receiving the highest degree of convergence from the feedback will not be those (or more accurately, will be only a small percentage of those) receiving the densest LOT inputs. Accordingly feedback probably serves to bring to firing threshold a collection of neurons that receive subthreshold input from the LOT. In simulation studies we have noted that this tends to differentiate further the responses of the pyriform cortex to similar LOT inputs (Lynch et al. 1988).

It might also be noted that the combinatorial nature of the pyriform system suggests one crucial function for the olfactory bulb, namely, the regulation of the total number of mitral cells that fire in response to an olfactory signal. This follows from the statistical fact that the number of neurons responding in the cortex increases exponentially with the size of the bulbar output. Clearly, then, some device must exist that regulates this variable, and the dense inhibitory network in the bulb seems particularly appropriate.

Synaptic potentiation resulting from learning would be a useful property in the pyriform cortex for a variety of reasons. First, it would increase the reliability and robustness of the pyriform response, thereby increasing the likelihood that a particular signal would be detected in a "noisy" environment. Second, it would allow the system to recognize partially degraded cues (that is, cues with missing elements) because a target neuron would require fewer potentiated than naive synapses to respond. Third, in studies using a simple simulation of the pyriform cortex, we have found that synaptic potentiation produces a type of categorical response when the cortex is provided with several examples of cues with shared elements (Lynch et al. 1988). In all, learning in the pyriform cortex serves to facilitate perception and to extract "group" information. Some of these points were considered in greater detail in an earlier paper (Lynch 1986).

Evidence that synapses in the pyriform cortex are modified by learning has been obtained in recent studies using electrical stimulation of the LOT as a cue in the successive odor discrimination paradigm described earlier. In those studies rats were first trained on a series of odor pairs and then tested with patterned electrical stimulation of the LOT. The animals quickly acquired a learned response to the stimulation (whether used as a positive or a negative cue), and this was accompanied by a stable facilitation of the LOT-pyriform evoked potential (Roman et al. 1987). Interestingly enough, naive rats did not show a stable synaptic potentiation to the same stimulation conditions, a result in accord with earlier findings (Racine et al. 1983). It appears that the acquisition of a learning set somehow adjusts the pyriform cortex so that synaptic potentiation and learning to LOT activity occurs. We return to this point in a later section.

The Dorsomedial Nucleus, Frontal Cortex, and Olfactory Memory
Slotnick and Kaneko (1981) appear to have been the first to identify the dorsomedial nucleus as a critical component in the circuitry subserving olfactory learning. They reported that intact rats acquire learning sets for odors but not for auditory or visual cues. Thus across days learning showed dramatic improvements with olfactory cues, as described, but much smaller changes were obtained with nonolfactory signals. Lesions to the DMN of the thalamus, the primary source of thalamic afferents of the frontal cortex, eliminated learning set performance, leaving the rats to respond to successive olfactory problems in much the same fashion as they did to auditory or visual problems [see also Staubli, Schottler et al. (1987)].

Eichenbaum et al. (1980) also examined the role of the DMN–frontal cortex system in olfactory learning and found that discrete lesions caused a profound impairment in go–no go performance (this task requires the rat to approach one cue and to withhold responses to a second). They also reported that damage to either of the two subdivisions of the frontal cortex innervated by the DMN produced effects restricted to either olfactory or nonolfactory tasks.

From these studies it appears that the DMN–frontal cortex system is vital to the process of associating appropriate response patterns to particular olfactory cues. In the case of Slotnick's experiments it is not implausible to imagine that the animal has lost the ability to form and use the context-dependent exclusion-inclusion rules that focus behavior to the appropriate stimuli and responses; on a given day's testing this might well manifest itself as an encoding problem because many more trials would be needed for a given datum (the correct cue) to be learned.

The organization of the olfactory connections of the DMN offers clues to a more specific hypothesis about its contributions to learning and memory [see Lynch (1986)]. In brief, the layer II neurons of the pyriform cortex, which are innervated by the LOT, project to a heterogeneous collection of larger cells in layer IV, some subset of which sends fibers to the medial section of the DMN. Given the number of cells in layer II and the DMN, this must be a highly convergent projection in which many cells in the cortex contact a much smaller number in the thalamus. If we assume that the neural representations for individual odors are formed in the olfactory cortex, then convergence would presumably result in DMN cells that respond to several different odors. It will be noted that in the successive discrimination problem the rat is required, first, to recognize many different smells and, second, to place each of these into one of two categories (correct or incorrect). Similarly, in nature quite different odors are categorized according to physical similarity and other characteristics into groups with common associations. Plant and animal odors are quite distinct; yet in each group there are subsets that can be classified as food. Different odors may also be related to single locations or objects. A convergent system such as the layer II–layer IV–DMN projections might well provide this type of categorization. According to this idea the information sent from the DMN to the cortex is not concerned with the identity of an odor but rather with its type.

Two things are needed for a system of this kind to work. First, some extrinsic input to the DMN is required to create a collection of cells that represent a class. Second, any given input from the olfactory cortex would have to have access to the cells of a particular class, because any odor could potentially be a member of that class. The second condition can be met by having the inputs from the pyriform cortex disperse widely throughout the DMN and then linking them to class cells through learning. The anatomical organization of the pyriform-DMN connection is in accord with this description. There are three likely sources of "typing" inputs to the DMN: the frontal cortex, the ventral striatum, or the hypothalamus. The hypothalamus could provide input relevant to the visceral and emotional events associated with an odor (for example, food, reward). The frontal cortex must receive a diverse collection of information through its intracortical connections, much of it presumably about events and objects in the external world. Thus one could imagine that hypothalamic and frontal inputs to the DMN set up categorical cells to which individual pyriform representations of odors become attached.

The output of the DMN to the frontal cortex is probably divergent in that a sizable collection of cells (in the cortex) receives input from a somewhat smaller group of thalamic neurons. The functions of the frontal cortex are a controversial subject, but the frontal cortex appears to play a general role in organizing response sequences, presumably through projections into the striatum and the ventral striatum. It will be recalled that layer II cells in the pyriform cortex project directly to that subdivision of the frontal cortex innervated by the pyriform target zone in the DMN. If the arguments developed to this point are correct, this sets up the possibility that information about the specific odor "now present" and its type or class becomes linked in the frontal cortex. Together these two lines of information would, according to the hypothesis being considered here, act on response sequences developed as part of the learning process.

The Hippocampus
There is now substantial literature linking the human hippocampus with the acquisition of data but not procedural memory. Damage to the hippocampus produces a "rapid forgetting" syndrome in which information seems to gain access to some type of memory system but then is lost (or, less likely, is no longer retrievable) after a short interval (Squire 1986). Some degree of retrograde amnesia also occurs after hippocampal and temporal lobe damage, but data memory established well in advance of the damage appears to be essentially intact.

Studies over the past thirty years have shown that hippocampal lesions in rats produce a variety of impairments and in particular a profound disturbance of spatial memories, but until recently there has been little evidence for a humanlike rapid forgetting syndrome. However, this effect was evident in animals tested in the described successive odor discrimination task. In those experiments rats were first trained over days on different odor pairs until asymptotic performance was reached, and new pairs were learned in five to ten trials. Lesions were then placed in the entorhinal zone interconnecting olfactory inputs and the hippocampus or in control sites.

The animals acquired new pairs of odors if tested with intertrial intervals of three minutes or less with about the same facility as controls in that after a few trials they reliably selected the correct odor. From this it can be concluded that sensory processing as well as procedural and short-term memory needed for the task were intact.

However, when tested one hour later, with the significance of the odors reversed, rats gave no evidence of having any memory from the first training episode. Thus control rats continued to respond to the former valence of the cues, and the lesioned animals exhibited no preference in their choices.

In a second variant of the experiment, the rats were trained using ten-minute intervals between trials; controls had no difficulty with these intervals, whereas the experimental rats were greatly impaired (Staubli, Ivy et al. 1985). The relationship between this pattern of deficits and the human hippocampal syndrome has been strengthened by recent experiments showing that the experimental rats perform normally on odors learned before the lesions were placed (Staubli et al. 1986). As well as showing that hippocampal lesions do not produce significant retrograde amnesia, this result indicates again that the hippocampus is not essential for the operation of learning sets (that is, procedures or rules used across a class of problems).

From earlier work by Slotnick and Kaneko (1981) it can be concluded that the hippocampus is also unnecessary for the formation of learning set memory. They showed that massive destruction of the posterior olfactory cortex, damage that severs the connections between olfaction and the hippocampus, did not prevent rats from acquiring learning sets (Slotnick and Katz 1974). Work by Cohen and Squire (1980) has established that procedural learning is intact in human amnesiacs, including those with extensive damage to the hippocampus and the surrounding temporal lobe.

Most but not all psychologists interpret the rapid forgetting effect as evidence that the hippocampus facilitates the encoding of data memory at sites elsewhere in the telencephalon. Although useful as a description of a behavioral syndrome, this explanation is very much a "black box" type of construction. It leaves unaddressed the questions of what type of operation the hippocampus exerts on the putative storage sites and the nature of the processing it carries out on the cue presented to it. One way of approaching these issues is to consider what is known of other functions of the hippocampus and to evaluate what its macroanatomical relationships suggest about its contributions to behavior.

O'Keefe and Nadel (1978) made the seminal observation that the hippocampus in rodents is extremely responsive to spatial cues. Thus individual neurons in the hippocampus appear to be "tuned" to complex distal cues that, according to these authors, are used by the animal to build and use a spatial "map." In a broader sense the hippocampus could serve to provide situational or contextual information [Kubie and Ranck 1984; Lynch 1986; Nadel et al. (1985) have advanced an idea similar to this]. As used here, "context" means a series of expectancies about objects or events that are likely to occur or be encountered in a complex environment. It provides for familiarity (and novelty) and in toto can be used to direct behavior into appropriate channels.

Context is obviously of vital significance to learning; for example, a novel odor in the olfactory discrimination test apparatus clearly means something different from a novel odor in the rat's home cage. According to this argument, during its first exposures to the cage, the rat builds a set of internal connections between hippocampal neurons such that cells responsive to external stimuli are linked together in patterns that reflect the order in which they are encountered during exploratory movements. (This process, which is similar to that envisioned by O'Keefe and Nadel, is discussed in more detailed "circuit" terms in section 2.3.)

Although indeed providing a kind of map, the collection of cells constituting the representation of the entire space also provides the brain with information about the specific environment within which it is located, information that can be used in directing the olfactory apparatus responsible for processing and storing odor perceptions. If this chain of events were to occur, then when the rat entered the cage, its hippocampus would exert a particular type of influence over the sensory pathways for smell. We can imagine that this influence would facilitate detection and storage.

The highly speculative hypothesis that the hippocampus provides contextual influences over sensory processing is consonant with the organization of olfactory-hippocampal relationships. As noted earlier, the hippocampus is the single site where olfactory and nonolfactory inputs of equivalent size become mixed in a large-scale matrix. Moreover, the hippocampus sends substantial projections to basal forebrain regions, including the nucleus accumbens septi and the nucleus of the diagonal band, that innervate both the olfactory bulb and the pyriform cortex. The first of these projects into the olfactory bulb, probably to innervate the inhibitory granule cells. It is not unreasonable to suppose that this relatively direct relationship allows the hippocampus to set thresholds for cell discharges and to shape the spike trains (frequency, duration, interburst intervals) going from the bulbar mitral cells to the layer II pyriform neurons. The second likely route for the hippocampus to affect encoding processes is through the nucleus of the diagonal band, which lies proximal to the deep layers of the pyriform cortex and, from the work of Valverde (1965), appears to project into them.

It might be noted here that the context hypothesis is not necessarily restricted to visual and spatial information. The hippocampus is also the recipient of auditory information (Deadwyler et al. 1979a,b, 1981; Rose et al. 1983), and one could imagine complexes of sounds and sights serving to orient the animal in such a way as to "expect" input of a particular type based on its prior experience.

Odors also become associated with specific objects in the environment, and, again because of the convergence of olfactory and nonolfactory signals, the hippocampus is a likely place for this to occur. In support of this, recent studies have shown that patient HM, who has sustained hippocampal and temporal lobe damage, is unable to associate odors with words (Eichenbaum et al. 1983). This type of specific association has two aspects to it: (1) expectancy, as in the case where an object associated with a strong odor might trigger sniffing or searching for an odor; and (2) recall, as when an odor triggers a memory of an object not present or a particular word. Expectancy is a simple case of the context hypothesis outlined earlier. Recall concerns the introspective observation that odors can trigger memories of objects but that objects do not elicit memories of odors. As discussed elsewhere (Lynch 1986) and illustrated in figure 2.1, this could reflect the fact that the hippocampus has access to the neocortex through the deep layers of the entorhinal cortex but lacks direct connections to the primary olfactory cortex. Accordingly it provides a vehicle through which olfaction can be routed to the neocortex but cannot be used in the reverse direction (neocortex to olfactory cortex).

To summarize, the hippocampus plays a crucial role in the encoding of fact or data memory but seems far less important in the learning of rules or procedures that apply to many problems of the same type. The fact memory function, according to the argument presented here, is one utilization of a particular type of associative operation carried out in the hippocampus. In olfaction the hippocampus is assumed to connect olfactory with nonolfactory information, including specific odors with specific objects. Distal cues also appear to become associated in the hippocampus and thereby provide information about spatial location. We assume that the animal uses the associations formed in the hippocampus as primary information (odor predisposes an animal to detect an object and to navigate in an environment) and as aggregate information to produce an output unique to particular environments. Finally, by organizing behavior appropriate to a context, the hippocampus is hypothesized to facilitate the detection and storage of new information.

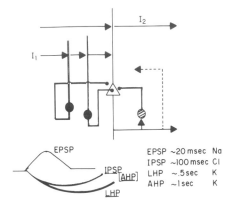

Figure 2.3
The various synaptic interactions on a pyramidal neuron. The pyramidal neuron is shown receiving (1) excitatory inputs from extrinsic afferent (I_n) and positive feedback from one of its collateral-generating EPSPs mediated by cations (Na$^+$), (2) inhibitory inputs from two types of feed-forward inhibitory interneurons and from feedback inhibitory interneurons generating two kinds of IPSPs mediated by Cl (IPSP) or K$^+$ (LHP). In addition, pyramidal neurons can generate an after-hyperpolarization (AHP) mediated by K$^+$.

2.3   Hippocampal Networks and Olfactory Memory

Aspects of Hippocampal Physiology

Excitation and Inhibition   Studies over the past several years, mostly using in vitro slices, have provided a clearer picture of the types of synaptic interrelationships occurring in the hippocampus. Here we simply list certain widely distributed characteristics that are especially pertinent to discussions of hippocampal networks. Figure 2.3 schematically illustrates a hippocampal cell with excitatory inputs from extrinsic and associational-feedback afferents terminating on dendritic spines. All connections of this type in the olfactory cortex and hippocampus so far examined have proven to produce short excitatory postsynaptic potentials (EPSPs). The excitatory afferents are also shown contacting two spineless interneurons that form synapses with the primary cell. Both cells are inhibitory, and their synapses produce hyperpolarization, one through chloride channels [the short inhibitory postsynaptic potential (IPSP)] and the other through receptor-gated potassium channels [the long hyperpolarization (LHP)]. The interneurons are low-threshold elements in that fewer afferents are needed to discharge them than are required to drive the primary cell to its spike discharge threshold. Together these cells constitute a powerful feed-forward inhibitory system. The target cell also contacts some of these interneurons and other interneurons, thereby setting up an inhibitory feedback system. Excitation of an input thus generates inhibitory and excitatory interactions on primary target cells with the degree of excitation depending on random convergence by the stimulated afferents. Inhibition increases the convergence requirement for spiking a primary cell, probably by shunting inward currents as much as by hyperpolarizing the cell.

Chronic recording studies have shown that pyramidal cells in the hippocampus fire at low baseline frequencies and are inclined to emit short bursts of three to four spikes (complex spikes) except when the animal enters particular places in the environment, at which time the neurons may generate longer bursts (Ranck 1973; Fox and Ranck 1975, 1981). Cells thought to be interneurons emit high-frequency trains of spikes. The short bursts of the pyramidal cells occur, to some degree at least, in synchrony with the hippocampal 5–7-Hz hippocampal theta rhythm, whereas the activity of the interneurons is clearly phase locked with this wave pattern.

Physiological Plasticity   One of the more important discoveries made in the study of hippocampal physiology is that synapses in the hippocampus exhibit a remarkably persistent potentiation following brief periods of high-frequency synaptic stimulation (Bliss and Lomo 1973; Bliss and Gardner-Medwin 1973). Subsequent work from several laboratories has identified several rules governing the induction of this long-term potentiation (LTP):

1. It requires convergent activity in a sizable number of synapses (the LTP convergence rule) (McNaughton et al. 1978).
2. Recent experiments have shown that the amount of convergence required varies inversely with the resting membrane potential of the target neuron; that is, depolarized cells are more readily potentiated than hyperpolarized ones (Wigstrom and Gustaffson 1983; Malinow and Miller 1986; Kelso et al., 1986).
3. The LTP effect is specific to those synapses activated cojointly; the strength of neighboring contacts is not increased (Lynch et al. 1977; Dunwiddie and Lynch 1978; Andersen et al. 1977).
4. LTP induction involves the activation of a specific class of acidic amino acid receptors [the NMDA (*N*-methy-D-aspartate) receptors] (Collingridge et al. 1983). These receptors are peculiar in that their associated channel is blocked by extracellular magnesium at resting membrane potential levels (Nowak et al. 1984; Mayer et al. 1984); reducing the membrane potential removes the

block, rendering the receptor-channel complex functional. This probably explains why LTP is sensitive to membrane potential (see item 2).

5. The induction of LTP probably involves alterations in postsynaptic calcium levels (Lynch et al. 1983); this may relate to the requirement for the activation of NMDA receptors because these entities appear to open calcium conducting channels (McDermott et al. 1986).

6. Structural changes accompany and correlate with LTP (Lee et al. 1980, 1981; Chang and Greenough 1984; Wenzel and Matthies 1985). The occurrence of morphological alterations provides a plausible explanation for the extraordinary persistence of LTP.

7. Biochemical mechanisms have been identified that are capable of eliciting stable morphological reorganization and have been shown to reproduce some of the correlates of LTP (Lynch and Baudry 1984).

Recent work from our laboratory has demonstrated links between the induction of LTP and the hippocampal theta rhythm and has provided insights into how the effect might be generated in the behaving animal. In those studies, stimulation was delivered in short high-frequency bursts that mimic one of the firing patterns of pyramidal neurons. Maximum LTP was produced when the number of bursts equaled the theta frequency, five per second (Larson et al. 1986). A plausible explanation for the efficiency of this pattern of stimulation became evident when the bursts were applied as pairs, with each member of the pair activating a separate set of inputs to the same target neuron. Under these conditions only the second member of the pair elicited LTP (Larson and Lynch 1986).

Additional studies led to the conclusion that the first input blocks the short feed-forward IPSP produced by a second input, thereby causing the second input to elicit prolonged EPSPs and a greater net depolarization of the target spines and dendrites; these effects are maximal at 200 msec after stimulation of the first input (Larson and Lynch 1986). Enhanced depolarization results in NMDA receptor activation, as indicated by the observation that antagonists of the receptor block some aspects of the response to the second burst and the LTP (Larson and Lynch, in press).

These results indicate that the physiological and chemical processes that initiate LTP are closely related to patterns of hippocampal activity observed in animals exploring their environments. This, coupled with the recent discovery (Morris et al. 1986; Staubli et al., in press) that antagonists of the NMDA receptor produce a profound and selective anterograde amnesia in rats encourage the conclusion that the processes responsible for LTP are involved in memory storage.

It should be noted that there is reason to suspect that LTP is not the only form of synaptic facilitation to follow high-frequency stimulation. In the physiological experiments just described, a 10–15-min period of decremental facilitation was found to be superimposed on LTP. Moreover, it appears that the stimulation parameters needed for this effect are different from those required for LTP (Larson et al. 1986).

Racine et al. (1983) reported that two forms of LTP followed several applications of lengthy trains of stimulation, one with a half-life of hours and a second with a half-life of several days. They also found that these two forms could be selectively manipulated, suggesting the possibility that they are mediated by different substrates. We have examined the duration of LTP in the field CA1 in rats with chronically implanted electrodes using the theta stimulation paradigm; about 50% of the animals showed a potentiation that declined little if at all during one or more weeks of testing. The ultimate duration of the LTP could not be established, but periods of months do not seem unlikely (Staubli and Lynch 1987). Whether the extremely stable LTP we observed is a property of field CA1 or is due to the patterned stimulation paradigm is a question that deserves further investigation.

Entorhinal Cortex to Dentate Gyrus: The Perforant Path

Organization of the Projections   The connections between the entorhinal cortex and the dentate gyrus arise in the layer II cells of the entorhinal cortex and terminate in the outer 75% of the dendritic field (the "molecular layer") of the dentate gyrus. These projections, which are known as the perforant path, are massive in that they generate about 95% of all synapses found in their target zones (Matthews et al. 1976). The number of synapses on a granule cell is unknown but about 10,000 seems reasonable (West and Andersen 1980). If we assume that the number of layer II entorhinal cells equals that of the granule cells (about 600,000), which from the relative areas occupied by the two groups of neurons is likely, then we can see that the perforant path–granule cell dendrites form a sparse matrix in which the probability of a given axon contacting a given granule cell dendrite is around 0.01. Multiple contacts from a single axon would lower this figure (2 contacts per fiber; density of the matrix, 0.005).

The outputs of the medial (nonolfactory) and lateral (olfactory) entorhinal cortices form separate medial and lateral perforant paths.

Small injections of anterograde transport markers into the medial entorhinal cortex result in labeled terminals occupying a segment of the septotemporal extent of the dentate gyrus that is far larger than the injected area of the entorhinal cortex; about 30% of the dentate gyrus receives projections from the smallest regions of the medial entorhinal cortex (<10%), according to one study (Wyss 1981). The nature of the topographical relationship was thought to be between the dorsoventral extent of the entorhinal cortex and the septotemporal dimension of the dentate gyrus (Hjorth-Simonsen 1972; Wyss 1981). More recent work by Ruth et al. (1982) indicates that a two-dimensional coordinate system is needed to describe the topography; these workers agree, however, that the medial perforant path projections are extremely divergent-convergent. Small injections in the lateral entorhinal cortex label synapses and terminals over most of the dentate gyrus (Wyss 1981; see also Ruth et al. 1983) (figure 2.4).

The diffuse nature of the perforant path–dentate gyrus system in toto does not mean that organizational rules are not found at the level of individual axons. Figure 2.4 illustrates one possibility in which the collaterals of individual perforant axons do not ramify blindly in the dentate gyrus but restrict themselves to a series of thin planes cut at an angle to the septotemporal axis of the hippocampus. If the planes selected by a given collateral were randomly distributed, then the extremely divergent projections observed for groups of cells would be reproduced. Long collaterals of the type illustrated in figure 2.4 are commonly observed in Golgi and fiber stain preparations of the dentate gyrus. A system of this type would produce a different pattern of

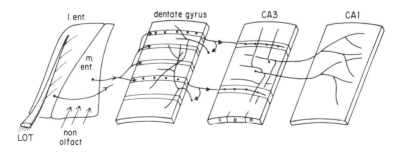

Figure 2.4
The anatomical connections between the entorhinal cortex and the various hippocampal subfields. The lateral entorhinal cortex receives fibers from the LOT, and the medial entorhinal cortex receives nonolfactory information. The lateral entorhinal cortex projects widely through the dentate gyrus, whereas the projections from the medial entorhinal cortex are more restricted and might be segregated into defined sections of the dentate gyrus. The projections of the dentate gyrus to field CA3 are topographically organized; those from CA3 to CA1 are widely spread in the septotemporal dimension.

activation in the dentate gyrus than a truly random organization, because it would result in the convergence of collaterals on narrow planes scattered along the longitudinal axis of the dentate gyrus. Thus activation of a subpopulation of layer II cells would produce activation of a group of granule neurons on a set of randomly distributed planes with a large number of intervening planes that lacked any stimulated cells (figure 2.4).

The greater divergence of the lateral perforant path suggests either that the planes innervated by the collaterals of individual axons are more widely separated than is the case for the medial perforant path fibers or that the olfactory projections do indeed ramify blindly and extensively.

Finally, it should be noted that both the lateral and the medial perforant paths generate a terminal field in the outermost branches of the CA3 pyramidal cells and that the lateral path also innervates a thin zone at the top of the CA1 pyramidal neurons. Physiological experiments indicate that these are extremely weak systems in that they do not produce robust EPSPs or drive their target cells (Andersen et al. 1966).

Lamination of the Perforant Path Terminal Fields   A striking aspect of the perforant path is the lamination (spatial restriction) of the terminal fields generated by the lateral (olfactory) and medial (nonolfactory) entorhinal cortices on the dendrites of the granule cells. Moreover, the proportion of the dendritic fields occupied by the two inputs varies along the mediolateral and septotemporal axis of the dentate gyrus; these gradients can be explained by the growth pathways followed by the perforant path axons during development and by the spatial pattern of proliferation and maturation exhibited by the granule cells [see Gall and Lynch (1980) for a discussion]. Accordingly it may not be wise to attribute too great a "computational" significance to the changes in the balance of innervation by the medial versus the lateral perforant path–dentate gyrus system. In any event the anatomy of the system does not provide strong clues as to whether lateral and medial pathways interact on the dendrites of the granule cells. However, the fact that spatial cues, which clearly have no olfactory correlates, "drive" cells in the hippocampus indicates that visual information by itself—and therefore probably the medial perforant path—is sufficient for triggering hippocampal circuitry. Sounds also activate granule cells by means of the perforant path (Deadwyler et al. 1979a,b; Rose et al. 1983).

Less is known about the functional efficacy of the lateral perforant path. Stimulation of the olfactory bulb evokes sizable responses in the dentate gyrus; assuming that a large number of cells in the bulb respond to odors, this could mean that olfactory inputs by themselves can activate the hippocampus. If olfactory and nonolfactory cues alone were to cause a meaningful number of granule cells to discharge, then a problem emerges when the two cues occur together. Combinatorial systems are extremely sensitive to the size of their inputs; the number of cells on which the inputs converge to a degree sufficient to produce spiking increases exponentially, not linearly, with input size. Accordingly mixing olfactory and nonolfactory cues that by themselves are adequately represented by granule cell responses would result in a large number of neurons that respond to the combined cue. This emphasizes the point that in a combinatorial system the number of elements in a given input must be regulated with some precision and/or the target network must possess means for adjusting the threshold of its elements to reflect the size of the input.

There does not appear to be an intra-entorhinal pathway that is appropriate for permitting the lateral and medial cortices to adjust the spike thresholds of their cells so that a normalized output occurs, but the feedback circuit from the hippocampus to the entorhinal cortex could serve this function. Adjustments of input vectors might be accomplished by either decreasing the frequency of cell firing or by reducing the number of cells firing or both.

Feed-forward and feedback inhibition in the dentate gyrus itself could also be used to raise the threshold of the granule cells so that greater convergence of input would be required to spike cells (that is, more input fibers are needed). But in any case what emerges in the dentate gyrus will not be a simple combination or partial combination of cells responsive to either stimulus alone. Instead, some cells from each group plus a large number of granule cells that are not responsive to either alone will fire when presented with the combined stimulus.

Sparse quasi-random matrices of the type formed by the perforant path–dentate gyrus system are not appropriate for building associations such that a stimulus that triggers a collection of cells unique to it also activates selectively a second group of neurons previously linked to another stimulus (Lynch 1986). Mixed stimuli in these systems are more likely to generate a new population of responsive cells in the target array.

What, then, happens when odors and visual objects are present at the same time? One possibility is that attentional mechanisms force a shifting of inputs between the two modalities such that only one projection to the dentate gyrus is operative at any given time. In all, although the mixture of olfactory and nonolfactory signals on the dendrites of the granule cells makes these neurons the obvious sites for associating the two modalities, there are reasons for assuming otherwise. Experimental work is needed to clarify this point.

The Dentate Gyrus

The granule cells of the dentate gyrus are among the most unusual neurons in the brain. They undergo postnatal mitosis, generate extremely fine axons with enormous terminals, lack basal dendrites, and form synaptic boutons that can only be described as exotic. Equally important, particularly from the view of circuit analysis, the dentate gyrus possesses a peculiar type of commissural-associational system: The granule cells innervate a population of polymorph neurons that in turn project back to the inner 27% of the granule cell dendrites in the ipsi- and contralateral hippocampus, where they generate virtually the entire synaptic population (McWilliams and Lynch 1979). Thus, rather than using direct connections to generate the associational system, as is the case for the pyriform-entorhinal cortices and the pyramidal cells of the hippocampus, the dentate gyrus employs an intermediary cell. Moreover, the granule cells vastly outnumber the polymorph neurons (that is, many granule cells to one polymorph cell and one polymorph cell to many granule cells), making the feedback system massively convergent-divergent (figure 2.5).

The dentate gyrus–mossy fiber system is found in essentially the same form in all mammals, from marsupials to humans, and may occur in a primitive form in reptiles (Lacey 1978). Presumably the system evolved to its present state with the earliest mammalian hippocampus and has been conserved across all subsequent evolution. It is likely then that its abnormal features are in some way related to important functions.

An analysis of the functions of the dentate gyrus properly begins with its interconnections, that is, the commissural-associational feedback system. The polymorph cells contain GAD, the GABA-synthesizing enzyme; yet the terminals they generate are found on spines, and the synapses they form are essentially the same as excitatory contacts found throughout the hippocampus and the cortex (Kosaka et al. 1984). Moreover, stimulation of the commissural system produces monosynaptic negative-going potentials restricted to the inner portion of the dendrite (Deadwyler et al. 1975; West et al. 1975; McNaughton et al. 1981); this is strong evidence for a depolarizing (excitatory) potential.

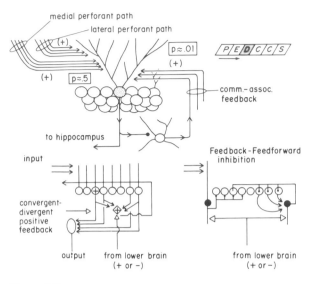

Figure 2.5
The organization of the dentate gyrus. (Top) A collection of granule cells receive excitatory inputs from the entorhinal cortex and the commissural-associational feedback system generated by the polymorph cells. (Bottom left) Convergent-divergent positive feedback. Note that modulatory influences (positive or negative) are exerted on the polymorph neuron. (Bottom right) Feed-forward and feedback inhibition, which are modulated by inputs from lower brain structures.

One explanation of these observations is that the polymorph neurons elicit normal EPSPs as well as depolarizing GABA responses of the type sometimes found in iontophoretic experiments (Alger and Nicoll 1979; Andersen et al. 1980). An interesting feature of the polymorph cells according to Lorente de No (1934) is that they lack basket contacts of the type known to be inhibitory at other cells in the forebrain. A system of this type would therefore constitute an excitatory feedback loop (granule cell–polymorph cell–granule cell) that would cycle unless suppressed by inhibitory contacts on the granule cells or by addition or subtraction of extrinsic afferents that control the spike thresholds of the polymorph neurons. The granule cells receive inhibitory inputs (feedback and feed-forward IPSPs), probably from interneurons located in the narrow zone immediately subjacent to their cell bodies. Interestingly enough, the infragranular and polymorph layers are targets for unusually high concentrations of cholinergic (from the septum), noradrenergic (from the brain stem), and serotoninergic (from the brain stem) fibers and terminals. Because granule cells lack basal dendrites, it can be assumed that these inputs innervate the interneuron and polymorph cell populations (see Mosko et al. 1973; Lynch et al. 1978; Rose and Schubert 1977). Conditions found in the dentate gyrus are thus appropriate for cycling activity with the duration or frequency of the cycles being dictated by extrahippocampal inputs. This argument is summarized in figure 2.5. Note that the extreme convergence-divergence of the system means that each granule cell receives input from a substantial portion of the polymorph cell population. A system such as this should react to virtually any event in the dentate gyrus and in turn will act diffusely on a large part of the granule cell population.

It is of interest in this context to note that granule cells fire at high frequencies for lengthy periods (seconds) when animals are moving. Moreover, one gains the impression from chronic recording studies that a large number of cells are active immediately before and during locomotor episodes (Deadwyler et al. 1979a,b; Rose et al. 1983). Since virtually all extrinsic (extrahippocampal) inputs to the dentate gyrus arise from the perforant path and given that this pathway conveys information about distal cues (odors, objects, spatial cues, sounds), the question of the origin of this movement-related influence becomes salient. The present interpretation of the commissural/associational (C/A) feedback loop provides one possibility, especially if we assume that the brain stem and septal inputs to the dentate gyrus are strongly influenced by systems that initiate locomotor responses.

From the anatomical arrangements, it is reasonable to assume that the granule cells have separate response modes that are activated when either the perforant path or the feedback system is stimulated. In the first case we can assume that the response is differentiated in that subgroups of granule cells, perhaps clustered in the manner described, are activated by different environmental stimuli. There are few neurobehavioral results pertinent to this suggestion, but several groups have reported the occurrence of a small number of granule cells that are coded for particular distal or spatial cues (Fox and Ranck 1981; O'Keefe and Nadel 1978). Because only a few cells react to any particular cue, we can conclude that the response of the dentate gyrus to the perforant path is, at least on some occasions, highly differentiated.

Conversely, the response of the granule cells to the feedback system is likely to involve a large percentage of the total cell population, in essence, an "en masse" reaction. The anatomy of the C/A feedback projections does, however, hint at the possibility that some structure may be found in the movement-related discharges of the granule cells. The ipsilateral (associational) and contralateral (commissural) projections exhibit opposing density gradients in the inner molecular layer of the dentate gyrus. The associational system is densest in the inner leaf of the dentate gyrus and produces a decreasing number of terminals as one proceeds toward the outer leaf of cells; the commissural terminals exhibit the opposite pattern, being most numerous in the outer leaf and decreasing in number toward the inner leaf (Gottlieb and Cowan 1973). If the postulated movement-related inputs to the polymorph cells were to be lateralized, then a movement to the left would trigger associational activity on one side of the hippocampus and commissural activity on the other. This in turn would favor firing by granule cells in the inner leaf in one dentate gyrus and in the outer leaf in the other.

To summarize, we suggest that the dentate gyrus exhibits a discrete response while the animal is optimally positioned for sampling external events and a second en masse type of behavior when it is moving vigorously. Olfaction may be exceptional in this scheme because smelling requires considerable muscle activity (whisker movement); moreover, because of the continuous presence of odors (to the animal), it might be possible for the animal to maintain contact with odors as it moves through the environment.

The Mossy Fiber–CA3 System
The mossy fiber system is marked by several unusual features, not the least of which is that it occupies a small portion of the pyramidal cell dendrite (see figure 2.6). Moreover, the enormous size of these

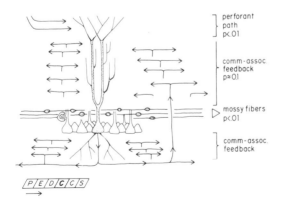

Figure 2.6
The organization of field CA3. A collection of CA3 pyramidal neurons is shown receiving (1) a narrow band of mossy fibers in the proximal apical dendrites, (2) relatively dense bands of commissural-associational feedback inputs on apical and basal dendrites, and (3) a narrow, sparse innervation from the perforant path on the distal apical dendrites.

EFFECTS OF INTERPOSED TOPOGRAPHY

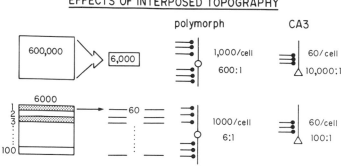

Figure 2.7
Numerical relationships between dentate gyrus and CA3 pyramidal neurons. (Top) In the absence of defined topography, 600,000 granule cells converge on 6,000 polymorph cells, which are assumed to have 1,000 contacts each, thus providing a 1 to 600 probability that a granule cell contacts a given polymorph neuron. Similarly, if we assume that a CA3 pyramidal neuron makes 60 contacts with mossy fibers, the probability that a granule cell contacts a CA3 pyramidal neuron would be 1 to 10,000. (Bottom) The corresponding number obtained by assuming the existence of a certain degree of topography in the organization of the projection from the granule cells.

contacts means that the packing density of the synapses in this zone is low. The net result of this is that each pyramidal cell samples only a few dozen granule cells, of which there are according to one count about 600,000. By combining these features, we arrive at an incredibly sparse matrix in which the probability of a particular axon contacting a particular dendrite would be of the order of less than 1 in 10,000. However, the true situation is considerably different because of yet another unusual (for the hippocampus) feature of the mossy fibers; they are topographically organized such that a narrow septotemporal segment of the dentate gyrus projects to an equivalently narrow septotemporal segment of the field CA3 (Blackstad et al. 1970; Lynch et al. 1973; Swanson et al. 1978) (see figure 2.4). Thus the potential pool of mossy synapses for a given pyramidal cell is reduced to a few thousand granule cells. Under this circumstance the density of the matrix can be assumed to be of the order of 1% (for example, <100 contacts per cell, 5,000 inputs). Thus topography converts the overall sparse matrix into a series of denser matrices (figure 2.7).

Note that the small number of mossy fiber synapses per cell means that only a few terminals will be active on a given pyramidal cell during stimulation of the granule cells by their afferents. It has been estimated that 200–500 synapses in the perforant path are needed to bring a granule cell to discharge (McNaughton et al. 1981), and like values have been deduced for the Schaffer-commissural projections to the pyramidal neurons of field CA1 (Andersen et al. 1980). These values are also reasonable if we assume that a single EPSP produces about 100 μV in the cell body near the spike initiation zone for the axon; that is, even with nonlinear summing resulting from shunting, 200 to 500 synapses should produce enough voltage to bring the cell to its spike discharge threshold. These numbers are clearly out of the question for the mossy fiber–CA3 connection.

How, then, do the granule cells excite the pyramidal neurons? The answer to this might lie in the unusual morphology of the mossy fiber terminal and its contact with the CA3 dendrite (Blackstad and Kjaerheim 1961). That is, the terminal is enormous and contains an extraordinary number of vesicles; moreover, each terminal envaginates a long spinous process on which it forms several synapses and makes contacts on the shaft of the CA3 dendrite directly. As a result of these arrangements, we can imagine that the discharge of one mossy axon results in transmitter release from a single terminal onto many synapses. This coupled with the fact that the contacts are immediately adjacent to the cell body might produce a situation in which depolarization of a given bouton would result in a much larger voltage change at the axon hillock than is the case for more typical synaptic systems. Coupled with the frequency facilitation that can be expected from the rapid firing of the granule cells, these features of the mossy synapses could compensate for their sparsity. Note, however, that judging from chronic unit data, it is clear that only a small percentage of the CA3 cells respond to specific cues (Fox and Ranck 1981).

It is noted that the topographic anatomy of the dentate gyrus–CA3 system has important consequences for the functioning of the much more diffuse perforant path systems. That is, it seems inevitable that convergence from the entorhinal cells activated by a particular cue onto a significant number of granule cells in the same septotemporal segment of the dentate gyrus is a requirement for the activation of a CA3 neuron. Grouping of granule neurons activated by a particular input into narrow segments into planes in parallel with the mossy fibers would satisfy this condition.

In all, the mossy fiber system can be viewed as a system in which each axon has concentrated its synaptic contributions to the target cell to a small region on the dendrite of that cell; in addition, all the mossy fiber terminals are concentrated in a narrow zone. It is possible that this serves to increase vastly the spatial and temporal summation of potentials elicited by a given axon and the mossy fibers in toto. By exploiting this feature, the mossy fiber boutons may have a range of potencies that is much greater than that for fibers that scatter their boutons across a broad dendritic field. The unusual packing density of vesicles in the mossy fiber boutons also suggests the possibility that these endings are capable of sustained high-frequency activity and thus an unusual degree of frequency facilitation.

The concentration of many synapses on a single bouton that engulfs an elaborate spine should result in a situation in which changes in ion concentrations in the target process are much greater than would occur in the one-terminal one-spine synapse configuration that characterizes much of the telencephalon. That is, the peculiar extended spine contacted by a mossy fiber presumably experiences the simultaneous action of several closely spaced synapses from a single bouton. It is also the case that the mossy fibers have extremely high levels of zinc and high levels of two and sometimes three neuropeptides (Gall et al. 1981). The significance of these chemical peculiarities is unknown, but they certainly imply that the mossy fiber synapse carries out unusual chemical activities. Activation of several mossy fiber axons that converge on a CA3 dendrite might well produce ionic and chemical changes in the target neuron that are greater than those seen when a large number of scattered synapses are activated in the spatially extended apical and basal dendrites of the pyramidal cell.

These points suggest to us that the mossy fiber system should exhibit plasticities of a type not found in other pathways. We are not aware of any chronic studies of the system, and only a few in vitro slice experiments have been reported. The mossy fiber synapse does appear to exhibit a powerful frequency facilitation effect and may also possess a potent but transient type of potentiation not found elsewhere. Specifically Hopkins and Johnston (1984) have reported that high-frequency stimulation causes a marked increase in postsynaptic responses that lasts for only 15–30 min. Although they refer to this as LTP, the transience of the effect indicates that it is in fact something quite different.

We have found that potentiation in the mossy fibers is synapse specific, in contrast to reports from other groups [Yamamoto and Chujo 1978; Misgeld et al. 1979; see Higashima and Yamamoto (1985) for a recent clarification], but we lack data on the stability of the effect (unpublished data).

Potentiation of the mossy fiber synapses is peculiar in another regard: It is not blocked by antagonists of NMDA receptors (Harris and Cotman 1986). This is consonant with the finding that NMDA binding sites are absent from the mossy fiber zone (Monaghan et al. 1983). It will be recalled that both short- and long-term potentiation are selectively blocked by NMDA receptor antagonists at other sites in the hippocampus. By combining these results, it is apparent that the mossy fibers possess a peculiar kind of transient potentiation effect that is in all probability selective to synapses receiving high-frequency stimulation; whether they also exhibit long-term potentiation is an open question.

Operations of the Dentate Gyrus–CA3 System
The following points have been made about the dentate gyrus as an intermediary between the olfactory cortex and hippocampal pyramidal cell fields:

1. The perforant path has olfactory and nonolfactory subdivisions, both of which generate sparse arrays in the dendrites of the granule cells.

2. A granule cell–polymorph cell–granule cell feedback loop exists that is probably excitatory in nature and is certainly massively convergent-divergent.

3. The granule cells fire at high rates in large numbers before and during movement; it was suggested that the feedback system is in part responsible for this.

4. The mossy fiber–CA3 system, in striking contrast to the systems preceding and following it, is topographically organized; despite this, the system constitutes a sparse matrix.

5. The mossy fiber bouton is remarkable in a number of respects, not the least of which is that it engulfs an elongated dendritic spine on which it forms a much greater than normal number of synapses. Moreover, the mossy fiber synapses exhibit a peculiar kind of transient potentiation.

6. The CA3 output, in marked contrast to the granule cell input, consists of a small percentage of the pyramidal cell population.

In the following sections, we consider some possible ways in which these features of the dentate gyrus–CA3 system, and in particular short-term potentiation and en masse activity, might contribute to behavior.

Short-Term Potentiation and Movement-Related Granule Cell Firing Mammals have elaborated the olfactory system, including the primary machinery for detection of odors, to a far greater degree than the other vertebrates. Because the hippocampus is a third-order olfactory structure, it follows that it plays a primary role in fundamental olfactory behavior. Certain groups and indeed perhaps most orders of mammals display remarkable abilities for tracking odors, and this constitutes a reasonable place to begin looking for hippocampal contributions to behavior.

Suppose that a given stimulus arriving through the entorhinal cortex evokes a response in a small number of granule cells on which sufficient perforant path fiber convergence occurs. In this initial state we imagine the inhibition on the pyramidal cells to be at some baseline value (figure 2.8a). If the animal moves or prepares to move, the polymorph cells are "released" and feedback spreads activity rapidly throughout the dentate gyrus on an ever-increasing number of granule cells. Two populations of granule cells are now present: those under the control of the feedback system and those receiving both feedback and perforant path input. If the perforant path signal increases in strength, either through the addition of cells in the entorhinal cortex as the cue is fully perceived or because of increased firing rates, then the second group of neurons could exhibit firing patterns distinctly different from those of the cells being activated by feedback alone. Thus correct approach (that is, toward the cue) is signaled by maintenance of a firing rate (or pattern) above a "noisy" background (figure 2.8b).

Note that intensity of movement is in some ways encoded within this system. That is, more intense locomotion produces greater feedback and thus more intense or widespread activation of granule cells. Under conditions of rapid walking, the input signal from the perforant path would have to increase more rapidly than when a more leisurely approach toward the cue is taken. If this did not occur, the "signal" portion of the granule cell response (that is, those cells responsive to the perforant path afferents activated by the external cue) would rapidly drop into the "noise."

Olfactory cues as targets are evanescent, and the strength of the signal is dependent on not only the animal's behavior but also wind conditions. Thus a signal may appear and disappear for intervals of uncertain length. If the cue is important, the brain must be prepared to direct behavior in an appropriate manner for extended periods in which the cue is absent. Furthermore, competing signals have to be ignored for some period after detection of the critical signal, even though the animal is presumably directing its attention toward olfaction.

This type of selectivity must be a major problem for a macrosomatic mammal. Let us suppose that an animal learns that an odor is of importance and that as a result the LOT and perforant path synapses that convey representations of the odor to the hippocampus are strengthened. On some subsequent occasion this odor is presented and produces a pronounced response in the dentate gyrus. The intense firing of a subgroup of granule cells causes a short-term potenti-

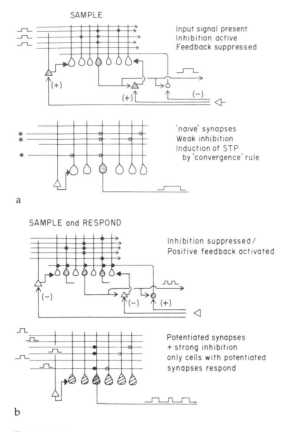

Figure 2.8
Various modes of functioning of the dentate gyrus. (a) Sample mode: An input signal is present in the perforant path while the inhibitory pathways are active and the polymorph cells are inhibited. Only the granule cells receiving large convergence from the input signal are activated and might eventually fire. Conversely, during periods of weak inhibition with feedback activated, a weaker input signal from the perforant path can fire a granule cell. (b) Sample and respond mode: If the inhibition is suppressed, a large number of granule cells fire repetitively. Conversely, in the presence of strong inhibition only cells that have previously potentiated some of their synapses will respond to an input signal in the perforant path.

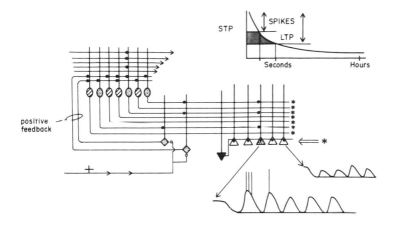

Figure 2.9
Mode of functioning of the dentate gyrus–CA3 system. With the positive feedback system activated and a large number of granule cells firing (en masse activity), convergence of inputs on CA3 pyramidal neurons produces the firing of a small number of CA3 pyramidal neurons. Also indicated are various forms of potentiation of synaptic contacts lasting from seconds [short-term potentiation (STP)] to hours [long-term potentiation (LTP)].

ation of the mossy fiber synapses formed between the granule cells and the CA3 pyramidal cells (figure 2.9). If the detected odor has been classified positively (by the pyriform-DMN system), then the animal will begin search behavior, which presumably involves a switch from intense sniffing mode to locomotion plus sniffing. Because the granule cells are discharging in response to the smell, the addition of locomotor cues will activate the polymorph C/A association, resulting in feedback to the granule cells. Because this is a positive feedback loop, the granule cells will continue to receive excitation while the animal is moving. By acting broadly, the excitatory loop will on occasion drive the granule cells whose synapses were potentiated; initially, when the potentiation is at a maximum, this will cause the target cells in field CA3 to spike, although perhaps not to the degree found when the odor is sampled under optimal conditions.

The mossy fiber system also activates a feed-forward chloride-dependent IPSP system and potassium-mediated late hyperpolarization (Brown and Johnston 1983). As the granule cells are acting en masse, virtually all of the feed-forward system in CA3 will be brought into play with the result that all pyramidal cells will be quickly inhibited. At some point the animal will again sample the odor; if this occurs during movement, granule cells responsive to the initially detected odor will receive both feedback and perforant path inputs, producing (hypothetically) intensive stimulation of the previously potentiated synapses in field CA3. Other odors will stimulate granule cells that will not have potentiated synapses in field CA3 and thus will fail to activate CA3 neurons. Thus movement and the granule cell discharges associated with it will functionally elevate the threshold of the CA3 pyramidal cells and suppress responses to signals other than those sampled (and potentiated) at the beginning of the episode.

In a mechanistic sense, then, we can imagine that detection followed by approach effectively "locks" the animal onto the detected cues. [Extrahippocampal circuitry could exaggerate this process. Freeman (1981) has argued that the brain imposes on the olfactory bulb a "search" pattern of activity that reflects the odor expected for a given occasion. The hippocampal output into the basal forebrain and then into the bulb might be capable of eliciting differential sensitivities appropriate for particular odors.]

Short-term potentiation may also be useful in a more subtle fashion. The animal must be able to distinguish the initial detection of an odor from the "redetection" of that odor—in some sense initial detection of an important odor has to set up an "expectancy" that this odor will occur again in the near future, an expectancy that produces a different response when the odor is encountered a second time (figure 2.10). If nothing else, this information is needed to evaluate actions carried out between the two sampling episodes and to provide certainty that the cue has been correctly identified. As a result of short-term potentiation, the CA3 response will be different in the redetection (potentiated) mode than in the detection (nonpotentiated)

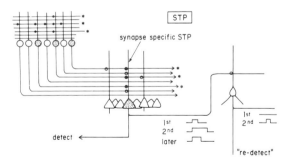

Figure 2.10
Role of short-term potentiation (STP) in redetection of signals. The initial detection of a signal (that is, odor) sets up a synapse-specific STP in the dendrites of some CA3 neurons. As a result, the responses of these neurons will be different in the redetection mode. This change in response can be reflected by the different activation of the target cells of CA3 (probably in CA1).

mode; similarly the target cells of field CA3 will reflect the degree of potentiation in the axons coming from field CA3.

It is noted that the system as described so far would not distinguish an odor approaching from an odor approached. That is, if the animal did not move after the first and second detections and if the odor was still present across the two sampling periods, then two successive responses would be generated, the same condition that holds in a search episode. To distinguish responses occurring with and without movement, the hippocampus could exploit the likelihood that the pattern of CA3 cell responses elicited by potentiated synapses against a background of movement-related inhibition will be different from that elicited without intervening inhibition.

To summarize, we suggest that the en masse activity of the granule cells activates a potent inhibitory system that suppresses responses to cues other than those just perceived and transiently alter the state of the CA3 cells such that their responses are different from those occurring in the absence of movement. Short-term potentiation in the mossy fiber system is postulated to facilitate detection and provide an altered response that denotes the reoccurrence of a recently detected odor.

Short-term potentiation anywhere in the chain leading from the olfactory nerve to the hippocampus could serve as the transient memory function described; however, the peculiar nature of the mossy fiber short-term potentiation suggests that it may be specialized for this role. Note also that the dentate gyrus–CA3 system is also the likely site for integration of movement and detection information, making it a plausible candidate for the generation of redetection signals.

The hypothesis described assumes specific (perforant path) and nonspecific (feedback-promoted) activation of granule cells. An alternative version in which the granule cells respond, because of prior learning and potentiation at their perforant path input, but generate a nonspecific mossy fiber output might also be worth considering. In this version specificity of the CA3 response would be imposed by the perforant path endings in the distal apical dendrites of the pyramidal cells (Hjorth-Simonsen 1972; Steward 1976; Wyss 1981) with the mossy fibers adding information about relative movement strength (figure 2.6). The distal perforant path endings appear to be quite weak at least in field CA1 (Andersen et al. 1980) and possibly in field CA3 as well (Rose, personal communication). Nonetheless, analysis of their interaction with other inputs, including the mossy fibers, might yet reveal a role for these afferents in shaping the CA3 cell response to activity in the entorhinal cortex.

Possible Functions of Topography   The narrow (septotemporally con-strained) projection field of the mossy fibers is most surprising given the much more diffuse nature of the systems that precede (perforant path) and follow (CA3 associational) it. Clearly the topographic or-ganization of the mossy fibers does not serve to transmit "maps" of any kind. As in all discussions of anatomical detail, the possibility must be held in mind that mossy fibers are the way they are because of developmental rather than functional constraints. However, as noted earlier, it seems that the transition from a low-order (quasi-random) design to a series of topographic combinatorial "chips" requires a number of specialized adjustments. Accordingly one sus-pects that mossy fiber organization, which in all probability has been maintained across the entire course of mammalian evolution, is es-sential to hippocampal operation. Here we consider four possibilities; others undoubtedly could be developed.

1. Septotemporal restriction provides a sort of timing device such that transverse processing across the hippocampus interacts at different times with slowly conducting septal and brain stem afferents.

2. The crude topographic organization of the medial perforant path is accompanied by a functional differentiation so that pro-jections from the entorhinal cortex to the dentate gyrus could present different types of information to different segments of the hippocampus, and the maintenance of this segregation is important for processing in field CA3. According to this idea, the topography of the mossy fibers is an "overreaction" to the less precise perforant path organization.

3. The narrow projection field of the mossy fibers reflects so far undiscovered patterns of perforant path afferents that are buried within the divergent-convergent nature of these afferents. The system of perforant path collateral restriction coupled with mossy fiber topography should cluster responses in field CA3; that is, it may serve to place a small number of pyramidal cells reacting to the same input closer together (within narrow sep-totemporal segments) than would be the case if the system were totally random.

4. Topography ensures that the CA3 cells will be activated by the mossy fibers in a temporal sequence, beginning with those py-ramidal neurons closest to the dentate gyrus. If the mossy fibers were to spread randomly throughout field CA3, then spatiotem-poral patterns of this type would be far less precise than would be the case in a rigidly topographic system.

The CA3 Associational System

In the preceding sections we hypothesized that the dentate gyrus–CA3 system serves to provide a kind of maintenance function in which short-term potentiation of the mossy fibers coupled with en masse activity of the granule cells provides a temporary record that previously learned events have occurred in a current behavioral episode. The utility of these mechanisms for tracking odors was stressed, but they could also prove useful in the vital function of associating odors with particular objects.

As noted, association in the sense of linking neural representations poses a problem for networks of the type under discussion. If we assume that an olfactory signal triggers a response in a certain percentage of hippocampal granule cells and that a comparable response is elicited by a nonolfactory cue, the question arises as to how both representations might be processed together in the hippocampus. Simply presenting them together will result in a response that is far larger than the simple addition of the two representations. Synaptic strengthening would then presumably occur between cells that are not part of either representation. One means for obviating this problem would be to present the stimuli sequentially and have the first leave a trace on its targets that remains until the second cue arrives. The cells activated by the second input could then be imagined to potentiate their outputs only on those neurons containing the trace. The difficulty with this lies in the fact that membrane depolarization, the obvious "trace" for an LTP-like learning mechanism, is very short-lived ($\ll$ 1 sec). Various forms of synaptic potentiation, however, possess temporal properties that seem more appropriate for a "trace." But for reasons just alluded to we cannot assume that the external cues that trigger potentiated synapses will be present when the second signal, to which it is to be associated, is presented.

En masse activity by stimulating a substantial portion of the total mossy fiber synaptic field over an interval of time provides one with means for overcoming this difficulty; that is, large-scale activation of the granule cells will produce much larger responses in those cells with recently potentiated synapses (and hence those cells that "represent" recently experienced cues) than it will on CA3 neurons receiving naive contacts from the mossy fibers. By using short-term potentiation, an environmental event that occurred in the recent past can leave a trace of some duration in the field CA3.

In this section we argue that the anatomy of the CA3 system coupled with the postulated maintenance characteristics of the dentate gyrus–CA3 projections are appropriate for obviating the difficulties inherent in forming associations in a combinatorial matrix.

Anatomical Organization   The CA3 pyramidal cells possess large, ramifying apical dendritic trees as well as an extensive "bushy" basal dendritic field. The great majority of both are occupied by fibers generated by CA3 neurons in the ipsi- and contralateral hippocampus (Blackstad 1956; Raisman et al. 1965). It can be assumed that these dendrites contain tens of thousands of synapses. If we assume values of >50,000 contacts with ~200,000 CA3 cells in each hippocampus, then it can be seen that the associational-commissural CA3 dendrite system is potentially a much denser matrix (that is, each pyramidal neuron could potentially be innervated by >10% of the total CA3 field) than those found in the dentate gyrus and the olfactory cortex (figure 2.6). In reality, it is likely that a given axon forms more than one bouton-spine contact per dendrite, thereby substantially reducing the matrix density; however, this is equally likely to be the case for the other systems so far discussed (with the exception of the mossy fibers), and it is reasonable to assume that the CA3 system matrix is an order of magnitude denser than the perforant path system, the pyriform-entorhinal associational system, etc.

It is unfortunate that the CA3 associational system has received little attention from anatomists and physiologists. Lorente de No (1934) describes three subfields: CA3c, CA3b, and CA3a, going from the hilus toward the fimbria. He argued that CA3c and CA3b generate a dense projection that passes on to field CA1 as the Schaffer collaterals, whereas CA3a emits a longitudinal associational projection (LAP) that interconnects CA3a segments along the septotemporal axis of the hippocampus.

Swanson et al. (1978) convincingly demonstrated that each of the subfields contributes to the Schaffer-commissural system and projects broadly throughout CA3c, CA3b, and CA3a; however, Swanson et al. also offer a suggestion that an LAP of the type reported by Lorente de No is present, at least in the ventral hippocampus, but not to the exclusion of CA3a projections to other areas of CA3 and CA1.

Swanson et al. (1978) also demonstrated that even restricted areas of the CA3 subfields generate projections that cover much of the ipsi- and contralateral hippocampus. From the Golgi work of Lorente de No it appears that individual CA3 cells project at right angles to the septotemporal axis of the hippocampus, and in unpublished studies we found this to be true for neurons filled with intracellular injections of horseradish peroxidase. Thus CA3 neurons may have a tendency to project initially at least along the plane of the mossy fibers. Whether all cells or a subpopulation contribute to the septotemporal spread of the associational system is unknown. In any event a line of cells lying along the trajectory of a collection of mossy fibers is likely to receive a denser projection from within the local field than from any other randomly selected plane of the hippocampus [also see Swanson et al. (1978) on possible gradients of terminal densities]. This takes on potential significance in light of the arguments about the significance of the topographic organization of the mossy fibers. That is, if this anatomical feature does indeed result in "clustering" of CA3 cells responsive to a given cue, then a denser within-"chip" associational system increases the likelihood of interconnections between these cells.

As noted, the topographic arrangement of the granule cells has the additional effect of predisposing CA3 to operate in a sequential fashion. The mossy fibers are thin, unmyelinated axons and therefore presumably slowly conducting. This, coupled with their tight topography, ensures that CA3a will receive input from the dentate gyrus with some delay after CA3c, the zone proximal to the dentate gyrus. The outputs of the pyramidal cells will therefore presumably impose EPSPs in a sequence. This could have important biophysical consequences.

There is evidence that the CA3 pyramidal cells innervate their targets, at least those in CA1, in a laminar fashion with CA3c fibers in more distal segment and CA3a axons terminating more proximal to the cell body layer (Swanson et al. 1978; Lynch et al. 1974). This could be quite useful in that the earlier arrival of the distal input would prevent it from being shunted by synaptic conductances closer to the cell body of the target neuron. This argument might be extended to convergence between afferents of the apical and basal dendrites. That is, there is probably an optimal timing of inputs between these, something that might require spatial segregation and sequential stimulation of the cells generating those afferents.

Possible Role of CA3 Associational Systems in Olfactory Behavior   Having briefly described the interconnections of field CA3, we can now turn to the question of its possible contributions to olfactory behavior. It will be recalled that the dentate gyrus–CA3 connections were postulated to provide information needed for tracking odors (short-term memory of what has been detected and approached). As might be inferred from the discussion of CA3 organization, we propose that this system serves to link odors with objects.

Imagine that during a learning episode the animal detects and approaches an odor, whereupon it encounters an object. The animal will alternate between sampling the odor and exploring and manipulating the object. These repeated episodes produce LTP in two collections of perforant path synapses, one activated by the odor and the other stimulated by the object. In field CA3 short-term potentiation will occur in two corresponding groups of mossy fiber synapses. As the animal moves between the two modes of behavior (olfactory and visual/tactile sampling), the en masse response of the granule cells will prolong the responses of the CA3 cells to the stimulus element just sampled. In this way the two populations of pyramidal cells representing the two sensory aspects of the cue will become simultaneously active for brief periods. Long-term potentiation is far more likely to occur on a depolarized background than on a hyperpolarized neuron. Therefore the en masse response of the granule cells will provide a target population of depolarized CA3 cells for the neurons firing in response to the now sampled element; other CA3 cells will be hyperpolarized by the feed-forward inhibitory system operating throughout the hippocampus because of en masse activation of the granule cells. Because of the dense matrix generated by the CA3 collateral system, we can assume that the axons generated by the active pyramidal neurons will converge on a substantial portion of the depolarized cells and thus potentiate. Sequential sampling will thus provide learned linkages between the cells responsive to the elements of the object-odor pair (figure 2.11). Note that this form of association differs radically from that described for the pyriform-entorhinal cortices and the dentate gyrus, where convergence occurred in a sparse matrix and in essence selected a population of target neurons that

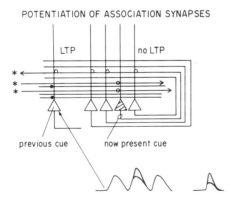

Figure 2.11
Proposed potentiation of association synapses. Two synapses on a CA3 pyramidal neuron that responded to a previous cue are activated (short-term potentiation + en masse activity) (solid contacts). The present cue activates a different CA3 pyramidal neuron, which sends a collateral contacting the previous cue neuron. The en masse activity of granule cells, coupled with STP, produces large depolarization in the previous cue neuron and potentiation of the associational synapse.

became a unitary representation of a complex cue (Lynch 1986). In the CA3 system two distinct representations are generated and maintained, and LTP serves to connect these without necessarily producing a third population of neurons that represent the combined signal.

Once the animal has associated an object with an odor, subsequent odor tracking episodes will result in a situation in which one group of CA3 cells (those firing to the odor) will produce potentiated responses on a second. This might provide the basis for recall. In a weaker sense it will "predispose" the hippocampus to detect an object because the odor-driven potentiated CA3 associational synapses will partially depolarize those CA3 neurons on which the mossy fibers activated by the visual aspects of the object converge. Thus learning provides for stimulus selectivity or, in a sense, expectancy.

Note that the occurrence of an odor response followed by an object response does not by itself tell the animal that the "expected" object has been located. That is, the object by itself in another environment might well trigger the same CA3 cells that respond when the object followed the odor. Information that the odor-object sequence has occurred is useful because it signals that a particular context is present. To "collect" this information, we apparently need a third cell that fires only if object and odor occur sequentially.

It hardly needs to be emphasized that the description of CA3 given here is extremely speculative and certainly simplistic. Hopefully it will be of use in identifying issues that should be resolved before formal models and hypotheses can be attempted. Vitally needed is a more complete description of the projections of the various subfields of CA3 and an analysis of the precise origins of the afferents of the basal dendritic field. Given their different morphologies, it can be assumed that apical and basal dendrites have different biophysical properties from which any number of crucial functional differences could emerge.

Microanatomical studies are also badly needed here (as elsewhere) to determine if individual axons obey constraints in their projection patterns (for example, do collaterals of CA3 initially travel along the trajectory of the mossy fibers?). Physiological experiments are required to determine the rules of plasticity of the various afferents and especially to test the postulated transient synapse-specific potentiation in the mossy fibers.

Data concerning interaction and convergence properties of the system are necessary for a description of the rules dictating how mossy fibers and commissural-associational synapses act together. Finally, the presence or absence of stable LTP in the mossy fibers needs to be

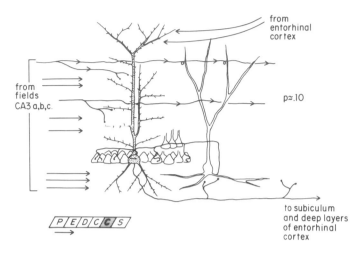

from
entorhinal
cortex

from
fields
CA3 a,b,c.

p≈.10

to subiculum
and deep layers
of entorhinal
cortex

| P | E | D | C | C | S |

Figure 2.12
The organization of CA1. A collection of CA1 pyramidal neurons is shown to receive a relatively dense innervation from the Schaffer-commissural pathways on both apical and basal dendrites. A small projection from the entorhinal cortex innervates the distal apical dendrites. A feed-forward inhibitory interneuron is also represented.

established using chronic recording techniques; the mossy fibers are exotic in so many regards that one would hardly be surprised if they possessed unique versions of synaptic potentiation.

CA3 to CA1: The Schaffer-Commissural System
The projections from CA3 to the field CA1 constitute what must be one of the most massive connections in the brain. They form the overwhelming majority of synapses in well-developed basal and apical dendritic trees and in fact are the only numerically significant afferents of field CA1 (figure 2.12). If we assume that a CA1 pyramidal cell has 50,000 synapses and given that there are ~400,000 CA3 pyramidal cells (counting both hippocampi), we can see that the system forms a dense matrix. Note also that field CA1 is most unusual in that it lacks a feedback (commissural-associational) system, of either the direct (for example, olfactory cortex–field CA3) or indirect (for example, dentate gyrus) variety. Clearly, then, field CA1 represents a relay station in which the output of the CA3 cells is combined or integrated in some fashion that does not occur in field CA3 itself and then is sent out of the pyramidal cell fields without further elaboration.

The question to ask, then, is, What is added at the level of CA1 that is lacking in CA3? One possibility is that the CA1 cells are a type of "and" neuron that discharges if two or more collections of CA3 outputs converge on them (Lynch 1986). We might imagine that the animal in a particular place in the environment rapidly samples two different distal cues, thereby activating two collections of CA3 neurons in rapid sequence, leading to intense depolarization and LTP in field CA1. Potentiation would require several such successive samplings and in the end would produce synapses sufficiently strong to fire the cell when few samples are taken. The resulting cells in CA1 would therefore be more complex in their requirements and thus more specific. O'Keefe (1979) has proposed that the stages of the hippocampus produce ever more precise definitions of spatial locations. This indeed would result from the hypothesis just described.

But the CA1 cell, if responsive in the manner postulated here, would also convey the information that previously established linkages were being activated in a current episode. For odors the cojoint activation of a CA1 neuron by odor- and object-driven CA3 neurons would signal that the searched-for object has been located. This information would not be available in field CA3 because the object-related cells there could fire when the object was presented alone in a nonolfactory context.

Odors are not only associated with specific objects; they also serve to define environments (think of bakeries, animal colonies, machine shops). In these instances the odor is not associated with a specific nonolfactory cue but instead is linked to a diverse collection of objects. In the framework of the present discussion an animal rapidly exploring a defined environment while a strong odor is present would form associations in field CA3 between cells responsive to the odor and those reacting to a number of different elements in the environment. The odor would thus become a "supercue" that predisposes the hippocampus to detect any of a collection of stimuli. If we assume that cells in CA1 are reliably discharged (because of prior LTP) by cojoint activity in CA3 cells and particular objects in the environment, then the collection of CA1 neurons can be viewed as a context signal that denotes the presence of a complex environment.

Odors would be especially useful in defining contexts in which the nonolfactory elements are some distance apart in time or space. Having the same odor-related cells active during the occurrence of two nonolfactory stimuli would provide a bridge between elements that would otherwise be difficult to connect. This could be valuable in nature where a "place" might incorporate a sizable territory or elements that are not tightly fixed in space. This arrangement would be all the more effective if the odor-related CA3 cells were able to discharge some subset of CA1 cells on which they converge with the object-related CA3 outputs. If so, the odor alone would elicit responses in two groups of CA1 cells: those innervated by it alone and those on which it had been potentiated cojointly with nonodor CA3 output. The first group of cells would serve as odor-recognition elements in search behavior; the cojointly potentiated cells would provide information about the context about to be entered. Statistically we can assume the existence of a third group of CA1 neurons: those in which both object- and odor-related CA3 discharges are needed for activation. These would serve to acknowledge that an object cue previously associated with the odor was in fact present in the context.

These postulates regarding the role of the CA3-CA1 system in olfaction should also be relevant to its functions in nonolfactory behavior. Consider the case in which an animal learns to recognize two stimuli that are constantly present in a particular environment.

If these cues are spatially contiguous, then continued exploration will lead to activation of one group of granule cell "chips," with the resultant short-term potentiation of the mossy fiber synapses, followed shortly by movement and en masse activation of the granule cells. As the second stimulus is detected, the perforant path is activated, leading to stimulation of a collection of CA3 neurons by means of the mossy fibers; the associational projections of these will then potentiate on those CA3 cells sufficiently depolarized by mossy fiber contacts that had moments before experienced potentiation, that is, those associated with the first cue. Viewing the cues in reverse order will lead to potentiation in the other direction—from the CA3 cells responsive to the first stimulus to cells driven by the second. This process could be repeated for successive cues until the animal returns to the starting point.

Note that potentiation will occur with decreasing strength across several stimuli as a function of the spatial and thus temporal distance between them, with a time constant dictated by the decay rate of short-term potentiation. In this way a spider web of connection patterns could be constructed in field CA3, with the strength of the links being inversely proportional to the distance between the objects represented by the nodal points in the network. We need not envision this network as cycling in the sense of connectionist models; instead it is postulated to be a complex series of predispositions such that activation of a set of dentate gyrus "chips" will predispose the hippocampus to detect any of several stimuli with the degree of predisposition related to the proximity of the stimulus to the object that initiated the activation sequence (figure 2.13).

Field CA1 in this model plays much the same role as it did for olfactory behavior; it registers the occurrence of an expected sequence

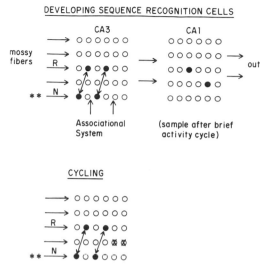

Figure 2.13
Formation of sequence recognition cells in CA1. Two successive signals R and N are associated in CA3 through the combination of short-term potentiation and the en masse activity of granule cells. This results in congruent firing of combinations of CA3 cells responding to both R and N and the emergence in CA1 of cells firing in response to the correct sequence R, N. In addition, the associational system would allow the cycling of neuronal activity in various subpopulations of CA3 neurons initiated by the firing of neurons to one signal.

of distal stimuli. LTP in field CA1 requires near simultaneous activity in a sizable collection of CA3 neurons (the convergence requirement). Therefore, for potentiation to occur in response to two spatial or object cues, the CA3 firing elicited by one cue must partially overlap with that of the second, even though the animal's sensory field is shifting from one cue to another. The combination of short-term potentiation in the mossy fibers, en masse activity of the granule cells, and LTP in the CA3 associational system might be sufficient to meet this requirement. That is, assume that the first cue produces rapidly decaying short-term potentiation in the mossy fibers and that en masse activity of the granule cells causes these synapses to continue to drive their CA3 targets as the animal begins its movement. In essence, the activity of the CA3 cells coded to the first cue is extended beyond the period in which the cue is being sampled. The potentiated associational synapses driven by the first group of CA3 neurons will cause the CA3 cells responsive to the second cue to become active early in the encounter with that cue. Moreover, the associational feedback from the second stimulus will add to the potentiated mossy fiber input to the CA3 cells related to the first cue, causing some of these to fire above baseline levels of activity. In all, the brief interval between successive samplings will be marked by a still shorter period in which two separate groups of CA3 cells are firing. As this is repeated several times, one can imagine that LTP will be generated on the CA1 cells on which the two groups of CA3 outputs converge. These neurons would then serve in future explorations to indicate that the learned association has occurred.

The version of CA3-CA3 and CA3-CA1 interactions just described requires processing of closely spaced cues and synaptic potentiation for a context memory to be established. Exponentially decaying short-term potentiation was envisioned to provide a bridge between cues, providing depolarized targets to produce LTP (generated by the just sampled cue) for cells firing in response to a now present cue. A complex and spatially extended environment would thus require learning of a large number of distal cues. However, the system might work by learning a few salient cues and then using convergence without learning to provide bridges between the cues.

Assume that the animal learns to associate two closely spaced stimuli by the mechanisms outlined. To the extent that partial temporal overlap occurs in the activity of the CA3 neurons coded to these cues, there will be other cells in CA3 that receive convergent inputs from the associational system activated by these two populations. Suppose that those cells receiving the highest degree of convergence, coupled with en masse mossy fiber activity and whatever peripheral inputs reach the hippocampus, are sufficiently depolarized to overcome feed-forward inhibition and therefore spike.

In essence this would be a secondary response to the activation of the encoded cells plus movement-generated input. The firing of these cells would lead to depolarization in a further collection of neurons that are weakly influenced by a subsequent weak peripheral stimulus; in this fashion a kind of chain of activity would be set up by a potent response of CA3 to well-learned environmental cues.

If at the end of the chain a second learned response were to occur, then this would be linked to the first stimulus by the events set in motion by that stimulus rather than through direct connections with it. Chains of activity set up in this way are contingent on the temporal summing properties of CA3 and CA1 cells; little work has been done in this area using multiple small collections of inputs to individual cells. But the idea is inherently attractive because it could provide for a dense (detailed) movement-dependent contextual map with a relatively limited amount of long-term synaptic potentiation. Note that psychologically the chain hypothesis context would be defined by a

TRIGGERED RECALL OF RECENT EVENTS

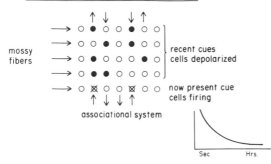

Figure 2.14
Possible recall mechanism in CA3. A number of cells that responded to recent cues have maintained some degree of potentiation in their mossy fiber contacts. The presence of a new cue and the firing of a new population of CA3 neurons activate the associational system, which, when coupled with en masse activity of the granule cells, brings the initial population of cells to firing threshold.

few major learned cues with a number of other stimuli playing an almost subliminal role.

Circumstances are also conceivable under which context is defined by a single dominant visual cue that is observed from several overlapping viewpoints. Rapid scanning and movement would produce a series of CA3 segments to be activated in rapid succession, through the en masse activity/short-term potentiation mechanism. In a sense any collection of CA3 cells responsive to one aspect of the cue would become interconnected with those collections responsive to all other aspects. On subsequent occasions short scanning episodes might be expected to elicit a broad CA3 response; in essence, the salient object would acquire a large representation in the hippocampus. This is an interesting special case; it is conceivable that at some size the representation becomes self-sustaining in that, if enough of it is triggered, the associational system would be sufficient to activate the remainder (figure 2.14). Objects reliably located near the dominant cue would then become associated with it in CA3 with associations in field CA1 signifying both that the cue is present and that an expected association has occurred. In this way, elements that bear no defined or constant spatial relationship to one another would become associated by means of the CA3 cells responsive to the dominant cues in much the way as suggested to occur for odors. In any event the possibility exists that signals present over large parts of the environment have larger representations in the dentate gyrus–CA3 system than do discrete elements in that environment.

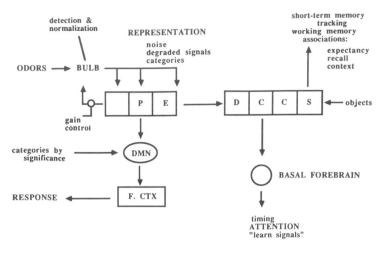

Figure 2.15
Summary of the different operations performed by the networks discussed in the text.

2.4   Discussion

Taxonomy of Memory

The analysis of olfactory projections through the forebrain in terms of "circuitries" indicates that different designs are found in different regions and suggests that these are linked to the different memory operations carried out by these stations (figure 2.15). However, the analysis also points to a taxonomy of memory that is somewhat different from that derived from behavioral and cognitive studies.

The suggestion made here (and earlier) is that the cortex-DMN system collects information that is shared by many physically distinct odors and thus categorizes odors on the basis of experience and then sends this information to cortical areas in which response patterns appropriate to the categories are initiated. In an earlier work (Lynch 1986) it was suggested that this might be considered as a kind of procedural memory, but the appropriateness of this term would depend on the particular definition of "procedural" that is used.

Procedural memory is often discussed in terms of habits or specific sensorimotor acts that are built up over many trials. The cortex-DMN-cortex system, as envisioned here, involves linking groups of sensory cues with groups of motoric sequences. It appears that development of the groups requires extensive training, but adding new stimulus representations to an already present group is rapid. In all, the dorsomedial nucleus system does not fit comfortably into typically defined memory categories.

Similarly, the olfactory (pyriform–lateral entorhinal) cortex-hippocampal system, although constituting a clearly defined circuit, contains sufficiently different subcomponents to suggest that important distinctions exist in their memory-related operations. One distinction touched on throughout the review concerned representation versus association, with representation being postulated as a pyriform-entorhinal operation and association relegated to the hippocampus. We posited that synaptic strengthening serves to stabilize perception and provides for recognition of previously experienced odors (Lynch 1986) even when degraded or obscured.

In preliminary studies using a simulation of a greatly simplified pyriform cortex, we found that synaptic potentiation also allows for the formation of categories or groupings based on physical similarity (Lynch et al. 1988). Thus in the olfactory cortex memory is intimately tied to the physical attributes of the stimulus rather than to its meanings, significance, or associations. It allows the animal to deal with novel odors in terms of their similarities to already learned ones and to provide for more reliable detection of significant smells.

The hippocampus, as previously suggested, is the likely site for association of olfactory and nonolfactory signals, but it is given a broader role in the present analysis (table 2.1):

1. Integration of information about motor activity and strength of the olfactory signal. Does an increase in the strength of an odor signify that an object is approaching or being approached?
2. Formation of a transient record that a known odor has occurred. This would allow the animal to maintain appropriate search or avoidance behaviors for some period after the signal is lost.

Table 2.1
Postulated hippocampal operations and their functions

Postulated hippocampal operation	Function
Short-term potentiation	Tracking; "stimulus locking"
Working memory	Detection; detection and approach
Association (odors:objects; objects:objects)	Expectancy (stimulus selection); recall; context; "maps"
Outputs	Recall signals: hippocampus → cortex (odors-objects); facilitation of recall process (objects-objects) Context signals: encoding; recall (memories stored by context and episode)

3. Association of the representation of an odor with nonolfactory signals. This permits an olfactory signal to predispose the hippocampus to detect and possibly "recall" those signals.
4. Association of a single olfactory cue with several nonolfactory stimuli and thereby use of the cue to identify a context or environment.

Some of these points were also applied to functions of the hippocampus unrelated to olfaction. The formation of associations between neural responses to environmental cues, a process postulated to be facilitated by the "maintenance" mechanism needed for olfactory tracking, could serve to establish predispositions for detection. Context emerges from the idea that higher levels of the hippocampus (CA1) respond to the sequential occurrences of previously associated response patterns to environmental objects.

The notion of context has much in common with the spatial map hypothesis advanced by O'Keefe and Nadel (1978); however, context, as used here, is not solely a spatial property (for example, odors can assist in developing a context), and it can be used in a nonspatial fashion (for example, search for odors in this environment). Recent data by Wible et al. (1986), indicating that hippocampal neurons respond to combinations of stimulus dimensions, are pertinent to this point. Note also that the discharge of "context cells" occurring because two previously associated cues have been detected in sequence, serves not only to inform the animal as to its position but also to notify it that the previous context is still present [see Deadwyler et al. (1985) and Eichenbaum et al. (1987) for data relevant to this issue].

In all, we are suggesting the idea that memories are "grouped" at each stage of the olfactory projections through the hippocampus and the thalamus but according to rules that vary across regions. Physical similarity (shared components) and learning produce odor categories (e.g., cheeses) in layer II of the pyriform-entorhinal cortices, whereas in the layer IV–DMN network a common valence or significance (for example, food) is suggested as a grouping principle. Associations based on spatiotemporal contiguity are hypothesized to occur in the hippocampus with the further suggestion that associations between associations result in the development of a context-recognition system. Later we speculate, admittedly in the absence of pertinent data, on the possibility that context serves to provide in the neocortex for further groupings based on temporal sequences or episodes. The extent to which the various grouping systems can be assigned to catego-

Table 2.2
Short-term potentiation by means of mossy fibers

Characteristics of mossy fibers
Multiple synapses per bouton
Engulfment of extended spines
Vesicle packing
Unusual biochemistry (Zn^{++}, peptides)
Possible unusual forms of synaptic plasticity
Observations
Large potentiation with rapid decay (Hopkins and Johnston 1985)
NMDA independent (Monaghan et al. 1985; Harris et al. 1986)
Synapse specific
May be hormone sensitive
Postulated functions
In tracking, allows for recognition that the now-perceived cue is the same as the one recently sampled; that is, response of CA3 cells to second sample will be larger and therefore will trigger a response in CA3 targets. CA1 cells act as "redetection" elements.
If hormone sensitive, permits differentiation according to significance, that is, longer, more pronounced potentiation to cues that trigger emotional responses.
Coupled with en masse activity of granule cells, generates new possibilities.

ries in current memory classification schemes is not apparent to us, and this question could be a useful subject for further inquiry.

The transient plasticity postulated here to assist in the tracking and associating of cues (tables 2.2 and 2.3) is similar to the "working memory" function ascribed to the hippocampus by Olton et al. (1979). Olton notes that rats are extremely proficient at remembering which arms of a radial maze they have entered on a given day. This memory appears to persist for about 4–5 hours [see also Gallagher et al. (1983)]. Olton argues that the rat forms a permanent memory at some extrahippocampal site of a given testing situation ("reference memory") and then on a given day uses the hippocampus to store a transient list of what it has done in that environment on this day. We speculate that contextual cues are represented in the hippocampus and that the transient memory is due to interactions (for example, approach) between these; we assume that memories, transient and otherwise, of events occurring within a given context are also stored outside the hippocampus, albeit with a facilitatory influence from that structure.

Table 2.3
En masse activity of granule cells

Function of movement-related positive feedback

When coupled with short-term potentiation and feed-forward inhibition:

(1) Provides targets for synaptic potentiation. Will produce large depolarizations in neurons driven by recently sampled cue. Associational synapses formed on these cells by axons from CA3 cells responding to cue will undergo potentiation.

(2) Prolongs firing of CA3 cells coded to a cue and only those cells after the cue is no longer sampled, allowing for congruent firing of CA3 cells to recently sampled cue with CA3 cells responding to present cue.

(3) Obviates the combinatorial explosion that would occur if two cues were simultaneously present. Allows for learning to link two collections of neurons, with the inputs to only one collection being active.

(4) Opens the possibility for "read-out" of memories of recent events, with likelihood of recall greatest for most recent events.

(5) May relate particular stereotyped movements with particular associations (left turn, expectancies, etc.). This follows from opposite density gradients of commissural and associational feedback.

Brain Size and the Behavioral Role of the Hippocampus

As noted in an earlier section, there is some reason to suspect that the increase in neocortical size that is tightly correlated with increases in absolute brain size [see Lynch (1986)] is accompanied by a type of "encephalization" in which the cortex comes to assume an ever-increasing role in all aspects of sensory information processing. If applicable to hippocampal functions, this effect could explain the baffling differences seen in the behavioral consequences of hippocampal damage in rodents versus humans.

For small-brained mammals, associations formed in the hippocampus could be primary in the sense that mapping of the environment and the map itself are developed and stored in the hippocampus; in larger-brained animals (for example, humans) the explosive growth of the neocortex probably offers opportunities for parallel and more efficient processing of certain functions carried out by the hippocampus. As an example, we might suggest the development in the cortex of egocentric spatial/cognitive maps, of the type envisioned by O'Keefe and Nadel (1978), that would render redundant the rather mechanistic series of "predisposition" and context cells we propose for the hippocampus (olfaction is the exception to this argument). But certain features of the hippocampus, notably the extraordinary dentate gyrus, its mossy fibers, and the massive associational system found in the pyramidal cell fields, do not appear to have been reproduced in the neocortex or elsewhere, and thus some capacities of the hippocampus are likely to remain unique to it.

To return to the theme mentioned earlier, we suggest that the function of the hippocampus is to generate an output signal informing the brain that a particular context has been entered into and is at that moment still present. For small-brained animals and for smell in all mammals, the specific information needed to determine context is probably also used in directing moment-to-moment behavior. For large-brained mammals, the contextual framework built on hippocampal associations might be an impoverished but more rapidly developed and easily triggered version of that found in the neocortex.

According to this argument, the en masse activity, short-term potentiation, and dense associational connections found in the hippocampus would in the human carry little specific information content (for example, event A follows event B). Instead it would provide a relatively simple but necessary cue identifying the now present context. But wouldn't this information also be present in the neocortex, as particular conceptual frameworks are activated by the environment? Probably so, but note that the specialized features of the hippocampus coupled with its strategic position between the cortex and the basal forebrain suggest that its signal would be both different in quality and in zones of influence. In the following section we consider this idea in more detail.

The Hippocampus and Memory Storage
The foregoing discussion leads to the question of the role of the hippocampus in memory storage and retrieval in extrahippocampal sites. As already noted, the anatomy of the olfactory system is sufficiently simple to suggest specific pathways through which the hippocampus might influence processing through the bulb and pyriform cortex. Coupling this with the idea of context, we can see that one possible function of the hippocampus would be to assess the environment and then to direct behavior and attention to specific types of cues (Lynch 1986). There is no reason why this argument could not be generalized to nonolfactory learning. The hippocampus has access to all areas of the neocortex by means of the basal forebrain and to a variety of specific regions through its outputs to the deep layers of the entorhinal cortex. Swanson and Kohler (1986) have recently shown that these entorhinal neocortex pathways are even more extensive than previously thought (Van Hoesen and Pandya 1975) and that the medial frontal area innervated by the lateral aspects of the dorsomedial nucleus is the target of a particularly dense projection. Because

this area also receives inputs from the subiculum (Swanson and Cowan 1977), it may constitute a primary target of the hippocampus.

The nature of hippocampal contributions to memory may depend on the extent to which information is stored in corticocortical networks or elsewhere, a parameter that again can be reasonably expected to reflect brain size and thus neocortical volume. The demonstration that hippocampal denervation produces anterograde amnesia for simple cues was made with olfactory stimuli, which are almost certainly processed by cortical (pyriform) tissue. One cannot assume that this holds true for discrete and prominent signals in other modalities that can be processed in precortical stages. Moreover, neocortical expansion may have added modes of memory storage that are not found at all in olfaction or other modalities in small-brained animals.

Tulving (1983) has made the important point that humans store memories in "episodes" containing temporal strings of events. He contrasts this with "semantic" memories, which consist of simple associations of facts (France:Paris). If the hippocampus does in fact define the continuing presence of a particular context, then we might imagine that particular patterns of activity within it define the onset and offset of particular episodes. That is, the continuous output from a particular collection of neurons in the presence of a set of contextual cues is postulated here to be a specialization of the hippocampus. The presence of such an output may be required by the neocortex to link ongoing events into a continuous string.

To speculate further, one could imagine that the hippocampal information also serves to facilitate the reactivation of the episodic string; this might serve to explain the temporally restricted and partial retrograde amnesia reported for humans with temporal lobe dysfunction. Two arguments mitigate against this idea: (1) Retrograde amnesia does not extend to established memories, and (2) human amnesiacs also probably experience a loss of recently acquired simple (semantic?) memories. Regarding the second point, Tulving indicates that even the simplest facts tend to be stored with information about the episode in which they were acquired. Thus the loss of context signals might impair retrieval. The persistence of old memories in the face of hippocampal damage constitutes a serious problem for any argument postulating a role for the hippocampus in retrieval. However, as Squire et al. (1984) note, the property of memory changes with time. One wonders if older records are accurately retained as "episodes" rather than being converted into a series of associated semantic memories. Episodic memory is labile and subject to distortion and in some senses is "reconstituted" on retrieval (Tulving 1983).

Possibly, then, the continuity of and triggers for memories in humans change with time, replacing a film of experience with a series of snapshots, thus eliminating the necessity of the hippocampus for retrieval.

Neurobiological Considerations
This discussion has wandered far from the subject of the structure and organization of brain circuitries and their functions in memory-related behavior. Perhaps this can be excused by an appeal to the argument that the analysis of structure-function relationships is necessarily a two-way street, especially when the structure is only partially understood. By way of concluding, we emphasize again areas in which neurobiological research is urgently needed if realistic and predictive network models are to be realized.

Three types of unanswered questions were identified:

1. "Microanatomy" of individual components in the olfactory chain. More specifically, we need to determine the degree to which the low order found in the projections of small areas of the cortex, hippocampus, etc. is a group or individual cell property. The occurrence of topography intercalated between quasi-random projections suggests that some organizing principle may be found in the distribution of individual axons.

2. Physiological experiments testing for interactions between afferents. Surprisingly little attention has been given to the issue of how afferents landing in different dendritic zones facilitate or block one another and at what temporal and spatial intervals these interactions occur. Reasonable predictions can be made on the basis of known physiology and established biophysical principles, but we suspect that temporal and activity pattern rules exist.

3. Chronic unit recording from animals engaged in appropriate behaviors. Appropriate behavior is difficult to define but, as we have tried to argue, can be predicted from already defined characteristics of networks. Neurobehavioral experiments should thus serve to test hypotheses and to provide essential information for model construction.

Computer simulations of networks are the next logical step in the type of analysis we have followed in this review. These should serve to organize data and focus hypotheses and to yield novel predictions across the dimension running from synaptology to behavior. Moreover, simulations provide tools for asking which anatomical and physiological features are pivotal in the "computational" properties of individual brain networks. Preliminary work has been done on layer II of the pyriform cortex because of its simplicity and well-studied neurobiological properties and because reasonable inferences can be made about its behavioral functions. Extending this to the hippocampus should be possible in the near future. It will indeed be fascinating to compare the results of such efforts with the findings being made using purely theoretical neuronal networks.

To summarize the last two sections, we suggest that the role of the hippocampus in memory is dependent on the size of the neocortex. In all animals the hippocampus uses its "maintenance" properties (short-term potentiation, en masse activity) to form associations between spatially and temporally dispersed stimuli and collects these to generate a context-specific response. In small-brained animals the associations are used as primary information and the context responses are used for negotiation through the environment and to direct behavior so as to be appropriate to it. This last function is needed for the rapid acquisition of new information because it involves the continued attention directed by continuous hippocampal output. In highly encephalized mammals, the associations (except those involving smell) formed in the hippocampus are redundant, as is the context map, at least so far as directing specific behaviors in particular environments is concerned. However, the context signals generated by the hippocampus are still required for rapid encoding of information and are possibly useful in recalling episodes.

2.5   Summary

In this chapter we discussed the anatomical organization and physiological operations of a collection of mammalian forebrain networks with regard to their contributions to memory; in essence, we attempted to deduce function (memory) from structure. We emphasized the hippocampal formation but attempted to place this region in the broader context of the olfactory networks within which it operates.

In the first part of the review we gave several reasons for choosing the olfactory system as a model for elucidating structure-function relationships, with the principal ones being anatomical simplicity and the fact that the olfactory networks are centered in the telencephalon, the brain subdivision thought to be responsible for most aspects of memory in mammals and especially humans.

In the second part of this chapter we summarized previous arguments (Lynch 1986) concerning the relationships between components of the olfactory networks extending through the forebrain and particular aspects of memory. We hypothesized the olfactory cortex to be a low-order combinatorial network with design rules that through learning allow for the assemblage of multicomponent odors into a unitary representation. This provides for a robust recognition memory.

We traced two pathways from the cortex, one through the thalamus into the frontal cortex and a second running into and through the hippocampus. We proposed that the cortex-thalamus-cortex path is a convergent-divergent network that serves to classify odor representations into a few categories defined by experience (for example, food, animal, plant) and to link these with appropriate response sequences.

We postulated the hippocampus to provide for associations between odors and objects and to recognize contextual cues needed to direct the animal toward olfactory signals. We believe that hippocampal output to the olfactory networks serves functions necessary for the efficient encoding of new odor memories in those networks.

In section 2.3 we dealt with intrahippocampal circuitries and their roles in memory. We briefly reviewed physiological properties and described a type of synaptic plasticity thought to be involved in the encoding of memory. Using these plasticity rules and the organization of hippocampal networks, we put forward the hypothesis that the hippocampus associates cues that occur in spatial/temporal sequence, that is, before and after particular locomotor movements. In the simplest olfactory case this information is useful in tracking because it informs the animal that a recently experienced odor has reoccurred. Coupled with associative learning in the hippocampus, it produces sequences of the type odor:movement:object. Elaboration of these basic processes results in groups or strings of learned sequences that together define environmental context. The three basic stages of hippocampal circuitry make quite different contributions to the extraction of information about the occurrence of sequences in the environment.

The dentate gyrus receives olfactory and nonolfactory cue information from the entorhinal cortex and produces a short-term potentiation of its mossy fiber contacts with the CA3 pyramidal cells. We postulated that movement or the "intention" to move disinhibits the convergent-divergent dentate gyrus associational system and thereby causes widespread firing of the granule cells (en masse activation). We raised the possibility that different movements activate different groups of granule cells.

En masse activity in the granule cells produces widespread feedforward hyperpolarization in the CA3 field that is partially offset in those cells with synapses potentiated by the cue present immediately before the onset of movement. The occurrence of a second environmental stimulus then activates a second group of CA3 neurons, the collaterals of which potentiate their synapses on those pyramidal cells partially depolarized by the previously potentiated synapses. We argued that the dense matrix generated by the CA3 associational system is needed for this type of association to occur. The output of field CA3 (the Schaffer-commissural projections) produces long-term potentiation on those cells cojointly innervated by the two separate collections of CA3 cells (those cells responsive to the first and second cues). In future episodes the presentation of one of the two cues predisposes field CA3 cells to respond to the second cue with field CA1 neurons firing if the "expected" cue does in fact occur.

The learned associations in the hippocampus contribute to memory in several ways. First, the hippocampus serves as a site in which particular types of associations are formed and "stored." In the olfactory modality it may well be the single site at which higher-order representations of odors and objects become linked so that an odor can produce the recall of the object (presumably by means of hippocampal output to the cortex) or a predisposition to perceive it. For other modalities it may well be the case that learned associations formed in the hippocampus are redundant to those found in the neocortex, at least in larger-brained and more encephalized animals.

The second role of the hippocampus is postulated to reflect the particular kind of associations it is assumed to create and to the pattern of its output connections. Through its connections with the basal forebrain, the hippocampus is well positioned to influence activity in all aspects of the cortical telencephalon; this provides a route through which context information (in the form of expected cue sequence) could direct attention and behavior in a manner consonant with past experience.

Acknowledgments

This work was supported by the Office of Naval Research under grant N00014-K-0333. We wish to thank Jackie Porter and Marla Lay for their expert and dedicated secretarial work.

References

Alger, B. E., and R. A. Nicoll. 1979. "GABA-mediated biphasic inhibitory response in hippocampus." *Nature* 281:315–317.

Alkon, D. 1984. "Calcium-mediated reduction of ionic currents: A biophysical memory trace." *Science* 226:1037–1045.

Andersen, P., T. W. Blackstad, and T. Lomo. 1966. "Location and identification of excitatory synapses on hippocampal pyramidal cells." *Experimental Brain Research* 1:236–248.

Andersen, P., B. Holmquist, and P. E. Voorhoeve. 1966. "Excitatory synapses on hippocampal apical dendrites activated by entorhinal stimulation." *Acta Physiologica Scandinavia* 66:461–472.

Andersen, P., H. Silfvenius, S. H. Sundberg, and O. Sveen. 1980. "A comparison of distal and proximal dendritic synapses on CA1 pyramids in guinea-pig hippocampal slices in vitro." *Journal of Physiology* 307:273–299.

Andersen, P., S. H. Sundberg, O. Sveen, and H. Wigstrom. 1977. "Specific long-lasting potentiation of synaptic transmission in hippocampal slices." *Nature* 266:736–737.

Andersen, P., R. Dingledine, L. Gjerstad, I. A. Landmoen, and A. Mosfeldt-Laursen. 1980. "Two different responses of hippocampal pyramidal cells to application of gamma-amino butyric acid." *Journal of Physiology* 305:279–296.

Anderson, J. R. 1976. *Language, Memory and Thought*. Hillsdale, N.J.: Erlbaum.

Blackstad, T. W. 1956. "Commissural connections of the hippocampal region in the rat with special reference to their mode of termination." *Journal of Comparative Neurology* 105:417–537.

Blackstad, T. W., and A. Kjaerheim. 1961. "Special axo-dendritic synapses in the hippocampal cortex: Electron and light microscopic studies in the layer of mossy fibers." *Journal of Comparative Neurology* 117:133–159.

Blackstad, T. W., K. Brink, J. Hem, and B. Jeune. 1970. "Distribution of hippocampal mossy fibers in the rat: An experimental study with silver impregnation methods." *Journal of Comparative Neurology* 138:433–450.

Bliss, T. V. P., and A. T. Gardner-Medwin. 1973. "Long-lasting potentiation of synaptic transmission in the dentate area of the unanesthetized rabbit following stimulation of the perforant path." *Journal of Physiology* (London), 232:357–374.

Bliss, T. V. P., and T. Lomo. 1973. "Long-lasting potentiation of synaptic transmission in the dentate area of the anesthetized rabbit following stimulation of the perforant path." *Journal of Physiology* (London), 232:331–356.

Brown, T. H., and D. Johnston. 1983. "Voltage-clamp analysis of mossy fiber synaptic input to hippocampal neurons." *Journal of Neurophysiology* 50:487–507.

Chang, F. L. F., and W. T. Greenough. 1984. "Transient and enduring morphological correlates of synaptic activity and efficacy change in the rat hippocampal slice." *Brain Research* 309:35–46.

Chronister, R. B., R. W. Sikes, and L. E. White, Jr. 1975. "Postcommissural fornix: Origin and distribution in the rodent." *Neuroscience Letters* 1:199–201.

Cohen, D. H. 1980. "The functional neuroanatomy of a conditioned response," in *Neural Mechanisms of Goal-Directed Behavior and Learning*, R. F. Thompson, L. H. Hicks, and V. B. Shvyrkov, eds. New York: Academic Press, 283–302.

Cohen, N., and L. R. Squire. 1980. "Preserved learning and retention of pattern analyzing skill in amnesia: Dissociation of knowing how and knowing what." *Science* 210:207–209.

Collingridge, G. L., S. J. Kehl, and H. McLennan. 1983. "The antagonism of amino-acid-induced excitation of rat hippocampal CA1 neurones in vitro." *Journal of Physiology* 334:19–31.

Deadwyler, S. A., M. West, and G. Lynch. 1979a. "Activity of dentate granule cells during learning: Differentiation of perforant path input." *Brain Research* 169:29–43.

Deadwyler, S. A., M. West, and G. Lynch. 1979b. "Synaptically identified hippocampal slow potentials during behavior." *Brain Research* 161:211–225.

Deadwyler, S. A., M. O. West, and J. H. Robinson. 1981. "Entorhinal and septal inputs differentially control sensory-evoked responses in rat dentate gyrus." *Science* 211:1131–1183.

Deadwyler, S. A., J. West, C. W. Cotman, and G. Lynch. 1975. "Physiological studies of the reciprocal connections between hippocampus and entorhinal cortex." *Experimental Neurology* 49:35–42.

Deadwyler, S. A., M. O. West, E. P. Christian, R. E. Hampson, and T. C. Foster. 1985. "Sequence-related changes in sensory-evoked potentials in the dentate gyrus: A mechanism for item-specific short-term information storage in the hippocampus." *Behavioral and Neural Biology* 44:201–212.

Dunwiddie, T. V., and G. S. Lynch. 1978. "Long-term potentiation and depression of synaptic responses in the rat hippocampus: Localization and frequency dependency." *Journal of Physiology* (London), 276:353–367.

Eichenbaum, H., K. J. Shedlack, and K. W. Eckmann. 1980. "Thalamocortical mechanisms in odor-guided behavior I. Effects of lesions of the medio dorsal thalamic nucleus and frontal cortex on olfactory discrimination in the rat." *Brain Behavior Evolution* 17:255–275.

Eichenbaum, H., M. Kuperstein, A. Fagan, and J. Nagode. 1987. "Cue-sampling and goal-approach correlates of hippocampal unit activity in rats performing an odor-discrimination task." *Journal of Neuroscience* 7(3):716–732.

Eichenbaum, H., T. H. Morton, H. Potter, and S. Corkin. 1983. "Selective olfactory deficits in case H.M." *Brain* 106:459–472.

Fox, S. E., and J. B. Ranck, Jr. 1975. "Localization and anatomical identification of theta and complex-spike cells in dorsal hippocampal formation of rats." *Experimental Neurology* 49:299–313.

Fox, S. E., and J. B. Ranck, Jr. 1981. "Electrophysiological characteristics of hippocampal complex-spike cells and theta cells." *Experimental Brain Research* 41:399–410.

Freeman, W. J. 1981. "A physiological hypothesis of perception." *Perspectives in Biological Medicine* 24:561–592.

Freeman, W. J. 1987. "Stimulation of chaotic EEG patterns with a dynamic model of the olfactory system." *Biological Cybernetics* 56:139–150.

Gall, C., and G. Lynch. 1980. "The regulation of fiber growth and synaptogenesis in the developing hippocampus," in *Topics in Developmental Biology*, G. K. Hunt, ed. New York: Academic Press, vol. 15, 159–180.

Gall, C., N. Brecha, T. Chang, and H. Karten. 1981. "Localization of enkephalins in rat hippocampus." *Journal of Comparative Neurology* 198:335–350.

Gallagher, M., R. A. King, and N. B. Young. 1983. "Opiate antagonists improve spatial memory." *Science* 221:975–976.

Gelperin, A., J. J. Hopfield, and D. W. Tank. 1986. "The logic of Limax learning," in *Model Neural Networks and Behavior*, A. I. Silverston, ed. New York: Plenum Press.

Gottlieb, D. I., and W. M. Cowan. 1973. "Autoradiographic studies of the commissural and ipsilateral association connections of the hippocampus and dentate gyrus of the rat I. The commissural connections." *Journal of Comparative Neurology* 149:393–422.

Haberly, L. B. 1985. "Neuronal circuitry in olfactory cortex: Anatomy and functional implications." *Chemical Senses* 10:219–238.

Harris, E. W., and C. W. Cotman. 1986. "Long-term potentiation of guinea-pig mossy fiber responses is not blocked by N-methyl-D-aspartate antagonists." *Neuroscience Letters* 70:132–137.

Higashima, M., and C. Yamamoto. 1985. "Two components of long-term potentiation in mossy fiber–induced excitation in hippocampus." *Experimental Neurology* 90:529–539.

Hjorth-Simonsen, A. 1972. "Projection of the lateral part of the entorhinal area to the hippocampus in the rat: An experimental analysis." *Journal of Comparative Neurology* 147:145–162.

Hjorth-Simonsen, A. 1973. "Some intrinsic connections of the hippocampus in the rat: An experimental analysis." *Journal of Comparative Neurology* 147:145–162.

Hopkins, W. F., and D. Johnston. 1984. "Frequency-dependent noradrenergic modulation of long-term potentiation in the hippocampus." *Science* 226:350–352.

Jerison, H. J. 1973. *Evolution of the Brain and Intelligence.* New York: Academic Press.

Jourdan, F. 1982. "Spatial dimension of olfactory coding: A representation of 14C-2-deoxyglucose patterns of glomerular labeling in the olfactory bulb." *Brain Research* 240:341–344.

Kandel, E. R., and J. H. Schwartz. 1982. "Molecular biology of learning: Modulation of transmitter release." *Science* 218:433–443.

Kelso, S. R., A. H. Ganong, and T. H. Brown. 1986. "Hebbian synapses in hippocampus." *Proceedings of the National Academy of Sciences USA* 83:5326-5330.

Kosaka, T., K. Hama, and J. Wu. 1984. "GABAergic synaptic boutons in the granule cell layer of rat dentate gyrus." *Brain Research* 293:353–359.

Kubie, J. L., and J. B. Ranck, Jr. 1984. "Hippocampal neuronal firing, context and learning," in *Neuropsychology of Memory,* L. Squire and N. Butters, eds. New York: Guilford Press, 417–423.

Lacey, D. J. 1978. "The organization of the hippocampus of the fence lizard: A light microscopic study." *Journal of Comparative Neurology* 182:247–264.

Lancet, D., C. A. Greer, J. S. Kauer, and G. M. Shepherd. 1982. "Mapping of odor-related neuronal activity in the olfactory bulb by high-resolution 2-deoxyglucose autoradiography." *Proceedings of the National Academy of Sciences USA* 79:670–674.

Larson, J., and G. S. Lynch. 1986. "Synaptic potentiation in hippocampus by patterned stimulation involves two events." *Science* 232:985–988.

Larson, J., and G. Lynch. In press. "Role of N-methyl-D-aspartate receptors in the induction of synaptic potentiation by burst stimulation patterned after the hippocampal θ-rhythm." *Brain Research.*

Larson, J., D. Wong, and G. Lynch. 1986. "Patterned stimulation at the theta frequency is optimal for induction of long-term potentiation." *Brain Research* 368(3):7–35.

Lee, K., M. Oliver, F. Schottler, and G. Lynch. 1981. "Electron microscopic studies of brain slices: The effects of high-frequency stimulation on dendritic ultrastructure," in *Electrical Activity in Isolated Mammalian CNS Preparations,* G. Kerkut, ed. New York: Academic Press, 189–212.

Lee, K., F. Schottler, M. Oliver, and G. Lynch. 1980. "Brief bursts of high-frequency stimulation produce two types of structural change in rat hippocampus." *Journal of Neurophysiology* 44:247–258.

Lorente de No, R. 1934. "Studies on the structure of the cerebral cortex II. Continuation of the study of the ammonic system." *Journal of Psychological Neurology* 46:113–177.

Loy, R., D. A. Koziell, J. D. Lindsey, and R. Y. Moore. 1980. "Noradrenergic innervation of the adult rat hippocampal formation." *Journal of Comparative Neurology* 184:699–710.

Lynch, G. 1986. *Synapses, Circuits and the Beginnings of Memory.* Cambridge, Mass.: MIT Press.

Lynch, G., and M. Baudry. 1984. "The biochemistry of memory: A new and specific hypothesis." *Science* 224:1057–1063.

Lynch, G. S., T. V. Dunwiddie, and V. Gribkoff. 1977. "Heterosynaptic depression: A postsynaptic correlate of long-term potentiation." *Nature* 266:737–739.

Lynch, G., G. Rose, and C. Gall. 1978. "Anatomical and functional aspects of the septo-hippocampal projections." *Functions of the Septo-Hippocampal System* (Liba Foundation Symposium, vol. 58). Amsterdam: Elsevier and North-Holland, 5–24.

Lynch, G., C. Gall, P. Mensah, and C. W. Cotman. 1973. "Horseradish peroxidase histochemistry: A new method for tracing efferent projections in the central nervous system." *Brain Research* 65:373–380.

Lynch, G., R. Granger, J. Larson, and M. Baudry. 1988. "Cortical encoding of memory: Hypothesis derived from analysis and simulation of physiological learning rule in anatomical structures," in *Neuronal Connections*, L. Nadel, L. A. Cooper, P. Culicover, and R. M. Harnish, eds. Cambridge, Mass.: MIT Press. A Bradford Book.

Lynch, G., J. Larson, S. Kelso, G. Barrionuevo, and F. Schottler. 1983. "Intracellular injections of EGTA block the induction of hippocampal long-term potentiation." *Nature* 305:719–721.

McClelland, J. C., D. E. Rumelhart, and PDP Research Group. 1986. *Parallel Distributed Processing*. Cambridge, Mass.: MIT Press.

McDermott, A. B., M. L. Mayer, G. L. Westbrook, S. J. Smith, and J. L. Barker. 1986. "NMDA receptor activation increases cytoplasmic calcium concentration in cultured spinal cord neurones." *Nature* 321:519–522.

McNaughton, B. L., and C. A. Barnes. 1977. "Physiological identification and analysis of dentate granule cell responses to stimulation of the medial and lateral perforant pathways in the rat." *Journal of Comparative Neurology* 175:439–454.

McNaughton, B. L., C. A. Barnes, and P. Andersen. 1981. "Synaptic efficacy and EPSP summation in granule cell of rat fascia dentata studied in vitro." *Journal of Neurophysiology* 46:952–966.

McNaughton, B. L., R. M. Douglas, and G. V. Goddard. 1978. "Synaptic enhancement in fascia dentata: Cooperativity among coactive afferents." *Brain Research* 157:277–293.

McWilliams, J. R., and G. S. Lynch. 1979. "Terminal proliferation in the partially deafferented dentate gyrus: Time courses for the appearance and removal of degeneration and the replacement of lost terminals." *Journal of Comparative Neurology* 187:191–198.

Malinow, R., and J. P. Miller. 1986. "Postsynaptic hyperpolarization during conditioning reversibly blocks induction of long-term potentiation." *Nature* 320:529–530.

Matthews, D. A., C. Cotman, and G. Lynch. 1976. "An electron microscopic study of lesion-induced synaptogenesis in the dentate gyrus of the adult rat I. Magnitude and time course of degeneration." *Brain Research* 115:1–21.

Mayer, M. G., G. L. Westbrook, and P. B. Guthrie. 1984. "Voltage-dependent block by Mg^{2+} of NMDA responses in spinal cord neurons." *Nature* 309:261–263.

Meiback, R. C., and A. Seigel. 1975. "The origin of fornix fibers which project to the mammillary bodies of the rat: A horseradish peroxidase study." *Brain Research* 88:518–522.

Meiback, R. C., and A. Seigel. 1977. "Efferent connections of the hippocampal formation in the rat." *Brain Research* 124:197–224.

Misgeld, U., J. Sarvey, and M. R. Klee. 1979. "Heterosynaptic postactivation potentiation in hippocampal CA3 neurons: Long-term changes of the postsynaptic potentials." *Experimental Brain Research* 37:217–229.

Mishkin, M., B. Malamut, and J. Bachevalier. 1984. "Memories and habits: Two neural systems," in *Neurobiology of Learning and Memory*, G. S. Lynch, J. L. McGaugh, and N. Weinberger, eds. New York: Guilford Press, 65–78.

Monaghan, D., V. R. Holets, D. W. Toy, and C. W. Cotman. 1983. "Anatomical distributions of four pharmacologically distinct 3H-L-glutamate binding sites." *Nature* 306:176–178.

Moore, R. Y., and A. Halaris. 1975. "Hippocampal innervation by serotonin neurons of the midbrain raphe in the cat." *Journal of Comparative Neurology* 164:171–184.

Morris, R. G. M., E. Anderson, G. Lynch, and M. Baudry. 1986. "Selective impairment of learning and blockade of long-term potentiation by an *N*-methyl-D-aspartate receptor antagonist, AP-5." *Nature* 319:774–776.

Mosko, S., G. Lynch, and C. W. Cotman. 1973. "The distribution of septal projections to the hippocampus of the rat." *Journal of Comparative Neurology* 152:163–174.

Mouly, A. M., M. Vigouroux, and A. Holley. 1985. "On the ability of rats to discriminate between microstimulations of the olfactory bulb in different locations." *Behavior and Brain Research* 17:45–58.

Nadel, L., J. Willner, and E. M. Kurz. 1985. "Cognitive maps and environmental context," in *Context and Learning,* D. Balsam and A. Tomic, eds. Hillsdale, N.J.: Erlbaum, 385–406.

Nowak, L., P. Bregestovski, P. Ascher, A. Herbet, and A. Prochiantz. 1984. "Magnesium gates glutamate-activated channels in mouse central neurones." *Nature* 307:462–465.

O'Keefe, J. 1979. "A review of the hippocampal place cells." *Progress in Neurobiology* 13:419–439.

O'Keefe, J., and L. Nadel. 1978. *The Hippocampus as a Cognitive Map.* London: Oxford University Press.

Olton, D. S., J. T. Becker, and G. E. Handelmann. 1979. "Hippocampus, space and memory." *Behavior and Brain Sciences* 2:313–365.

Overman, W. H., Jr., and R. W. Doty. 1980. "Prolonged visual memory in macaques and man." *Neuroscience* 5:1875–1831.

Racine, R. J., N. W. Milgram, and S. Hafner. 1983. "Long-term potentiation phenomena in the rat limbic forebrain." *Brain Research* 260:217–231.

Raisman, G., W. D. Cowan, and T. P. S. Powell. 1965. "The extrinsic afferent, commissural and associational fibers of the hippocampus." *Brain Research* 88:963–996.

Ranck, J. B., Jr. 1973. "Studies on single neurons in dorsal hippocampal formation and septum in unrestrained rats." *Experimental Neurology* 41:462–531.

Rolls, E. T. 1984. "Neurophysiological investigations of different types of memory in the primate," in *Neuropsychology of Memory,* L. R. Squire and N. Butters, eds. New York: Guilford Press, 269–278.

Roman, R., U. Staubli, and G. Lynch. 1987. "Evidence for synaptic potentiation in a cortical network during learning." *Brain Research* 418:221–226.

Rose, G., and P. Schubert. 1977. "Release and transfer of ^{3}H-adenosine derivative in the cholinergic septal system." *Brain Research* 121:353–357.

Rose, G., D. Diamond, and G. Lynch. 1983. "Dentate granule cells in the rat hippocampal formation have the behavioral characteristics of theta neurons." *Brain Research* 266:29–37.

Ruth, R. D., J. J. Collier, and A. Routtenberg. 1982. "Topography between the entorhinal cortex and the dentate septotemporal axis in rats I. Medial and intermediate entorhinal projecting cells." *Journal of Comparative Neurology* 209:69–78.

Schacter, D. L. 1985. "Multiple forms of memory in humans and animals," in *Memory Systems of the Brain,* N. Weinberger, J. McGaugh, and G. Lynch, eds. New York: Guilford Press, 351–379.

Schwartz, S. P., and P. D. Coleman. 1981. "Neurons of origin of the perforant path." *Experimental Neurology* 74:305–312.

Shepherd, G. M. 1979. *The Synaptic Organization of the Brain,* second edition. New York: Oxford University Press.

Slotnick, B. M., and N. Kaneko. 1981. "Role of mediodorsal thalamic nucleus in olfactory discrimination learning in rats." *Science* 214:91–92.

Slotnick, B. M., and H. M. Katz. 1974. "Olfactory learning-set formation in rats." *Science* 185:796–798.

Squire, L. S. 1986. "Mechanisms of memory." *Science* 232:1612–1619.

Squire, L. R., C. Cohen, and L. Nadel. 1984. "The medial temporal region and memory consolidation: A new hypothesis," in *Memory Consolidation*, H. Weingartner and E. Parker, eds. Hillsdale, N.J.: Erlbaum, 185–209.

Standing, L. 1973. "Learning 10,000 pictures." *Quarterly Journal of Experimental Psychology* 25:207–222.

Staubli, U., and G. Lynch. 1987. "Stable hippocampal long-term potentiation elicited by 'theta' pattern stimulation." *Brain Research* 435:227–234.

Staubli, U., G. Ivy, and G. Lynch. 1985. "Denervation of hippocampus causes rapid forgetting of olfactory memory in rats." *Proceedings of the National Academy of Sciences USA* 81:5885–5887.

Staubli, U., D. Fraser, R. Faraday, and G. Lynch. 1987. "Olfaction and the 'data' memory system in rats." *Behavioral Neuroscience* 101:757–765.

Staubli, U., D. Fraser, M. Kessler, and G. Lynch. 1986. "Studies on retrograde and anterograde amnesia of olfactory memory after denervation of the hippocampus by entorhinal cortex lesions." *Behavioral and Neural Biology* 46(3):432–444.

Staubli, U., F. Schottler, D. Nejat-Bina, and G. Lynch. 1987. "Role of dorsomedial thalamic nucleus and piriform cortex in processing olfactory information." *Behavioral and Brain Research* 25:117–129.

Staubli, U., O. Thibault, M. DiLorenzo, and G. Lynch. In press. "Antagonism of NMDA receptors impairs acquisition but not retention of olfactory memory." *Behavioral Neuroscience*.

Steward, O. 1976. "Topographic organization of the projections from the entorhinal area to the hippocampal formation of the rat." *Journal of Comparative Neurology* 167:285–314.

Steward, O., and S. A. Scoville. 1976. "Cells of origin of entorhinal cortical afferents to the hippocampus and fascia dentata of the rat." *Journal of Comparative Neurology* 169:347–370.

Swanson, L. W., and C. M. Cowan. 1977. "An autoradiographic study of the organization of the efferent connection of the hippocampal formation in the rat." *Journal of Comparative Neurology* 172:49–84.

Swanson, L. W., and W. D. Cowan. 1975. "Hippocampal-hypothalamic connections: Origin in subicular cortex, not Ammon's horn." *Science* 189:303–304.

Swanson, L. W., and C. Kohler. 1986. "Anatomical evidence for direct projections from the entorhinal area to the entire cortical mantle in the rat." *Journal of Neuroscience* 6:3010–3023.

Swanson, L. W., P. E. Sawchenko, and W. M. Cowan. 1981. "Evidence for collateral projections by neurons in Ammon's horn, the dentate gyrus, and the subiculum: A multiple retrograde labeling study in the rat." *Journal of Neuroscience* 1:548–559.

Swanson, L. W., J. M. Wyss, and W. N. Cowan. 1978. "An autoradiographic study of the organization of intrahippocampal association pathways in the rat." *Journal of Comparative Neurology* 181:681–716.

Teyler, T. J., and P. Discenna. 1986. "Long-term potentiation as a candidate mnemonic device." *Brain Research Review* 7:15–28.

Thompson, R. F. 1986. "The neurobiology of learning and memory." *Science* 233:941–947.

Tulving, E. 1983. *Elements of Episodic Memory*. Oxford: Clarendon Press.

Valverde, F. 1965. *Studies on the Piriform Lobe.* Cambridge, Mass.: Harvard University Press.

Van Hoesen, G. W., and D. N. Pandya. 1975. "Some connections of the entorhinal (area 28) and perirhinal (area 35) cortices of the rhesus monkey III. Efferent connections." *Brain Research* 95:39–59.

Weinberger, N. M. 1980. "Neurophysiological studies of learning in association with the pupillary dilation conditioned reflex," in *Neural Mechanisms of Goal-Directed Behavior and Learning*, R. F. Thompson, L. H. Hicks, and V. B. Shvyrkov, eds. New York: Academic Press, 241–246.

Weinberger, N. M. 1982. "Effect of conditioned arousal on the auditory system," in *The Neural Basis of Behavior*, A. L. Beckman, ed. Jamaica, N.Y.: Spectrum, 63–91.

Wenzel, J., and H. Matthies. 1985. "Morphological changes in the hippocampal formation accompanying memory formation and long-term potentiation," in *Memory Systems of the Brain*, N. Weinberger, J. McGaugh, and G. Lynch, eds. New York: Guilford Press, 156–170.

West, M. D., and A. H. Andersen. 1980. "An allometric study of the ara dentata in the rat and mouse." *Brain Research Review* 2:97–110.

West, J. R., S. A. Deadwyler, C. W. Cotman, and G. S. Lynch. 1975. "Time-dependent changes in commissural field potentials in the dentate gyrus following lesions of the entorhinal cortex in adult rats." *Brain Research* 97:215–233.

Wible, C. G., R. L. Findling, M. Shapiro, E. J. Lang, S. Crane, and D. S. Olton. 1986. "Mnemonic correlates of unit activity in the hippocampus." *Brain Research* 399:97–110.

Wigstrom, H., and B. Gustafsson. 1983. "Facilitated induction of long-lasting potentiation during blockade of inhibition." *Nature* 301:603–605.

Woody, C. D. 1982. *Memory, Learning, and Higher Function: A Cellular View.* New York: Springer.

Wyss, J. M. 1981. "Autoradiographic study of the efferent connections of entorhinal cortex in the rat." *Journal of Comparative Neurology* 199:495–512.

Yamamoto, C., and T. Chujo. 1978. "Long-term potentiation in thin hippocampal sections studied by intracellular and extracellular recordings." *Experimental Neurology* 58:242–250.

Zimmer, J. 1971. "Ipsilateral afferents to the commissural zone of the fascia dentata demonstrated in decommissurated rats by silver impregnation." *Journal of Comparative Neurology* 23:393–416.

3

A Basic Circuit of Cortical Organization

Gordon M. Shepherd

The intrinsic organization of the cerebral cortex is crucial to the neural basis of human cognitive functions. There are three main types of cortex: paleocortex (consisting of the regions that receive olfactory input), archicortex (the hippocampus), and neocortex (that part of the cerebral mantle that has proliferated so extensively in the human). Anatomists have defined each of these regions in terms of different cell layers, cell types, and connections with other regions. The traditional view arising from this work is that perception and memory and other higher cognitive functions in the human depend primarily on principles of organization that are special for the intrinsic neocortical circuits [see, for example, Lorente de No (1938), Edelman and Mountcastle (1979), and Schmitt et al. (1981)].

A complementary view is that behind the differences in anatomical structure is a more fundamental plan of intrinsic organization that is similar in the three types (Shepherd 1974, 1979). This view arose from a study of olfactory cortex (Haberly and Shepherd 1973) and was originally set forth as follows:

> It is suggested that the study of synaptic organization provides a basis for distinguishing certain characteristics of local organization that may be termed cortical. . . . It implies that certain modes of information processing are possible with a cortical type of organization that are not possible with other, noncortical, types. (Shepherd 1974, p. 258)

The test for this fundamental plan is thus at the level of local circuit organization, that is, at the level of the individual cortical neuron and the local circuits and microcircuits it forms through synapses with its neighbors. These circuits form functional modules that carry out a range of specific operations. Many recent studies suggest that this type of modularization is widespread in the nervous system and that in terms of gene expression it is an effective mechanism for laying down neural circuits during development.

An understanding of cortical function at this level thus requires an approach that bridges traditional anatomical distinctions and is concerned with the basic rules for the organization of intrinsic cortical circuits. This type of approach is necessarily multidisciplinary, requiring *anatomical* methods for identification and characterization of neuronal morphologies, fine structure, and synaptic connections; *physiological* methods for describing impulse and synaptic properties; *neurochemical* methods for characterizing biochemical pathways, transmitters, modulators, and second messengers; *genetic* and *immunological* methods for identifying gene products and mechanisms of development; and *computational* methods for testing models of neuronal and synaptic circuit function.

The purpose of this review is to summarize recent work in the different types of cortex in order to test and update the original hypothesis: that there is a set of basic principles that governs the organization of intrinsic circuits in the main types of cerebral cortex. We consider what kinds of insights this gives us into the neural basis of behavior mediated by the mammalian neocortex, particularly the higher cognitive functions of humans. An underlying premise of this review is that the principles of organization have practical implications for the construction of neural networks that can more accurately simulate human cognitive functions.

3.1   Plan of Review

In order to characterize and compare the organization of different types of cortex, we need a common framework and a common vocabulary. For this purpose the present discussion is organized around the concept of a *basic circuit*. This concept is based on the fact that any region of the nervous system can be characterized in terms of three possible neural components: *inputs,* which bring information from other regions; *output* neurons, which send the output of their region (and thus constitute inputs to other regions); and *intrinsic* neurons, whose processes are confined within their region (Shepherd 1979). The organization of neural regions consists of the interconnections and interactions of this triad of fundamental components. Because the interconnections and interactions can vary greatly, we begin by focusing on the single type of connection between the components that is most numerous and most important for the overall function of the region. Taken together, this minimum of essential connections and operations constitutes the basic circuit for that region.

A second useful concept is that in the cortex, as in most regions of the brain, the functions of local circuits and microcircuits tend to fall into two main categories: those related primarily to reception of information from other regions (*input processing*) and those related to generation of output to other regions (*output control*) [see Shepherd (1979)]. Recognition of these two general types not only aids in characterizing and comparing circuit elements in different regions but also gives insight into the logic of gene expression underlying the assembly of the circuits during development.

These concepts create a useful framework for identifying the fundamental plan of organization of each of the cortical regions at the microcircuit level, and they confer the added benefit of providing a common vocabulary facilitating comparisons between them. We therefore adopt this strategy, recognizing that it is only a first step in dealing with the complexities of cortical organization and function.

The plan of this review is to summarize, first, studies of the synaptic organization of olfactory cortex as the simplest model for cortical microcircuits. This will be compared with the models that have emerged from studies of the hippocampus and submammalian general cortex, which is generally regarded as an evolutionary precursor of the mammalian neocortex. We will see that the basic circuits for these three types are similar in their fundamental rules of construction. We then consider the mammalian neocortex and find that similar rules of microcircuit organization can be identified there, with a first stage of elaboration in the association cortex and additional stages in the sensory cortex.

From this analysis it will appear that there is an underlying logic to the construction of cortical local circuits and microcircuits that provides a common modular framework that is adapted to generate the special properties of the neocortex. The common framework and its adaptations give insight into the neural basis of cortical organization. This should facilitate construction of more accurate and realistic neural network models of higher cortical functions in humans.

3.2   The Paleocortex

The rationale for using the olfactory cortex as a model for cortical organization was made explicit a number of years ago (Shepherd 1974):

> We may note certain features of the prepyriform cortex that are distinctive in its synaptic organization: (1) there is a parallel orientation of apical dendritic trees of the principal neurons; (2) there is a non-repeating sequence of layers in relation to the vertical extent of the principal neurons; (3) the principal neurons

are graded in terms of vertical extent and dendritic geometry; (4) the principal axon collaterals give rise to internal feedback circuits that are widespread and excitatory to principal as well as intrinsic neurons; and (5) inhibitory actions by intrinsic neurons onto principal neurons are profound and long lasting. . . . These features are shared by the prepyriform cortex with other parts of the cerebral cortex—the hippocampus . . . and the neocortex. (p. 257)

The paleocortex is usually equated with the olfactory cortex, defined as those regions of the cerebrum receiving inputs from the olfactory bulb. Because the olfactory bulb relays sensory information from olfactory receptors, olfactory cortex is the only type of cortex to receive sensory information without a relay in the thalamus.

The olfactory cortex is commonly divided into five main regions: anterior olfactory nucleus, pyriform (formerly called prepyriform) cortex, olfactory tubercle, corticomedial nuclei of the amygdala, and transitional entorhinal cortex (Price and Powell 1971). Classically these are all similar in having a three-layer structure. This is a simple consequence of the fact that most of the pyramidal cell bodies lie in a sheet several hundred microns below the cortical surface, thus giving rise to a superficial (molecular) layer, the cell body layer, and a deep layer. The pyriform cortex is commonly regarded as the main olfactory cortex because it projects through the mediodorsal thalamus to the prefrontal neocortex and thereby subserves olfactory perception. We therefore focus on the basic circuit that has emerged from studies of the pyriform cortex.

Principal (Output) Neuron
The output neuron of the pyriform cortex is the pyramidal cell (Cajal 1955) (see figure 3.1). The cell body has a pyramidal shape because it gives rise to a single apical dendrite from the side farthest from the origin of the axon and to several basal dendrites near the axonal origin. Both this form of cell body and the division of dendrites are fundamental for the olfactory cortical output neuron and indeed for most output neurons of all types of cortex. Some output neurons lack basal dendrites and therefore appear to represent a simpler subtype.

The apical dendrites have a radial orientation and branch and terminate near the cortical surface. The trunk and especially the branches are studded with small processes called spines (Haberly 1983). Basal dendrites are also covered with spines. Most of the syn-

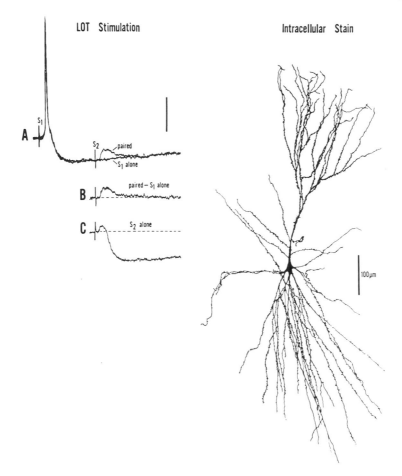

Figure 3.1
(Right) Intracellularly stained pyramidal neuron in the pyriform (olfactory) cortex of the opossum. Afferent fibers in the lateral olfactory tract (LOT) terminate in the upper half of the apical dendritic tree. (Left) Response of this pyramidal neuron to single or paired valleys in the LOT. S_1 and S_2 indicate brief electric stimuli delivered to the LOT. Intracellular potential calibration bar indicates 20 mV. (A) Response to S_2 consists of early EPSP giving rise to an action potential followed by a long-lasting IPSP. (B) Difference between S_2 responses in (A). (C) S_2 response alone, just subthreshold for eliciting an impulse. Note that the response blocks the S_2 IPSP, revealing a long-lasting EPSP.

aptic inputs to pyramidal neurons are made on the spines. This is another characteristic of pyramidal neurons in most areas of the cortex.

The axon arises from an axon hillock on the cell body or, quite often, on one of the trunks of the basal dendrites. Most axons give rise to collateral branches (Haberly and Bower 1984), which issue at more or less right angles from the parent axon. Deep collaterals give off terminal branches in the deep layer; recurrent collaterals ascend to the molecular layer and extend for varying distances through their region of origin to certain neighboring regions (Price 1973). Deep collaterals make type I (presumably excitatory) synapses mainly on deep interneurons. Recurrent collaterals make type I synapses on the basal and apical dendrites of pyramidal neurons or on interneuronal dendrites in the superficial layer (Haberly and Presto 1986). There are thus two basic types of axon collateral connection: directly onto the same or other pyramidal neurons and onto interneurons. These two types are important components of the basic circuits of other cortical regions, as we will see.

Input Fibers

The main type of specific input to the olfactory cortex is olfactory, carried by axons of the output neurons (mitral and tufted cells) of the olfactory bulb. The axons are gathered in the lateral olfactory tract (LOT), from which numerous collaterals arise, more or less at right angles, to connect to all the olfactory cortical regions. A cardinal feature of this connection is that all the axons terminate in the most superficial layer of the cortex, where they make type I (excitatory) synapses on the spines of the distal branches of the apical dendrites of the pyramidal neurons.

This relay of specific sensory information through distally situated synapses is counterintuitive to the general notion that distal synapses provide mainly for slow, weak background modulation of impulse generation in the axon hillock. In fact, the afferent relay in the olfactory bulb also occurs through distal synapses [on the mitral and tufted cells; see Pinching and Powell (1971)], and a similar organization is seen in the retina for transfer of visual information (Dowling 1968). It appears, therefore, that, rather than being disadvantageous, the siting of inputs on the spines of distal dendrites confers some key advantages for the transfer and processing of specific information. This is such an important feature that we can regard it as a primary rule of connection for olfactory cortex. We will see that this rule applies in the other types of cortex as well.

Apart from the specific sensory input, the olfactory cortex also receives inputs from other sources in the brain. These include reciprocal connections from target regions, commissural fibers through the anterior commissure, and axons from brain stem centers.

Interneurons

The main type of interneuron in the pyriform cortex is the polymorphic cell, so-called because it gives rise to dendrites of various sizes and orientations (Haberly 1983). Most of these cells are located in the deep layer. The inputs to these cells are still being worked out; they appear to include external inputs from other brain regions and internal input from the axon collaterals of pyramidal neurons. The axons of these cells for the most part ascend and branch in the cell body and superficial layers, where synapses are made on the pyramidal neurons. These synapses are morphologically type II (Haberly and Behan 1983), correlated with the presumed inhibitory action of these neurons on the pyramidal cells.

A second type of interneuron, located in the superficial layer, has been recently described. It is believed that its dendrites receive most of their inputs from the afferent fibers and their collateral branches, and its axon makes synapses mainly on the apical dendrites of the pyramidal neurons (Haberly 1985). These interneurons are also believed to have an inhibitory action on the pyramidal neurons.

Thus the olfactory cortex contains two main types of interneuron, each of which receives different types of input and has inhibitory actions on different parts of the pyramidal cell dendritic tree.

Basic Circuit

The principal features discussed so far may be summarized in a basic circuit diagram, as indicated in figure 3.2.

We see first that the organization of the olfactory cortex is dominated by processing of the specific sensory input. This involves elaboration of an apical dendrite and reception of the input by means of synapses on spines on the distal branches. Other external inputs to the pyramidal neurons are made mainly on spines on the basal dendrites. This suggests that a primary function of the apical dendrite is to permit processing of the olfactory input separately from the processing of other inputs that occurs in the basal dendrites.

A second aspect of organization evident in figure 3.2 is that, in addition to receiving external inputs, pyramidal neurons also receive intrinsic inputs from themselves through axon collaterals. When a pyramidal neuron generates an impulse output in its axon, the output not only goes to distant targets but also invades the axon collaterals,

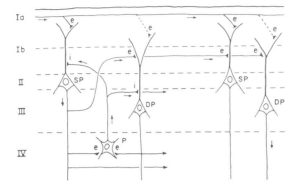

Figure 3.2
Basic circuit diagram summarizing the synaptic organization of mammalian olfactory cortex, as originally proposed by Haberly and Shepherd (1973). Layers shown on left. DP, deep pyramidal neuron; SP, superficial pyramidal neuron; P, polymorphic neuron; e, excitatory synapse; i, inhibitory synapse.

where it excites nearby pyramidal neurons through their basal dendrites and distant pyramidal neurons through synapses on their apical dendrites.

A third important component of organization is the interneuronal population. There are two types, according to location. The superficial type, activated by olfactory fibers, mediates mainly feedforward inhibition onto the shafts of apical dendrites of pyramidal neurons and thus contributes to processing of the olfactory input. The deep (polymorphic) type is a convergence point for external inputs from central brain regions as well as intrinsic inputs from pyramidal cell axon collaterals and thus can mediate both feed-forward and feedback inhibition (Biedenbach and Stevens 1969; Haberly and Shepherd 1973). This inhibition has multiple sites on pyramidal neurons: apical dendritic branches, apical dendritic trunk, basal dendrites, and soma–axon hillock–initial segment region.

Functional Properties　The main functional properties related to these aspects of anatomical organization can be summarized in relation to the excitatory and inhibitory components of the local circuits, as indicated in figure 3.3. With regard to initial processing of the olfactory input, many studies have shown that the olfactory axons are excitatory to the pyramidal neurons [reviewed in Halasz and Shepherd (1983)].

The properties of the apical dendrites are obviously critical for the mechanisms of synaptic integration that underlie the processing of the sensory information. Intracellular recordings have been obtained

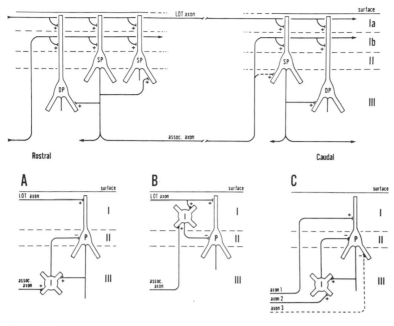

Figure 3.3
Circuit diagrams of mammalian olfactory cortex showing details of excitatory and inhibitory components based on recent studies (Haberly and Bower 1984). (Top) Summary of excitatory (+) inputs to pyramidal neurons, through LOT axons and intrinsic collaterals. (Bottom) Summary of inhibitory (−) subcircuits. (A) Feedback inhibition. (B) Feed-forward inhibition. (C) Three types of connections for mediating IPSPs through intrinsic collateral axons (I–III).

from pyramidal neurons, both in vivo and in the slice preparation, in order to test for these properties. The recordings show that the olfactory axon synapses on the distal spines generate large EPSPs, which spread to the cell body to generate impulses in the axon hillock regions (Biedenbach and Stevens 1969; Haberly 1973a,b; Haberly and Shepherd 1973; Satou et al. 1983). Thus far no evidence has been obtained for voltage-gated channels in the dendritic membranes contributing to these synaptic responses. This may be correlated with the fact that the olfactory pyramidal neuron has a relatively short apical dendrite, only a few hundred microns in length, probably providing for rather tight coupling between the distal synapses and the axon hillock by passive electronic spread of current alone. However, voltage-gated properties are so widespread in both neuronal and non-neuronal cell membranes that they seem likely to be present to some degree in olfactory pyramidal neuron dendrites, a point that requires further study. In other cortical regions we will see that there is ample evidence for voltage-gated properties in dendritic membrane, either at branch points or possibly in the dendritic spines themselves.

The second component of organization to be considered is the axon collaterals of the pyramidal neurons. Physiological studies (Haberly 1973a,b; Haberly and Bower 1984) suggest that these have an excitatory action on the pyramidal neurons themselves, presumably on basal dendrites of nearby cells and apical dendrites of distant cells, as indicated by the anatomy (see figure 3.3). The clear implication from the basic circuit is that the ensemble of pyramidal neurons activated by a specific *external* array of sensory fibers leads to activation of a specific *internal* array of axon collaterals. There is a rostral-caudal gradient in the proportions of external compared with internal inputs (Haberly and Bower 1984). The pyramidal neurons excited by the internal array presumably include some neurons originally activated by the external input and some that were not activated.

An important aspect of the anatomy of the cortex is that the collaterals of the input axons tend to arise at right angles and run in parallel from their origin in the LOT, whereas the collaterals of the pyramidal neurons tend to run orthogonally to the input collaterals (Cajal 1955). Thus there is a rather strict geometric latticelike arrangement of the two types of fiber, external and internal. This implies some relatively strict constraints on the way that the excitation-reexcitation sequence gives rise to a pattern of output from the cortex. Recent studies have emphasized that, rather than keeping track of topographical relations, this kind of organization is best suited for mediating combinatorial types of computations. The operation of olfactory cortex in this manner as a content-addressable memory "for association of odor stimuli with memory traces of previous odor stimuli" (p. 232) has been suggested by Haberly (1985) (also J. Bower, personal communication). This aspect of olfactory organization is considered in more detail elsewhere in this volume (chapter 2). We will see that other types of cortex are also well suited for combinatorial computations.

We consider finally the functional properties of the olfactory cortical interneurons (see figure 3.3). The response of pyramidal neurons to a volley in the input fibers in the LOT consists of an EPSP (the excitatory synapses in the distal spines) followed by an IPSP (see figure 3.1). It has been believed for many years that this represents a recurrent IPSP mediated by the polymorphic interneurons after activation by the pyramidal cell axon collaterals (Biedenbach and Stevens 1969; Haberly and Shepherd 1973; Satou et al. 1984). The IPSPs have brief and long-duration components, reflecting different GABA receptors linked to different membrane conductances (Satou et al. 1984). Recent studies indicate that, in addition, the superficial interneurons contribute a feed-forward inhibition to the pyramidal neurons (Haberly 1985). Autoradiographic studies of the localization of radioactively labeled GABA and immunocytochemical studies utilizing specific antibodies to the GABA-synthesizing enzyme GAD are needed to test the notion that both types of interneuron release GABA as the neurotransmitter at their synapses.

It should be emphasized that here, as elsewhere in the nervous system, inhibition is located not only at the soma–axon hillock region, as commonly believed, but has different roles depending on different sites of action. Thus the small number of inhibitory synapses (from superficial interneurons) in the distal apical dendrites of the pyramidal neurons can nonetheless make a powerful contribution to integration of the spine responses during input processing (Shepherd 1974; Shepherd and Brayton 1987). Inhibitory fibers near the apical dendritic trunk provide the polymorphic cells with a critical role in gating the transfer of information from the level of input processing in the apical branches to the level of output control in the axon hillock. Polymorphic cells also contribute inhibition to integration in the basal dendrites and exert global inhibition on impulse generation at the level of output control.

3.3   The Archicortex

The archicortex includes the hippocampus and dentate fascia. Our focus is on the hippocampus because it is the part whose output goes to distant regions.

As in the olfactory cortex, Nissl stains reveal a sheet of pyramidal cell bodies, imparting a three-layer structure, with a superficial (molecular) layer and a deep layer. The main types of neuronal elements and their relationships were revealed by the classical studies of Golgi, Cajal, and Lorente de No. The well-known summary diagram of Cajal (1955) is shown in figure 3.4. I note only those aspects most relevant to my present concern with microcircuit organization.

Principal (Output) Neuron
The principal neuron of the hippocampus is the pyramidal neuron. The classical studies showed that the sheet of these neurons is divided into four subregions on the basis of their morphology and their intrinsic connections.

In the superior region (also called CA1 and CA2), the pyramidal neurons give rise to an apical dendrite and several basal dendrites. The apical dendrite differs from its olfactory counterpart in details of its branching pattern (see h in figure 3.4) but is similar in its general form and orientation and in the many spines that cover the trunk and

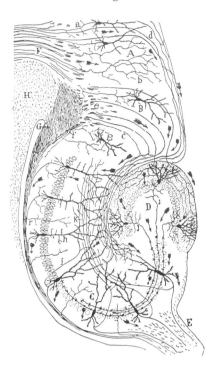

Figure 3.4
Summary diagram of the neuronal organization of the mammalian hippocampus (Cajal 1955).

especially the branches. There are several basal dendrites, which are also covered with spines.

In the inferior region (also called CA3 and CA4), the pyramidal neurons have larger cell bodies, thicker apical dendrites, and longer dendritic branches (C in figure 3.4). Near its origin the apical trunk has an elaborate network of short sinuous processes. These are specialized for receiving synapses of mossy fibers (j) from the neighboring dentate fascia (D).

The pyramidal neurons of the superior and inferior regions are also distinctive in their pattern of axon collaterals. In the superior region these remain mostly in the deep layer (r), where they make synaptic connections onto polymorphic interneurons. In the inferior region there is in addition a separate type, the so-called Schaffer collaterals, which recur to the superficial layer (k) and make synaptic connections onto the pyramidal cell apical dendrites.

The targets of the output axons are a third difference between the superior and inferior regions. From the pyramidal neurons in the superior region the axons are directed mainly to a neighboring cortical region, termed the subiculum (Swanson 1981). The subiculum projects through the precommissural part of the fornix to the lateral septum and several other basal forebrain regions and through the postcommissural part of the fornix to the hypothalamus (ventromedial nucleus and mammillary bodies). The pyramidal neurons of the inferior region, on the other hand, send their axons directly through the precommissural pathway to the lateral septum. In addition, recent work has demonstrated projections to the accumbens nucleus, the infralimbic cortex, and the prefrontal cortex (in the rat) (Fenno et al. in press). Commissural fibers arise mainly in the inferior region as well.

Input Fibers
The primary input to the hippocampus is commonly regarded to be from the entorhinal cortex. This is a center for multisensory integration and an important station in the limbic system. The entorhinal axons form the so-called perforant pathway and make type 1 excitatory synaptic connections on spines of the distal apical dendrites of hippocampal pyramidal neurons and on spines of the distal dendrites of granule cells in the dentate fascia.

The hippocampus also receives a specialized input, in the form of mossy fibers from the dentate. Because the dentate receives its main input by means of the perforant fibers and sends all its output exclusively to the inferior region of the hippocampus through the mossy fibers, the mossy fibers may be regarded as a pathway through which the entorhinal cortex can send preprocessed information to a part of the hippocampus in parallel with direct input of entorhinal information. In this regard the dentate functions like layer IV in primary sensory regions of the neocortex.

The perforant fibers correspond, in the sensory information they carry and their site of input in apical dendrites, to the olfactory input to the olfactory cortex. Other types of input come mainly from the septal nuclei, commissural fibers, and brain stem centers. These may be regarded as central inputs. The septal fibers make synapses on several targets within the hippocampus, including pyramidal neurons.

Interneurons
The interneurons in the hippocampus are of two types, depending on whether the cell bodies are located in the superficial or deep layers. The cell bodies in the superficial layer tend to have flattened dendritic trees, and their axons ramify in the deep layer, making synaptic contacts on the shafts of apical dendritic branches of the pyramidal neurons. The cell bodies in the deep layer are more polymorphic in

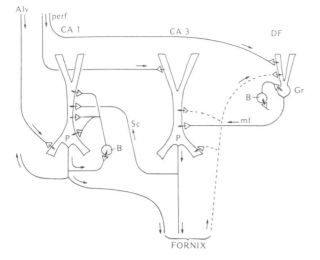

Figure 3.5
Basic circuit diagram of the mammalian hippocampus [modified from Shepherd
(1979)]. Alv, alveus; perf, perforant fibers; P, pyramidal cell; B, basket cell; Sc, Schaffer
collateral; mf, mossy fiber; Gr, granule cell; CA1, CA3, regions of hippocampus; DF,
dentate fascia; sub, subiculum.

shape; their axons ramify extensively, many of the branches forming
basketlike terminal arborizations around the cell bodies and axon
hillocks of the pyramidal neurons. Both types of interneuron are
GABA-ergic, as demonstrated by immunocytochemical localization of
GAD (Ribak et al. 1978) and other methods. Both make type II
synapses and are presumed to function as inhibitory interneurons on
the pyramidal neurons.

Basic Circuit
The organization of the hippocampus may be summarized in a basic
circuit as depicted in figure 3.5. First, with regard to circuit elements
involved in input processing, the restriction of the input from the
entorhinal cortex to the distal branches of the apical dendrites of the
pyramidal neurons is notable. This input is excitatory, the synapses
are located on spines, and there is at present a strong presumption
that the transmitter is glutamate or glutamatelike [reviewed in Walaas
(1983)]. These features are strikingly similar to those in the olfactory
cortex described earlier. It appears that initial input processing of the
multisensory information from the entorhinal cortex involves integrative mechanisms similar to those for the specific olfactory information
to the olfactory cortex. In both regions, siting on the apical dendrites

ensures that this initial stage of input processing will be carried out without interference from other inputs sited on the basal dendrites.

A second similarity is the fact that axon collaterals make direct excitatory connections from one pyramidal cell to another, and these connections are made on the apical dendrites. Thus in both regions external excitation can be followed by internal reexcitation to produce a more complicated activation pattern. In the hippocampus, however, these collaterals arise only from the inferior regions and are directed mainly to the superior region. Although there is preferential orientation of pyriform association collaterals, it appears that the internal reexcitation is more stereotyped in the hippocampus.

The interneurons in the hippocampus are also similar to their olfactory counterparts in that they are divided into superficial and deep populations, make type II inhibitory synapses at different locations on the pyramidal neurons, are activated by afferent inputs in the superficial layer and by both afferent inputs and axon collaterals in the deep layer, and use GABA as the inhibitory transmitter. The actions of the superficial neurons appear to be directed mainly at input processing in the apical dendrites; the actions of deep interneurons are involved in input processing in the basal dendrites and in output control near the axon hillock region.

Functional Properties   One of the attractions of the hippocampus as a model for cortical organization is that the arrangement of its neural elements has implied a simple sequence of activity from input to output (Andersen et al. 1973). This may be summarized in relation to the basic circuit diagram of figure 3.5.

The sequence begins with the input from the entorhinal cortex through the perforant pathway. These fibers deliver synaptic excitation to the apical dendrites of the pyramidal neurons and the dendrites of the dentate granule cells. The granule cells in turn deliver synaptic excitation through their mossy fibers to the bases of the apical dendritic trunks of the pyramidal neurons in the inferior region. These CA3 and CA4 cells then deliver synaptic excitation to the mid-apical branches of CA1 and CA2 cells through the Schaffer collaterals.

A comparison of this sequence with that in the olfactory cortex is provided in figure 3.6. In the pyriform cortex the sequence is relatively generalized, with external excitation delivered throughout the cortex followed by internal reexcitation also spreading throughout the cortex; the example of a rostral-caudal gradient is illustrated. In the hippocampus there are different amounts of external excitation delivered to CA1 and CA3, feed-forward excitation from the den-

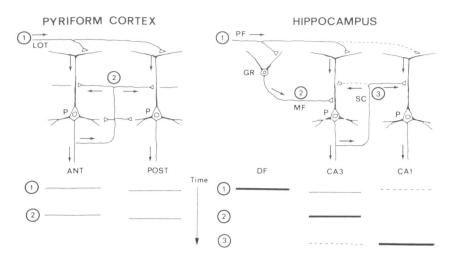

Figure 3.6
Comparison between the functional organization of the pyriform cortex and the hippocampus with regard to sequences of activity elicited by afferent input. (Top) Basic circuit diagrams. For pyriform cortex the sequence involves (1) activation of lateral olfactory tract (LOT) followed by (2) intrinsic reexcitatory collaterals. P, pyramidal neuron. For the hippocampus the sequence involves (1) input activity carried in perforant fibers (PF); (2) feed-forward excitation through mossy fibers (MF) arising from granule cells (GR); (3) feed-forward excitation through Schaffer collaterals (SC). CA3, CA1, regions of the hippocampus. (Bottom) Diagrams indicating the relative timing of activity in the pyramidal neurons and granule cells during the sequences of activity. More intense activity is shown by thick lines; weak activity is shown by dashed lines.

tate to only CA3, and internal reexcitation to CA3 and CA1. Thus the hippocampus appears to be more strictly differentiated on a regional basis in its combinations of excitation patterns than the pyriform cortex.

The final patterns of activity depend on multiple factors underlying input processing and output control. Recent physiological studies have focused particularly on two types of mechanisms involved in input processing in the apical dendrites. The first mechanism concerns the synaptic receptors activated by the excitatory inputs. There is considerable evidence that glutamate is released from the terminals and that it acts on two types of receptors: those that control cation fluxes that depolarize the postsynaptic membrane much as at many other glutamate synapses elsewhere in the nervous system, and those that are linked to voltage-dependent channels, the so-called NMDA receptors (Fagg et al. 1986). These receptors, and their possible involvement in long-term potentiation, go beyond the scope of the present review; they are discussed by Lynch and Baudry in chapter 2 of this volume.

A second type of mechanism involved in input processing in the apical dendrites involves the contribution of voltage-gated channels. The earliest intracellular studies of pyramidal neurons suggested the presence of active responses in the apical dendrites that could function as boosters for generating impulse responses in the axon hillock region (Spencer and Kandel 1961). Subsequent work, in vivo and especially in the slice preparation, has provided ample evidence of these regenerative properties (Benardo et al. 1982). The activity reflects a strong contribution of regenerative calcium currents (Traub and Llinas 1979).

In hippocampal pyramidal neurons it has been assumed that these voltage-dependent channels are sited at points of bifurcation of the larger branches, where they can be activated by summed currents from many synaptic responses. An alternative possibility is that they are located in the dendritic spines themselves (Jack et al. 1975). Testing of this possibility has been beyond the means of experimental methods, but it has been analyzed by computational simulations. The results from several groups (Miller et al. 1985; Perkel and Perkel 1985; Shepherd et al. 1985; Rall and Segev 1986) have shown that placement of the regenerative conductances in the spines confers several properties that could make powerful contributions to integrative actions within the apical dendrites. These properties include (1) amplification of the synaptic response in the spine, with correspondingly greater electrotonic spread to the cell body; (2) pseudosaltatory conduction of the amplified response from spine to spine; (3) generation of logic functions by interactions of individual spines; and (4) generation of complex integrative properties through activation of spine clusters. We return to the significance of these properties in section 3.7.

In addition to providing insights into possible functions, these computational studies have stimulated attempts to obtain more direct experimental evidence regarding properties of dendrites and spines. One approach has been to make patch recordings from dendrites of neurons in culture. An initial study of hippocampal neurons in culture has confirmed that their dendrites contain voltage-gated ionic conductances (Masukawa et al. 1985). The types thus far identified include conductances that pass either depolarizing or hyperpolarizing currents in response to membrane depolarization and those that pass depolarizing currents in response to membrane hyperpolarization. Work is in progress to characterize these conductances pharmacologically and to relate them to known channel types. Work is also in progress on the spines themselves to analyze their mechanical and electrical responses to application of transmitter substances and volt-

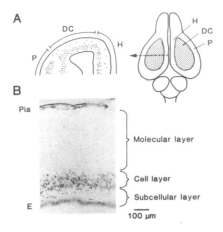

Figure 3.7
Overview of the structure of submammalian cortex, as exemplified by the turtle dorsal cortex. (A, right) Dorsal surface of the brain showing positions of the hippocampus (H), visual dorsal cortex (DC), and pyriform cortex (P). (A, left) Frontal cross section at the level indicated by arrow. (B) Histological section showing basic three-layer structure of dorsal cortex. Afferent fibers enter near surface, just below pia; ependyma (E) below lies the ventricle (Connors and Kriegstein 1986).

age steps in primary cultures (S. J. Smith, personal communication). This work should provide a firmer basis for the computational simulations and lead to an expanded view of the contribution of spine properties to the steps involved in input processing in the apical dendrites.

3.4 Submammalian General Cortex

Both the olfactory cortex and the hippocampus are present in the mammal, together with the neocortex. Before we turn to the mammalian neocortex, it is of interest to consider its phylogenetic ancestry. Mammals are believed to have evolved from a reptilianlike ancestor, which also gave rise to the reptiles. Reptiles have, in addition to the paleocortex and the archicortex, an intervening region of dorsal pallium that is commonly regarded as homologous to the neocortex (figure 3.7; Smith et al. 1980; Kriegstein and Connors 1986). Because many reptiles have changed little over the millennia, it is reasonable to presume that their dorsal cortex is similar to the basic form out of which evolved the mammalian neocortex. Analysis of its intrinsic organization may therefore give insight into the basic plan underlying neocortical microcircuits.

In recent years the turtle has become a useful model for analysis of the synaptic organization of reptilian cortex. The afferent and efferent connections of the turtle dorsal cortex have a number of similarities with those of the mammalian neocortex. Physiological studies have taken advantage of the fact that the turtle brain survives well in vitro (Nowycky et al. 1978; Mori et al. 1981a–c) and thus is an ideal preparation for intracellular analysis. We therefore focus on the turtle as a model.

Principal (Output) Neuron
In the turtle dorsal cortex, as in the other types of cortex, the output neuron is the pyramidal cell. The cell bodies lie within a sheet situated deep within the cortical gray matter (see figure 3.7). Each cell gives rise to several apical dendrites, which issue directly from the cell body or from a short common apical trunk. The dendrites branch sparingly as they ascend toward the cortical surface and are covered with spines. Basal dendrites are directed downward; branching is more extensive in the lateral than in the medial cortex. The turtle pyramidal cell thus resembles its olfactory and hippocampal counterparts and shows regional variation in its morphology as in the hippocampus.

The axon issues from the deeper aspect of the cell body or a basal dendritic trunk. It commonly gives rise to collateral branches that ramify both below and above the cell layer. The laminar organization of these collaterals is not as distinct as in the hippocampus or even in the olfactory cortex.

Input Fibers
We focus on the visual area of the dorsal cortex, which receives the visual input relayed by thalamocortical fibers. These fibers terminate within the most superficial layer of the cortex, in a zone approximately 100 μm just below the pial surface (see figure 3.7). Within this layer are the terminal branches of the apical dendrites of pyramidal neurons and the cell bodies and dendrites of stellate neurons. Anatomical studies have shown that the afferent terminals make type I, presumably excitatory, synapses on spines of the pyramidal neurons and branches of the stellate neurons. These studies have further shown that each stellate cell on average receives more than six times as many afferent synapses as each pyramidal cell (Smith et al. 1980).

This arrangement of the visual cortex, with the afferent fibers terminating in the most superficial zone, is significant for functional organization and for comparison with other types of cortex, as is discussed later.

Interneurons

The main type of interneuron is the stellate cell, found either in the superficial or deep layer. The cell body is usually elongated in the horizontal plane. From either pole several dendrites arise and branch sparingly, with a horizontal orientation. The surfaces of the branches are smooth, which puts these cells in the class of aspiny stellate cells.

The stellate cells receive inputs from the thalamocortical afferents, as already noted. On the output side, the axons of the stellate cells are presumed to make synapses on dendritic shafts in the superficial layer and pyramidal cell bodies. These synapses have type I morphology, with pleomorphic vesicles and symmetric contacts, correlated with inhibitory actions. Immunohistochemical studies have provided evidence that these cells contain GABA and its synthetic enzyme, GAD (Blanton et al. 1985).

Basic Circuit

The main connections between these neural elements were deduced from the anatomical studies of Ebner's laboratory (Smith et al. 1980) and have been strongly supported and extended by comprehensive electrophysiological study (Connors and Kriegstein 1986; and Kriegstein and Connors 1986). The basic circuit that has emerged as a consensus from this work is shown in figure 3.8. Similarities with the other two types of cortex, olfactory and hippocampal, are immediately evident. Before assessing these similarities, let us first summarize the circuit with reference to the same organizational principles employed previously.

In terms of input processing the turtle visual cortex is dominated, like the other two types, by processing of its specific sensory input from the thalamus. This input (1 in figure 3.8) arrives at the surface, where excitatory synapses are made on spines of the distal branches of the apical dendrites of pyramidal neurons (a). As far as is known, other external inputs (for example, cortical association fibers) are made on other parts of the apical or the basal dendrites. Thus the distal apical dendrites appear to be elaborated for the primary function of receiving and processing the primary sensory input.

In addition to this primary external input, pyramidal neurons also receive internal inputs from themselves and from each other by means of direct connections by their axon collaterals (3). The evidence thus far indicates that the axon collaterals make excitatory synapses on spines on the apical branches, probably more on proximal parts, as shown in figure 3.8.

Output control over pyramidal cell firing is exerted in two main ways. One is by *feed-forward inhibition*. As shown in figure 3.8, this

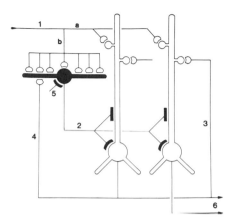

Figure 3.8
Basic circuit diagram of the synaptic organization of the turtle visual cortex combining recent neuroanatomical and neurophysiological findings. Following the same convention used in figures 3.2, 3.3, 3.5, and 3.6, the numbers indicate the sequence of activity that is set up by afferent activity: (1) thalamocortical input to pyramidal neurons (a) and interneurons (b); (2) feed-forward inhibition; (3) reexcitation through intrinsic axon collaterals; (4) feedback excitation-inhibition; (5) stellate-stellate inhibition; (6) output to other cortical sites and to subcortical regions (Kriegstein and Connors 1986).

involves synaptic excitation of stellate interneurons (1b), which then inhibit the pyramidal neurons through synapses located mainly on their cell bodies and proximal apical dendritic trunks (2). The other is by *feedback inhibition*. The pathway for this involves pyramidal cell recurrent axon collaterals, which not only make direct connections to other pyramidal neurons but also make connections onto the stellate inhibitory interneurons (4). Stellate cell inhibition of pyramidal cell output is subject to further control by stellate-stellate interactions (5).

Functional Considerations   The quantitative study by Smith et al. (1980), showing that up to six times as many thalamocortical synapses are made on the stellate cells as on the apical dendrites of pyramidal neurons, implies that the thalamic input can weakly excite the distal apical dendrites and strongly excite stellate cells, resulting in strong inhibition of the pyramidal neurons in response to a thalamic volley. The electrophysiological studies have borne out this prediction; single shocks delivered to the surface layer containing the input fibers elicit a brief, short-latency, relatively weak excitation in most pyramidal neurons, accompanied by a strong and prolonged inhibition (Kriegstein and Connors 1986). Because stellate neurons are strongly excited by these volleys, responding with large EPSPs that give rise to bursts of spikes, it seems likely that they are a major element in mediating the pyramidal cell inhibition.

The membrane mechanisms underlying pyramidal cell excitation and inhibition are of some interest. With regard to excitation, Connors and Kriegstein (1986) observed small-amplitude spikes in somatic recordings and inferred that electrogenic sites are found in the dendrites. Their data in fact suggested that voltage-sensitive sodium channels are present in somatic, perisomatic, and distal dendritic membranes. Thus the turtle cortical pyramidal neuron resembles the hippocampal pyramidal neuron with regard to evidence for voltage-gated channels in distal dendrites. Kriegstein and Connors (1986) recall the observation by Ebner and Colonnier (1975) of "large, organelle-filled spines on the distal dendrites of turtle pyramidal cells" and their speculation that "these might be sites of active electrical processes." Thus one may hypothesize that input processing within the distal apical branches involves interactions between active spines.

With regard to membrane properties underlying the postsynaptic inhibition, the electrophysiological studies have provided evidence for two mechanisms, short term and long term. Sensitivity to Cl^- and blockade by bicuculline indicate that the early IPSP is mediated by GABA, acting on a $GABA_A$ receptor linked to a Cl^--selective channel. The late IPSP, which is not sensitive to Cl^- and is not blocked by bicuculline, appears to be mediated by another ion, probably K^+ (Kriegstein and Connors 1986). Similar types of brief and long-term inhibition have been reported in turtle mitral cells (Mori et al. 1981a; Nowycky et al. 1981) and in the other types of pyramidal neurons: olfactory (Satou et al. 1982), hippocampal (Newberry and Nicoll 1984), and neocortical (Connors et al. 1982). Because the stellate neurons are the only GABA-ergic neurons in the cortex, it may be presumed that they are responsible for both types of IPSP. Here, as elsewhere, it remains to be determined whether they are mediated by the same or by different subpopulations of stellate cells. In the turtle olfactory bulb the different types are mediated by the same granule cell population, implying that GABA can act on different receptors at the same synapse (Mori et al. 1981a,b).

It remains to consider the recurrent excitatory collaterals onto pyramidal neurons. These are not organized in as strict a laminar fashion as in the olfactory and hippocampal cortex, and physiological evidence for their actions is accordingly more limited. Several properties of the pyramidal neurons point to their presence. These include sustained barrages of EPSPs in response to glutamate ionophoresis, synchronous epileptiform burst discharges, and location of current sources and sinks during the response to thalamic volleys (Kriegstein and Connors 1986). One assumes that there is some order to the projection of these recurrent collaterals, but this remains for future experiments to elucidate.

3.5   The Mammalian Neocortex

In considering the neocortex, one is faced with the problem of dealing with its complexity. On the one hand, it can be considered a single entity, defined by the fact that it is a pallium constructed of six histological layers. This is traditionally the main criterion by which it is distinguished from the other types of cortex and from subcortical structures. On the other hand, there is considerable variation in the layers in different parts of the cortex, correlated with differences in input and output connections. This forms the basis for parcellation of the neocortex into many different anatomical and correspondingly functional regions, a tendency that reaches its apogee in the human. Correlated with this is the appearance of multiple cell subtypes within the different regions and multiple intracortical and intercortical connections.

As indicated in the beginning of this chapter, the strategy used to deal with this problem is to identify the three elements of the synaptic triad and characterize their organization in terms of the two overall functions common to all neural regions. In the neocortex we obviously run the greatest risk of losing important aspects of organization and function by this approach. However, if a basic circuit can be thus determined, the principles of its organization can be compared with those of the other types of cortex, and the circuit elaborations that underlie the differentiation of functions in particular regions can be more clearly characterized.

An immediate advantage of this approach is that one is concerned mainly with the neural elements and types of circuit connections that are most common to all regions. In fact, an important development in recent years is an emerging consensus on what constitutes this basic minimum of elements and connections (Jones 1986). I take advantage of this consensus in the following brief summary.

Principal (Output) Neuron

It is generally agreed that in virtually all regions of the neocortex the axons that leave the cortex to carry information to other regions arise from pyramid-shaped neurons. This feature is thus shared with all the other types of cortex we have considered. Because of the larger number of layers and the corresponding greater thickness of the

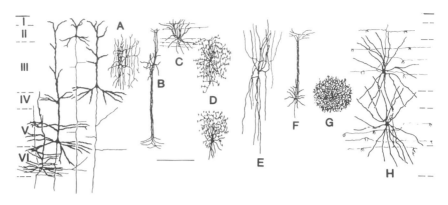

Figure 3.9
The main types of neurons in the primate motor cortex, based on Golgi stains in the sensorimotor areas. On the left are shown pyramidal neurons with cell bodies in different layers. The full extents of the dendritic arbors and axon collaterals are not shown. The rest of the figure shows different types of interneurons. (A) Cell with axonal arcades. (B) Double bouquet cell. (C) Basket cell. (D) Chandelier cells. (E) Bitufted dendritic cell, usually a peptidergic cell. (F) Small spiny cell of layer IV with ascending axon. (G) Neurogliaform cell. (H) Basket cell. Horizontal calibration bar: 100 mm (Jones 1986).

neocortex, its pyramidal neurons vary in shape and size. Some typical examples are shown in figure 3.9. It can be seen that all have in common an apical dendrite that ascends toward the surface, giving rise to branches along the way. The branches are covered with spines. Neither the amount of branching nor the investiture with spines is adequately represented in the low-magnification views of figure 3.9. The pyramidal cells also give rise to several basal dendrites, which branch sparingly and are invested with spines.

The axon arises from the cell body or the origin of a basal dendrite. It characteristically gives off one or more collateral branches. These branches ramify locally and recur to ramify in other layers. The amount of branching is variable and may be quite extensive. There is a suggestion that some collaterals may be specific for certain layers, but this is not as distinct as, for example, the Schaffer collaterals in the hippocampus.

An important principle that has emerged with the use of retrograde HRP tracing is that pyramidal neurons in different layers tend to be associated with different output targets. The general rule is that connections go from pyramidal neurons in layers II and III to other cortical regions, from layer V to subcortical sites such as the superior colliculus, and from layer VI to the thalamus. This of course does not preclude multiple output targets for some axons by means of collateralization (A. M. Thierry, personal communication).

Input Fibers

The traditional way of characterizing inputs to the cortex is to begin with primary sensory cortex, where the situation is clearest. In the primary visual areas, for example, the thalamocortical input fibers from the lateral geniculate nucleus terminate mainly in layer IV on spiny stellate cells in that layer. A similar arrangement is seen in the primary sensory areas for somesthesia and audition.

This focus, on the thalamocortical input to layer IV, has provided the basis for much of our present understanding of the sequence of activation of cortical mechanisms (Edelman and Mountcastle 1978). However, some limitations have become evident in recent years. First, it has become evident that the input fibers send some collaterals to other layers. Second, it has been realized that sensory terminals in layer IV may also make synapses on basal dendrites of layer III pyramidal neurons and on apical dendrites passing through layer IV from pyramidal neurons in deeper layers (Peters and Feldman 1977). Third, physiological studies have suggested properties of pyramidal neurons apparently more dependent on different classes of input fibers from the thalamus than on sequences of activity within the cortex (Stone 1983).

These considerations, together with the fact that the primary visual area accounts for only some 3% of the entire neocortex (Rakic 1981), suggest that one might enlarge one's view by focusing on other areas and types of inputs. Quantitatively the dominant input to most areas of cortex is made up of fibers from other areas. These include ipsilateral corticocortical association fibers, and contralateral corticocortical fibers passing through the corpus callosum. These fibers project mainly to the superficial layers (I–III) (Goldman-Rakic 1981). The precise sites of these synapses are still being worked out, but it seems likely that they include spines of distal apical dendrites in layer I, spines of apical and possibly basal dendrites of pyramidal neurons in layers II and III, and spines of various types of interneurons whose cell bodies are in those layers.

It is evident that these corticocortical input fibers bear a similarity in their mode of termination to the specific inputs to the other types of cortex we have considered. This will be useful in constructing the basic circuit later.

Interneurons

The neocortex contains an unusual variety of intrinsic neurons. Some typical examples are shown in figure 3.9A–H. By far the most numerous and best known in primary sensory cortex is the spiny stellate cell found in layer IV (figure 3.9F). This receives type I (excitatory) afferent synapses on its dendritic spines and in turn makes type I synapses on spines of pyramidal cell dendrites, primarily in the superficial layers. It should be noted that this is the only excitatory interneuron we have encountered in the different types of cortex; the closest similarity would be with the granule cells of the dentate fascia, which feed excitation forward onto CA3 pyramidal neurons.

Most of the other main types of neocortical interneuron have aspiny dendrites. It is not our purpose to document these different types but rather to inquire whether they share any common properties. The answer, from recent studies, is affirmative. Thus most of these cells are believed to make type II synapses and to function as inhibitory interneurons. All of these aspiny intrinsic neurons appear to use GABA as their inhibitory transmitter; conversely, all of the GABA-ergic cells in the cortex are interneurons. A further generalization is that most neuropeptides present in the cortex are localized within interneurons, and these may in fact form a distinct subclass within the interneuronal population (Jones and Hendry 1986). Cortical peptides appear to be transcribed and translated from separate genes rather than by means of intracellular processing of common gene products.

Jones et al. have hypothesized, therefore, that most cortical interneurons arise from a family of closely related precursors and during development become differentiated for specific functions dependent on their laminar localization, dendritic patterns, axonal arborizations, and species of neuroactive peptides. They have suggested that, among other possible functions, the peptides may act as specific growth factors and might thus play a role in processes of differentiation, growth, and cell-cell recognition. In their differentiated forms the interneurons obviously mediate quite distinct types of inhibition; the best examples thus far identified are the basket cells (figures 3.9C,H), which make inhibitory synapses on the soma and proximal dendrites of pyramidal cells, and chandelier cells (figure 3.9D), which make inhibitory synapses only on the initial segments of the pyramidal cell axons.

Basic Circuit
In constructing a basic circuit for the neocortex, we follow the rationale developed in the preceding section and emphasize those aspects related to corticocortical organization. Of particular interest in this respect are those parts of cortex that lack the prominent laminar IV population of stellate cells. These constitute the agranular cortex, characteristic of the motor cortex and other parts of the frontal lobe, and parts of the cingulate and related cortical areas. Many so-called

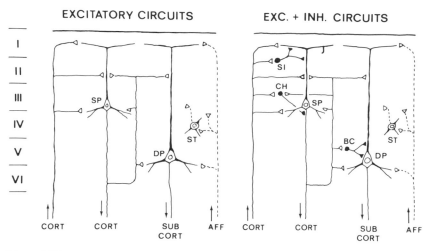

EXCITATORY CIRCUITS

EXC. + INH. CIRCUITS

Figure 3.10
Excitatory and inhibitory subcircuits of the mammalian neocortex. (Left) Excitatory subcircuits. Inputs from other cortical areas are shown on the left (CORT); thalamocortical afferents are shown on the right (AFF), with dashed lines. Cell types: SP, superficial pyramidal neuron; DP, deep pyramidal neuron; ST, stellate cell. (Right) Several of the main types of inhibitory subcircuits: feed-forward inhibitory connections through superficial inhibitory neurons (SI) and chandelier cells (CH) and feedback connections through basket cells (BC). Compare these circuits with their counterparts in figures 3.3 and 3.6.

higher association areas of the frontal, parietal, and temporal lobes also have relatively small populations of layer IV granule cells [see, for example, Brodal (1981)]. Building on the analysis of the paleocortex, we first assess excitatory circuits and then incorporate inhibitory connections.

As shown in figure 3.10 (left), fibers from other areas of the cortex (CORT) terminate mainly in the superficial layers, where they make excitatory synapses on dendrites of pyramidal neurons. In layer I these synapses are on spines of distal apical branches, but in layers II and III they may be on basal and apical dendrites. Input processing of corticocortical information thus appears to bear some similarity to input processing of specific sensory information in the other types of cortex, but with the possible difference that some of the information may be processed through basal and apical dendrites. Whether this implies transmission of different types of information in basal and apical dendrites is not known. As in the other types of cortex, the input is excitatory onto dendritic spines.

The second type of excitatory connection to be considered is that made by the axon collaterals of the pyramidal neurons. As indicated in figure 3.10 (left), the collaterals from superficial pyramidal neurons recur to make excitatory connections at several levels, and there is the strong presumption that many of these are made onto the same and neighboring pyramidal neurons. One therefore has pathways for recurrent reexcitation of pyramidal neurons as in the other types of cortex. Collaterals from deep pyramidal neurons would also contribute to these reexcitatory actions (not shown in figure 3.10 for simplicity). Thus far it is not known whether the axon collaterals in the neocortex have specific dendritic targets.

It is evident that inhibitory control over excitatory circuits is exerted at many points through the multiplicity of types of inhibitory neuron. Thus, as indicated in figure 3.10 (right), some of these cells make inhibitory synapses in the superficial layers (SI), on apical dendrites of pyramidal neurons. It is presumed that these interneurons are excited by the input fibers terminating in these layers and thus can contribute to mechanisms of input processing. This feed-forward inhibition might be similar in principle to its counterpart in the other types of cortex. Other inhibitory interneurons, especially the chandelier cells (CH in figure 3.10) and basket cells (BC), have their synapses placed to subserve mechanisms of output control in the pyramidal neurons. Depending on their type of input, these interneurons could be elements in feed-forward (from input fibers) or feedback (from recurrent collaterals) pathways.

We finally consider those regions of the cortex that receive primary sensory afferents. These afferents, indicated in figure 3.10 by dashed lines, terminate mainly in layer IV on stellate cells, which then make excitatory connections onto pyramidal neurons (Gilbert and Wiesel 1979). There are parallel pathways for different classes of afferents, such as from X and Y cells in the lateral geniculate nucleus. There is strong evidence that in addition to stellate cells these primary afferents make synapses on spines of pyramidal cell dendrites at several levels in the cortex.

How does one incorporate this arrangement for processing of specific sensory input into the basic circuit for the neocortex? As noted, the spiny stellate cell of lamina IV is unique among cortical neurons. Its essential role appears to be to provide an intrinsic relay of specific sensory information within the cortex itself. It is as if an extra step of input processing must be interposed between the thalamus and the cortical pyramidal cells in order to have the incoming information in a form appropriate for processing in the pyramidal cells. In this respect the stellate cells function like granule cells in the cerebellum in relation to Purkinje cells, and granule cells in the dentate fascia vis-à-vis the hippocampus. Just as the hippocampus has an intrinsic plan that is largely independent of the dentate, so the neocortex can be considered to have an intrinsic organization that is largely independent of the spiny stellate cell. In many regions of the cortex this basic circuit carries out most of the essential operations; in primary sensory and related granular areas of the cortex, the spiny stellate cell is added, so to speak, to preprocess the input information.

These considerations indicate some of the ways in which the basic circuits for the neocortex and the other cortical types may be related. We summarize further the common principles in section 3.7.

Functional Considerations   Among the many studies of cortical physiology, certain results are particularly relevant for assessing the functional properties of the neocortical basic circuit and can be briefly summarized.

First, intracellular recordings from pyramidal neurons indicate membrane properties generally similar to those of hippocampal pyramidal neurons. The presence of voltage-sensitive channels for Na, Ca, and K in or near the cell soma (Stafstrom et al. 1984) resembles the findings in the turtle cortex and in the hippocampus. The similarities with the turtle have suggested that the pyramidal neurons are homologous and that their functional characteristics have been highly conserved during evolution (Connors and Kriegstein 1986).

Second, the membrane properties of apical dendrites are still not well understood. Thus far there has been limited evidence for active properties, except during early development (Purpura et al. 1965). It is assumed that EPSPs recorded in the soma are conducted passively, but the possibility remains that active properties contribute. This is particularly relevant for the spines on distal branches of the apical and basal dendrites. As already mentioned, computer simulations have indicated that interactions between active spines would greatly enhance the spread of responses toward the cell body and could also provide the basis for logic operations during synaptic integration within the dendritic tree. The simulations further indicate that it could be difficult to distinguish active from inactive spines using only somatic recordings (T. Woolfe and G. M. Shepherd, unpublished data).

Third, single input volleys characteristically elicit an excitatory-inhibitory sequence in pyramidal neurons. This sequence is similar to that in pyramidal neurons in the other types of cortex (see figure 3.1) and supports the notion that the basic circuits are similar.

Fourth, the basic circuit for the neocortex appears to be dominated by the presence of powerful local circuits for excitation and reexcitation and for feed-forward and feedback inhibition. The balance between excitation and inhibition is obviously critical for normal function. These considerations apply also to the other types of cortex.

In all types disturbances of this balance lead to epileptic seizure activity.

3.6 Synthesis of Principles

The general conclusion arising from this survey is that the basic circuits for the four types of cortex are similar. The synaptic organization of each type appears to arise from a similar set of neural elements, which may be summarized in the following manner.

Each cortex has as its principal output neuron a pyramidal type of cell, with apical and basal dendritic compartments. Different subtypes may be elaborated within a given region or in different parts of the same region. Each subtype tends to have its cell bodies and basal dendrites in a specific layer, whereas the apical dendrites extend through different layers or sublayers. Each subtype thus is a substrate for integrating a different combination of inputs; each in turn has an output to a distinct target or group of target regions.

Specific inputs to the three types of simple cortex are made onto the apical dendrites of the pyramidal neurons. This rule of connectivity also appears to apply to many areas of the neocortex. In these four types the input fibers make excitatory synapses onto spines of the distal apical branches. There is also a feed-forward inhibitory pathway, in which input fibers make excitatory synapses on interneurons, which make inhibitory synapses on apical dendritic branches and pyramidal cell somata.

Input processing within pyramidal neurons takes place in the apical dendrites by a series of integrative steps. This begins with the response in the individual spine, then interactions between individual spines, interactions between clusters of spines, interactions between branches, and finally spread of integrated potentials to the cell body and axon hillock, where the impulse output is generated in the axon. Integrative interactions at successive levels are determined by several factors: the spatial distribution of excitatory and inhibitory inputs; neurotransmitter and neuromodulatory actions, including second-messenger actions; impedance matching of electrotonic properties; and distribution of voltage-gated membrane channels. Similar principles apply to input processing in the basal dendrites.

Output control is mediated by inhibitory interneurons. One type is the feed-forward inhibitory interneuron, which enables the afferent (preprocessed) input to impose its own control on output. The second type is the feedback inhibitory interneuron, activated by collaterals of the pyramidal cell axon. This enables the pyramidal cell "postprocessed" output to add self-inhibition to its own control and to provide for lateral inhibition of neighboring cells. Both of these mechanisms are well known in sensory systems and appear to be embedded in these cortical circuits.

Reexcitation of pyramidal cells is mediated by direct connections from their axon collaterals. This is targeted especially for specific levels of apical and basal dendrites. Through these connections the cortical output is recombined with the original cortical input to give rise to new combinations of input information to the apical dendrites. The reexcitatory circuits are crucial to the patterns of cortical output that develop over time.

Ontogeny of Basic Circuit Elements
These considerations thus suggest that the different types of cortex have a similar basic circuit for their local organization. This implies that a common set of rules may underlie the genetic expression of the neural elements that form these circuits. A relatively simple set of rules can be envisaged that would include the following: expression of the pyramidal neuron type or subtypes, guidance to their laminar localization, ingrowth of input fibers specified by lamina, formation of input synapses, formation of axon collateral and output synapses, and expression of interneurons and formation of their synapses. Significant progress has already been made toward characterizing these rules. Rakic (1981) has suggested that the primate neocortex develops on the basis of radial columnar units, within which the laminar position of a neuron is determined by the time of its genesis and its rate of migration from the proliferative zone.

A relatively limited set of mechanisms suggests that a considerable economy may have been achieved by constructing all types of cortex according to some common rules. The elaboration of the differences between the different types could then have arisen from a limited number of further genetic instructions, from gene polymorphisms, or posttranscriptional or posttranslational steps, perhaps affecting only individual elements within the basic circuit plan. Just as different types of receptor molecules and enzymes can belong to the same gene family, so could the different types of cortex have derived from the same gene family.

Much further work will be required to test this hypothesis. One kind of test is provided by the recent study of Rakic et al. (1986) on the ontogeny of synapses in primate cortex. They found that the number and density of synapses in different regions follow a similar time course of overproduction followed by reduction during the early period of postnatal development. Thus, rather than a sequence in which specific sensory areas develop first, followed by association areas, the cortex seems to be laid down as a whole. Studies such as this may therefore enable the analysis of ontogenic sequences and phylogenetic comparisons to converge onto the same principles for construction of the basic circuit for cortical organization.

3.7   General Discussion

The work reviewed in this chapter supports the general proposition that at the level of synaptic circuits there are basic principles common to all the main types of cerebral cortex. The main conclusion is that a set of neural elements and their circuit connections can be identified in the simplest, olfactory, type of cortex and that this set forms a basic circuit that can also be identified in the other types of cortex: the hippocampus, the submammalian general cortex, and the neocortex of mammals, including primates and humans. What is the relevance of this conclusion for human cognitive functions?

Toward a Theory of Cortical Function

Contemporary thought on neocortical organization is dominated by the concept of the cortical column as a basic module. This has been shown to provide a basic framework for organization of both primary sensory (Edelman and Mountcastle 1978) and association (Goldman-Rakic 1981) areas, although the precise nature of the column as a functional module is still controversial (Crick and Asanuma 1986). Within a column there is a radial alignment of neurons and connections (Lorente de No 1938; Szentagothai 1975). The present concept of the basic circuit is entirely compatible with this scheme, the skeleton organization within a column being represented by the basic circuit.

In order to develop a comprehensive theory of cortical functions, we need to incorporate the concepts of the basic circuit and the cortical column into an overall scheme for the ontogeny and phylogeny of the cortex. The ontogeny of the basic circuit has already been discussed in terms of its development within a radial columnar unit. With regard to phylogeny, it can be argued that the evolution of cortical function cannot be considered adequately with a focus only on the neocortex. This reflects a general principle of animal organization. For example, the origins of the vertebrates are to be found in the invertebrates; the origins of the hand are to be found in primitive limbs of crossopterygians. Applying this reasoning, one can find the origins of neocortical functions in the common elements shared with the simpler types of cortex reviewed here. One of the aims of this review is to encourage workers on the neocortex to take this broader phylogenetic view and to incorporate the results of studies on these other types of cortex in the synthesis of concepts of cortical function.

In this endeavor it is important to realize that the aim is not to conclude that all types of cortex have the same organization and function. The fact that a basic circuit can be discerned in all the types of cortex considered here is analogous to the fact that the same set of bones provides the basic structure for the limbs of all terrestrial vertebrates. We understand the functions of the hand in terms of the ways that these skeletal elements have become adapted by evolutionary processes to perform a variety of general and special maneuvers. Similarly the basic circuit contains the main neural elements that have been subjected to adaptive pressures in the evolution of cortical function. The basic circuit has responded to these pressures by addition of numbers and types of output neurons, generation of new varieties of interneurons, and elaboration of specific intracortical connections through its excitatory and inhibitory axon collateral systems. In addition to these anatomical features, it is worth considering that novel physiological properties may have appeared; of prime interest in this respect are the deployment of active membrane properties in dendritic trees, as discussed previously, and the elaboration of second messengers and related biochemical mechanisms. Thus, rather than leading to the conclusion that all types of cortex have the same functions, the basic circuit provides the means for assessing the ways that the cortex has responded to evolutionary pressures to generate the functions unique to the neocortex and to humans.

The Cortex and Cognitive Functions
It is a reasonable presumption that the cognitive abilities of the human evolved in parallel with the development of cortical function. Thus by similar reasoning an understanding of the neural basis of cognition will require not only studies of the neocortex alone but also a broader comparison with the other types of cortex. A goal of this endeavor should be to try to identify neural elements and properties that are crucial for generating specific aspects of cognitive functions. The basic cortical circuit provides a useful tool for this type of analysis.

At present the most promising areas for making this correlation appear to be in sensory perception and memory. With regard to sensory perception, the fact that both the pyriform cortex and the dorsal general cortex receive specific sensory inputs shows that the basic cortical circuit is fully capable of receiving and processing specific sensory information per se. However, in the neocortex those roles appear to require, for the visual, auditory, and somatosensory modalities, a modified compound circuit containing the added stellate cell state. This added stage may provide for more rapid processing of these sensory inputs, as would be required for our ability to perceive, recognize, and act quickly on visual, auditory, and tactile information. It may also play a role in the more analytical aspects of perception, particularly in relation to the parceling of visual, auditory, and somatosensory cortex into regions for multiple representations of different submodalities. The basic circuit itself would be adapted to these different perceptual operations by elaboration of specific types of synaptic connections and functional properties, as described previously for the generation of phylogenetic diversity. The axon collateral systems would appear to be particularly well suited for carrying out the combinatorial and synthetic operations within each cortical area.

Although lower levels of visual perception may depend on the stellate stage of processing, even in the primary visual cortex the synapses of thalamocortical input fibers on the stellate cells account for only a few percent of the total (Rakic 1981). Thus, even in the granular cortex the basic circuit provides for most of the processing. Higher levels of visual perception involve areas of association cortex in which processing is increasingly less topographical and more combinatorial. The surprising result is that this resembles the kind of processing carried out in the olfactory cortex. Haberly (1985) has pointed out that the neural mechanisms for odor discrimination by the olfactory cortex may resemble those for recognition of faces by the temporal association cortex. The way in which the olfactory cortex uses neural space to encode information about different molecules may thus resemble mechanisms for abstraction of complex spatial areas in the visual association cortex. This supports the suggestion that our concepts of the neural basis of perception should draw on studies of all types of cortex and all sensory modalities.

With regard to memory, there are two areas where studies of the neural properties of the basic circuit appear to have direct bearing at the cognitive level. These concern the briefest time intervals, up to a second or so, and, at the other extreme, the longest time intervals, of months and years.

For brief time periods the single impulse (1 msec duration) and classical postsynaptic potential (20–30 msec duration) are too brief; the problem has been to identify mechanisms that can prolong these initial types of responses over the time taken for rapid recognition and recall. The traditional view is that brief inputs trigger impulse discharges that are prolonged by the action of "reverberating circuits" set up by recurrent excitatory axon collaterals (Forbes 1922; Lorente de No 1938). Modern research is adding other candidate mechanisms. One is voltage-gated channels in the somatic and dendritic membranes, which enable neurons to respond to inputs with a variety of tonic or bursty firing patterns (Jahnsen and Llinas 1985). Another is second-messenger systems, which convert the response of a ligand-gated receptor molecule into prolonged biochemical effects, including prolonged actions on membrane conductances.

There is also evidence that some activity may propagate extremely slowly (< 1 m/sec) through intrinsic cortical axons. All of these mechanisms would appear to be at the disposal of the basic circuit in mediating the shortest-term processes of memory storage and recall.

At the other extreme, much of the current work on the most enduring types of memory is focused on the model of LTP in pyramidal neurons. As already discussed, the dendritic spines of pyramidal neurons are considered to be the prime sites for the long-term changes in synaptic efficacy associated with LTP and with long-term memory in general. To recapitulate briefly, the spines are the sites of input synapses in all the major types of cortex. The small size of the spines means that a microcompartment is created in which any electrical, ionic, biochemical, or structural change has a maximal effect on transmission at the synapse. The small size of the spine stem provides an effective means for regulating transmission from the synapse to the rest of the neuron. The possible presence of active membrane channels contributes more powerful, nonlinear actions to these properties.

If the dendritic spines are likely sites for activity-dependent changes underlying long-term memory, one has to account in addition for mechanisms of read-in and readout. Read-in may be fairly direct, because the sites of input to the pyramidal neuron are the dendritic spines themselves. Readout, or recall, would appear to require more complicated mechanisms for accessing appropriate populations of spines in appropriate sequences. This type of function is likely mediated through the corticocortical and recurrent collateral systems. These systems provide for the activation of a rich repertoire of spine combinations, and the closed loops set up by the recurrent nature of the connections can provide for the appropriate sequencing of the activation. In this view a long-term memory is stored within a population of spines distributed over a population of cortical neurons and recalled by an appropriate sequence of spine activation by intrinsic fiber systems. The basic circuit provides a local spine population and a local sequence of activation; connections between basic circuit loci or modules provide for the sequences that coordinate global recall.

Neural Network Simulations of Cognitive Functions
We have discussed cortical organization in relation to generation of cognitive functions; we turn now to cortical organization in relation to the construction of neural network models for simulating those functions. A priori one might expect that, having identified the neural elements and properties that are crucial for generating specific aspects of cognitive functions as in the previous section, one would simply proceed to build those elements and properties into network models and simulate those functions. This has not yet occurred, for present-day neural networks in general are based instead on multiple simple summing nodes with extensive, reciprocal connections [see Hopfield (1982) and Rumelhart and McClelland (1986)]. These networks represent interesting physical models of the behavior of systems and are important for developing conceptual frameworks and vocabularies for analyzing how systems carry out computations that generate properties resembling perception or memory. Unfortunately these models capture little of the real neural architecture of cortical neurons, and their insight into how the real architecture generates real cognitive functions is therefore necessarily limited.

A key question revolves around the units of which a cortical computational network should be built. This question has been addressed in thoughtful reviews by Crick and Asanuma (1986) and Sejnowski (1986). There is general agreement that cortical neurons cannot be adequately represented by single summing nodes. In particular, the dendrites need to be included in any functional representation of the neuron, as was first suggested by Rall (1959). A conceptual framework within which dendritic trees contain several levels of functional units for integration of synaptic inputs was introduced some years ago [Shepherd (1972); see also Koch et al. (1982)]. The importance of the dendrites was explicit in the original formulation of the cortical basic circuit (Shepherd 1974) and has been amply documented for the different types of cortices in the present review.

The tremendous expansion of computational capacity made possible by the presence of multiple functional units within cortical dendrites is being increasingly recognized. Crick and Asanuma (1986), for example, in noting the evidence that cortical dendrites have active properties, remark that

> it would make a tremendous difference if the dendrites were not purely passive. . . . A single neuron, rather than being a single integrating device . . . may be a more complex processing unit, with each dendritic branch acting . . . as an integrating unit for its own inputs. . . . It is obvious that a lot needs to be learned about

dendritic behavior before theorists have a solid body of facts to build on. (pp. 364–365)

This argument supports the postulate that dendrites contain multiple computational units and that the dendritic spine is the basic computational unit of cortical neurons (Shepherd 1986). For network modelers it is relevant to note that

> the significance of large numbers of spine units in distal dendrites is that it takes advantage of moving those synaptic inputs away from having an immediate, direct, obligatory effect on soma output, and making their effects contingent on specific combinations of inputs and cascades of nonlinear interactions between the spines. (Shepherd 1986, p. 95)

The challenge for network modelers is to expand their view of the neuron to include these properties of the dendrites. It is not unreasonable to conjecture that key aspects of cognitive function depend on these intraneuronal properties. Apart from their relevance to the computational basis of perception and memory, the generation of logic operations in distal cortical dendrites by means of spine interactions might be directly related to the human capacity for abstract thought and mathematical reasoning. It is a possibility well worth pursuing in future network models.

In addition to dendritic trees the recurrent axon collateral systems of the basic cortical circuit seem to be crucial for inclusion in network models. Because of the way that they form closed loops embracing differing extents of the cortex, these axons and their collaterals have the intrinsic property of mediating iterative operations, as already discussed. They thus may generate the algorithms through which sequences of computations are carried out. This not only is important for the processing of input information but also can serve as the means for generating a program of output control in the performance of a motor function or abstract thought. If the association systems together with the computational units distributed in the dendritic trees function in this manner, then one has left the domain of computer technology, with its distinction between software and hardware, and begun to enter the domain of the brain, where these distinctions disappear. As Galifret (1986) has observed:

> The distinction between hardware and software, though useful for computer science, cannot be transposed into the domain of the brain; the knowledge, the program, is an integral part of the neural machinery, indissociable from its basic structure. (p. 12)

To put it succinctly: In the brain the hardware is the software and the software is the hardware.

This raises the question of exactly what kinds of computations underly cognitive functions. Sejnowski (1986) has discussed this question with great insight:

> The key issue about which we know least is the style of computation in cerebral cortex. . . . Information processing and memory share the same circuitry in cerebral cortex, in contrast with digital computers where the memory and central processing unit are physically separated. The style of computation and the style of memory must therefore be closely related. . . . The performance of algorithms can be seamlessly improved by experience. (pp. 372–373)

Construction of realistic neural models of cognitive functions will therefore depend on the identification of computational modes of cortical neurons and successful simulations of those modes. We already know about several modes (for example, analog versus digital, synchronous versus asynchronous). Realistic networks need to reflect these different modes. Perhaps the most relevant aspect of the cortical basic circuit in this respect is that it constitutes a multifunctional unit. By themselves, the dendritic trees, or the recurrent collaterals, can individually mediate only limited types of operations; together they function in a coordinated manner to express a variety of computational modes. Network models that incorporate the basic circuit are thus likely to express more accurately the actual mechanisms through which the cortex mediates higher cognitive functions in the human.

Acknowledgments

I am grateful to L. B. Haberly, T. J. Sejnowski, A. Peters, E. G. Jones, L. M. Masukawa, P. Rakic, P. Goldman-Rakic, and B. W. Strowbridge for stimulating discussions. This work was supported by the National Institutes of Health under grant NS-07609 and by the Office of Naval Research under grant N00014-86-K-0145.

References

Andersen, P., B. H. Blond, and J. H. Dudar. 1973. "Organization of the hippocampal output." *Experimental Brain Research* 17:152–168.

Benardo, L. S., L. M. Masukawa, and D. A. Prince. 1982. "Electrophysiology of isolated hippocampal pyramidal dendrites." *Journal of Neuroscience* 2:1614–1622.

Biedenbach, M. A., and C. F. Stevens. 1969. "Synaptic organization of cat olfactory cortex as revealed by intracellular recording." *Journal of Neurophysiology* 32:204–214.

Blanton, M., J. Shea, and A. R. Kriegstein. 1985. "Stellate neurons in the turtle dorsal cortex contain aminobutyric acid and its synthetic enzyme." *Society of Neuroscience Abstracts* 8:237.

Brodal, A. 1981. *Neurological Anatomy*, third edition. New York: Oxford University Press.

Cajal, S. R. 1955. *Studies on the Cerebral Cortex*. London: Lloyd-Luke.

Connors, B. W., and R. D. Chervin. 1986. "Physiological evidence for periodicity and directionality of lateral excitatory connections in rat neocortex." *Society of Neuroscience Abstracts* 12:350.

Connors, B. W., and A. R. Kriegstein. 1986. "Cellular physiology of the turtle visual cortex: Distinctive properties of pyramidal and stellate neurons." *Journal of Neuroscience* 6:164–177.

Connors, B. W., M. J. Gutnick, and D. A. Prince. 1982. "Electrophysiological properties of neocortical neurons in vitro." *Journal of Neurophysiology* 48:1302–1320.

Crick, F., and C. Asanuma. 1986. "Certain aspects of the anatomy and physiology of the cerebral cortex," in *Parallel Distributed Processing*, J. L. McClelland and D. E. Rumelhart, eds. Cambridge, Mass.: MIT Press, 333–371.

Dowling, J. E. 1968. "Synaptic organization of the frog retina: An electron microscopic analysis comparing the retinas of frogs and primates." *Proceedings of the Royal Society of London*, sec. B, 170:205–228.

Ebner, F. F., and M. Colonnier. 1975. "Synaptic patterns in the visual cortex of turtle." *Journal of Comparative Neurology* 160:51–79.

Edelman, G. M., and V. B. Mountcastle. 1978. *The Mindful Brain: Cortical Organization and the Group-Selective Theory of Higher Brain Function*. Cambridge, Mass.: MIT Press.

Fagg, G. E., A. C. Foster, and A. H. Ganong. 1986. "Excitatory amino acid synaptic mechanisms and neurological function." *Trends in Pharmacological Science* 6:357–363.

Fenno, F., A. M. Thierry, and J. Glowinski. In press. "Anatomical and electrophysiological evidence for a direct projection from Ammon's horn to the medial prefrontal cortex in the rat." *Experimental Brain Research*.

Forbes, A. 1922. "The interpretation of spinal reflexes in terms of present knowledge of nerve conduction." *Physiology Review* 2:361–414.

Galifret, Y. 1986. "Esprit, es-tu là?" in his *Avatars de la Psychologie*. Paris: Nouvelles Editions Rationalistes, 5–17.

Gilbert, C. D., and T. N. Wiesel. 1979. "Morphology and intracortical projections of functionally characterized neurons in the cat visual cortex." *Nature* 280:120–125.

Goldman-Rakic, P. S. 1981. "Development and plasticity of primate frontal association cortex," in *The Organization of the Cerebral Cortex*, F. O. Schmitt, F. G. Worden, G. Adelman, and S. G. Dennis, eds. Cambridge, Mass.: MIT Press, 69–97.

Haberly, L. B. 1973a. "Summed potentials evoked in opossum prepyriform cortex." *Journal of Neurophysiology* 36:775–788.

Haberly, L. B. 1973b. "Unitary analysis of opossum prepyriform cortex." *Journal of Neurophysiology* 36:762–787.

Haberly, L. B. 1983. "Structure of the pyriform cortex of the opossum I. Description of neuron types with Golgi methods." *Journal of Comparative Neurology* 213:163–187.

Haberly, L. B. 1985. "Neuronal circuitry in olfactory cortex: Anatomy and functional implications." *Chemical Senses* 10:219–238.

Haberly, L. B., and M. Behan. 1983. "Structure of the pyriform cortex of the opossum III. Ultrastructural characterization of synaptic terminals of olfactory bulb afferent fibers and association fibers." *Journal of Comparative Neurology* 219:448–460.

Haberly, L. B., and J. M. Bower. 1984. "Analysis of association fiber system in pyriform cortex with intracellular recording and staining techniques." *Journal of Neurophysiology* 51:90–112.

Haberly, L. B., and S. Presto. 1986. "Ultrastructural analysis of synaptic relationships of intracellularly stained pyramidal cell axons in pyriform cortex." *Journal of Comparative Neurology* 248:464–474.

Haberly, L. B., and G. M. Shepherd. 1973. "Current-density analysis of summed evoked potentials in opossum prepyriform cortex." *Journal of Neurophysiology* 36:789–802.

Halasz, N., and G. M. Shepherd. 1983. "Neurochemistry of the vertebrate olfactory bulb." *Neuroscience* 10:579–619.

Hopfield, J. J. 1982. "Neural networks and physical systems with emergent collective computational abilities." *Proceedings of the National Academy of Science USA* 79:2554–2558.

Jack, J., D. Noble, and R. Tsien. 1975. *Electric Current Flow in Excitable Cells.* Oxford: Oxford University Press.

Jahnsen, H., and R. Llinas. 1985. "Ionic basis for the electroresponsiveness and oscillatory properties of guinea-pig thalamic neurones in vitro." *Journal of Physiology* (London) 349:227–247.

Jones, E. G. 1986. "Neurotransmitters in the cerebral cortex." *Journal of Neurosurgery* 65:135–153.

Jones, E. G., and S. H. C. Hendry. 1986. "Co-localization of GABA and neuropeptides in neocortical neurons." *Trends in Neuroscience* 9:71–76.

Koch, C., T. Poggio, and V. Torre. 1982. "Retinal ganglion cells: A functional interpretation of dendritic morphology." *Philosophical Transactions of the Royal Society of London.* ser. B, 298:227–264.

Kriegstein, A. R., and B. W. Connors. 1986. "Cellular physiology of the turtle visual cortex: Synaptic properties and intrinsic circuitry." *Journal of Neuroscience* 6:178–191.

Lorente de No, R. 1938. "The cerebral cortex: Architecture, intracortical connections and motor projections," in *Physiology of the Nervous System,* J. F. Fulton, ed. Oxford: Oxford University Press, 291–339.

Masukawa, L. M., A. Hansen, and G. M. Shepherd. 1985. "Single channel currents recorded from dendritic membranes of cultured dissociated neurons from the rat hippocampus." *Society of Neuroscience Abstracts* 11:1183.

Masukawa, L. M., B. W. Strowbridge, J. Kim, D. D. Spencer, and G. M. Shepherd. 1987. "Electrical responses of human epileptic cortical tissue." *Biophysical Journal* 51:67A.

Miller, J., W. Rall, and J. Rinzel. 1985. "Synaptic amplification by active membrane in dendritic spines." *Brain Research* 325:325–330.

Mori, K., M. C. Nowycky, and G. M. Shepherd. 1981a. "Analysis of a long-duration inhibitory potential in mitral cells in the isolated turtle olfactory bulb." *Journal of Physiology* 314:311–320.

Mori, K., M. C. Nowycky, and G. M. Shepherd. 1981b. "Analysis of synaptic potentials in mitral cells in the isolated turtle olfactory bulb." *Journal of Physiology* 314:295–309.

Mori, K., M. C. Nowycky, and G. M. Shepherd. 1981c. "Electrophysiological analysis of mitral cells in the isolated turtle olfactory bulb." *Journal of Physiology* 314:281–294.

Mori, K., M. C. Nowycky, and G. M. Shepherd. 1983. "Synaptic excitatory and inhibitory interactions at distal dendritic sites on mitral cells in the isolated turtle olfactory bulb." *Journal of Neuroscience* 4:2291–2296.

Newberry, N. R., and R. A. Nicoll. 1984. "A bicuculline-resistant inhibitory postsynaptic potential in rat hippocampal pyramidal cells in vitro." *Journal of Physiology* 348:239–254.

Nowycky, M. C., K. Mori, and G. M. Shepherd. 1981. "GABAergic mechanisms of dendrodendritic synapses in isolated turtle olfactory bulb." *Journal of Neurophysiology* 46:639–648.

Nowycky, M. C., U. Waldow, and G. M. Shepherd. 1978. "Electrophysiological studies in the isolated turtle brain." *Society of Neuroscience Abstracts* 4:583.

Perkel, D. H., and D. J. Perkel. 1985. "Dendritic spines: Role of active membrane in modulating synaptic efficacy." *Brain Research* 325:331–335.

Peters, A., and M. L. Feldman. 1977. "The projection of the lateral geniculate nucleus to area 17 of the rat cerebral cortex IV. Terminations upon spiny dendrites." *Journal of Neurocytology* 6:669–689.

Pinching, A. J., and T. P. S. Powell. 1971. "The neuropil of the periglomerular region of the olfactory bulb." *Journal of Cell Science* 9:379–409.

Price, J. L. 1973. "An autoradiographic study of complementary laminar patterns of termination of afferent fibers of the olfactory cortex." *Journal of Comparative Neurology* 150:87–108.

Price, J. L., and T. P. S. Powell. 1971. "Certain observations on the olfactory pathway." *Journal of Anatomy* 110:105–126.

Purpura, D. P., R. J. Shofer, and T. Scarff. 1965. "Properties of synaptic activities and spike potentials of neurons in immature neocortex." *Journal of Neurophysiology* 28:925–942.

Rakic, P. 1981. "Developmental events leading to laminar and areal organization of the neocortex," in *The Organization of the Cerebral Cortex*, F. O. Schmitt, F. G. Worden, G. Adelman, and S. G. Dennis, eds. Cambridge, Mass.: MIT Press, 7–28.

Rakic, P., J.-P. Bourgeois, M. F. Eckenhoff, N. Zecevic, and P. S. Goldman-Rakic. 1986. "Concurrent overproduction of synapses in diverse regions of the primate cerebral cortex." *Science* 232:232–235.

Rall, W. 1959. "Branching dendritic trees and motoneuron membrane resistivity." *Experimental Neurology* 1:491–527.

Rall, W., and I. Segev. 1986. "Functional possibilities for synapses on dendrites and dendritic spines," in *New Insights into Synaptic Function*, G. Edelman, W. Gall, and M. Cowan, eds. New York: Neuroscience Research Foundation and Wiley, 606–636.

Ribak, C. E., J. E. Vaughn, and K. Saito. 1978. "Immunocytochemical localization of glutamic acid decarboxylase in neuronal somata following colchicine inhibition of axonal transport." *Brain Research* 140:315–332.

Rumelhart, D. E., and J. L. McClelland, eds. 1986. *Parallel Distributed Processing: Explorations in the Microstructure of Cognition*. Cambridge, Mass.: MIT Press.

Satou, M., K. Mori, Y. Tazawa, and S. F. Takagi. 1982. "Two types of postsynaptic inhibition in pyriform cortex of the rabbit: Fast and slow inhibitory postsynaptic potentials." *Journal of Neurophysiology* 48:1142–1156.

Satou, M., K. Mori, Y. Tazawa, and S. F. Takagi. 1983. "Interneurons mediating fast postsynaptic inhibition in pyriform cortex of the rabbit." *Journal of Neurophysiology* 50:89–101.

Schmitt, F. O., F. G. Worden, G. Adelman, and S. G. Dennis. 1981. *The Organization of the Cerebral Cortex*. Cambridge, Mass.: MIT Press.

Sejnowski, T. J. 1986. "Open questions about computation in cerebral cortex," in *Parallel Distributed Processing*, J. L. McClelland and D. E. Rumelhart, eds. Cambridge, Mass.: MIT Press, 372–389.

Sejnowski, T. J., P. K. Kienker, and G. M. Shepherd. 1985. "Simple pattern recognition models of olfactory discrimination." *Society of Neuroscience Abstracts* 11:970.

Shepherd, G. M. 1972. "The neuron doctrine: A revision of functional concepts." *Yale Journal of Biology and Medicine* 45:584–599.

Shepherd, G. M. 1974. *The Synaptic Organization of the Brain.* New York: Oxford University Press.

Shepherd, G. M. 1979. *The Synaptic Organization of the Brain,* second edition. New York: Oxford University Press.

Shepherd, G. M. 1985. "The olfactory system: The uses of neural space for a nonspatial modality," in *Contemporary Sensory Neurobiology,* M. Correia and A. A. Perachio, eds. New York: A. R. Liss, 99–114.

Shepherd, G. M. 1986. "Apical dendritic spines of cortical pyramidal cells: Remarks on their possible roles in higher brain functions, including memory," in *Synapses, Circuits, and the Beginnings of Memory,* G. Lynch, ed. Cambridge, Mass.: MIT Press, 85–98.

Shepherd, G. M., and R. K. Brayton. 1979. "Computer simulation of a dendrodendritic synaptic circuit for self- and lateral inhibition in the olfactory bulb." *Brain Research* 175:377–382.

Shepherd, G., and R. Brayton. 1987. "Logic operations are properties of computer-simulated interactions between excitable dendritic spines." *Neuroscience* 21:151–165.

Shepherd, G. M., R. K. Brayton, J. F. Miller, I. Segev, J. Rinzel, and W. Rall. 1985. "Signal enhancement in distal cortical dendrites by means of interactions between active dendritic spines." *Proceedings of the National Academy of Science USA* 82:2192–2195.

Smith, L. M., F. F. Ebner, and M. Colonnier. 1980. "The thalamo-cortical projection in *Pseudemys* turtles: A quantitative electron microscopic study." *Journal of Comparative Neurology* 190:445–461.

Spencer, W. A., and E. R. Kandel. 1961. "Electrophysiology of hippocampal neurons IV. Fast prepotentials." *Journal of Neurophysiology* 24:272–285.

Stafstrom, C. E., P. C. Schwindt, J. A. Flatman, and W. E. Crill. 1984. "Properties of subthreshold response and action potential recorded in layer V neurons from cat sensorimotor cortex in vitro." *Journal of Neurophysiology* 52:244–263.

Stone, J. 1983. *Parallel Processing in the Visual System.* New York: Plenum.

Swanson, L. W. 1981. "A direct projection from Ammon's horn to prefrontal cortex in the rat." *Brain Research* 217:150–154.

Szentagothai, J. 1975. "The module-concept in cerebral cortex architecture." *Brain Research* 95:475–496.

Traub, R. D., and R. Llinas. 1979. "Hippocampal pyramidal cells: Significance of dendritic ionic conductances for neuronal function and epileptogenesis." *Journal of Neurophysiology* 42:476–496.

Walaas, I. 1983. "The hippocampus," in *Chemical Neuroanatomy,* P. C. Emson, ed. New York: Raven, 337–358.

4

Learning and Representation in Connectionist Models

Terrence J. Sejinowski and
Charles R. Rosenberg

Expert performance is characterized by speed and effortlessness, but this fluency requires long hours of effortful practice. We are all experts at reading and communicating with language. We forget how long it took to acquire these skills because we are now so good at them and we continue to practice every day. As performance on a difficult task becomes more automatic, it also becomes more inaccessible to conscious scrutiny. The acquisition of skilled performance by practice is more difficult to study and is not as well understood as memory for specific facts (Anderson 1982; Norman 1982; Squire 1986, Tulving 1985).

In connectionist models information is represented as patterns of activity in a large number of simple processing units. Memory and processing are closely intertwined in a network. Information can be stored by changing the connection strengths or weights on the links between the processing units. By studying the properties of relatively simple connectionist models, researchers may be able to gain insights into the different ways information processing is organized in the nervous system.

The earliest network models of associative memory were based on correlations between input and output patterns of activity in linear processing units (Hinton and Anderson 1981). These models have several features that make them attractive: The synaptic strengths are computed from information available locally at each synapse in a single trial; the information is distributed in a large number of connection strengths; the recall of stored information is associative; and the network can generalize to new input patterns that are similar to stored patterns. There are also severe limitations with this class of linear associative matrix models, including interference between stored items, especially between ones that are related, and inability to make decisions that are contingent on several inputs. New network models and network learning algorithms have been introduced recently that overcome some of the shortcomings of the associative matrix models of memory. These learning algorithms require many training examples to create the internal representations needed to perform a task skillfully and to generalize properly, which makes this type of learning a candidate model for skill acquisition.

4.1   Neural Network Models of Learning

Organizing Principles

Neural Networks   Neurons are highly specialized processing units. Their relatively slow processing time is compensated for by their large number and high connectivity. There are many types of neurons that have highly specific patterns of connectivity. Some are primarily inhibitory; others are primarily excitatory. Unfortunately the detailed patterns of connectivity in the cerebral cortex have not yet been determined. Processing within neurons can be complex, although within the basic limitations on speed and accuracy imposed by the biophysical properties of ions and membranes. The dendrites in some neurons integrate incoming information through nonlinear spatiotemporal interactions between synapses. Synaptic strengths are variable on many time scales and can facilitate or habituate with activity. The anatomical arrangements found in the cerebral cortex are outlined by Crick and Asanuma (1986), and the physiological properties of cortical cells are summarized by Sejnowski (1986).

The degree of neural detail that should be included in a model depends on the level under investigation. Biophysical properties may be crucial when modeling synaptic plasticity, but only a general rule for modification may be needed to model information storage at the circuit level. The style of processing and memory, such as the degree to which information is localized or distributed in the network, could well be general properties, whereas the actual codes used are probably specific to the detailed circuits. If there are no general properties of cortical processing, then nothing short of detailed simulations of actual circuits will yield any insights, but there is hope that at least some general insights will be possible. Churchland (1986) has emphasized the importance of computational network models in providing generalizations and guidance at both the neural and cognitive levels of description.

As a first step toward understanding neural networks, we study network models constructed from simple processing units that have only the most basic properties of neurons and attempt to explore their computational capabilities: What are the possible ways to represent sensory information in a collection of these units? What are the computational capabilities of different patterns of connectivity in the network? What computations can the network not perform? Even the simplest networks have complex behaviors that are not easy to describe analytically, so much of the research is empirical and exploratory. Also, there are so many architectures—the number of layers, feedback between layers, and local patterns of connectivity—that much guidance is needed from the general organization of cortical circuits, such as the columnar organization of the cerebral cortex and the hierarchical arrangements of cortical mappings (Adrian 1953; Hubel and Wiesel 1962; Mountcastle 1978; Allman et al. 1983; Van Essen and Maunsell 1983). Once we have gained some insight into the capabilities of these simple models, we can compare their performance with human performance on similar tasks and continue to improve the models.

Representations   In this chapter we present a network model that pronounces English text by transforming letters into elementary speech sounds, or phonemes. How many neurons are involved in the representation of letters and phonemes in the cerebral cortex? A related question is, How much overlap is there between the populations of neurons? To be more specific, when the word "cat" is pronounced, how localized is the representation for the production of the sound of the letter "a" and how different is it from the sound of the letter "a" in "gate"? Almost nothing is known about these issues in part because recordings have not been made from cortical neurons in humans. Two extreme possibilities are that each item is assigned to a single neuron, the so-called grandmother cell hypothesis (Barlow 1972; Feldman 1986), or that a large number of the neurons in a brain area are used to represent an item, sometimes called the holographic hypothesis (Longuet-Higgins 1968; Willshaw 1981). Almost certainly the number of neurons involved is intermediate between these extremes and depends on the item.

The nature of internal representations in the transformations of letters to sounds can be studied by constructing network models that can perform the same task. The networks we present here are much too simple to serve as a literal model for the real neural networks in the human speech areas. However, we have been able to explore many interesting questions, including the properties of distributed internal representations and their consequences for learning strategies. Several general principles emerge based on the qualitative similarities between the performance of the network model and human abilities.

Associative Matrix Models

The goal of early models of memory (Steinbuch 1961; Anderson 1970; Kohonen 1970; Longuet-Higgins 1968) was to perform content-addressable recall of information represented as vectors. Given an input vector ι_b and an associated output vector o_a, the correlation matrix is defined as

$$K_{ab} = \varepsilon o_a \iota_b, \tag{4.1}$$

where ε is the strength of the association. If ι_b is identified with the rate of firing of the bth presynaptic element and o_a is identified with the rate of firing of the ath postsynaptic element, then K_{ab} can be computed after modifying the synapses between the input and output neurons according to the learning rule suggested by Hebb (1949), which states that the strength of the synapse should increase whenever there is a simultaneous presynaptic spike and a postsynaptic spike. An important property of the correlation matrix is that it depends only on information that is available locally at a synapse. Nonlocal modification rules that require information from disparate parts of a network are more difficult to implement.

Each component of the input and output vectors is identified with the firing rate of a neuron. The associative matrix model assumes that the output firing rate is a linear summation of all the weighted inputs. Given an input vector η_b, the output vector ϕ_a is given by

$$\phi_a = \varepsilon \sum_{b=1}^{n} K_{ab} \eta_b, \tag{4.2}$$

where n is the number of components of the input vector. By substituting the expression for K_{ab} in equation (4.2), we can rewrite the output vector as

$$\phi_a = \varepsilon o_a \sum_{b=1}^{n} \iota_b \eta_b. \tag{4.3}$$

Thus the output of the network is proportional to the stored output vector and the amplitude depends on the inner product or overlap between the input vector and the stored input vector.

Several pairs of inputs and outputs can be stored this way in the same network:

$$K_{ab} = \sum_{\alpha=1}^{A} \varepsilon_\alpha o_a^\alpha \iota_b^\alpha, \tag{4.4}$$

where o_a^α and ι_b^α are A pairs of input and output vectors, respectively, and ε_α is the association strength of the αth pair. The output vector can similarly be related to the stored vectors:

$$\phi_a = \sum_{\alpha=1}^{A} \varepsilon_\alpha o_a^\alpha \sum_{b=1}^{n} \iota_b^\alpha \eta_b. \tag{4.5}$$

However, as the number of stored vectors increases, so does the interference between them (Anderson 1970). Crosstalk between the stored input vectors can be minimized by orthogonalizing them (Kohonen 1984).

Hebbian synaptic plasticity is probably the simplest local rule that can be used for associative storage and recall of information. Evidence supporting Hebbian plasticity has recently been found in the hippocampus (Kelso et al. 1986), and detailed correlation matrix models of the hippocampus are now being explored (Lynch 1986; Rolls 1986; McNaughton and Morris 1987). However, there are many other uses for Hebbian synaptic plasticity, such as plasticity during development (Linsker 1986), unsupervised learning (Sutton and Barto 1981; Tesauro 1986; Finkel and Edelman 1985), and rapid changes in the topology of a network (von der Malsburg and Bienenstock 1987). As a consequence, experimental evidence for Hebbian modification of synaptic strength does not necessarily imply associative storage.

Numerous variations have been proposed on the conditions for Hebbian plasticity (Levy et al. 1984). One problem with any synaptic modification rule that can only increase the strength of a synapse is the eventual saturation of the synaptic strength at its maximum value. Nonspecific decay is one solution to this problem. Sejnowski (1977a,b) suggested that specific decreases in the strength of a plastic plastic synapse should be considered and proposed that the change in strength of a plastic synapse should be proportional to the covariance between the presynaptic firing and the postsynaptic firing:

$$K_{ab} = \sum_{\alpha=1}^{A} \varepsilon_\alpha (o_a^\alpha - \bar{o}_a)(\iota_b^\alpha - \bar{\iota}_b), \tag{4.6}$$

where $\bar{o}_a$ is the average firing rate of the output neuron and $\bar{\iota}_b$ is the average firing rate of the input neuron [see also Chauvet (1986)]. According to this modification rule, the strength of the synapse should increase if the firings of the presynaptic and postsynaptic elements are positively correlated, decrease if they are negatively correlated, and remain unchanged if they are uncorrelated. Evidence for a decrease in the strength of synapses in the hippocampus under the predicted conditions has recently been reported by Levy et al. (1983). Similar modification rules have also been suggested for plasticity during development (Cooper et al. 1979; Bienenstock et al. 1982).

Improvements have recently been made to associative matrix models by introducing feedback connections, so that they are auto-associative, and by making them nonlinear (Anderson and Mozer 1981; Sejnowski 1981; Hopfield 1982; Kohonen 1984; Toulouse et al. 1986). However, this class of models still has a severe computational limitation in that all the processing units in the network are constrained by either the inputs or the outputs, so that there are no free units that could be used to form new internal representations. What representations should be used if the network is deeply buried in the association cortex far from sensory inputs and motor outputs? Some other principles must be specified for forming these internal representations. Nevertheless, given that good representations already exist, the associative matrix model is still a viable one for the fast storage of novel events and items.

Nonlinear Processing Units

In the model neuron introduced by McCulloch and Pitts (1943), the output could only take the value 0 or 1, like the all-or-none nature of the action potential. This binary model does not take into account the graded responses of neurons, which can be expressed as an average rate of firing. There are two ways to make the output of the processing unit graded. First, the output of the processing unit can be made probabilistic, with a probability proportional to its average rate of firing. Second, the output of a processing unit can be made a real number between 0 and 1. Both of these possibilities are illustrated in this section.

The output function of a more realistic model neuron is shown in figure 4.1. This function has a sigmoid shape: It monotonically increases with input; it is 0 if the input is negative; and it asymptotically approaches 1 as the input becomes large. This roughly describes the firing rate of a neuron as a function of its integrated input: If the input is below threshold, there is no output, the firing rate increases with the input, and it saturates at a maximum firing rate. The behavior of the network does not depend critically on the details of the sigmoid function, but the one we used is given by

$$s_i = P(E_i) = \frac{1}{1 + e^{-E_i}},$$ (4.7)

where s_i is the output of the ith unit and the total input E_i is

$$E_i = \sum_j w_{ij} s_j,$$ (4.8)

where w_{ij} is the weight from the jth to the ith unit. The weights can

Neurons as Processors

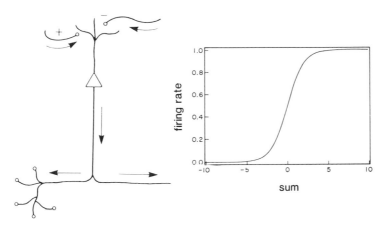

Figure 4.1
(Left) Schematic model of a processing unit receiving inputs from other processing units. (Right) Transformation between summed inputs and output of a processing unit as given by equation (4.7).

have positive or negative real values, representing an excitatory or inhibitory influence.

In addition to the weights connecting them, each unit also has a threshold. In some learning algorithms the thresholds can also vary. To make the notation uniform, we implemented the threshold as an ordinary weight from a special unit, called the true unit, that always has an output value of 1. This fixed bias acts like a threshold whose value is the negative of the weight.

The properties of the nonlinear processing units used here have some properties that make them similar to real neurons: (1) the integration of diverse excitatory and inhibitory signals arriving from other units, although with low accuracy; (2) an output signal that is a nonlinear transformation of the total integrated input, including a threshold; and (3) a complex pattern of interconnectivity. Many other properties of neurons are not taken into account but could be incorporated into subsequent models. The goal here is to explore the processing capabilities of the simplest classes of nonlinear networks, particularly those properties that arise through the patterns of connections in the network.

Nonlinear Networks with One Layer of Connections
In a network of processing units a subset receives information from outside the network while another subset provides the output from

the network. Patterns of activity in the group of input units are transformed into patterns of activity in the output units by direct connections and through connections with additional internal units that play the role of interneurons. In general, it is difficult to analyze the performance and computational capabilities of nonlinear network models, but by making restrictions on the connectivity, it is possible to make progress. The small networks that we can study at present should be considered part of a larger system.

When there are feedback connections in a network, the units may reverberate without settling down to a stable output. In some cases oscillations may be desirable, but otherwise special provisions must be made to suppress them. One method that has been thoroughly explored is the use of symmetric connectivity. Networks with reciprocal symmetric connections, first introduced by Hopfield (1982) in the context of binary-valued processing units, were the starting point for the study of learning algorithms in Boltzmann machines by Hinton and Sejnowski (1983). Another method, extensively studied by Grossberg (1976), is the use of lateral shunting inhibition. But it is easiest to avoid oscillations by not considering any feedback connections.

In a feed-forward network there is no dynamic feedback so that information can flow only from the input layer to the output layer. The simplest class of feed-forward networks are ones that have no internal or "hidden" units. In this case each output unit acts independently in response to input patterns in its "receptive field," defined here as the group of input units that drives the output unit, in analogy with the concept of a receptive field for sensory neurons. The output unit is most strongly driven by patterns of activity in its receptive field that are congruent to the excitatory connections and that avoid the inhibitory ones.

A simple learning procedure exists for automatically determining the weights in a single-layer feed-forward network. It is an incremental learning procedure that requires a teacher to provide the network with examples of typical input patterns and the correct outputs; with each example the weights in the network are slightly altered to improve the performance of the network. If a set of weights exists that can solve the classification problem, then convergence theorems guarantee that such a set of weights will be found.

These learning procedures are error correcting in the sense that only information about the discrepancy between the desired outputs provided by the teacher and the actual output given by the network is used to update the weights. The LMS algorithm of Widrow and Hoff (1960) applies to units that have continuous-valued outputs, and the perceptron learning algorithm of Rosenblatt (1959) applies to binary-valued units. The LMS algorithm is described here. Define the difference between the desired outputs s_i^* and the actual outputs s_i as

$$\delta_i = s_i^* - s_i. \tag{4.9}$$

The LMS learning algorithm requires that the weight from input unit s_j to the ith output unit should be altered by

$$\Delta w_{ij} = \delta_i s_j. \tag{4.10}$$

This is a gradient descent procedure because on each step the squared error averaged over all input patterns is reduced.

There is an interesting relationship between this error-correcting procedure and the Rescorla-Wagner theory for classical conditioning. Rescorla and Wagner (1972) state that "organisms only learn when events violate their expectations. Certain expectations are built up about the events following a stimulus complex; expectations initiated by the complex and its component stimuli are then only modified when consequent events disagree with the composite expectation" (p. 75). Thus it is the difference between the expected and the actual outcomes that determines whether strengths are modified. Sutton and Barto (1981) have shown that the mathematical formalism introduced by Rescorla and Wagner is identical with the Widrow-Hoff LMS algorithm.

Recently Gluck and Bower (1986, 1987) have applied the LMS algorithm to category learning in humans. In three experiments subjects learned to categorize diseases in hypothetical patients from patterns of symptoms. The adaptive network model was a better predictor of human performance than probability matching, exemplar retrieval, or simple prototype matching. The model correctly predicted a counterintuitive phenomenon called base-rate neglect that has been frequently observed in studies of likelihood judgments: When one disease is far more likely than another, the model predicts that subjects will overestimate the diagnostic value of the more valid symptom for the rare disease. Thus the subjects consistently overestimated the degree to which evidence that was representative or typical of a rare event was actually predictive of it (Kahneman and Tversky 1972).

The patterns that can be correctly classified with a one-layer network are limited to those that are geometrically equivalent to regions of a vector space bounded by a plane (Minsky and Papert 1969). Single-layer networks are severely limited in the difficulty of the problem that they can solve, but this deficiency can be partially overcome by preprocessing the inputs through a layer of units that serve as feature detectors so that the information needed to solve the problem is made explicitly available (Rosenblatt 1959; Gamba et al. 1961). The required features may be different for each problem.

An impressive example of how clever coding can turn a difficult problem into one that can be learned in one layer of weights is the study of verb learning by Rumelhart and McClelland (1986a). The goal of their network was to take as input English verbs and produce as output their past tenses. Their coding scheme decomposed the ordered string of letters in words into unordered triples. These triples in turn were coded into patterns on 460 input units. The same coding was used for the 460 output units, each of which received a connection from all the input units, making a total of 231,600 weights. Their network was equivalent to a single-layer Boltzmann machine, which we discuss in the next section.

One problem with single-layer networks is the lack of internal degrees of freedom. Can the learning algorithm be generalized to networks with more than one layer of weights? If so, then the need to hand-code the features for each problem would be alleviated and much more difficult problems could be solved by the same type of supervised learning paradigm. It had been thought for many years that such a learning algorithm was not possible for multilayered networks [Minsky and Papert (1969, p. 232); see also Arbib (1987)].

Nonlinear Network Models with Hidden Units
A network without hidden units is limited in what it can learn. Adding a single intermediate layer of hidden units suffices to perform any desired transformation. Consider, for example, the case of binary units. If there are N input units, then there are 2^N possible input patterns. Dedicate one hidden unit to each of these input patterns and connect it to the input units in the following way: Set the weight from an input unit to the hidden unit to $+1$ if the input unit is on or to -1 if the input unit is off, and set the threshold of the hidden unit to the total number of input units that are on. For any given input pattern only one hidden unit will be activated, which in turn can activate any desired output pattern. In this way any problem can be solved, but at the expense of a huge number of hidden units that grows exponentially with the number of input units. With continuous-valued units the analysis is more difficult, but similar theorems can be proved (Kolmogorov 1957; Palm 1978, 1979).

In practice, only a small subset of all possible transformations are ever needed and only a small number of hidden units are available. The challenge is to find the appropriate set of hidden units for each problem. One possibility is to have the network discover the proper features without supervision from a teacher. There are several unsupervised learning procedures that can automatically model structure from the environment (Kohonen 1984; Grossberg 1976; Rumelhart and Zipser 1985; Pearlmutter and Hinton 1986). One problem with unsupervised learning is that all the hidden units may discover the same features. Competition through mutual inhibition is one solution that enforces diversity (Feldman 1982), and others have been suggested (Reggia 1985; Baum et al. 1987). Another problem is that not all the structure in the inputs may be relevant to the solution of a particular problem. Feedback of information from the environment about the desired performance is needed.

One class of supervised learning algorithms for multilayered networks uses reinforcement signals from a teacher that tell the network whether or not the output is correct (Sutton and Barto 1981; Barto 1985; Klopf 1986; Tesauro 1986; Gluck and Thompson 1986). This is the minimum amount of information needed to help direct the hidden units toward good features, but there is so little information that the networks improve slowly and hesitatingly. Recently a new class of algorithms was discovered that directly generalizes the class of error-correcting learning procedures to multilayered networks. Two examples are reviewed here: the Boltzmann machine and backpropagation. [See also Arbib (1987) for a review that includes a valuable historical perspective on earlier work.]

Boltzmann Machines   Hinton and Sejnowski (1983, 1986) introduced a stochastic network architecture, called the Boltzmann machine, for solving optimization problems (Marr and Poggio 1976; Ballard et al. 1983; Hopfield and Tank 1986). The processing units in a Boltzmann machine are binary, like the perceptron, but they are updated probabilistically using the same output function in figure 4.1. As a consequence, the internal state of a Boltzmann machine fluctuates even for a constant input pattern. The amount of fluctuation is controlled by a parameter that is analogous to the temperature of a thermodynamic system. Fluctuations allow the system to escape from local traps into which it would get stuck if there were no noise in the system. Another important difference with the perceptron is that all the units in a Boltzmann machine are symmetrically connected; this allows an "energy" to be defined for the network and ensures that the network will relax to an equilibrium state that minimizes the energy (Hopfield 1982). Smolensky (1983, 1986) has studied the same architecture using "harmony," which is the negative of energy, as the global function.

The Boltzmann machine has been applied to a number of constraint satisfaction problems in vision, such as figure-ground separation in image analysis (Sejnowski and Hinton 1986; Kienker et al. 1986), and generalizations have been applied to image restoration (Geman and Geman 1984) and binocular depth perception (Divko and Schulten 1986). Riley and Smolensky (1984) have used harmony theory to study problem solving. The number of times that the network must be updated to reach an optimal solution can be very large when the units are stochastic; an alternative architecture that converges more quickly, although not necessarily to the optimal solution, is based on continuous-valued units (Hopfield 1984; Hopfield and Tank 1985, 1986). This deterministic system is like a "mean field" approximation to the stochastic system.

Boltzmann machines have an interesting learning algorithm that allows "energy landscapes" to be created through training by example. Learning in a Boltzmann machine has two phases. In the training phase a binary input pattern is imposed on the input group and on the correct binary output pattern. The system is allowed to relax to equilibrium at a fixed "temperature" while the inputs and outputs are held fixed. At equilibrium the average fraction of the time a pair of units is on together, the co-occurrence probability p_{ij}^+, is computed for each connection. In the test phase the same procedure is followed with only the input units clamped, and the average co-occurrence probabilities p_{ij}^- are again computed. The weights are then updated according to

$$\Delta w_{ij} = \varepsilon(p_{ij}^+ - p_{ij}^-), \tag{4.11}$$

where the parameter ε controls the rate of learning. A co-occurrence probability is related to the correlation between the firing or activation of the presynaptic and postsynaptic units and can be implemented by a Hebb synapse. In the second phase, however, the change in the synaptic strengths is anti-Hebbian because it must decrease with increasing correlation. Notice that this procedure is also error correcting, for no change will be made to the weight if the two probabilities are the same. The perceptron learning procedure follows as a special case of the Boltzmann learning algorithm when there are no hidden units and the probability function reduces to a step function.

The Boltzmann learning algorithm has been applied to a variety of problems, such as bandwidth compression (Ackley et al. 1985), the learning of symmetry groups (Sejnowski et al. 1986), and speech recognition (Prager et al. 1986). One of the practical limitations of simulating a Boltzmann machine on a conventional digital computer is the excessive time required to come to equilibrium and collect statistics. A special-purpose VLSI chip is being designed to speed up the learning (Alspector and Allen 1986).

Back-Propagation   Another error-correcting learning procedure, introduced by Rumelhart et al. (1986) and called error back-propagation, generalizes the Widrow-Hoff algorithm. The network is a multilayered feed-forward architecture that uses the same processing units described in equation (4.7) and figure 4.1. There may be direct connections between the input layer and the output layer as well as through the hidden units. A superscript is used to denote the layer for each unit, so that $s_i^{(n)}$ is the ith unit on the nth layer. The final output layer is designated the Nth layer.

The first step is to compute the output of the network for a given input. The goal of the learning procedure is to minimize the average squared error between the computed values of the output units and the correct pattern s_i^* provided by a teacher:

$$\text{Error} = \sum_{i-1}^{J} (s_i^* - s_i^{(N)})^2, \tag{4.12}$$

where J is the number of units in the output layer. This is accomplished by first computing the error gradient on the output layer,

$$\delta_i^{(N)} = (s_i^* - s_i^{(N)})P'(E_i^{(N)}), \tag{4.13}$$

and then propagating it backward through the network layer by layer:

$$\delta_i^{(n)} = \sum_j \delta_j^{(n+1)} w_{ji}^{(n)} P'(E_i^{(n)}), \tag{4.14}$$

where $P'(E_i)$ is the first derivative of the function $P(E_i)$ in figure 4.1.

These gradients are the directions that each weight should be altered to reduce the error for a particular item. To reduce the average error for all the input patterns, the gradients must be averaged over all the training patterns before updating the weights. In practice, it is sufficient to average over several inputs before updating the weights. Another method is to compute a running average of the gradient with an exponentially decaying filter:

$$\Delta w_{ij}^{(n)}(u + 1) = \alpha \Delta w_{ij}^{(n)}(u) + (1 - \alpha)\delta_i^{(n+1)} s_j^{(n)}, \tag{4.15}$$

where α is a smoothing parameter (typically 0.9) and u is the number of input patterns presented. The smoothed weight gradients $\Delta w_{ij}^{(n)}(u)$ can then be used to update the weights:

$$w_{ij}^{(n)}(t + 1) = w_{ij}^{(n)}(t) + \varepsilon \Delta w_{ij}^{(n)}, \tag{4.16}$$

where t is the number of weight updates and ε is the learning rate (typically 1.0). The error signal is back-propagated only when the difference between the actual and the desired values of the outputs is greater than a margin of 0.1. This ensures that the network does not overlearn on inputs that it is already getting correct. This learning algorithm can be generalized to networks with feedback connections and multiplicative connections (Rumelhart et al. 1986), but these extensions will not be discussed further.

The definitions of the learning parameters here are somewhat different from those in Rumelhart et al. (1986). In the original algorithm ε is used rather than $(1 - \alpha)$ in equation (4.15). Our parameter α is used to smooth the gradient in a way that is independent of the learning rate ε, which appears only in the weight update [equation (4.16)]. Our averaging procedure also makes it unnecessary to scale the learning rate by the number of presentations per weight update.

The back-propagation learning algorithm has been applied to several problems, including knowledge representation in semantic networks (Hinton 1986; Rumelhart 1986), bandwidth compression by dimensionality reduction (Saund 1986; Zipser 1986), speech recognition (Ellman and Zipser 1986; Watrous et al. 1986), conversion of text to speech (Sejnowski and Rosenberg 1987), and backgammon (Tesauro and Sejnowski 1988). In the next section we give a detailed description of how back-propagation was applied to the problem of converting English text to speech.

Biological Plausibility   Neither the Boltzmann machine nor the error back-propagation scheme is meant as a literal model of real neural circuitry. They are also quite different from each other—the Boltzmann machine uses binary stochastic units in a symmetric network, whereas back-propagation uses real-valued deterministic units in a feed-forward network—but both architectures have learning algorithms that depend on gradient descent in the space of weights, which can have high dimensionality. The class of gradient descent algorithms for learning in large networks may have general properties that are already present in the simplest members. Other more elaborate gradient descent learning algorithms, which are more biologically plausible, are also being explored (Parker 1986; Le Cun 1985).

The network models we review in this section make a number of assumptions that should be critically examined. First, the networks are based on a highly idealized version of real neurons, and many constraints concerning patterns of connectivity found in the nervous system are not incorporated into the models. Second, human learning is often imitative rather than instructive, so that children, for example, are exposed to many positive examples and are not always corrected when they make mistakes.

At this early stage in exploring the capabilities of network models at the psychological level, it is more helpful to discover the general properties of networks before studying the properties of highly specialized networks. The network models are sufficiently general that they can be applied to several different levels of investigation. A processing unit, for example, can be identified with a group of neurons rather than a single neuron and the activity level of the unit identified with the average firing rate within the group. Also, the "teacher" in a supervised learning algorithm should not be taken too literally. For example, one brain area can serve as the teacher and provide the information needed to train another brain area. In the next section we consider the problem of pronouncing English text. The teacher can be a part of the brain that already contains the correct pronunciation of words, and during the learning process the pronunciations become associated with the spellings of the words. Little is known about the neurophysiological basis of human language abilities, so a detailed comparison with real brain circuits is not yet possible.

Thus the present network model should not be considered a neural model but rather a model system in which to explore issues of representation and learning in large populations of neurons. The general insights that are found can be used to explore more detailed brain models and may even help in analyzing recordings from neurons in the cerebral cortex.

4.2   NETtalk

The problem of pronouncing written English text illustrates many of the features of skill acquisition and expert performance. In reading aloud, we first recognize letters and words from images on our retinas. Several words can be processed in one fixation so that a significant amount of parallel processing must be involved. At some point in the central nervous system the information encoded visually is transformed into articulatory information about how to produce the correct speech sounds. Finally, intricate patterns of activity occur in the motor neurons that innervate muscles in the larynx and mouth, and sounds are produced. The key step that we are concerned with in this section is the transformation between the highest sensory representations of the letters and the earliest articulatory representations of the phonemes.

English pronunciation has been extensively studied by linguists, and much is known about the correspondence between letters and phonemes (Venezky 1970). English is a particularly difficult language to master because of its irregular orthography. For example, the "a" in almost all words ending in "ave," such as "brave" and "gave," is a long vowel, but not in "have," and there are some words such as "read" that can vary in pronunciation. The problem of reconciling rules and exceptions in converting text to speech shares some characteristics with difficult problems in artificial intelligence that have traditionally been approached with rule-based knowledge representations, such as natural language translation (Haas 1970).

In this section we describe a network that learns to pronounce English text. The model, which we call NETtalk, demonstrates that even a small network can capture a significant fraction of the regularities in English pronunciation as well as absorb many of the irregularities. In commercial systems such as DECtalk (Digital Equipment Corporation), a look-up table (of about a million bits) is used to store the phonetic transcription of the most common words, and phonological rules are applied to words that are not in the dictionary (Allen 1987; Klatt 1980). The result is a string of phonemes that can then be converted to sounds with digital speech synthesis. NETtalk is designed to perform the task of converting strings of letters to strings of phonemes. Earlier work on NETtalk was described by Sejnowski and Rosenberg (1986, 1987).

Network Architecture
NETtalk is a feed-forward network that uses the back-propagation learning algorithm. We have also used the Boltzmann learning algorithm on this problem, but the results are not reported here. The network is hierarchically arranged into three layers of units: an input layer, an output layer, and an intermediate, or "hidden," layer, as illustrated in figure 4.2. Information flows through the network from bottom to top. First, the letter units at the base are clamped; then the states of the hidden units are determined by equations (4.2) and (4.3); finally, the states of the phoneme units at the top are determined.

Representations of Letters and Phonemes   The standard network has seven groups of units in the input layer, and one group of units in each of the other two layers. Each input group encodes one letter of the input text, so that strings of seven letters are presented to the input units at any one time. The desired output of the network is the correct phoneme, associated with the center, or fourth, letter of this seven-letter "window." The other six letters (three on either side of

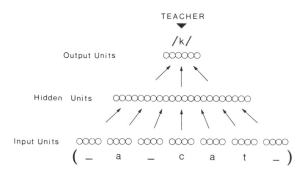

Figure 4.2
Schematic drawing of the NETtalk network architecture. Window of letters in an English text is fed to an array of 203 input units, as shown on the bottom of the pyramid, with 7 groups of 29 units in each group. Information from these units is transformed by an intermediate layer of 80 hidden units. Each hidden unit receives inputs from all the input units on the bottom layer and in turn sends its output to all 26 units in the output layer. The output pattern of activity is then used to choose the closest phoneme and stress corresponding to the middle letter. During learning, a teacher provides the correct output vector and the error is used to update the weights in the network. An example of an input string of letters from a training text is shown below the input groups, and the output phoneme for the middle letter is shown above the output layer. There are 309 units and 18,629 weights in the network, including a variable threshold for each unit.

the center letter) provide a partial context for this decision. The text is stepped through the window letter by letter. At each step the network computes a phoneme, and after each word the weights are adjusted according to how closely the computed pronunciation matched the correct one.

We chose a window with seven letters for two reasons. First, Lucassen and Mercer (1984) have shown that a significant amount of the information needed to pronounce a letter correctly is contributed by the nearby letters (figure 4.3). Second, we were limited by our computational resources to exploring small networks, and it proved possible to train a network with a seven-letter window in a few days. The limited size of the window also meant that some important nonlocal information about pronunciation and stress could not be properly taken into account by our model (Church 1985). The main goal of our model is to explore the basic principles of distributed information coding in a real-world domain rather than to achieve perfect performance.

The letters and phonemes are represented in different ways. The letters are represented locally within each group by twenty-nine dedicated units, one for each letter of the alphabet plus an additional three

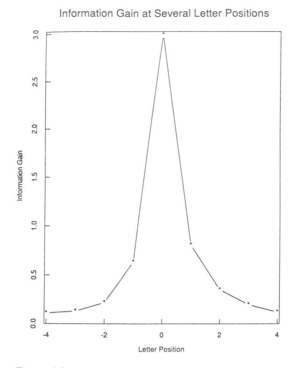

Figure 4.3
Mutual information provided by neighboring letters and the correct pronunciation of the center letter as a function of distance from the center letter. Data from Lucassen and Mercer (1984).

units to encode punctuation and word boundaries. Only one unit in each input group is active for a given input. The phonemes, in contrast, are represented in terms of twenty-one articulatory features, such as point of articulation, voicing, and vowel height, as summarized in table 4.1. Five additional units encode stress and syllable boundaries, making twenty-six output units. This is a distributed representation because each output unit participates in the encoding of several phonemes (Hinton et al. 1986).

The hidden units neither receive direct input nor have direct output but are used by the network to form internal representations appropriate for mapping letters to phonemes. The goal of the learning algorithm is to search effectively the space of all possible weights for a network that performs the mapping.

Learning   We used two texts to train the network: phonetic transcriptions from the informal continuous speech of a child (Carterette

Table 4.1
Articulatory representation of phonemes and punctuations

Symbol[a]	Phoneme[b]	Articulatory features[c]
/a/	f*a*ther	Low, Tensed, Central2
/b/	*b*et	Voiced, Labial, Stop
/c/	b*ou*ght	Medium, Velar
/d/	*d*ebt	Voiced, Alveolar, Stop
/e/	b*a*ke	Medium, Tensed, Front2
/f/	*f*in	Unvoiced, Labial, Fricative
/g/	*g*uess	Voiced, Velar, Stop
/h/	*h*ead	Unvoiced, Glottal, Glide
/i/	P*e*te	High, Tensed, Front1
/k/	*K*en	Unvoiced, Velar, Stop
/l/	*l*et	Voiced, Dental, Liquid
/m/	*m*et	Voiced, Labial, Nasal
/n/	*n*et	Voiced, Alveolar, Nasal
/o/	b*oa*t	Medium, Tensed, Back2
/p/	*p*et	Unvoiced, Labial, Stop
/r/	*r*ed	Voiced, Palatal, Liquid
/s/	*s*it	Unvoiced, Alveolar, Fricative
/t/	*t*est	Unvoiced, Alveolar, Stop
/u/	l*u*te	High, Tensed, Back2
/v/	*v*est	Voiced, Labial, Fricative
/w/	*w*et	Voiced, Labial, Glide
/x/	*a*bout	Medium, Central2
/y/	*y*et	Voiced, Palatal, Glide
/z/	*z*oo	Voiced, Alveolar, Fricative
/A/	b*i*te	Medium, Tensed, Front2 + Central1
/C/	*ch*in	Unvoiced, Palatal, Affricative
/D/	*th*is	Voiced, Dental, Fricative
/E/	b*e*t	Medium, Front1 + Front2
/G/	si*ng*	Voiced, Velar, Nasal
/I/	b*i*t	High, Front1
/J/	*g*in	Voiced, Velar, Nasal
/K/	se*x*ual	Unvoiced, Palatal, Fricative + Velar, Affricative (Compound: /k/ + /S/)
/L/	bott*le*	Voiced, Alveolar, Liquid
/M/	absy*m*	Voiced, Dental, Nasal
/N/	butto*n*	Voiced, Palatal, Nasal
/O/	b*oy*	Medium, Tensed, Central1 + Central2
/Q/	*qu*est	Voiced, Labial + Velar, Affricative, Stop
/R/	bi*r*d	Voiced, Velar, Liquid
/S/	*sh*in	Unvoiced, Palatal, Fricative

Table 4.1 *(Continued)*

Symbol[a]	Phoneme[b]	Articulatory features[c]
/T/	*th*in	Unvoiced, Dental, Fricative
/U/	b*oo*k	High, Back1
/W/	b*ou*t	High + Medium, Tensed, Central2 + Back1
/X/	e*x*cess	Unvoiced, Affricative, Front2 + Central1 (Compound: /k/ + /s/)
/Y/	c*u*te	High, Tensed, Front1 + Front2 + Central1
/Z/	lei*s*ure	Voiced, Palatal, Fricative
/@/	b*a*t	Low, Front2
/!/	*Naz*i	Unvoiced, Labial + Dental, Affricative (Compound: /t/ + /s/)
/#/	e*x*amine	Voiced, Palatal, + Velar, Affricative (Compound: /g/ + /z/)
/*/	*o*ne	Voiced, Glide, Front1 + Low, Central1 (Compound: /w/ + /^/)
/|/	log*i*c	High, Front1 + Front2
/^/	b*u*t	Low, Central1
/-/	Continuation	Silent, Elide
/–/	Word boundary	Pause, Elide
/./	Period	Pause, Full Stop
<	Syllable boundary	Right
>	Syllable boundary	Left
1	Primary stress	Strong, weak
2	Secondary stress	Strong
0	Tertiary stress	Weak
–	Word boundary	Right, left, boundary

a. The symbols for phonemes are a superset of ARPAbet and are associated with the sound of the italicized part of the adjacent word.

b. Compound phonemes were introduced when a single letter was associated with more than one primary phoneme.

c. Two or more of the following twenty-one articulatory feature units were used to represent each phoneme and punctuation. Position in mouth: Labial = Front1, Dental = Front2, Alveolar = Central1, Palatal = Central2, Velar = Back1, Glottal = Back2. Phoneme type: Stop, Nasal, Fricative, Affricative, Glide, Liquid, Voiced, Tensed. Vowel height: High, Medium, Low. Punctuation: Silent, Elide, Pause, Full stop. The continuation symbol was used when a letter is silent. Stress and syllable boundaries were represented with combinations of five additional units, as shown at the end of this table. Stress was associated with vowels, and arrows were associated with letters. The arrows point toward the stress and change direction at syllable boundaries. Thus the stress assignments for "atmosphere" are 1 < > 0 >>> 2 <<. The phoneme and stress assignments were chosen independently.

and Jones 1974) and Merriam-Webster's *Pocket Dictionary* (1974). The corresponding letters and phonemes were aligned, and a special symbol for continuation, -, was inserted whenever a letter is silent or part of a graphemic letter combination, as in the conversion from the string of letters "phone" to the string of phonemes /f-on-/ (see table 4.1). Two procedures were used to move the text through the window of seven input groups. For the corpus of informal continuous speech the text was processed in order with word boundary symbols between the words. Several words or word fragments could be within the window at the same time. For the dictionary the words were placed in random order and moved through the window individually.

The weights were incrementally adjusted during the training according to the discrepancy between the desired and the actual values of the output units. For each phoneme this error was "back-propagated" from the output to the input layer using the learning algorithm introduced by Rumelhart et al. (1986) and described in the previous section. Each weight in the network was adjusted after every word to minimize its contribution to the total mean squared error between the desired and the actual output. The weights in the network were always initialized to small random values uniformly distributed between −0.3 and 0.3; this was necessary to differentiate the hidden units.

A simulator was written in the C programming language for configuring a network with arbitrary connectivity, training it on a corpus and collecting statistics on its performance. A network of 10,000 weights had a throughput during learning of about 2 letters/ sec on a VAX 780 FPA. After every presentation of an input the inner product of the output vector was computed with the codes for each of the phonemes. The phoneme that made the smallest angle with the output was chosen as the "best guess." Slightly better performance was achieved by choosing the phoneme whose representation had the smallest Euclidean distance from the output vector, but these results are not reported here. All performance figures reported in the next section refer to the percentage of correct phonemes chosen by the network. The performance was also assayed by "playing" the output string of phonemes and stresses through DECtalk, bypassing the part of the machine that converts letters to phonemes.

Performance

Continuous Informal Speech   Carterette and Jones (1974) provide phonetic transcriptions of children and adults that were taped during

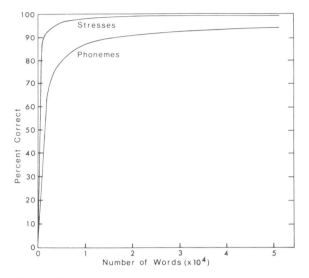

Figure 4.4
Learning curves for phonemes and stresses during training on the 1,024-word corpus of continuous informal speech. The percentage of correct phonemes and stresses are shown as functions of the number of training words.

informal sessions. This was a particularly difficult training corpus because the same word was often pronounced several different ways; phonemes were commonly elided or modified at word boundaries, and adults were about as inconsistent as children. We used the first two pages of transcriptions, which contain 1,024 words from a child in the first grade. The stresses were assigned to the transcriptions so that the training text sounded natural when played through DECtalk. The learning curve for 1,024 words from the informal speech corpus is shown in figure 4.4. The percentage of correct phonemes rises rapidly at first and continues to rise at a slower rate throughout the learning, reaching 95% after 50,000 words. Primary and secondary stresses and syllable boundaries are learned quickly for all words, and the network achieved nearly perfect performance by 5,000 words. When the learning curves are plotted on double logarithmic scales, they are approximately straight lines; thus the learning follows a power law, which is characteristic of human skill learning (Rosenbloom and Newell 1986).

The distinction between vowels and consonants is made early; however, the network predicts the same vowel for all vowels and the same consonant for all consonants, which results in a babbling sound. A second stage occurs when word boundaries are recognized, and the output then resembles pseudowords. After just a few passes through the network many of the words are intelligible, and by ten passes the text is understandable.

When the network makes an error, it often substitutes phonemes that sound similar. For example, a common confusion is between the "th" sounds in "thesis" and "these," which differ only in voicing. Few errors in a well-trained network are confusions between vowels and consonants. Some errors are actually corrections to inconsistencies in the original training corpus. Overall the intelligibility of the speech is quite good.

Does the network memorize the training words, or does it capture the regular features of pronunciation? As a test of generalization, a network trained on the 1,024-word corpus of informal speech was tested without training on a 439-word continuation from the same speaker. The performance was 78%, which indicates that much of the learning was transferred to novel words even after a small sample of English words.

Is the network resistant to damage? We examined performance of a highly trained network after making random changes of varying size to the weights. As shown in figure 4.5a, random perturbations of the weights uniformly distributed on the interval $[-0.5, 0.5]$ have little effect on the performance of the network, and degradation is gradual with increasing damage. This damage causes the average magnitude of each weight to change by 0.25; this can be considered the roundoff error that can be tolerated before the performance of the network begins to deteriorate. With 4 binary bits it is possible to specify 16 possible values, or -2 to $+2$ in steps of 0.25. This range covers almost all the weights, which have an average magnitude of 0.8. Hence the minimum information needed to specify each weight in the network is about 4 bits.

If the damage is not too severe, relearning is much faster than the original learning starting from the same level of performance, as shown in figure 4.5b. Similar fault tolerance and fast recovery from damage has also been observed in networks constructed using the Boltzmann learning algorithm (Hinton and Sejnowski 1986).

Dictionary The Merriam-Webster *Pocket Dictionary* we used has 20,012 words. A subset of the 1,000 most commonly occurring words was selected from this dictionary based on frequency counts in the Brown corpus (Kuchera and Francis 1967). The most common English words are also among the most irregular, so this was also a test of the capacity of the network to absorb exceptions. We were particularly interested in exploring how the performance of the network and

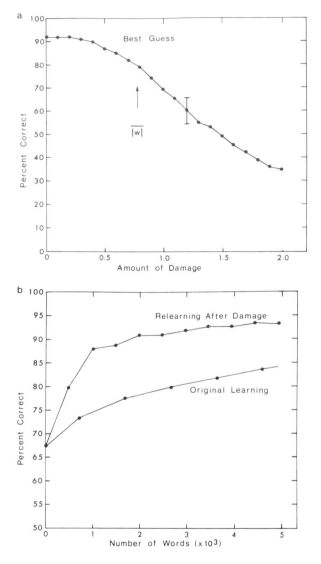

Figure 4.5
Damage to the network and recovery from damage. (a) Performance of a network as a function of the amount of damage to the weights. The network had been previously trained on 50 passes through the corpus of continuous informal speech. The weights were then damaged by adding a random component to each weight uniformly distributed on the interval $[-d, d]$, where d is the amount of damage plotted on the abscissa. The performance shown is the average of at least two disrupted networks for each value of d. For $d = 1.2$, 22 disrupted networks were tested to obtain a standard deviation of 6%. The average absolute value of the weights in the network was $|w| = 0.77$, and the standard deviation was $\sigma = 1.2$. There was little degradation of the best

learning rate scale with the number of hidden units. With no hidden units the performance rises quickly and saturates at 82%, as shown in figure 4.6a. This represents the part of the mapping that can be accomplished by linearly separable partitioning of the input space (Minsky and Papert 1969). Hidden units allow more contextual influence by recognizing higher-order features among combinations of input units.

The rate of learning and asymptotic performance increases with the number of hidden units, as shown in figure 4.6a. The best performance achieved with 120 hidden units was 98%, significantly better than the performance achieved with continuous informal speech, which was more difficult because of the variability in real-world speech. Different letter-to-sound correspondences are learned at different rates; two examples are shown in figure 4.6b. The ability of a network to generalize was tested on a large dictionary. Using weights from a network with 120 hidden units trained on the 1,000 words, the average performance of the network on the dictionary of 20,012 words was 77%. With continued learning the performance reached 85% at the end of the first pass through the dictionary, indicating a significant improvement in generalization. Following five training passes through the dictionary, the performance increased to 90%.

The number of input groups was varied from three to eleven. Both the speed of learning and the asymptotic level of performance improved with the size of the window. The learning curve with 11 input groups and 80 hidden units was about 7% higher than a network with 7 input groups and 80 hidden units up to about 25,000 words of training and reached 97.5% at 55,000 words, compared with 95% for the network with 7 input groups.

Adding an extra layer of hidden units also improved the performance somewhat. A network with 7 input groups and two layers of 80 hidden units each was trained first on the 1,000-word dictionary. Its performance after 55,000 words of training was 97%, and its generalization was 80% on the 20,012-word dictionary without additional training and 87% after the first pass through the dictionary with

---

guesses until $d = 0.5$, and the falloff with increasing damage was gentle. (b) Retraining of a damaged network compared with the original learning curve starting from the same level of performance. The network was damaged with $d = 1.2$ and was retrained using the same corpus and learning parameters that were used to train it. There is a rapid recovery phase during the first pass through the network, followed by a slower healing process similar in time course to the later stages of the original training. These two phases can be accounted for by the shape of the error metric in weight space, which typically has deep ravines (Hinton and Sejnowski 1986).

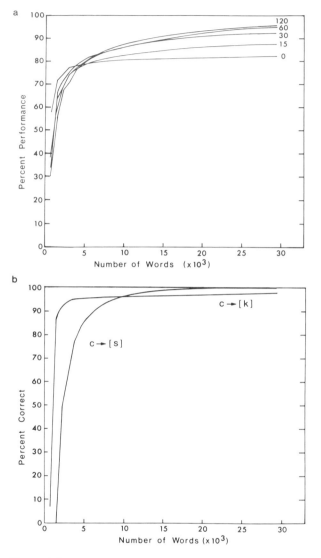

Figure 4.6
(a) Learning curves for training on a corpus of the 1,000 most common words in English using different numbers of hidden units, as indicated for each curve. The percentage of phonemes correctly assigned by the network is shown as a function of the number of training words. For the case with no hidden units, the input units were directly connected to the output units. (b) Performance during learning of two representative phonological rules, the hard and soft pronunciation of the letter "c." Note that the soft "c" takes longer to learn but eventually achieves perfect accuracy. The hard "c" occurs about twice as often as the soft "c" in the training corpus. Children show a similar difficulty with learning to read words with the soft "c" (Venezky and Johnson, 1973).

training. The asymptotic performance after 218,000 words of training on the dictionary was 91%. Compared to the network with 120 hidden units, which had about the same number of weights, the network with two layers of hidden units was better at generalization but about the same in absolute performance.

Analysis of Hidden Units
There are not enough hidden units in even the largest network that we studied to memorize all the words in the dictionary. The standard network with 80 hidden units had 18,629 weights, including variable thresholds. If we allow 4 bits of accuracy for each weight, as indicated by the damage experiments, the total storage needed to define the network is about 10 kilobytes or 80,000 bits. In comparison, the 20,012-word dictionary, including stress information, requires nearly 2,000,000 bits of storage. This data compression is possible because of the redundancy in English pronunciation. By studying the patterns of activation among the hidden units, we were able to understand some of the coding methods that the network had discovered.

The standard network used for analysis had 7 input groups and 80 hidden units and had been trained to 95% correct on 1,000 dictionary words. The levels of activation of the hidden units were examined for each letter of each word using the graphical representation shown in figure 4.7. On average, about 20% of the hidden units are highly activated for any given input, and most of the remaining hidden units have little or no activation. Thus the coding scheme cannot be described as either a local representation, which would activate only one or two units, or a "holographic" representation, in which all the hidden units participate to some extent. It is apparent, even without using statistical techniques, that many hidden units are highly activated only for certain letters or sounds or letter-to-sound correspondences. Some of the hidden units can be assigned unequivocal characterizations, such as one unit that responds only to vowels, but most of the units participate in more than one regularity.

To test the hypothesis that letter-to-sound correspondences are the primary organizing variable, we computed the average activation level of each hidden unit for each letter-to-sound correspondence in the training corpus. The result was 79 vectors with 80 components each, one vector for each letter-to-sound correspondence. A hierarchical clustering technique was used to arrange the letter-to-sound vectors in groups based on a Euclidean metric in the 80-dimensional space of hidden units. The overall pattern, as shown in figure 4.8, is striking: The most important distinction is the complete separation of consonants and vowels. However, within these two groups the clus-

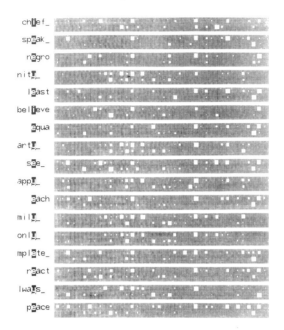

Figure 4.7
Levels of activation in the layer of hidden units for a variety of words, all of which produce the same phoneme, /E/, on the output. The network had 7 input groups and 80 hidden units. The input string is shown on the left with the center letter emphasized. The level of activity of each hidden unit is shown on the right, in two rows of 40 units each. The area of the square is proportional to the activity level. Only a few units were highly activated, and most were inactive.

tering has a different pattern. For the vowels the next most important variable is the letter, whereas consonants are clustered according to the similarity of their sounds. The same clustering procedure is repeated for three networks starting from different random starting states. The patterns of weights are completely different, but the clustering analysis reveals the same hierarchies, with some differences in the details, for all three networks.

4.3   The Spacing Effect

In section 4.2 we demonstrated that a small network was able to perform a difficult task in a way that was quite different from most previous methods used to solve the problem. Information about particular words are stored in the network in a distributed fashion. New words can be added to the network, but they must be added in a way that is compatible with the previously stored information. As a conse-

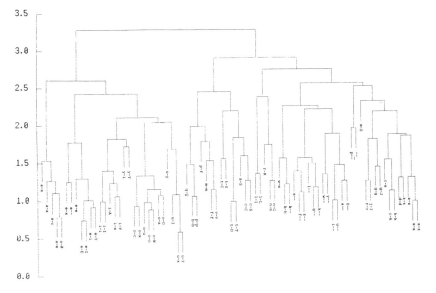

Figure 4.8
Hierarchical clustering of hidden units for letter-to-sound correspondences. The vectors of average hidden unit activity for each correspondence, shown at the bottom of the binary tree, were sequentially grouped according to an agglomerative method using complete linkage (Everitt 1974). The horizontal scale gives the Euclidean distance between the farthest elements in two groups when a pair was merged.

quence, the representation of information affects the training strategy for learning new words. In this section we compare the performance of humans on learning paired associates with the performance of the network on a similar task in the domain of pronunciation. More details about these simulations are presented by Rosenberg and Sejnowski (1986).

Spaced versus Massed Practice
In 1885 Ebbinghaus noted that "with any considerable number of repetitions a suitable distribution of them over a space of time is decidedly more advantageous than the massing of them at a single time" (Ebbinghaus 1885, p. 89). Since then, the spacing effect has been found across a wide range of stimulus materials and tasks, semantic as well as perceptual and motor, and has even been found when the repetitions are across modality, or across languages if bilinguals are employed as subjects [see Hintzman (1974) for a review]. The ubiquity of these results suggests that spacing reflects something of central importance in memory. However, despite over a hundred years of research, there is no adequate, or at least simple, explanation for the spacing effect.

Perhaps the most popular account of the spacing effect is the encoding variability hypothesis, which assumes that stimuli are encoded relative to the context, or environment, in which they occur and that the probability of recall is greater when the context at retrieval is similar to the context at encoding. Another explanation is that the subject habituates to repeated presentations of the same item and therefore cannot process the later presentations as well as the first. Jacoby (1978) has suggested that less conscious "processing effort" is made by the subjects to subsequent presentations when they are massed rather than spaced. Although each of these explanations can account for some of the experimental data, none can account for all experiments (Hintzman 1976).

These theories attempt to explain spacing in terms of such concepts as encoding, habituation, and consolidation, which make little reference to the actual form of the memory representation. Another approach is to seek an explanation at the level of the representation: It may matter how the information is stored in the system. One way to explore this possibility is to construct explicit models that incorporate particular memory representations and learning mechanisms and to test them with the same experimental paradigms that have been used to study human memory.

In this section we demonstrate that the spacing effect also occurs in NETtalk when the same experimental paradigm used to study the spacing effect on humans is applied to the network described in section 4.2. The window size was reduced from seven to five to speed training. There were 231 units and 10,346 connections in the version of the network used in the present experiments.

Experimental Design

The design was modeled after Glenburg's Experiment 1 (Glenberg 1976). In this experiment subjects were presented with paired associates, repeated twice at spacings of approximately 0, 1, 4, 8, 20, and 40 intervening items, and tested at retention intervals of approximately 2, 8, 32, and 64 items. Each pair was composed of two four-letter common nouns "constructed to avoid common pre-experimental associations, rhymes, and orthographic similarities" (table 4.2). During testing only the stimulus word was presented, and the subject was to recall the associated response term. Glenberg's results are reproduced here as figure 4.9. A significant interaction is found between spacing (lag) and the retention interval. At short retention intervals massed repetitions lead to a higher probability of recall, whereas at long retention intervals distributed repetitions are advantageous. Glenberg also noted that retention at the 64-item re-

Table 4.2
Examples of some training distractors and target items used in the
experiments on spacing in NETtalk[a]

Letters	Phonemes	Stress
Distractors[a]		
file	fAl-	>1<<
all	cl-	1<<
second	sEkxnd	>1<0<<
take	tek-	>1<<
together	txgED--R	>0>1<<0<
neck	nEk-	>1<<
atmosphere	@tmxsf-Ir-	1<>0>>>2<<
Random target items		
fozepd	WdicnK	1<121>
sccfyk	p-UdSp	>202<1
bmyqcl	bzgTlz	0>><<>
grtufh	KCczOL	>1<010
eqhxxu	ANT|vM	>01<>2
ncssvr	zTSdWg	<<12>2
wxsale	RKpfl|	1<1110
djzxde	Yby´yI	20>>2>
·kmfjqi	WGenGN	1><102

a. Training distractors were part of the original training corpus and were
presented between training sessions on the target items and during the retention interval.

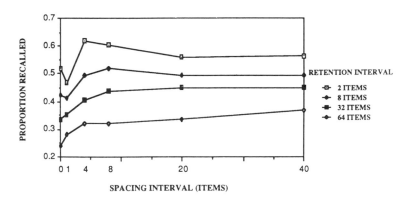

Figure 4.9
The proportion of response terms recalled as a function of spacing interval and retention interval. After Glenberg (1976).

tention interval is a monotonic and negatively accelerating function of spacing.

As in Glenberg's experiment, we measured the retention of target stimuli repeated a certain number of times at various spacing intervals as a function of the retention interval. If NETtalk exhibits the spacing effect, then long-term retention of these items should be better when a large number of other items intervene between successive repeats of the target (distributed practice). Conversely short-term retention of the target items should be better when fewer items are presented between repeats (massed practice).

Pre-Experimental Training   The network was first trained on the 1,000 most common English words taken from the Brown corpus. The network cycled through this 1,000-word corpus eleven times. The performance of the network at this point in training, as determined by the percentage of the correct phonemes "guessed," was 85% and could have been improved with further practice. The weight values of the network were stored following this initial training and served as a common starting point for all of the subsequent experimental trials.

Target Stimuli   In order to force new learning to take place, random character strings of length six were employed as target stimuli. Thus there was no orderly relation between the cue and the response. Whatever performance level NETtalk was able to reach on these items could not have been due to the utilization of rules acquired either before or after the study. Twenty six-letter cues were generated by choosing six letters at random (with replacement) out of the twenty-six letters of the English alphabet. Likewise, the response terms associated with each of these cues were randomly generated phoneme and stress strings, also six characters in length. There were fifty-three possible phonemes and five possible stress characters. In generating the target stimuli, two "phonemes," the space between words (_) and the period (.), were not possible choices. The frequency of occurrence of the characters in natural language were not taken into account in this selection process. Some of these items and several items from the training corpus are presented in table 4.2.

Procedure   The 20 target items were tested individually on separate trials. A trial consisted of, first, reading in the pre-experimental weights, presenting a target item 2, 10, or 20 times, and then measuring the retention of the target as it was interfered with by subsequent learning. Furthermore, each target was presented at each of 6 spacing intervals, with either 0 (massed), 1, 4, 8, 20, or 40 (distributed) intervening items. Thus 18 trials were devoted to each target item (3 repetition groups × 6 spacing intervals). Between successive repeats of the target, words were presented from the original training corpus. Following the last repeat, the training corpus was again presented, and retention of the response terms of the target item was assessed after every item by presenting the cue term and measuring the mean squared difference between the output of the network and the correct response. The error defined in equation (4.12) was used to define the response accuracy for the word:

$$\text{Accuracy} = 1 - \frac{\sum_{l=1}^{L} \text{Error}_l}{L}, \tag{4.17}$$

where L is the number of letters in the word. Note that this measure of accuracy is more sensitive than the performance accuracy given earlier, which measured only the correct choices made by the network. Learning was turned off (achieved by setting the learning rate to 0) for these tests, so that no changes were made to the strengths of the connections in the network.

Results   Accuracy, as defined by equation (4.17) was averaged over the 20 target items and plotted as a function of spacing interval for each repetition group at retention intervals of 2, 8, 32, and 64 in figure 4.10, following Glenberg (1976). A significant spacing effect was observed in NETtalk: Retention of nonwords after a 64-item retention interval was significantly better when presented at the longer spacings (distributed presentation) than at the shorter spacings. In addition, a significant advantage for massed presentations was found for short-term retention of the items. Although stimulus materials, response measures, and procedure differ sufficiently to make direct comparison impossible, the overall pattern of these results resembles that found by Glenberg (1976) in an experiment using human subjects. We obtained our results without making additional assumptions or including additional mechanisms such as consolidation, rehearsal, or attention. Nor were explicit assumptions made about a continuously changing context other than the context implicitly provided by the network.

Recency effects, similar to those reported here, are common in the literature and have been reported in many spacing experiments [for example, Peterson et al. (1963) and Sperber (1974)]. This short-term advantage for massed practice is commonly discussed with reference to a limited-capacity memory buffer. The present experiments indi-

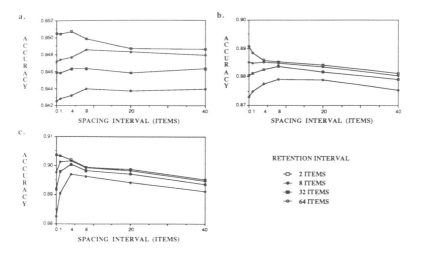

Figure 4.10
Mean response accuracy plotted as a function of spacing interval at 2-, 8-, 32-, and 64-item retention intervals for the (a) 2, (b) 10, and (c) 20 repetition groups.

cate that some of the effects for which such a mechanism is designed to account can be produced without a separate buffer.

A Possible Explanation for the Spacing Effect
Why should NETtalk exhibit these characteristics? The answer depends on the learning procedure and the way in which the resulting knowledge is represented in the network.

The learning algorithm alters the weights by a small amount after each training word in a direction that minimizes the average error. A network with n weights can be considered a point in the n-dimensional Euclidean space of weights, and this point moves through the space during learning along a trajectory that brings it closer to a point in the space where the error over the entire training corpus is minimal. After reaching such a point, the network is stable; that is, further training on the same vocabulary will not change the weights. If a new word that is irregular is introduced, then the network must accommodate the new word in such a way that the pronunciations of the old words are not altered. Our hypothesis is that distributing practice leads to a more stable position in the weight space upon the re-presentation of the training corpus.

For the sake of simplicity, consider only three connections from the entire network, so that they can be represented in a three-dimensional space (see figure 4.11). Suppose further that, as in the

Weight Space Projection

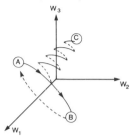

Figure 4.11
Idealized trajectories in weight space during learning for massed (dark) and distributed (light) conditions. Point A is a set of weights that is optimum for the pre-experimental training corpus (the assumed starting point for all experimental trials); point B is an optimum for the target item, and point C is an optimum for both the target and the training corpus. See text for explanation.

present simulations, this network has been trained on a large pre-experimental training corpus and that it has reached a point where the error is at a local minimum for these items (point A). Now a new and unusual target item is presented in either a massed or spaced condition to the network. If the target is presented several times back to back, as in the massed condition, minimizing the error following each presentation leads the weights down a path toward a nearby point that is optimal for this target item, perhaps even reaching it (point B). But because this trajectory will have taken the network some distance away from the starting point, this new position is not likely to be stable to the re-presentation of the training corpus, and so the massed learning of the new item will be lost quickly.

Assuming, however, that there is a point that is optimal for both the training corpus and the target item (point C in figure 4.11), alternating presentations of the target with items from the training set is one way of moving closer to this highly stable point. On the first presentation of the target item the error gradient for that item is estimated and the error is reduced by adjusting the weights in the direction of the steepest descent (to position 1). So far, this procedure has been identical with that for the massed condition, so the network is at the same point in weight space. Now, however, instead of presenting the target again, an item from the original training corpus is presented. Again the weights are adjusted to minimize the error on the item (to position 2), only this time the direction of movement is more likely to be toward point A than point B, because A is a global minimum for the training corpus. Presenting the target again will cause a movement back toward B (to position 3), and so on. We see that distributing practice causes the network to weave through the weight space, allowing it to search for a point that is good for both the training corpus and the target item. The network therefore has a better chance of finding the overall optimal position (point C) than it would if practice were massed, and its encoding of the target item will consequently be more able to withstand interference resulting from further training on both types of material.

Discussion

In all the experiments we updated the weights after every word. Another way to learn new items is to update the weight values less frequently. Instead of learning in small increments, one could also collect data over many trials and then take one big jump. Although this procedure (within its resolution) overcomes the problems associated with presentation order (such as the spacing effect), it may be hazardous because new information is integrated at a slow rate. Both of these time scales for modification might be used in the nervous system. Hinton (personal communication) has suggested that each synapse could have one component that changes its value rapidly and another component that changes more gradually. Fast learning could be done with the fast component of the weight, and only an average of the fast synaptic changes could be committed to long-term storage. This allows new regions of the weight space to be temporarily explored without "forgetting" the previous knowledge.

The explanation of the spacing effect that we offer here is not meant as an alternative to previous suggestions; it is a different type of explanation, relying as it does on the underlying structure of the representations. The decline in learning rate as local optima are approached is reminiscent of the process of habituation: Less is effectively learned each time the item is repeated. Other aspects of our model bear a resemblance to encoding variability to the extent that items are encoded relative to the current state of the network, which is in a state of continual flux. And if we identify Jacoby's processing effort with the degree of change required to construct a distributed representation, then our simulations can be considered support for this proposal as well. Nevertheless, although these concepts of habituation, encoding variability, and processing effort may be reinterpreted within the framework of connectionist models such as ours, they are at a different level of explanation.

Our results are limited to a particular network architecture in a particular domain. To what extent is this conclusion dependent on the details of our model? If the spacing effect is a direct consequence of incremental learning in memory systems that use distributed representations, as we suspect, then the same effects of massed and distributed learning should occur in other task domains and with other network architectures that also have learning algorithms with distributed representations, such as Boltzmann machines (Hinton and Sejnowski, 1983; Ackley et al. 1985). We predict as well that the same general principles may underlie the spacing effect in human learning.

4.4 Conclusions

NETtalk is an illustration in miniature of many aspects of learning. First, the network starts with considerable "innate" knowledge of input and output representations chosen by the experimenters and with no knowledge specific for English—the network could have been trained on any language with the same set of letters and phonemes. Second, the network acquires its competence through practice, goes through several distinct stages, and reaches a significant level of performance. Finally, the information is distributed in the network such that no single unit or link is essential. As a consequence, the network is fault tolerant and degrades gracefully with increasing damage. Moreover, the network recovers from damage much more quickly than it takes to learn initially. In addition to these features, the effect of temporal ordering during training on new words is remarkably similar to that in humans.

Despite these similarities with human learning and memory, NETtalk is too simple to serve as a good model for the acquisition of reading skills in humans. The network attempts to accomplish in one stage what occurs in two stages of human development. Children learn to talk first, and only after representations for words and their meanings are well developed do they learn to read. It is also likely that we have access to articulatory representations for whole words in addition to our ability to use letter-to-sound correspondences, but there are no word-level representations in the network. It is perhaps surprising that the network is capable of reaching a significant level of performance using a window of only seven letters. This approach would have to be generalized to account for prosodic features in connected text, and a human level of performance would require the integration of information from several words at once.

NETtalk can be used as a research tool to explore many aspects of network coding, scaling, and training in a domain that is far from trivial. Those aspects of the network's performance that are similar to human performance are good candidates for general properties of network models; more progress may be made by studying these aspects in the small test laboratory that NETtalk affords. Our exploration of the spacing effect is an example of how a general property of human memory can be studied in a much simpler model system. When NETtalk deviates from human performance, there is good reason to believe that a more detailed account of brain circuitry may be necessary.

After training many networks, we concluded that many different sets of weights give about equally good performance. Although it was possible to understand the function of some hidden units, it was not possible to identify units in different networks that have the same function. However, the activity patterns in the hidden units could be interpreted in an interesting way. Patterns of activity in groups of hidden units could be identified in different networks that serve the same function, such as distinguishing vowels from consonants. This suggests that the detailed synaptic connectivity between neurons in the cerebral cortex may not be helpful in revealing the functional properties of a neural network. It is not at the level of the synapse or the neuron that one should expect to find invariant properties of a network but at the level of functional groupings of cells. Techniques that are developed to uncover these groupings in model neural networks could be of value in uncovering similar cell assemblies in real neural networks.

Acknowledgments

We thank Alfonso Caramazza, Francis Crick, Stephen Hanson, Geoffrey Hinton, Thomas Landauer, James McClelland, George Miller, David Rumelhart, and Stephen Wolfram for helpful discussions about language and learning. We are indebted to Stephen Hanson and Andrew Olson, who made important contributions in the statistical analysis of the hidden units, and to Thomas Landauer, who suggested that the spacing effect could be studied with NETtalk. Peter Brown, Edward Carterette, Howard Nusbaum, and Alex Waibel assisted in the early stages of development. Bell Communications Research generously provided computational support.

Terrence J. Sejnowski is supported by grants from the National Science Foundation, the System Development Foundation, the Sloan Foundation, General Electric Corporation, the Allied Corporation Foundation, the Richard Lounsbery Foundation, the Seaver Institute, and the Air Force Office of Scientific Research. Charles R. Rosenberg is supported in part by grants from the James S. McDonnell Foundation, by IBM under grant 487906, by the Defense Advanced Research Projects Agency of the Department of Defense, by the Office of Naval Research under contracts N00014-85-C-0456 and N00014-85-K-0465, and by the National Science Foundation under Cooperative Agreement DCR-8420948 and grant IST8503968.

References

Ackley, D. H., G. E. Hinton, and T. J. Sejnowski. 1985. "A learning algorithm for Boltzmann machines." *Cognitive Science* 9:147–169.

Adrian, E. D. 1953. *The Physical Background of Perception*. Oxford: Clarendon Press.

Allen, J. 1987. *From Text to Speech: the MITalk System*. Cambridge: Cambridge University Press.

Allman, J. M., J. F. Baker, W. T. Newsome, and S. E. Petersen. 1983. "Visual topography and function: Cortical visual areas in the owl monkey," in *Cortical Sensory Organization. Vol. 2, Multiple Visual Areas*, C. N. Woolsey, ed. Clifton, N.J.: Humana Press.

Alspector, J., and R. B. Allen. 1986. *A VLSI Model of Neural Nets*. Technical Memorandum TM ARH002688. Morristown, N.J.: Bellcore.

Anderson, J. A. 1970. "Two models for memory organization using interacting traces." *Mathematical Biosciences* 8:137–160.

Anderson, J. A., and M. C. Mozer. 1981. "Categorization and selective neurons," in *Parallel Models of Associative Memory*, G. E. Hinton and J. A. Anderson, eds. Hillsdale, N.J.: Erlbaum Associates.

Anderson, J. R. 1982. "Acquisition of cognitive skill." *Psychological Review* 89:369–406.

Arbib, M. A. 1987. *Brains, Machines and Mathematics*, second edition. New York: McGraw-Hill.

Ballard, D. H., G. E. Hinton, and T. J. Sejnowski. 1983. "Parallel visual computation." *Nature* 306:21–26.

Barlow, H. B. 1972. "Single units and sensation: A neuron doctrine for perceptual psychology?" *Perception* 1:371–394.

Barto, A. G. 1985. "Learning by statistical cooperation of self-interested neuronlike computing elements." *Human Neurobiology* 4:229–256.

Baum, E. B., J. Moody, and F. Wilczek. 1987. *Internal Representations for Associative Memory*. Technical Report. Santa Barbara, Cal.: Institute for Theoretical Physics, University of California.

Bienenstock, E. L., L. N. Cooper, and P. W. Munro. 1982. "Theory for the development of neuron selectivity: Orientation specificity and binocular interaction in visual cortex." *Journal of Neuroscience* 2:32–48.

Bounds, D. G. 1986. "Numerical simulations of Boltzmann machines," in *Neural Networks for Computing* (AIP Conference Proceedings), J. S. Denker, ed. New York: American Institute of Physics, vol. 151, 59–64.

Carterette, E. C., and M. G. Jones. 1974. *Informal Speech*. Los Angeles, Calif.: University of California Press.

Chauvet, G. 1986. "Habituation rules for a theory of the cerebellar cortex." *Biological Cybernetics* 55:201–209.

Church, K. 1985. "Stress assignment in letter to sound rules for speech synthesis," in *Proceedings of the 23rd Annual Meeting of the Association for Computational Linguistics*, D. Walker, ed. Morristown, NJ: ACL, 246–253.

Churchland, P. S. 1986. *Neurophilosophy*. Cambridge, Mass.: MIT Press.

Cohen, M. A., and S. Grossberg. 1983. "Absolute stability of global pattern formation and parallel memory storage by competitive neural networks." *IEEE Transactions on Systems, Man and Cybernetics* 13:815–825.

Cooper, L. N., F. Liberman, and E. Oja. 1979. "A theory for the acquisition and loss of neuron specificity in visual cortex." *Biological Cybernetics* 33:9–28.

Crick, F. H. C., and C. Asanuma. 1986. "Certain aspects of the anatomy and physiology of the cerebral cortex," in *Parallel Distributed Processing: Explorations in the Microstructure of Cognition. Vol. 2, Psychological and Biological Models*, J. L. McClelland and D. E. Rumelhart, eds. Cambridge, Mass.: MIT Press, 333–371.

Divko, R., and K. Schulten. 1986. "Stochastic spin models for pattern recognition," in *Neural Networks for Computing* (AIP Conference Proceedings), J. S. Denker, ed. New York: American Institute of Physics, vol. 151, 129–134.

Ebbinghaus, H. 1885. *Memory: A Contribution to Experimental Psychology*. Berlin: Privat Docent in Philosophy at the University of Berlin. Reprinted in 1964 by Dover (New York).

Ellman, J., and D. Zipser. 1987. *Learning the Hidden Structure of Speech*. Technical Report 8701. San Diego, Cal.: University of California, Institute for Cognitive Science.

Everitt, B. 1974. *Cluster Analysis*. London: Heinemann.

Fahlman, S. E., G. E. Hinton, and T. J. Sejnowski. 1983. "Massively parallel architectures for AI: NETL, THISTLE and Boltzmann machines." *Proceedings of the National Conference on Artificial Intelligence*. Los Altos, Cal.: William Kauffman, Inc., 109–113.

Feldman, J. A. 1982. "Dynamic connections in neural networks." *Biological Cybernetics* 46:27–39.

Feldman, J. A. 1986. *Neural Representation of Conceptual Knowledge*. Technical Report TR-189. Rochester, N.Y.: University of Rochester, Department of Computer Science.

Feldman, J. A., and D. H. Ballard. 1982. "Connectionist models and their properties." *Cognitive Science* 6:205–254.

Finkel, L. H., and G. M. Edelman. 1985. "Interaction of synaptic modification rules within population of neurons." *Proceedings of the National Academy of Sciences USA* 82:1291–1295.

Gamba, A. L., G. Gamberini, G. Palmieri, and R. Sanna. 1961. "Further experiments with PAPA." *Nuovo Cimento*, suppl., 20(2):221–231.

Geman, S., and D. Geman. 1984. "Stochastic relaxation, Gibbs distributions, and the Baysian restoration of images." *IEEE Transactions on Pattern Analysis and Machine Intelligence* 3:79–92.

Glenberg, A. M. 1976. "Monotonic and nonmonotonic lag effects in paired-associate and recognition memory paradigms." *Journal of Verbal Learning and Verbal Behavior* 15:1–16.

Gluck, M. A., and G. H. Bower. 1986. "Conditioning and categorization: Some common effects of informational variables in animal and human learning." *Proceedings of the Eighth Annual Conference of the Cognitive Science Society*. Hillsdale, N.J.: Erlbaum Associates, 126–140.

Gluck, M. A., and G. H. Bower. 1987. "From conditioning to category learning: An adaptive network model." Unpublished.

Gluck, M. A., and R. F. Thompson. 1986. "Modeling the neural substrates of associative learning and memory: A computational approach." *Psychological Review* 94(2):176–191.

Grossberg, S. 1976. "Adaptive pattern classification and universal recoding I. Parallel development and coding of neural feature detectors." *Biological Cybernetics* 23:121–134.

Haas, W. 1970. *Phonographic Translation*. Manchester: Manchester University Press.

Hebb, D. O. 1949. *Organization of Behavior*. New York: Wiley.

Hinton, G. E. 1986. "Learning distributed representations of concepts." *Proceedings of the Eighth Annual Conference of the Cognitive Science Society*. Hillsdale, N.J.: Erlbaum, 1–12.

Hinton, G. E., and J. A. Anderson. 1981. *Parallel Models of Associative Memory*. Hillsdale, N.J.: Erlbaum Associates.

Hinton, G. E., and T. J. Sejnowski. 1983. "Optimal perceptual inference." *Proceedings of the IEEE Computer Society Conference on Computer Vision and Pattern Recognition*. Silver Spring, Md.: IEEE Computer Society Press, 448–453.

Hinton, G. E., and T. J. Sejnowski. 1986. "Learning and relearning in Boltzmann machines," in *Parallel Distributed Processing: Explorations in the Microstructure of*

Cognition. Vol. 2, Psychological and Biological Models, J. L. McClelland and D. E. Rumelhart, eds. Cambridge, Mass.: MIT Press, 282–317.

Hinton, G. E., J. L. McClelland, and D. E. Rumelhart. 1986. "Distributed representations," in *Parallel Distributed Processing: Explorations in the Microstructure of Cognition. Vol. 1, Foundations,* D. E. Rumelhart and J. L. McClelland, eds. Cambridge, Mass.: MIT Press, 77–109.

Hintzman, D. L. 1974. "Theoretical implications of the spacing effect," in *Theories in Cognitive Psychology: The Loyola Symposium,* R. L. Solso, ed. Hillsdale, N.J.: Erlbaum Associates, 77–99.

Hintzman, D. L. 1976. "Repetition and memory," in *The Psychology of Learning and Motivation,* G. H. Bower, ed. New York: Academic Press, vol. 10, 47–91.

Hopfield, J. J. 1982. "Neural networks and physical systems with emergent collective computational abilities." *Proceedings of the National Academy of Sciences USA* 79:2554–2558.

Hopfield, J. J. 1984. "Neurons with graded response have collective computation abilities." *Proceedings of the National Academy of Sciences USA* 81:3088–3092.

Hopfield, J. J., and D. Tank. 1985. "Neural computation of decision in optimization problems." *Biological Cybernetics* 52:141–152.

Hopfield, J. J., and D. Tank. 1986. "Computing with neural circuits: A model." *Science* 233:624–633.

Hubel, D. H., and T. N. Wiesel. 1962. "Receptive fields, binocular interactions, and functional architecture in the cat's visual cortex." *Journal of Physiology* 160:106–154.

Jacoby, L. L. 1978. "On interpreting the effects of repetition: Solving a problem versus remembering a solution." *Journal of Verbal Learning and Verbal Behavior* 17:649–667.

Kahneman, D., and A. Tversky. 1972. "Subjective probability: A judgment of representativeness." *Cognitive Psychology* 3:430–454.

Kelso, S. R., A. H. Ganong, and T. H. Brown. 1986. "Hebbian synapses in hippocampus." *Proceedings of the National Academy of Sciences USA* 83:5326–5330.

Kienker, P. K., T. J. Sejnowski, G. E. Hinton, and L. E. Schumacher. 1986. "Separating figure from ground with a parallel network." *Perception* 15:197–216.

Klatt, D. 1980. "Software for a cascade/parallel formant synthesizer." *Journal of the Acoustical Society of America* 67:971–995.

Klopf, A. H. 1986. "A drive-reinforcement model of single neuron function: An alternative to the Hebbian neuronal model, in *Neural Networks for Computing,* J. S. Denker, ed. New York: American Institute of Physics, 265–270.

Kohonen, T. 1970. "Correlation matrix memories." *IEEE Transactions on Computers* C21:353–359.

Kohonen, T. 1984. *Self-Organization and Associative Memory.* New York: Springer-Verlag.

Kolmogorov, A. N. 1957. "On the representation of continuous functions of one variable by superposition of continuous functions of one variable and addition." *AMS Translation* 2:55–59.

Kuchera, H., and W. N. Francis. 1967. *Computational Analysis of Modern-Day American English.* Providence, R.I.: Brown University Press.

Le Cun, Y. 1985. "A learning procedure for asymmetric network." *Proceedings of Cognitiva* 85:599–604.

Levy, W. B., J. A. Anderson, and W. Lehmkuhle. 1984. *Synaptic Change in the Nervous System.* Hillsdale, N.J.: Erlbaum Associates.

Levy, W. B., S. E. Brassel, and S. D. Moore. 1983. "Partial quantification of the associative synaptic learning rule of the dentate gyrus." *Neuroscience* 8:799–808.

Linsker, R. 1986. "From basic network principles to neural architecture: Emergence of orientation columns." *Proceedings of the National Academy of Sciences USA* 83:8779–8783.

Longuet-Higgins, H. C. 1968. "Holographic model of temporal recall." *Nature* 217:104–107.

Lucassen, J. M., and R. L. Mercer. 1984. "An information theoretic approach to the automatic determination of phonemic baseforms." *Proceedings of the IEEE International Conference on Acoustics, Speech and Signal Processing.* Silver Spring, Md.: IEEE Press, 42.5.1–42.5.4.

Lynch, G. 1986. *Synapses, Circuits, and the Beginnings of Memory.* Cambridge, Mass.: MIT Press.

Lyons, J. 1971. *Introduction to Theoretical Linguistics.* Cambridge: Cambridge University Press.

Marr, D., and T. Poggio. 1976. "Cooperative computation of stereo disparity." *Science* 194:283–287.

McClelland, J. L., and D. E. Rumelhart. 1986. *Parallel Distributed Processing: Explorations in the Microstructure of Cognition. Vol. 2, Psychological and Biological Models.* Cambridge, Mass.: MIT Press.

McCulloch, W. S., and W. H. Pitts. 1943. "A logical calculus of ideas immanent in nervous activity." *Bulletin of Mathematical Biophysics* 5:115–133.

McNaughton, B. L., and R. G. Morris. 1987. "Hippocampal synaptic enhancement and information storage within a distributed memory system." *Trends in Neuroscience* 10:408–415.

Minsky, M., and S. Papert. 1969. *Perceptrons.* Cambridge, Mass.: MIT Press.

Mountcastle, V. B. 1978. "An organizing principle for cerebral function: The unit module and the distributed system," in *The Mindful Brain,* G. M. Edelman and V. B. Mountcastle, eds. Cambridge, Mass.: MIT Press, 7–50.

Norman, D. A. 1982. *Learning and Memory.* San Francisco, Calif.: Freeman.

Palm, G. 1978. "On representation and approximation on nonlinear systems." *Biological Cybernetics* 31:119–124.

Palm, G. 1979. "On representation and approximation of nonlinear systems II. Discrete time." *Biological Cybernetics* 34:49–52.

Parker, D. B. 1986. "A comparison of algorithms for neuron-like cells," in *Neural Networks for Computing,* J. S. Denker, ed. New York: American Institute of Physics, 327–332.

Pearlmutter, B. A., and G. E. Hinton. 1986. "G-Maximization: An unsupervised learning procedure for discovering regularities," in *Neural Networks for Computing,* J. S. Denker, ed. New York: American Institute of Physics, 333–338.

Peterson, L. R., R. Wampler, M. Kirkpatrick, and D. Saltzman. 1963. "Effect of spacing presentations on retention of a paired-associate over short intervals." *Journal of Experimental Psychology* 66:206–209.

Prager, R. W., T. D. Harrison, and F. Fallside. 1986. *Boltzmann Machines for Speech Recognition.* Technical Report TR.260. Cambridge: Cambridge University, Engineering Department.

Reggia, J. A. 1985. "Virtual lateral inhibition in parallel activation models of associative memory." *Proceedings of the 9th International Joint Conference on Artificial Intelligence.* Los Altos, Calif.: Morgan Kauffman, 244–248.

Rescorla, R. A., and A. R. Wagner. 1972. "A theory of Pavlovian conditioning: Variations in the effectiveness of reinforcement and nonreinforcement," in *Classical Conditioning II: Current Research and Theory,* A. H. Black and W. F. Prokasy, eds. New York: Appleton-Crofts, 64–99.

Riley, M. S., and P. Smolensky. 1984. "A parallel model of (sequential) problem solving." *Proceedings of the Sixth Annual Conference of the Cognitive Science Society*. Hillsdale, N.J.: Erlbaum Associates, 286–292.

Rolls, E. T. 1986. "Information representation, processing and storage in the brain: Analysis at the single neuron level," in *Neural and Molecular Mechanisms of Learning*. Berlin: Springer-Verlag.

Rosenberg, C. R., and T. J. Sejnowski. 1986. "The spacing effect on NETtalk, a massively-parallel network." *Proceedings of the Eighth Annual Conference of the Cognitive Science Society*. Hillsdale, N.J.: Erlbaum Associates, 72–89.

Rosenblatt, F. 1959. *Principles of Neurodynamics*. New York: Spartan Books.

Rosenbloom, P. S., and A. Newell. 1986. "The chunking of goal hierarchies: A generalized model of practice," in *Machine Learning: An Artificial Intelligence Approach*, R. S. Michalski, J. G. Carbonell, and T. M. Mitchell, eds. Los Altos, Calif.: Morgan Kauffman, vol. 2, 247–288.

Rumelhart, D. E. 1986. "Learning paradigms in connectionism." Paper presented at the Symposium on Connectionism: Multiple Agents, Parallelism and Learning. Geneva, Switzerland, September 9–12, 1986.

Rumelhart, D. E., and J. L. McClelland. 1986a. "On learning the past tenses of English verbs." in *Parallel Distributed Processing: Explorations in the Microstructure of Cognition. Vol. 2, Psychological and Biological Models*, J. L. McClelland and D. E. Rumelhart, eds. Cambridge, Mass.: MIT Press.

Rumelhart, D. E., and J. L. McClelland. 1986b. *Parallel Distributed Processing: Explorations in the Microstructure of Cognition. Vol. 1, Foundations*. Cambridge, Mass.: MIT Press.

Rumelhart, D. E., and D. Zipser. 1985. "Feature discovery by competitive learning." *Cognitive Science* 9:75–112.

Rumelhart, D. E., G. E. Hinton, and R. J. Williams. 1986. "Learning internal representations by error propagation," in *Parallel Distributed Processing: Explorations in the Microstructure of Cognition. Vol. 1, Foundations*, D. E. Rumelhart and J. L. McClelland, eds. Cambridge, Mass.: MIT Press.

Saund, E. 1986. "Abstraction and representation of continuous variables in connectionist networks." *Proceedings of the Fifth National Conference on Artificial Intelligence*. Los Altos, Calif.: Morgan Kauffmann, 638–644.

Sejnowski, T. J. 1977a. "Statistical constraints on synaptic plasticity." *Journal of Mathematical Biology* 69:385–389.

Sejnowski, T. J. 1977b. "Storing covariance with nonlinearly interacting neurons." *Journal of Mathematical Biology* 4:303–321.

Sejnowski, T. J. 1981. "Skeleton filters in the brain," in *Parallel Models of Associative Memory*, G. E. Hinton and J. A. Anderson, eds. Hillsdale, N.J.: Erlbaum Associates, 189–212.

Sejnowski, T. J. 1986. "Open questions about computation in cerebral cortex," in *Parallel Distributed Processing: Explorations in the Microstructure of Cognition. Vol. 2, Psychological and Biological Models*, J. L. McClelland and D. E. Rumelhart, eds. Cambridge, Mass.: MIT Press, 372–389.

Sejnowski, T. J., and G. E. Hinton. 1987. "Separating figure from ground with a Boltzmann machine," in *Vision, Brain and Cooperative Computation*, M. A. Arbib and A. R. Hanson, eds. Cambridge, Mass.: MIT Press.

Sejnowski, T. J., and C. R. Rosenberg. 1986. *NETtalk: A Parallel Network That Learns to Read Aloud*. Technical Report 86/01. Baltimore, Md.: Johns Hopkins University, Department of Electrical Engineering and Computer Science

Sejnowski, T. J., and C. R. Rosenberg, 1987. "Parallel networks that learn to pronounce English text." *Complex Systems* 1:145–168.

Sejnowski, T. J., P. K. Kienker, and G. E. Hinton. 1986. "Learning symmetry groups with hidden units: Beyond the perceptron." *Physica* 22D:260–275.

Smolensky, P. 1983. "Schema selection and stochastic inference in modular environments." in *Proceedings of the National Conference on Artificial Intelligence.* Los Altos, California: William Kauffman, 378–382.

Smolensky, P. 1986. "Information processing in dynamical systems: Foundations of harmony theory," in *Parallel Distributed Processing: Explorations in the Microstructure of Cognition. Vol. 2, Psychological and Biological Models,* J. L. McClelland and D. E. Rumelhart, eds. Cambridge, Mass.: MIT Press, 194–281.

Sperber, R. D. 1974. "Developmental changes in effects of spacing of trials in retardate discrimination learning and memory." *Journal of Experimental Psychology* 103:204–210.

Squire, L. R. 1986. "Mechanisms of memory." *Science* 232:1612–1619.

Steinbuch, K. 1961. "Die lernmatrix." *Kybernetik* 1:36–45.

Sutton, R. S., and A. G. Barto. 1981. "Toward a modern theory of adaptive networks: Expectation and prediction." *Psychological Review* 88:135–170.

Tesauro, G. 1986. "Simple neural models of classical conditioning." *Biological Cybernetics* 55:187–200.

Tesauro, G., and T. J. Sejnowski. In press. "A parallel network that learns to play backgammon." *Artificial Intelligence Journal.*

Toulouse, G., S. Dehaene, and J.-P. Changeux. 1986. "Spin glass model of learning by selection." *Proceedings of the National Academy of Sciences USA* 83:1695–1698.

Tulving, E. 1985. "How many memory systems are there?" *American Psychologist* 40(4):385–398.

Van Essen, D. C., and J. H. R. Maunsell. 1983. "Hierarchical organization and functional streams in the visual cortex." *Trends in Neuroscience* 6:370–375.

Venezky, R. L. 1970. *The Structure of English Orthography.* The Hague: Mouton.

Venezky, R. L., and D. Johnson. 1973. "Development of two letter-sound patterns in grades one through three." *Journal of Educational Psychology* 64:109–115.

von der Malsburg, C., and E. Bienenstock. 1987. "A neural network for the retrieval of superimposed connection patterns." *Europhysics Letters* 3:1243–1249.

Watrous, R. L., and L. Shastri. 1986. *Learning Phonetic Features Using Connectionist Networks: An Experiment in Speech Recognition.* Technical Report MS-CIS-86-78. Philadelphia, Penn.: University of Pennsylvania Department of Electrical Engineering and Computer Science.

Widrow, G., and M. E. Hoff. 1960. "Adaptive switching circuits." Institute of Radio Engineers Western Electronic Show and Convention. *Convention Record,* vol. 4, 96–194.

Willshaw, D. 1981. "Holography, associative memory, and inductive generalization," in *Parallel Models of Associative Memory,* G. E. Hinton and J. A. Anderson, eds. Hillsdale, N.J.: Erlbaum Associates, 83–104.

Zipser, D. 1986. *Programming Neural Nets to Do Spatial Computations.* ICS Technical Report 8608. San Diego, Calif.: University of California, Institute for Cognitive Science.

II

Psychological Dimensions of Memory Function in Humans

5

Review of Event-Related Potential Studies of Memory

Marta Kutas

It is no easy matter to describe our conscious experience of memory in either psychological or physiological terms. No doubt, part of the difficulty stems from our inability to observe memory operations in action. It is my aim here to show that some relevant evidence can be provided by investigating the electrical activity of the brain generated when our memories are presented and tested under certain experimental conditions.

5.1 Event-Related Brain Potentials

In 1929 Hans Berger, a German psychiatrist, demonstrated that he could monitor some of the electrochemical signals by which brain cells communicate with each other with relative ease. He did so by placing two large pads soaked in saline on the front and back of a person's head and amplifying the voltage difference between them; he referred to these voltage oscillations as the electrical record of the brain (that is, the *elektrenkephalogramm*, or EEG). Although he was unable to turn this finding into a theory of the neural basis of mentation, Berger was successful in showing that the frequency content of the EEG changed with mental activity, such as reading or arithmetic, relative to periods of rest. Today more sophisticated analyses of the relation between information processing and EEG in the frequency domain are complemented by studies of brain waves in the time domain. For example, it is possible to examine voltage fluctuations that are synchronized (time-locked) to a stimulus, response, or event in the environment; these are called evoked potentials (EPs) or event-related potentials (ERPs). The term "event-related" has been adopted because it subsumes both potentials that are evoked by an external stimulus and potentials that are not evoked but instead are elicited by an event. Events may include the absence of an expected stimulus (for example, omitted stimulus response), preparation to take in information (for example, contingent negative variation), and preparation to initiate and perform a movement (for example, the *bereitschafts* or readiness potential). However, although a single ERP is easy to elicit, its characteristics are not as easy to decipher without specialized, computerized techniques. This is primarily because a single ERP is small relative to the co-occurring unsynchronized background EEG and can be masked by larger potentials, such as those associated with body and eye movements and changes in skin resistance (influenced by sweating).

In the normal adult the mean amplitude of an evoked response (10 μV) may be as small as one-tenth the amplitude of the background EEG (100 μV). This signal-to-noise problem typically is remedied by calculating an average of the brain's responses across repetitions of an evoking stimulus or an eliciting event. The utility of the averaging procedure is based on the assumption that the evoked response to a stimulus is the same on each repetition whereas the background EEG is not; thus the random activity cancels, and a consistent response or signal emerges. There are clearly violations of this assumption that show that some ERP components and background activity are correlated (Pritchard et al. 1985; Jasiukaitis, in press). Nonetheless, on occasion, this assumption can be relaxed so that ERPs to more natural stimulation can be investigated. For example, much of "cognitive" ERP research utilizes the repetition of stimuli that are conceptually rather than physically identical. This is particularly true of language research, in which it has proven unnecessary to repeat the same word again and again in order to obtain an average. Rather, it has been possible to average across experimentally defined categories, such as words that follow from the preceding context versus those that do not [for a review, see Kutas and Van Petten (in press) and Rugg et al. (1986)].

Cognitive ERP research is a subclass of EP research that includes studies in which variations in ERP components are related to variations in cognitive processes. Some ERP researchers in this class hypothesize about the functional organization of the brain for certain processes on the basis of interactions between the scalp distribution of the associated ERP components and experimental variables. Others use the ERP as a measure of a cognitive process in much the same way as some behavioral psychologists use reaction time. To some extent these particular ways of utilizing ERP in the study of human cognition are dictated by the fact that, at present, the generators of most ERPs are unknown. However, it is an empirical question as to whether the knowledge of the source of an ERP component will reveal much about its functional significance.

It is generally believed that ERP activity seen at the scalp is the summation of graded postsynaptic potentials (PSPs) generated by the depolarization and hyperpolarization of brain cells; these can be either excitatory (EPSPs) or inhibitory (IPSPs). Several factors—including the number, location, orientation, and synaptic connectivity of the neural elements involved, the location of the recording electrodes, and the properties of the electrically conductive medium—are crucial determinants of the extracellular potentials that are recorded in any particular case (Allison et al. 1986). Because a potential of a given polarity at the scalp can represent depolarization generated locally or hyperpolarization generated at a distance or vice versa, the polarity of a potential per se cannot be used to infer its neurophysiological basis. Moreover, given that extracellular potentials from different sources overlap in time and space according to the principle of superposition, it is not possible to determine either the number or the location of active sources from surface ERP recordings alone.

Nonetheless many ERP researchers do make tentative inferences about the source of a component from its distribution on the scalp. Because this approach is successful on occasion, it is a reasonable first step if neuropsychological, behavioral, and field potential principles are taken into account. For example, there is good correspondence between the distribution of movement-related potentials and the organization of the motor cortex (Vaughan et al. 1968). In contrast, the scalp distribution of the auditory evoked potential (AEP) reveals little about its source; the AEP is largest on top of the head at the vertex, not over the auditory cortex as would be expected from anatomical considerations alone. However, potential field theory predicts that many potentials with generators in each cerebral hemisphere appear largest at the midline locations on top of the head. For reasons such as this, hypotheses about ERP source localization need to be evaluated in light of converging evidence from many disciplines.

One approach that has been adopted recently by those interested in localizing the ERP generators of potentials such as brain stem evoked responses (BERs) and auditory N1 or P3 components has been that of "informed" modeling. The general idea has been to develop a model composed of the fewest number of equivalent dipoles that will account for the scalp potential fields obtained under a specified set of circumstances and then to test this model with real ERP data. The choice of dipoles is influenced by anatomical, neuropsychological, and potential field considerations. Thus far the modelers have restricted themselves to early or exogenous ERPs; however, the concept should apply equally well to later or endogenous ERP components (Scherg and von Cramon 1985a,b; Wood 1982).

Yet another approach to source localization has been to examine ERPs from patients with circumscribed brain lesions. Of course, such

lesion data are subject to all the usual criticisms leveled against interpretations about brain functions from lesions. In addition, the interpretation of ERP changes, at least in some patients, is complicated by
changes in conductance resulting from skull defects or scar tissue
(Nunez 1981). Nonetheless, ERP investigations of brain-damaged individuals have led to some interesting and testable hypotheses regarding the source of various ERP components and, in turn, about
the perceptual and cognitive processes they underlie (Knight et al.
1981; Neville et al. 1979; Johnson and Fedio 1984; Knight 1984; Wood
et al. 1984; Wood et al. 1982; Stapleton et al. 1987).

Recently, several ERP investigators have suggested that ERP localization from scalp distributions could benefit from detailed mappings
utilizing as many electrodes as possible (32–50 being a good starting
range). Numerous recording sites have, in fact, been utilized by those
researchers who have recorded ERP activity in the depths of the
brain. In so doing, they have been able to show that there are characteristic patterns of depth ERP activity coincident with particular scalp-
recorded potentials. Certain regions of the brain are characterized
by high-amplitude activity, and in some cases potentials change or
reverse polarity at what are presumed to be borders of anatomical
structures.

Given that depth recordings are generally obtained from the brains
of epileptics, albeit from the "normal" side, there has been a remarkable consistency of findings for the P3 component, the most heavily
investigated potential thus far (Halgren et al. 1980; Wood et al. 1980).
Specifically, several laboratories have observed that a P3-like component undergoes polarity inversion in the hippocampal-amygdala region. Nevertheless it has proven extremely difficult to equate the
intracerebral recordings of P3-like activity with the scalp-recorded
activity [see Halgren et al. (1986) for criteria necessary for generator
identification]. In fact, the consensus from depth recordings of the P3
in humans is that the scalp-recorded activity does not appear to be
generated in one place, such as the amygdala or hippocampus, but
seems to receive contributions from several regions, including the
medial temporal and frontal lobes and probably other brain areas yet
unexplored. Data from normal monkeys and monkeys with lesions of
the hippocampus and amygdala are consistent with this tentative
conclusion (Paller et al. 1982, 1984; Paller 1986).

It may well be the case that, on occasion, neither the source of a
cognitive process nor that of its ERP signature will be found in a
single distinct anatomical locus. Rather, the processing transactions
for any given cognitive event may be distributed at synaptic junctions

throughout the brain, and it is the sum or envelope of this wide-spread activity that is reflected in the ERPs we record. This is a likely possibility whether the ERPs reflect the postsynaptic activity of neurons carrying specific information about events or the action of diffuse modulatory systems [see Pineda (1987) for evidence on the role of the locus ceruleus on P3 generation and Halgren and Smith (1987) for similar thoughts along these lines]. It has been claimed that many of the brain's functions are best modeled by systems that are parallel and functionally distributed (see chapter 4 in this volume). For processes for which this is an apt description, the morphology and coherence among ERPs recorded in various places throughout the depths may be useful in delineating the elements of such distributed functional units. Similar analyses can be applied to reveal relationships among scalp-recorded ERPs (Gevins et al. 1985).

In any case, lack of knowledge or agreement on the anatomical sources of a component need not detract from its utility. Several early (less than 100 msec) EP measures are used daily by neurologists to test the integrity of the central nervous system and by audiologists to determine hearing thresholds in infants and other difficult-to-test individuals (Halliday 1982). In a similar manner, despite our lack of knowledge about their generators, information about various cognitive processes can be gleaned from the potentials occurring later (greater than 50–100 msec).

ERPs and Cognitive Processes
Although an in-depth review of ERPs in cognition is outside the scope of this chapter, a few general remarks are in order. [For detailed reviews, see Gaillard and Ritter (1983), Hillyard and Kutas (1983), and Karrer et al. (1984).] Cognitive ERP researchers have attacked many problems within developmental, experimental, and cognitive psychology. The questions they have posed have been essentially the same as those asked by cognitive scientists or neuroscientists using other dependent measures. In addition, cognitive ERP researchers have examined the timing of the processes under study and/or hypothesized about the brain areas that might be involved in their execution.

The following are but a small sample of the types of questions that have been asked by various cognitive ERP researchers: What system or process is facilitated when we find that reaction times are speeded by a prior cue (Duncan-Johnson and Donchin 1982)? Is a serial stage, a cascade, a continuous flow model, etc. the most appropriate for describing how certain tasks are carried out (Coles et al. 1985)? How many tasks can we perform simultaneously (Wickens et al. 1983;

Wickens 1984)? How is the functional organization of the brain altered by early experience (Neville and Lawson 1987)? What role does prior context play in the comprehension of a single word (Kutas and Hillyard 1980)? What are the mechanisms by which we turn our attention to some items and ignore others (Hansen and Hillyard 1983)? Which aspects of attentional deployment are under conscious control and which are not (Naatanen 1982)? What makes some events more memorable than others (Sanquist et al. 1980)? How similar are processes of recognition and recall (Paller et al. 1987)? What areas of the brain are involved in the formation and retrieval of episodic memories (Halgren and Smith, 1987)?

Although many of these are the same questions that an experimenter collecting reaction times might ask, there is ample data suggesting that ERPs and reaction times do not measure the same underlying processes. In some cases ERP and reaction time measures are highly correlated; however, there are circumstances under which they are not (Friedman et al. 1978; Kutas et al. 1977; Ritter et al. 1979; Brookhuis et al. 1981). This is to be expected to the extent that the processes indexed by reaction times and ERP components only partially overlap. For example, most of the evidence on the relationship between the P3 and the reaction time indicates that P3 latency reflects primarily the nonmotor subset of the processes that determine behavioral reaction times. In fact, it is the possibility that ERPs allow access to processes that are relatively impenetrable with traditional behavioral measures that makes them particularly appealing tools for investigating human cognition and memory, despite their cost (Regan 1972). In addition, ERPs provide a means of viewing the neuroanatomical basis of various cognitive processes in functional rather than purely connectionist ("static") terms.

5.2   ERPs and Memory

Some data relevant to our understanding of memory have come from ERP studies conducted outside the explicit domain of memory research. This is not surprising given that some aspect of every process must engage either a memory operation or utilize a memory store. Take, for example, the most basic memories that are programmed into our genes (DNA) and manifested in the anatomical, biochemical, and physiological organization of our brains. These organizations at different levels define the limits of the substrates within which our future memories are formed (Galambos and Hillyard 1981). Moreover, there is ample evidence demonstrating that these prewired connections in the human brain are indeed altered by experience.

In a series of elegant studies Neville demonstrated that ERPs are a useful physiological tool in investigations of early experiences on brain development. She combined behavioral and ERP approaches to show that early auditory deprivation (that is, congenital deafness) modifies the functional organization of both sensory and language systems in the human brain. For instance, she found that the refractory periods of the N1-P2 components of the ERPs elicited by simple light flashes were different in normally hearing and congenitally deaf adults, but only for stimuli presented outside the fovea (Neville et al. 1983). Thus congenital deafness altered the time course of the "physiologic memory" of at least a subset of the neurons involved in the processing of stimuli in the visual periphery. Specifically, the N1 generators in the deaf returned to "normal" functioning after rapid stimulation more quickly than they did in normally hearing individuals. Such a finding implies that the deaf ought to have either greater sensitivity or more efficient intake of peripheral visual stimuli. In fact, the results of a subsequent study showed that congenitally deaf individuals were better than hearing ones at detecting infrequent occurrences of apparent motion in the periphery (Neville and Lawson 1987). Thus it appears that ERPs are sensitive indexes of the functional organization of the brain and changes therein—processes that encompass a large part of the brain bases of learning and memory (in my opinion).

Perhaps another type of "memory" (although I view them as the same) is reflected by the brain changes that occur when a person learns to ride a bicycle or use a typewriter. Procedural memories such as these include the store(s) of skill-based information that is acquired by doing and, in turn, accessed through performance (Squire 1982). It is possible to record ERPs during skill acquisition and to assess corresponding changes in their morphologies, scalp distributions, or other parameters. So far, however, only a few ERP studies have examined changes in movement-related potentials recorded from the human scalp with the acquisition of a motor skill (Taylor 1978) or even during learning of paired associates (Horst et al. 1980) or concepts (Stuss and Picton 1978). Future studies with normal and memory-impaired individuals may reveal much about the laying down of procedural memories (for example, the extent to which procedural learning and traces are lateralized and/or involve different brain regions during acquisition) that are not easily accessible by other currently available methodologies.

As with most behavioral investigations, most ERP studies of memory have dealt with the formation and retrieval of episodic memories. That is, they have been designed to probe the nature of the processes engaged when a subject recognizes or recalls one or more items presented during an experimental episode. The majority of these studies have been concerned with memory for the contents of the items presented (declarative memory). Although rarely noted, I believe it is important to keep in mind that such tests almost invariably involve the language system, whereas similar memories outside the laboratory environment, as well as many tests of "procedural" memory, need not. In the following sections I review studies of short- and long-term memory using the ERP method.

ERPs are sensitive indicators of both physical and categorical changes in the environment. In fact, many of the best-studied ERP components have been described as responses to change or deviation from a train of prior stimuli. In some cases this response to change is considered to be conscious, whereas in others it is unconscious or involuntary. In either case, an appreciation of change requires memory for or some trace of the immediate past. The notion that some cognitive ERP is elicited as a direct or indirect consequence of comparing the eliciting stimulus to a preexisting trace or template plays at least a small part in almost every description of psychological processes underlying various cognitive ERP components. For example, Naatanen (1982) mentions templates in his discussion of several of the ERP components recorded during selective attention paradigms. Similarly Squires et al. (1976) based their theory of the P3b on a decaying "trace" of the stimuli. Similar proposals in terms of orienting and match/mismatch have been offered for the P3a, frontal P3, N2, and N400 components. Insofar as each of these potentials can be associated with more specific cognitive processes or modulation thereof, the body of knowledge on the nature and organization of memories in the human brain will be advanced.

ERP Studies of Recognition and Recall: Short-Term Memory
Since the early 1970s several cognitive ERP researchers have conducted experiments with the expressed purpose of finding out more about memory. All of these investigations were carried out within the context of a particular theoretical view of the memory process under study. In most cases both the hypothetical models of memory being tested and the experimental paradigms used in the testing were borrowed from the domain of experimental psychology. A good example is the Sternberg memory scanning paradigm (Sternberg 1969).

In a typical trial from a Sternberg experiment, a subject is presented with a memory set of 1 to N items followed shortly by a probe, target, or test item to which the subject must respond as quickly as possible with one of two buttons. One response indicates recognition of the probe as a member of the original memory set and the other the decision that it was not. Sternberg argued that, by manipulating the number of items in the memory set and measuring the response latency [that is, the reaction time (RT)] to the probe, it was possible to estimate the speed of the search process through short-term memory. He modeled performance in this task using a four-stage serial model composed of (1) stimulus encoding, (2) serial comparison, (3) binary decision, and (4) response organization and execution. Sternberg proposed that the intercept of the function relating probe RT to memory set size was an estimate of the time needed to perform all but the serial comparison stage and that the slope of the RT–memory set size function was an estimate of the time needed to search through memory and scan each item.

Sternberg argued that separate processing stages were empirically justifiable to the extent that one could find experimental variables that affected only one processing stage and did not interact with variables affecting the other processing stages. Although such variables as stimulus legibility, size of positive set, response type, and relative frequency of response type were identified for each of the proposed processing stages, respectively, RT measures did not provide a means for determining the relative durations of the stimulus encoding, decision, and response execution stages (that is, to fractionate the zero intercept time of the RT–memory set size function).

It is just such an analytic problem that the ERP approach in combination with RT measures can overcome. Specifically, it has been proposed that various ERPs, such as the N2 and P3 components, can be used to *estimate* the timing and duration of the component processes that underlie reaction times. The most heavily investigated ERP in this regard has been a positive component variously referred to as the P3, P3b, P300, and LPC. The P3 is a wave of positive polarity at the scalp (relative to an ear, mastoid, or noncephalic reference), with maximum amplitudes at midline centroparietal locations.

P3's can be obtained in a wide variety of tasks [for a review, see Pritchard (1981) and Sutton and Ruchkin (1984)]. Within most of these tasks, P3 amplitude is most sensitive to the subjective probability of stimulus categories and task relevance: The more relevant and the less probable a given stimulus class, the larger the P3 elicited [see Fabiani et al. (1988) and Johnson (in press)]. Although the original discovery of the P3 showed a positive peak with a mean latency around 300 msec poststimulus onset, it has been shown that P3 peaks may vary in latency between 300 and 1,000 msec, increasing in latency as a function of task complexity (Kutas and Donchin 1978). Although reaction times collected concurrently with the P3 likewise increase as a function of processing complexity, the two measures are not always highly correlated. For example, the P3-RT correlation is appreciably larger under task instructions that emphasize *accuracy* of response than under those that emphasize *speed* of response (Kutas et al. 1977).

This type of finding led to the proposition that P3 latency and RT are determined by two partially overlapping sets of processes. Subsequent research has been aimed at pinpointing the processes underlying or at least preceding P3 elicitation. Because infrequently occurring stimuli in a categorization task elicit large P3's relative to those elicited by the stimuli in the more frequently occurring category (under certain conditions), Donchin suggested that the latency of the P3 was a *relative marker* of stimulus categorization or evaluation time. Several studies have since indicated that the processes that must be completed before P3's are emitted are related to stimulus evaluation as opposed to response execution. For instance, both stimulus-response compatibility and crossed versus uncrossed hand manipulations had substantial deleterious effects on RT with only minimal effects or no effect on the associated P3's (McCarthy and Donchin 1981; Magliero et al. 1984; Ragot 1984; Mulder et al. 1984). Also consistent with this view of the P3 as reflecting primarily stimulus- as opposed to response-related processing are the findings in which P3's were elicited by infrequent auditory probes in dual-task situations. On the whole these studies showed that P3's to the probes were reduced in amplitude whenever the other task made heavy demands on "perceptual resources" but not when the task demands were predominantly "motor" in nature (Isreal, Chesney et al. 1980; Isreal, Wickens et al. 1980; Wickens and Kessel 1980).

Insofar as this view of P3 and its relation to RT is valid, ERP researchers hoped to combine P3 and RT measures in Sternberg's memory scanning paradigm to get estimates of the duration of each component stage [for another review, see Mulder (1986)]. The initial studies demonstrated that reliable ERP components could be elicited during this task and indicated a tendency for the P3 component to increase in latency with memory set size up to seven items but not beyond (Adam and Collins 1978). Subsequent studies have confirmed this relationship within the visual modality and elaborated the model by fractionating the memory scanning process by means of a series of regressions using P3 latencies and RTs. To reiterate, the working hypothesis is that RT is a composite measure of stimulus evaluation and response processes, whereas P3 latency is an approximate measure of the duration of stimulus evaluation. Within the context of the Sternberg paradigm, P3 latency is presumed to reflect the time necessary for the buildup of evidence about the presence or absence of a target in a visual display (Mulder 1986).

Sternberg's memory scanning model was modified as follows:

1. The slope of the P3 latency–memory set size function rather than that of the RT–memory set size function provides an estimate of serial comparison time.

2. The intercept of this P300 latency function gives an estimate of stimulus encoding time.

3. The interval between the peak of the P300 and the behavioral RT is a measure of the relative timing of response-related processes.

4. The slope of the P300 minus RT function is an estimate of the binary decision time.

5. The intercept of the P300 minus RT function reflects the time taken to translate and organize the response.

Several investigators have applied this modification of Sternberg's model to assess age-related changes in visual memory scanning (Marsh 1975; Ford et al. 1979; Pfefferbaum et al. 1980; Wickens et al. 1987). Although the results are somewhat variable, there are some consistencies [for an in-depth review, see Bashore (in press)]. For example, both RTs and P3 peak latencies are longer in the elderly than in the young. However, although advancing age steepens the slope of the RT–memory set size function, it does not affect the slope of the P3 latency–memory set size function (see figure 5.1). Ford et al. (1980) interpreted these findings to mean that the apparent slowing of memory scanning in the elderly is not due to a mental lapse in their rate of serial comparisons but rather to a moderate decrease in their speed of stimulus encoding and to a significant delay in their response organization and execution. In addition, the results of several studies including concurrent recordings of ERPs and speed-accuracy trade-off assessments in the Sternberg paradigm indicate that the elderly tend to have a more conservative response criterion than the young (Strayer et al., 1987). Bashore also emphasized the importance of differential response strategies in the young and old in accounting for the apparently different effects of age on response latencies as measured by RTs and those measured by peak P3's. Bashore found that, when he regressed the processing latency measures of the elderly onto those of the young across tasks of increasing complexity, as suggested by Cerella (1985), the RT data indicated that age had multiplicative effects, whereas the P3 data indicated that age had additive effects.

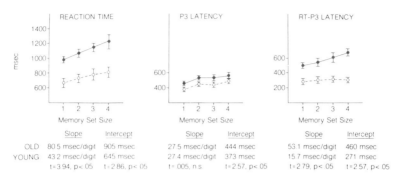

Figure 5.1
Means and standard errors for reaction time (RT), P3 latency, and RT-P3 latency as a function of memory set size for old (solid circles and line) and young (open circles and dashed line) subjects. P3 latencies are collapsed across electrode location and response type; RTs are collapsed across response type. Linear equations describing these RT, P3 latency, and RT-P3 latency measures were fitted by the method of least squares. t-tests comparing young and old subjects were performed on the slope and intercept data. Below each figure is a table of the slope and intercept of that function for old and young subjects. The value of the t-test comparing young and old subjects and an indication of whether it exceeded the $p < 0.05$ level of significance appear below the values of the slopes and intercepts. From Ford et al. (1979).

In conclusion, a cursory examination of the literature dealing with the Sternberg task reveals that Sternberg's original conception of search through short-term memory is neither entirely accurate nor all encompassing (Eriksen and Schultz 1979; McClelland 1979; Meyer et al. 1985). Nonetheless, insofar as the task is used to assess the differential capabilities of two or more experimental groups (as with the young and elderly), it appears as if a combination of ERP and RT measures provides greater precision than does either measure alone. At the least, this combined approach has consistently suggested what may turn out to be a general processing principle of aging, namely, the tendency for the elderly to employ a strategy of opting for accuracy at the expense of speed.

ERPs and Working Memory
The critical role of subject strategy in memory processes has also been highlighted in a series of studies originating from within the ERP research tradition. This line of investigation evolved from the attempts of ERP researchers to determine the consequences of P3 elicitation. The literature on the conditions that give rise to the P3 component is not detailed here [for reviews, see Donchin (1981), Pritchard (1981), and Sutton and Ruchkin (1984)]. Suffice it to say that

Donchin (1981, p. 508) has incorporated much of the available evidence into the proposition that "the P300 is intimately involved with the process of memory modification." Donchin's argument presumes that events are remembered if they require, on their occurrence, a restructuring of mental representations and that it is this process of "context updating" that is reflected in P3 elicitation. Hence one consequence of P3 elicitation is enhanced memorability: Events that elicit a P300 are remembered better than events that do not. Moreover, the larger the P3 elicited by a stimulus, the greater the chance that the stimulus will be remembered. In his most recent formulations, Donchin has argued that context updating is essential to maintain working memory, the temporary storage of information processing. In many respects Donchin's view of working memory converges with that proposed by Baddeley and Hitch (1974) as an alternative to a short-term memory store.

The first attempts by Donchin's group to test his views on the relation between P3 amplitude and memory seemed to go in favor of the Karis et al. hypothesis (Karis et al. 1981). Karis et al. briefly reported the results of two experiments wherein subjects were presented with lists of words, half of which were dim in intensity and half of which were bright. The different conditions included both incidental and intentional memory instructions, responding to only one or both classes of stimuli, and recognition and free recall performance. In general, the results suggested that recalled words were associated with larger P300's on initial presentation than words that were not recalled. However, Karis et al. noted substantial individual variation in the presence and size of this P3 memory effect.

Large individual variability in the relation between P3 amplitude and memory performance was likewise obtained in Karis's next study based on a von Restorff paradigm (von Restorff 1933); however, in this case, they explained these differences in terms of rehearsal and recall strategies. Specifically, Karis et al. (1984) found that all subjects produced large P3's to infrequent occurrences of a word typed in a smaller or larger size (that is, isolates) than the others in the list; however, only the three subjects who reported using a rote rehearsal strategy had larger P300's for words recalled than for words not recalled. The three subjects who reported using elaborative rehearsal techniques (that is, relating list items to each other or to personal experiences and/or world knowledge) elicited P3's of equal amplitude regardless of subsequent memory performance, whereas the results of the six other subjects were intermediate. The group differences were present to all the stimuli, albeit largest for the isolates.

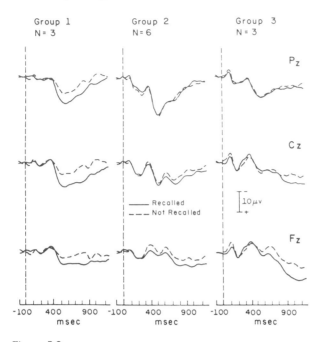

Figure 5.2
Group averages for isolates at three mid-line electrode sites (Fz, frontal; Cz, central; Pz, parietal). Average ERP to words recalled and not recalled are superimposed. Note that members of group 1 are the rote memorizers, and members of group 3 are the elaborators. From Karis et al. (1984).

The two groups differed in other respects as well. As a group the rote memorizers recalled fewer words than did the "elaborators." However, the members of the rote group recalled significantly more of the isolates than other word types, whereas the elaborators remembered about the same percentage of all word types. Finally, although P3 amplitude was not predictive of subsequent recall in the elaborators, a broad, positive "slow wave" with a frontal distribution was (see figure 5.2).

This proposed interaction among P3 amplitude, memory, and subject's strategy was examined in several subsequent studies by Donchin's group. In one, Fabiani et al. (1986) evaluated the relationship between P3 amplitude and subsequent recall under conditions in which the recall test was incidental to the subject's instructed task of counting male or female names. Fabiani et al. assumed that, because the subjects had no reason to expect a recall test, they would not use elaborative strategies to rehearse the stimuli and therefore would show a positive correlation between P3 amplitude and recall. The stimuli consisted of a Bernoulli sequence of male and female names

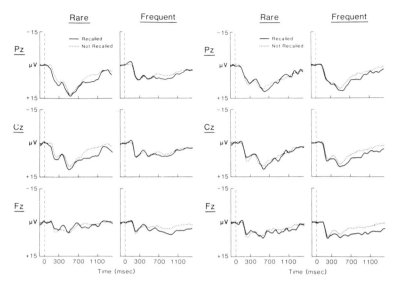

Figure 5.3
(Left) Grand average waveforms from the first block of the name isolate of subjects in the count-rare group ($N = 23$). Rare names and frequent names were sorted on the basis of their subsequent recall. (Right) Grand average waveforms from the first block of the name isolate of subjects in the count-frequent group ($N = 18$). Rare names and frequent names were sorted on the basis of their subsequent recall. From Fabiani et al. (1986).

(with no name repeated) occurring in categories with unequal probabilities (20/80 or 80/20). Across subjects, each of the categories occurred with a high or low probability and was or was not counted.

Probably owing to the incidental nature of the memory task, subjects performed very poorly, recalling only 16% of the names presented. It was nonetheless possible to compare ERPs elicited by recalled and not recalled names because of the large number of subjects employed. Visual inspection of the raw waveforms sorted as a function of subsequent recall (note the unequal number of trials in the two categories in figure 5.3) indicates some memory-related differences in these ERP comparisons. In the ERPs elicited by the frequent category, the memory effect is long lasting (400–1,100 msec) and equipotential in amplitude across the scalp, regardless of whether the stimuli were counted or uncounted. In the ERPs elicited by the rare category, the memory effect appears to be later (800–1,100 msec) and centroparietal in distribution and interacts with the counting task (see figure 5.3). The authors discounted these effects by stating that these grand average waveforms included substantial latency variability in the P3 peak.

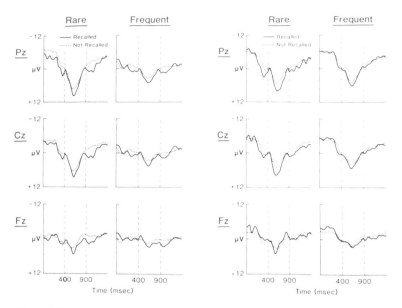

Figure 5.4
(Left) Latency-adjusted grand average waveforms from the first block of the name isolate of subjects in the count-rare group ($N = 23$). Rare names and frequent names were sorted on the basis of their subsequent recall. The two vertical dashed lines indicate the limits of the time window in which P300 was identified. The baseline for the waveforms was taken at the beginning of the window. (Right) Latency-adjusted grand average waveforms from the first block of the name isolate of subjects in the count-frequent group ($N = 18$). Rare names and frequent names were sorted on the basis of their subsequent recall. From Fabiani et al. (1986).

The memory-related ERP effects obtained after the data have been subjected to a latency adjustment procedure are shown in figure 5.4. In this analysis the ERPs elicited by all conditions show a memory effect at the P3 peak, larger for recalled than not recalled names. Across the different experimental conditions and stimulus categories, the distribution of the memory effect varies from equipotential to somewhat parietal; in any case latency adjustment appears to alter not only the peakedness of the late positivities but also their scalp distributions (relative to those of the unadjusted waveforms). In addition, the ERPs elicited by rare names that were counted are characterized by a later memory-related effect. Fabiani et al. (1986) suggested that this effect may be a second P3 after the categorization P3, elicited when the subject relates the name to a known person or song. Moreover, they argued that, in so doing, subjects increase the probability of recall of that word. This proposition was supported by the presence of a second P3 only in the averages of recalled names; however, it is inconsistent with the main proposition that the relation between P3 amplitude and recall is abolished by elaboration. Although Fabiani et al. concluded that these data were evidence of a strong relationship between P300 amplitude and subsequent recall, they did not provide compelling evidence that it was indeed the P3 and only the P3, rather than a temporally overlapping process, that varied with memory.

In the next study in this series, Fabiani et al. (n.d.) directly manipulated subjects' rehearsal strategies by means of instructions in a von Restorff paradigm. Rote memory instructions required subjects to repeat each word as it was presented, whereas elaboration instructions urged subjects to combine words into images, sentences, or stories. Both free recall and size recall were assessed throughout the experiment. The results generally confirmed those obtained in the Karis et al. study; different rehearsal strategies were associated with different patterns of overall recall. Overall recall was better under elaborate than rote strategies. The ERP data likewise replicated the findings of Karis et al.; the relationship between P3 amplitude and subsequent recall was more pronounced under rote than elaborate instructions, whereas the relation between a later ERP effect and recall was present only under elaborate instructions. As in the previous experiment, however, the exact nature (amplitude and scalp distribution) of these memory-related ERP effects appeared to be influenced by the latency adjustment procedure. This is especially important, given that there is some controversy in the literature as to whether it is the P3 per se whose amplitude variation predicts recall (Halgren and Smith 1987; Paller et al. 1987).

Insofar as the concept of working memory underlying Donchin's laboratory research is equivalent to that outlined by Baddeley and Hitch (1974), it may be possible to determine more precisely the cognitive process that the ERP memory effect reflects. Baddeley and Hitch fractionated working memory into at least three subcomponents: a central executive component and two supplementary slave systems (an articulatory loop and a visuospatial scratch pad). The central executor is assumed to be responsible for control processes, the articulatory loop for the maintenance of speech-based material through subvocalization, and the visuospatial store for maintenance of spatially coded information. There is strong evidence supporting the articulatory loop and some controversy as to the need for a visuospatial scratch pad (Phillips and Christie 1977; Baddeley and Lieberman 1980). In any case, although Donchin's group has not identified the P3–working memory relation with any particular aspect of working memory, some preliminary data on this issue was presented during Donchin's presentation at the Eighth International

Conference on Event-Related Slow Potentials of the Brain (EPIC VIII) held in Stanford, California, in June 1986.

As a start, Allison Fox in Michie's laboratory in Australia attempted to replicate Donchin's data on the relations among P3 amplitude, memory, and rehearsal strategy in a von Restorff paradigm. The only obvious difference between her study and that of Fabiani et al. was that Fox controlled subjects' elaborative strategies by instructing them to form visual images. Fox and her colleagues obtained behavioral data in agreement with those of Fabiani et al. Fox's ERP data, likewise, revealed an influence of strategy, although the pattern of effects differed somewhat from those of Donchin's group. Specifically, strategy altered the apparent scalp distribution of the memory-related differences in response to the isolates: Both groups had an effect over the parietal site, whereas the rote memorizers also had an equivalent-size effect at the frontal recording site.

With these findings in hand, Fox made use of the Baddeley model of working memory by combining the von Restorff paradigm and the strategy manipulation with one of two interference tasks, each assumed to engage different aspects of working memory. These tasks were performed on single letters presented one at a time between the words of the von Restorff paradigm. In the verbal interference task subjects were required to decide whether or not the target letter rhymed with the letter "e." In the visual inference task, subjects were asked to image the letter and determine whether or not it contained a curve.

In terms of memory performance both interference tasks were most detrimental under rote memory instructions. As for the ERPs, under rote instructions verbal interference enhanced the difference between recalled and nonrecalled items, whereas visual interference abolished the recall difference. In contrast, under the elaborate instructions verbal interference abolished the ERP recall effect, whereas visual interference enhanced the original parietal effect and revealed one at the frontal site. Although detailed analyses are necessary to determine what these data say about either P3 or Baddeley's model of working memory, these preliminary data are quite promising. There does indeed seem to be some relation between working memory and late component(s) of ERPs that is altered by the nature of rehearsal strategies.

Again, although it is not clear that the observed ERP effects can be attributed to modulation of the P300 component, unequivocally such data bode well for future ERP studies of working memory. At the least, the results of such investigations may offer practical suggestions as to the nature of the tasks that people can perform simultaneously without a drop in processing efficiency and those that will create trouble when performed in unison. Such studies also allow tests of the hypothesized subcomponents of working memory. In addition, these ERP findings suggest that it might be possible to alter the efficacy of dual (and perhaps multiple) task performance by altering people's processing and/or rehearsal strategies.

ERP Indexes of Encoding

Converging evidence for a possible relationship between the formation of memory traces and variation in the amplitude of the ERP in the latency range of the P3 component has come from other quarters of ERP research. In particular, several ERP researchers have looked to see whether any part of the ERP can be a metric of encoding operations within episodic memory. Extrapolating from the findings that ERPs do vary with information processing, these researchers assumed as a working hypothesis that various ERP components might provide indexes of the "unobservable processes, correlated with instructions to the subjects and the subsequent mental activity [that] determine the extent to which the studied material is retained" (Tulving 1983, p. 153). Many of these experiments were conducted within the levels-of-processing framework because it has been one of the more influential encoding-based theories of episodic memory (Craik and Tulving 1975; Craik and Lockhart 1972).

Traditionally cognitive psychologists have assessed the effect of differential encoding on memory by asking subjects to perform different orienting tasks with the same set of materials and comparing their percent correct recognitions or recall across the tasks. The results of such experiments have demonstrated that the nature of the orienting task can have profound effects on the memory scores. For example, under many, although not all, experimental procedures, semantic-level analyses lead to better retention than nonsemantic analyses. Such results have been interpreted to mean that the nature of initial encoding is a major determinant of whether or not an item will be remembered. Among proponents of the levels-of-processing framework of memory such results led to the proposition that memory performance is a function of "depth" of initial encoding. Depth refers to the amount of semantic processing (semanticity) that an item has received, although there is no one measure of semanticity that can be applied across all experimental paradigms.

Given the overwhelming evidence that orienting tasks have such a marked influence on memory performance, it is easy to forget that neither differential encoding nor the link between differential encoding and memory are direct observations. Rather, their existences have been inferred from the effects of task instructions on performance measures obtained minutes or hours after the subject's initial exposure to the material to be remembered. Because the ERP is an online reflection of at least some of the physiological activity of the brain during stimulus encoding, insofar as it can be related to variations in encoding operations, it can be used as a converging measure either to undermine or to reinforce hypotheses about the role of encoding in episodic memory. Thus it has been of some interest to determine how experimental manipulations of encoding are reflected in the ERP and the extent to which such ERP effects correlate with subsequent memory performance. For example, if depth of processing is a viable concept in memory trace formation, it is possible that some ERP parameter might vary systematically with fluctuations in depth and thereby serve to measure it. It is just such a hope that spurred several ERP investigators to record ERPs within typical levels-of-processing paradigms.

Before detailing the results of these studies, I must point out two of the assumptions implicit in using ERPs in this way: (1) ERP waveforms that are similar in morphology reflect the engagement of qualitatively similar processes, whereas those that are different reflect the activity of qualitatively distinct processes; (2) amplitude and latency changes in ERP components reflect quantitative, not qualitative, differences in processing. These working assumptions are based on some general observations that ERP researchers have made over the years. Namely, quantitative manipulations, such as increasing the brightness or the loudness of stimuli, typically lead to larger amplitudes or shorter latencies for the early sensory components of the ERP, whereas a qualitative change, such as a difference in the modality of presentation, yields a qualitatively different set of sensory components. Some cognitive ERP components have been shown to behave in a similar fashion. For example, variations in semantic expectancy are mirrored in quantitative changes in N400 amplitude, whereas deviations from a physical expectancy are associated with a late positive complex (Kutas and Hillyard 1980). Although such simple notions probably do not capture all the complexities of a working brain, working assumptions are easiest to relinquish in the face of direct contradictory evidence rather than theoretical possibilities.

Sanquist et al. (1980) were the first to compare the ERPs collected during three different orienting tasks. The tasks, which necessitated yes/no judgments about two words according to one of three criteria (for example, orthographic similarity, rhyming, and synonymy), were ones that had previously been shown to yield different levels of retention. And indeed Sanquist et al. obtained the expected results:

(1) Semantic judgments led to better subsequent recognition than did rhyme judgments, which in turn led to better recognition than judgments about the case (upper or lower) in which the two words were printed. (2) In addition, "same" judgments were followed by better recognition than were "different" judgments for the phonemic and semantic but not orthographic conditions.

Likewise the ERP data indicated an interaction between the orienting task and the type of judgment (for example, same or different): The ERPs elicited by "same" judgments were quite similar across all three tasks, whereas those elicited by "different" judgments were not (see figure 5.5). Specifically, "same" judgment ERPs were characterized by a late positivity whose duration increased steadily from the orthographic to the semantic task. On the other hand, "different" judgment ERPs were characterized by a large negativity (around 400 msec) in the semantic task, a moderate-size negativity in the phonemic task, and positivity with a negative notch in the orthographic task.

If these waveform differences are interpreted as previously discussed, then one conclusion would be that the processing of same and different items differs qualitatively in at least one operation. By contrast, the processing differences among the three orienting tasks seems to be quantitative rather than qualitative in nature. These ERP patterns are thus inconsistent with the view that the different orienting tasks invariably engage qualitatively distinct operations. The decision to respond "same" appears to involve similar encoding operations regardless of the linguistic dimension along which the judgments are being made, whereas the decision to respond "different" appears to call on qualitatively different encoding operations for semantic versus other types of processing. The varying durations of the late positivity in association with "same" responses across tasks probably reflects quantitative differences in the use of a particular cognitive process, the psychological identity of which remains uncertain at present. In any case the data patterns converge with behavioral data, suggesting that no simple concept such as depth of encoding is likely to explain the differential memory performance across these particular tasks [reviewed in Tulving (1983)]. At the least, another variable is necessary to account for the different encoding required by "same" versus "different" judgments in the phonemic and semantic tasks.

The Sanquist et al. data might have revealed more about the relationships among ERP parameters, encoding, and memory performance if it had allowed comparisons among the ERPs elicited during each of the orienting tasks, averaged as a function of subsequent

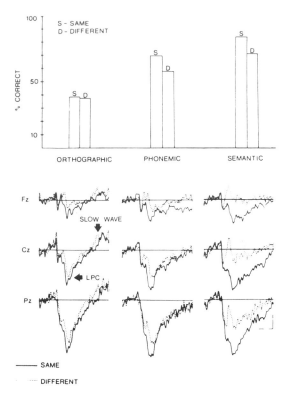

Figure 5.5
Percent correct recognition for each comparison criterion and judgment type. Shown below each comparison criterion are the grand average ERPs elicited by the second word in a pair for that condition. ERPs were digitized at the rate of 102.4 samples per second for a 2,500-msec epoch. Stimulus onset occurred following a 500-msec baseline. Calibrations: 500 msec and 5 μV, negativity upward. From Sanquist et al. (1980).

recognition performance and same/different judgments. Unfortunately there were not enough trials to generate all the subaverages necessary to make these comparisons. To the extent that this comparison was carried out (for example, for the semantic task ERPs), the data implied different encodings for items that would or would not be subsequently recognized. However, it is impossible to say this with certainty because the recognized/unrecognized comparison was confounded with the same/different judgment, in that subjects recognized many more "same" than "different" words. On the other hand, if this ERP pattern was not due to the confounding with response type, then it suggests substantial overlap between the encoding of "same" items that will not be recognized and those judged to be "different" (at least in the semantic domain).

Another ERP study (Paller et al., 1987) conducted within the levels-of-processing tradition included a sufficient number of trials to allow comparisons among the ERPs elicited during initial encoding as a function of subsequent recognition in both semantic and nonsemantic orienting tasks. These comparisons revealed that the type of memory-related ERP effect observed by Sanquist et al. appears to be more robust in semantic as opposed to nonsemantic tasks (although there is a possibility of a "floor effect" confound in the nonsemantic tasks).

By including two nominally semantic (for example, "Is it living?" or "Is it edible?") and two nominally nonsemantic tasks (for example, "Are there exactly two vowels?" or "Are the first and last letters in alphabetical order?"), Paller et al. also were able to assess the generality of their findings. In so doing, they found that it was an oversimplification to assume that processing during two semantic or two nonsemantic tasks were equivalent by virtue of their being deemed so by the experimenter. The ERPs elicited by the two semantic tasks and those elicited by the two nonsemantic tasks differ either in morphology or distribution over the scalp (see figure 5.6). By inference, so did at least some of the neural and perceptual and cognitive processing underlying the different tasks.

Moreover, whereas neither nonsemantic task elicited a significant memory-related ERP effect, one was associated with a large late positivity and the other was not. Thus Paller et al. concluded that the memory-related ERP effect could be dissociated from the P3. This finding, together with the observation that the ERP differences based on subsequent recognition and recall have a scalp distribution different from that of the typical P3 component, further suggested that the two ERP effects are independent. Of course, under some experimental conditions the P3 component might still vary in amplitude with

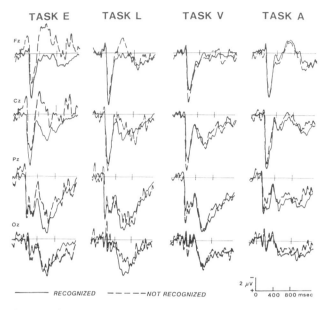

Figure 5.6
Grand average ERPs associated with each processing task; averaged based on later recognition performance. Note the ERP difference between words later recognized (solid lines) and words not recognized (dashed line) was greater in the two semantic task, especially task E. From Paller et al. (1987).

some aspect of memory. However, Paller et al.'s results imply that attributing variation in a late positivity to variation in the P3 component per se be done with great care [also see Halgren and Smith (1987)].

Finally, Paller et al. observed that the ERP signs of subsequent recognition during initial encoding are similar regardless of the nature of task decision (that is, yes or no). Items followed by a "yes" response did, however, evoke a slightly larger late ERP difference between subsequently recognized and unrecognized items than those followed by a "no" response. On the average, items associated with "yes" decisions were better recognized than those associated with "no" decisions. Perhaps some combination of the reduced priming (reflected in larger negativity) and decreased "additional" processing (reflected in less of a memory-related enhancement in the positivity) could account for the worse recognition of "no" items.

This set of observations may be important because it is the inability of the original levels-of-processing framework to account for the differential memorability of items associated with yes/no, same/different, or congruent/incongruent responses, especially within the semantic domain, that led to its reformulation. Within the revision, differential elaboration was invoked to account for the observation that congruent items are better remembered than incongruous ones (Craik and Jacoby 1979). For example, Craik and Tulving (1975) suggested that the congruity between a context and a target allowed the formation of an integrated memory unit that, once formed, could be elaborated, whereas incongruous context-target pairings did not, thus producing the observed differences in their retention. It is unclear whether this explanation implies that elaboration is a part of the encoding process or an adjunct to it. Moreover, this description provides no information about the time course of elaboration, if such a unitary process exists. Furthermore, the invocation of the "congruity" variable implies that there may be a special relationship between episodic memory and the rich store of preformed associations embodied in one's knowledge and experience with a language.

Interactions of Semantic and Episodic Memory
It was within the context of such questions that Neville et al. (1986) decided to use the ERP to examine the relationship between initial processing and subsequent memory. In particular, they wanted to determine how and when semantic congruity and elaboration contributed to episodic memory trace formation and recognition. This line of research drew on a relatively established ERP measure of semantic congruity. It has been found that during silent reading the differential processing of words that fit a given context and those that do not is apparent in the visual ERP within 200 msec of a word's presentation. Semantically incongruous or anomalous words within a sentence elicit ERPs characterized by a large negative component peaking around 400 msec (N400), whereas highly predictable, congruous endings elicit ERPs with a positive peak around 350 msec (Kutas and Hillyard 1980). The results of several investigations aimed at validating the N400 as a measure of semantic processing have led to the working hypothesis that N400 may be an index of semantic expectancy (Kutas and Hillyard 1984; Kutas et al. 1984). In these studies semantic expectancy was defined operationally in terms of cloze probability (Taylor 1953). However, in my view the semantic expectancy of an item is a function of a multitude of factors (automatic and under attentional control) that heighten the activation of particular semantic concepts relative to others. Lexical associations, the frequency of usage of a word in the language, grammatical, semantic, thematic, and pragmatic constraints, etc. may under certain circumstances contribute to a word's semantic expectancy. To date, it has been found that N400 amplitude bears an inverse relationship to be-

havioral measures of semantic priming; priming, in this case, refers to the increased speed or efficiency of processing of an item following a semantically related one relative to its following an unrelated item (Bentin et al. 1985; Fischler et al. 1983). Thus knowledge of the relations between congruity and recognition memory, between congruity and the N400, and between subsequent memory and the ERP was combined in the hopes of leading to a better understanding of why semantic incongruity results in poor memory performance.

Both experiments reported by Neville et al. (1986) obtained the typical N400 effect, namely, greater negativity in association with words that do not fit a preceding context (for example, type of weapon–sheep) than in association with words that do fit (for example, A type of insect–ant). Shortly after the initial presentation subjects were asked to differentiate the "old" words (sheep, ant) presented in isolation from their original context from an equal number of "new" words. Both studies replicated the common behavioral finding of better recognition for words that were congruous than those that were incongruous. Thus to some extent there was an inverse correlation between the average size of the N400 wave elicited by a word and the likelihood that it would be recognized in a test. However, the data clearly demonstrated that congruity per se (as reflected in N400 amplitude) could not account for memory performance singlehandedly. Incongruous words elicited N400's of equivalent amplitudes whether or not they were subsequently recognized. In fact, the ERPs elicited by incongruous words showed no effect of recognition until 500 msec or so (that is, past the N400 peak); the processes involved in recognition memory appeared to influence the amplitude of a late, broad positivity (P650). Likewise the responses to congruous words displayed a greater positivity for the to-be-recognized words (see figure 5.7). Whether the reduced positivity to congruous words that would not be recognized was due to variation solely in the amplitude of the late positivity or to the presence of an enhanced N400 could not be determined. However, congruent items that will not be recognized do seem to elicit a modest-sized N400.

Several aspects of these data are quite informative. First, we can note that the brain's response to each congruous word is not fully determined by the experimenter's classification of the stimuli. If the decreased N400 elicited by some congruous items (relative to incongruous items) reflects the fulfillment of a semantic expectancy, then clearly not all congruous items are equally expected. Because Neville et al. did not attempt to equate the degree of semantic expectancy among the congruous items, fluctuation in this variable may have accounted for the differential recognition and ERP responses within

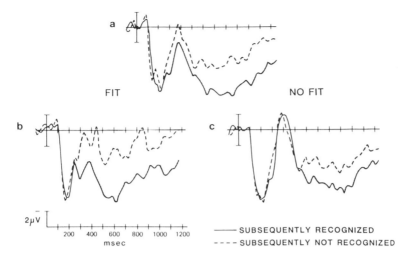

Figure 5.7
ERPs recorded from Cz in the judgment task of Experiment 2 averaged according to subsequent recognition in the recognition test. (a) ERPs averaged across fit and no-fit words. (b) ERPs averaged for fit words and (c) no-fit words. Solid line, subsequently recognized; dashed line, subsequently not recognized. From Neville et al. (1986).

the set of congruent words. However, it is also possible that these differences reflect individual variation in unconscious semantic priming or in the attention paid to the preceding phrase, which was supposed to set up the expectancy. In any case these data suggest that it is not objective congruity per se but rather degree of semantic expectancy or priming that accounts for the enhanced recognition of congruous relative to incongruous words. An alternative view also consistent with these data would say that the amplitude of the N400 elicited by a particular word is related to the number of elements in the lexicon that were activated to some degree in an attempt to interpret the word given the context. A large N400 would indicate some minimal activation of many lexical items (possibly "logogens") in the search for meaning. In this view incongruous words are difficult to remember because their activations do not differ from those of the numerous other words that received some activation.

At present, it is unclear what other processes involved in the formation of the memory traces for congruous words are reflected in the ERP waveforms. Neville et al. proposed that the enhanced positivity following the N400 was associated with increased elaborative processing; however, other candidates have not been ruled out. In any case the ERP data suggest that this same process also was invoked during the analysis of incongruous words, albeit to a lesser degree and with a delayed onset. It appears as if semantic priming might hasten the onset of this additional encoding process, thereby enhancing the subsequent recognizability of the primed word. This proposition assumes that semantic priming aids in the formation and storage of episodic memories by taking advantage of the existing organization of semantic memory.

I examined these issues in a subsequent experiment in which I analyzed the ERPs elicited by congruous and incongruous endings sorted as a function of recall. After reading 160 sentences for content, subjects were asked to recall the final word of each sentence on receiving all but the final word as a cue. It was important to determine whether or not cued recall would result in ERP patterns similar to that for recognition; such data were necessary before generalizations about the underlying mechanisms could be made. Moreover, the proposed hypothesis that semantic priming was involved in episodic retention needed to be tested. If semantic priming was instrumental in episodic memory, then incongruous sentence endings that were somehow related to the expected completions ("The game was called when it started to umbrella.") should be recalled better than incongruous endings that were not so related ("George was fired but he could not tell his fog."). This prediction was based on a previous observation (Kutas et al. 1984) that related incongruities ("umbrella") elicited smaller N400's than unrelated incongruities ("fog").

As predicted, when cued with a sentence fragment, not only was recall better for congruous (68%) than incongruous sentences but semantically related incongruities were recalled significantly more often than unrelated incongruities (41% versus 7%). The ERP data likewise showed the expected pattern: positivity in response to congruous endings, large N400's to unrelated semantic anomalies, and somewhat smaller N400's to semantically related anomalies. In addition, related incongruities elicited a late positive component over the front of the head that was not evident in response to unrelated anomalies. Sorting these initial responses as a function of recall revealed a pattern of differences quite similar to that previously obtained for recognition (see figure 5.8). On average, greater priming (as reflected in smaller N400's) indicated better recall regardless of congruity, although words with equal amplitude N400's could be associated with different recall performance. In addition, ERP signs of recall appeared to be earlier and more robust for congruous than incongruous endings.

All of the ERP data discussed are consistent with the hypothesis that there is substantial overlap between the operations involved in comprehension and those involved in the formation of episodic mem-

BEST COMPLETIONS   RELATED ANOMALIES

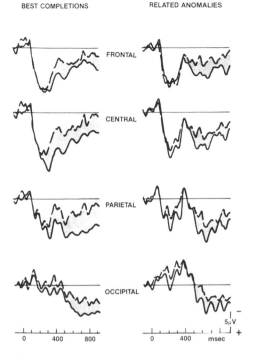

FRONTAL

CENTRAL

PARIETAL

OCCIPITAL

5μV

0   400   800   0   400   msec

Figure 5.8
Grand average (ERPs) elicited by comparisons of congruous ("best completions") and incongruous ("related anomalies") during initial encoding averaged as a function of subsequent recall. Solid line, subsequently recalled; dashed line, subsequently not recalled.

ory traces for verbal materials. This proposed overlap reflects the intimate use of semantic memory during episodic memory trace formation. The similarity of semantic and episodic memory mechanisms also has been discussed by other ERP investigators (Fischler et al. 1984; Halgren and Smith, in press). Semantic priming (measured by means of increased RTs or decreased N400 amplitudes) and aspects of repetition priming (not discussed here) are presumed to be a consequence of the efficient use of the structure of semantic memory. In this view semantic priming aids memory by affording the to-be-remembered item access to an organized semantic memory, thereby leading to greater ease of comprehension and storage. A strong test of this idea, however, must await the results of memory experiments in which episodic and semantic relationships are dissociated [such as in the RT experiments of Neely (1977)]. Nonetheless the ERP data suggest that semantic expectancy exerts at least some of its influence on the processing and retention of a word within half a second of its initial encoding, not just during the memory test. Similar conclusions can be drawn about the role of familiarity on recognition memory on the basis of ERP experiments not reviewed here [see, for example, Johnson et al. (1985), Smith et al. (1986), and Halgren and Smith (1987) for the role of the medial temporal lobe in such processes].

These data converge with others in suggesting that comprehension aids memory (Bransford et al. 1977). Accordingly one means of improving retention is to improve comprehension. The ERP data further suggest that the context in which an idea is presented has a significant impact on its comprehensibility. A context that can draw on existing mental schema and/or an existing network of semantic associations generally leads to quicker and greater understanding than one that cannot make use of well-traveled pathways in semantic memory. Practically, "new" items are best taught (that is, learned and remembered) in the context of what is already known, although it is also important to note the features of the new item that distinguish it from the old.

5.3   Practical Conclusions

Because ERPs can, in theory, provide an online assessment of a subset of the brain processes at any given moment, regardless of their accessibility to conscious awareness, they might seem to be an excellent way of tracking memory operations in the brain. In theory they are. However, before ERPs can be so used online in a training situation, it is essential to determine their sensitivity to hypothetical memory processes and/or performance variables. That is, it is necessary to validate the proposed relationships between any ERP parameter and any memory process. This is no small task. Years of research have shown that memory is not a unitary concept (witness the proliferation of memory terminology). Moreover, demonstrating a reliable and valid relationship may be difficult for the very reason that ERPs are useful, namely, because they reflect the activity of multiple processes, at least some of which are outside of awareness and therefore cannot be discussed, although they may nonetheless have behavioral consequences.

The main thrust of this chapter has been a review of the ERP studies that have been designed to validate relationships between various ERP parameters and memory processes. Much of this work has revolved around use of the P3 component of the ERP to study what has been variously called short-term or working memory. At one level the results of these experiments have converged with data from other disciplines in demonstrating that working memory is

1. Limited in capacity (<7 bits).
2. Takes time to search (30–45 msec per item).
3. Consists of more than one subcomponent (for example, "central executor" + articulatory loop + possibly "visuospatial scratch pad").

The results indicate that these various subcomponents of working memory are differentially utilized by subjects, with the difference being one of strategy. There is also evidence that a subject's natural strategy can be altered according to the desired behavioral outcome. If overall recall is the desired goal, then "elaboration" is the preferred strategy. On the other hand, if certain items need to be remembered at the expense of others, then rote memorization is the strategy of choice.

In addition, P3 studies of working memory have suggested that slowed search through the short-term store of information is not invariably attributable to slowing of mental processes. For example, the elderly seem to have relatively normal mental scanning rates but are slower in performing a scanning task because they tend to be cautious about responding and slower at controlling their musculature. A similar combined ERP-RT approach could be directed at assessing the effects of number of important variables (stress, lack of sleep, noisy environment, number of simultaneous tasks that need to be performed, etc.) not only on performance but on the speed of stimulus evaluation. Perhaps slowing in different processing or execution stages could be remedied by different training algorithms. For example, if ERP assessment revealed that stress acts to retard motor output but not to scramble the underlying mental processes, it might be possible to alter the required behavioral response so that it is less susceptible to fluctuations in muscle control.

The bulk of the remaining research on ERPs and memory has dealt with the role of encoding in episodic memory trace formation and retrieval. To date, ERP data have highlighted the critical roles of semantic priming and comprehension in episodic memories, but the role of other factors remains to be assessed. For example, it should be possible to examine the encoding and performance consequences of stimulus repetition or different modes of practice (for example, massed versus spaced) to determine which factors truly act during encoding and which have their impact during a subsequent process such as consolidation or during retrieval. Moreover, by using ERP technology across verbal units larger than the word (averaging across sentences or sentence fragments), researchers can assess the time course of recognition or recall. Finally, such analyses will allow tracking some of the brain processes involved in memory operations for which people are behaviorally amnestic, namely, those that cannot be consciously accessed. However, it is important to remember that these advances occur during the testing of theories of memory developed in a basic research environment and that the outcome of the tests can be no better than the theories they were designed to test.

Acknowledgments

Some of the work reported here has been supported by the National Science Foundation under grant BNS 83-09243, the National Institute of Neurological and Communicative Disorders and Stroke under grant NS 17778, and the National Institute of Child Health and Human Development under grant HD 22614. M. Kutas is supported by an RCDA Award from the National Institutes of Mental Health (MH 00322). Special thanks to C. Van Petten, K. A. Paller, and S. A. Hillyard for their editorial comments on previous versions of this manuscript.

References

Adam, N., and G. I. Collins. 1978. "Late components of the visual evoked potential to search in short-term memory." *Electroencephalography and Clinical Neurophysiology* 44:147–156.

Allison, T., C. C. Wood, and G. McCarthy. 1986. "The central nervous system," in *Psychophysiology, Systems, Processes, and Applications*, M. G. H. Coles, E. Donchin, and S. W. Porges, eds. New York: Guilford Press, 5–25.

Baddeley, A. D., and G. J. Hitch. 1974. "Working memory," in *Recent Advances in Learning and Motivation*, G. Bower, ed. New York: Academic Press, vol. 8.

Baddeley, A. D., and K. Lieberman. 1980. "Spatial working memory," in *Attention and Performance VIII*, R. S. Nickerson, ed. Hillsdale, N.J.: Erlbaum Associates, 521–539.

Bashore, T. R., A. Osman, and E. H. Heffley. 1988. "Mental slowing in the elderly: A cognitive psychophysiological analysis." Unpublished.

Bentin, S., G. McCarthy, and C. C. Wood. 1985. "Event-related potentials, lexical decision and semantic priming." *Electroencephalography and Clinical Neurophysiology* 60:343–355.

Berger, H. 1929. "Uber das Elektrenkephalogramm des Menschen." *Archiv für Psychiatrie Nervenkrankheiten* 87:527–570.

Bransford, J. D., N. S. McCarrell, J. J. Franks, and K. E. Nitsch. 1977. "Coming to understand things we could not previously understand," in *Perceiving, Acting and Knowing: Toward an Ecological Psychology*, R. E. Shaw and J. D. Bransford, eds. Hillsdale, N.J.: Erlbaum Associates, 431–466.

Brookhuis, K. A., G. Mulder, L. J. M. Mulder, A. B. M. Mulder, H. J. Gloerich, J. J. Van Dellen, J. J. Van der Meere, and H. Ellerman. 1981. "Late positive components and stimulus evaluation time." *Biological Psychology* 13:107–123.

Cerella, J. 1985. "Information processing rates in the elderly." *Psychological Bulletin* 98:67–83.

Coles, M. G. H., G. Gratton, T. R. Bashore, C. W. Eriksen, and E. Donchin. 1985. "A psychophysiological investigation of the continuous flow model of human information processing." *Journal of Experimental Psychology: Human Perception and Performance* 11:529–553.

Craik, F. I. M., and L. L. Jacoby. 1979. "Elaboration and distinctiveness in episodic memory," in *Perspectives on Memory Research: Essays in Honor of Uppsala University's 500th Anniversary*, L.-G. Nilsson, ed. Hillsdale, N.J.: Erlbaum Associates, 145–166.

Craik, F. I. M., and R. S. Lockhart. 1972. "Levels of processing: A framework for memory research." *Journal of Verbal Learning and Verbal Behavior* 11:671–684.

Craik, F. I. M., and E. Tulving. 1975. "Depth of processing and the retention of words in episodic memory." *Journal of Experimental Psychology: General* 104:268–294.

Donchin, E. 1981. "Surprise! . . . Surprise?" *Psychophysiology* 18:493–513.

Duncan-Johnson, C. C., and E. Donchin. 1982. "The P300 component of the event-related brain potential as an index of information processing." *Biological Psychology* 14:1–52.

Eriksen, C. W., and D. W. Schultz. 1979. "Information processing in visual search: A continuous flow conception and experimental results." *Perception and Psychophysics* 25:249–263.

Fabiani, M., D. Karis, and E. Donchin. 1986. "P300 and recall in an incidental memory paradigm." *Psychophysiology* 23:298–308.

Fabiani, M., D. Karis, and E. Donchin. n.d. "The effects of mnemonic strategy manipulation in a von Restorff paradigm." Unpublished.

Fabiani, M., G. Gratton, D. Karis, and E. Donchin. 1988. "The definition, identification, and reliability of measurement of the P300 component of the event-related brain potential," in *Advances in Psychophysiology*, P. K. Ackles, J. R. Jennings, and M. G. H. Coles, eds. Greenwich, Conn.: JAI Press, vol. 2.

Fischler, I., P. A. Bloom, D. G. Childers, A. A. Arroyo, and N. W. Perry, Jr. 1984. "Brain potentials during sentence verification: Late negativity and long-term memory strength." *Neuropsychologia* 22:559–568.

Fischler, I., P. A. Bloom, D. A. Childers, S. E. Roucos, and N. W. Perry, Jr. 1983. "Potentials related to sentence verification." *Psychophysiology* 20:400–409.

Ford, J. M., W. T. Roth, R. C. Mohs, W. F. Hopkins, III, and B. S. Kopell. 1979. "Event-related potentials recorded from young and old adults during a memory retrieval task." *Electroencephalography and Clinical Neurophysiology* 47:450–459.

Friedman, D., H. G. Vaughan, Jr., and L. Erlenmeyer-Kimling. 1978. "Stimulus and response related components of the late positive complex in a visual discrimination task." *Electroencephalography and Clinical Neurophysiology* 45:319–330.

Gaillard, A. W. K., and W. Ritter, eds. 1983. *Tutorials in Event-Related Potential Research: Endogenous Components*. Amsterdam: North-Holland.

Galambos, R., and S. Hillyard. 1981. "Electrophysiological approaches to human cognitive processing." *Neurosciences Research Program Bulletin* 20:141–265.

Gevins, A. S., J. C. Doyle, B. A. Cutillo, R. E. Schaffer, R. S. Tannehill, and S. L. Bressler. 1985. "Neurocognitive pattern analysis of a visuospatial task: Rapidly shifting foci of evoked correlations between electrodes." *Psychophysiology* 22:32–43.

Halgren, E., and M. E. Smith. 1987. "Cognitive evoked potentials as modulatory processes in human memory formation and retrieval." *Human Neurobiology* 6:129–140.

Halgren, E., J. M. Stapleton, M. Smith, and I. Altafullah. 1986. "Generators of the human scalp P3(S)," in *Frontiers of Clinical Neuroscience. Vol. 3, Evoked Potentials*, R. Q. Cracco and I. Bodis-Wollner, eds. New York: Alan R. Liss, 269–286.

Halgren, E., N. K. Squires, C. L. Wilson, J. W. Rohrbaugh, T. L. Babb, and P. H. Crandall. 1980. "Endogenous potentials generated in the human hippocampal formation and amygdala by infrequent events." *Science* 210:803–805.

Halliday, A. M., ed. 1982. *Evoked Potentials in Clinical Testing*. Edinburgh: Churchill Livingstone.

Hansen, J. C., and S. A. Hillyard. 1983. "Selective attention to multidimensional auditory stimuli in man." *Journal of Experimental Psychology: Human Perception Performance* 9:1–19.

Hillyard, S. A., and M. Kutas. 1983. "Electrophysiology of cognitive processing." *Annual Review of Psychology* 34:33–61.

Horst, R. L., R. Johnson, Jr., and E. Donchin. 1980. "Event-related brain potentials and subjective probability in a learning task." *Memory and Cognition* 8:476–488.

Isreal, J. B., G. L. Chesney, C. D. Wickens, and E. Donchin. 1980. "P300 and tracking difficulty: Evidence for multiple resources in dual-task performance." *Psychophysiology* 17:259–273.

Isreal, J. B., C. D. Wickens, G. L. Chesney, and E. Donchin. 1980. "The event-related brain potential as an index of display-monitoring workload." *Human Factors* 22:211–224.

Jasiukaitis, P. In press. "The effect of pre-stimulus alpha activity on the P300." *Psychophysiology.*

Johnson, R. E., Jr. In press. "The amplitude of the P300 component of the event-related potential: Review and synthesis," in *Advances in Psychophysiology*, P. K. Ackles, J. R. Jennings, and M. G. H. Coles, eds. Greenwich, Conn.: JAI Press, vol. 3.

Johnson, R. E., Jr., and P. Fedio. 1984. "ERP and P300 activity in patients following unilateral temporal lobectomy." *Society for Neuroscience Abstracts* 10:847.

Johnson, R. E., Jr., A. Pfefferbaum, and B. S. Kopell. 1985. "P300 and long-term memory: Latency predicts recognition performance." *Psychophysiology* 22:497–507.

Karis, D., M. Fabiani, and E. Donchin. 1984. "P300 and memory: Individual differences in the von Restorff effect." *Cognitive Psychology* 16:177–216.

Karis, D., T. Bashore, M. Fabiani, and E. Donchin. 1981. "P300 and memory." *Psychophysiology* 19:328.

Karrer, R., J. Cohen, and P. Tueting, eds. 1984. *Brain and Information: Event-Related Potentials.* New York: New York Academy of Sciences.

Knight, R. T. 1984. "Decreased response to novel stimuli after prefrontal lesions in man." *Electroencephalography and Clinical Neurophysiology* 59:9–20.

Knight, R. T., S. A. Hillyard, D. L. Woods, and H. J. Neville. 1981. "The effects of frontal cortex lesions on event-related potentials during auditory selective attention." *Electroencephalography and Clinical Neurophysiology* 52:571–582.

Kutas, M., and E. Donchin. 1978. "Variations in the latency of P300 as a function of variations in semantic categorization," in *New Perspectives in Event-Related Potential Research*, D. Otto, ed. Washington, D.C.: US Environmental Protection Agency, 198–201.

Kutas, M., and S. A. Hillyard. 1980. "Reading senseless sentences: Brain potentials reflect semantic incongruity." *Science* 207:203–205.

Kutas, M., and S. A. Hillyard. 1984. "Brain potentials during reading reflect word expectancy and semantic association." *Nature* 307:161–163.

Kutas, M., and C. Van Petten. In press. "Event-related brain potential studies of language," in *Advances in Psychophysiology*, P. K. Ackles, J. R. Jennings, and M. G. H. Coles, eds. Greenwich, Conn.: JAI Press.

Kutas, M., T. Lindamood, and S. A. Hillyard. 1984. "Word expectancy and event-related brain potentials during sentence processing," in *Preparatory States and Processes*, S. Kornblum and J. Requin, eds. Hillsdale, N.J.: Erlbaum Associates, 217–237.

Kutas, M., G. McCarthy, and E. Donchin. 1977. "Augmenting mental chronometry: The P300 as a measure of stimulus evaluation time." *Science* 197:792–795.

McCarthy, G., and E. Donchin. 1981. "A metric for thought: A comparison of P300 latency and reaction time." *Science* 211:77–80.

McClelland, J. L. 1979. "On time relations of mental processes: A framework for analyzing processes in cascade." *Psychological Review* 86:287–330.

Magliero, A., T. R. Bashore, M. G. H. Coles, and E. Donchin. 1984. "On the dependence of P300 latency on stimulus evaluation processes." *Psychophysiology* 21:171–186.

Marsh, G. R. 1975. "Age differences in evoked potential correlates of a memory scanning process." *Experimental Aging Research* 1:3–16.

Meyer, D., S. Yantis, A. M. Osman, and J. E. K. Smith. 1985. "Temporal properties of human information processing: Tests of discrete versus continuous models." *Cognitive Psychology* 17:445–518.

Mulder, G. 1986. "Memory search paradigms and practice effects," in *Cognitive Psychophysiology: Studies in ERPs*, W. C. McCallum, R. Zappolli, and F. Denoth, eds. Amsterdam: Elsevier, 57–63.

Mulder, G., A. B. M. Gloerich, K. A. Brookhuis, H. J. van Dellen, and L. J. M. Mulder. 1984. "Stage analysis of the reaction time process using brain-event related potentials and reaction time." *Psychological Review* 46:15–32.

Naatanen, R. 1982. "Processing negativity: Evoked-potential reflection of selective attention." *Psychological Bulletin* 92:605–640.

Neely, J. H. 1977. "Semantic priming and retrieval from lexical memory: Roles of inhibitionless spreading activation and limited-capacity attention." *Journal of Experimental Psychology: General* 106:226–254.

Neville, H. J., and D. Lawson. 1987. "Attention to central and peripheral visual space in a movement detection task II. Congenitally deaf adults." *Brain Research* 405:268–283.

Neville, H. J., M. Kutas, and A. Schmidt. 1982. "Event-related potential studies of cerebral specialization during reading II. Studies of congenitally deaf adults." *Brain and Language* 16:316–337.

Neville, H. J., A. Schmidt, and M. Kutas. 1983. "Altered visual-evoked potentials in congenitally deaf adults." *Brain Research* 266:127–132.

Neville, H. J., M. Kutas, G. Chesney, and A. Schmidt. 1986. "Event-related brain potentials during the initial encoding and subsequent recognition memory of congruous and incongruous words." *Journal of Memory and Language* 25:75–92.

Neville, H. J., E. Snyder, R. Knight, and R. Galambos. 1979. "Event-related potentials in language and non-language tasks in patients with alexia without agraphia," in *Human Evoked Potentials Applications and Problems*, D. Lehmann and E. Callaway, eds. New York: Plenum Press, 269–283.

Neville, H. J., E. Snyder, D. Woods, and R. Galambos. 1982. "Recognition and surprise alter the human visual evoked response." *Proceedings of the National Academy of Sciences USA* 79:2121–2123.

Nunez, P. L. 1981. *Electric Fields of the Brain*. New York: Oxford University Press.

Paller, K. A. 1986. "Effects of medial temporal lobectomy in monkeys on brain potentials related to memory." Ph.D. dissertation. University of California, San Diego. Unpublished.

Paller, K. A., M. Kutas, and A. Mayes. 1987. "Neural correlates of encoding in an incidental learning paradigm." *Electroencephalography and Clinical Neurophysiology* 67:360–371.

Paller, K. A., S. Zola-Morgan, L. R. Squire, and S. A. Hillyard. 1982. "Late positive event-related potentials in cynomolgus monkeys (*Macaca fascicularis*)." *Society for Neuroscience Abstracts* 8:975.

Paller, K. A., S. Zola-Morgan, L. R. Squire, and S. A. Hillyard. 1984. "Monkeys with lesions of hippocampus and amygdala exhibit event-related brain potentials that resemble the human P300 wave." *Society for Neuroscience Abstracts* 10:849.

Pfefferbaum, A., J. M. Ford, W. T. Roth, and B. S. Kopell. 1980. "Age differences in P3-reaction time associations." *Electroencephalography and Clinical Neurophysiology* 49:257–265.

Phillips, W. A., and D. F. M. Christie. 1977. "Components of visual memory." *Quarterly Journal of Experimental Psychology* 29:117–133.

Pineda, J. 1987. "Endogenous event-related potentials in nonhuman primates: The role of the noradrenergic locus coeruleus system." Ph.D. dissertation. University of California, San Diego. Unpublished.

Pritchard, W. S. 1981. "Psychophysiology of P300: A review." *Psychological Bulletin* 89:506–540.

Pritchard, W. S., M. E. Brandt, S. A. Shappell, T. J. O'Dell, and E. S. Barratt. 1985. "P300 amplitude/pre-stimulus EEG power relationships." *Psychophysiology* 22:609–610.

Ragot, R. 1984. "Perceptual and motor space representation: An event-related potential study." *Psychophysiology* 21:159–170.

Regan, D. 1972. *Evoked Potentials in Psychology, Sensory Physiology, and Clinical Medicine.* London: Chapman and Hall.

Restorff, H. von. 1933. "Uber die Wirkung von Bereichsbildungen im Spurenfeld." *Psycholigische Forschung* 18:299–342.

Ritter, W., R. Simson, H. G. Vaughan, and D. Friedman. 1979. "A brain event related to the making of a sensory discrimination." *Science* 203:1358–1361.

Rugg, M., A. Kok, G. Barrett, and I. Fischler. 1986. "ERPs associated with language and hemispheric specialization: A review," in *Cognitive Psychophysiology: Studies in ERPs,* W. C. McCallum, R. Zappolli, and F. Denoth, eds. Amsterdam: Elsevier, 273–300.

Sanquist, T. F., J. W. Rohrbaugh, K. Syndulko, and D. B. Lindsley. 1980. "Electrocortical signs of levels of processing: Perceptual analysis and recognition memory." *Psychophysiology* 17:568–576.

Scherg, M., and D. von Cramon. 1985a. "A new interpretation of the generators of BAEP waves I–V: Results of a spatio-temporal dipole model." *Electroencephalography and Clinical Neurophysiology* 62:290–299.

Scherg, M., and D. von Cramon. 1985b. "Two bilateral sources of the late AEP as identified by a spatio-temporal dipole model." *Electroencephalography and Clinical Neurophysiology* 62:32–44.

Smith, M. C., L. Theodor, and P. E. Franklin. 1983. "The relationship between contextual facilitation and depth of processing." *Journal of Experimental Psychology: Learning, Memory and Cognition* 9:697–712.

Smith, M. E., J. M. Stapleton, and E. Halgren. 1986. "Human medial temporal lobe potentials evoked in memory and language tasks." *Electroencephalography and Clinical Neurophysiology* 63:145–159.

Squire, L. 1982. "The neuropsychology of human memory." *Annual Review of Neuroscience* 5:241–273.

Squires, K., C. Wickens, N. Squires, and E. Donchin. 1976. "The effect of stimulus sequence on the waveform of the cortical event-related potential." *Science* 193:1142–1146.

Stapleton, J. M., E. Halgren, and K. A. Moreno. 1987. "Endogenous potentials after anterior temporal lobectomy. *Neuropsychologia* 25:549–557.

Sternberg, S. 1969a. "The discovery of processing stages: Extensions of Donders' method." *Acta Psychologica* 30:276–315.

Sternberg, S. 1969b. "Memory-scanning: Mental processes revealed by reaction-time experiments." *American Scientist* 57:421–457.

Strayer, D. L., C. D. Wickens, and R. Braune. 1987. Adult age differences in the speed and capacity of information processing II. An electrophysiological approach." *Psychology and Aging* 2(2):99–110.

Stuss, D. T., and T. W. Picton. 1978. "Neurophysiological correlates of human concept formation." *Behavioral Biology* 23:135–162.

Sutton, S., and D. S. Ruchkin. 1984. "The late positive complex: Advances and new problems," in *Brain and Information: Event-Related Potentials*, R. Karrer, J. Cohen, and P. Tueting, eds. New York: New York Academy of Sciences, 1–23.

Taylor, M. 1978. *"Bereitschaftspotential* during the acquisition of a skilled motor task." *Electroencephalography and Clinical Neurophysiology* 45:568–576.

Taylor, W. L. 1953. " 'Cloze' procedure: A new tool for measuring readability." *Journalism Quarterly* 30:415.

Tulving, E. 1983. *Elements of Episodic Memory*. Oxford: Clarendon Press.

Vaughan, H. G., Jr., L. D. Costa, and W. Ritter. 1968. "Topography of the human motor potential." *Electroencephalography and Clinical Neurophysiology* 25:1–10.

Wickens, C. D. 1984. "Processing resources in attention," in *Varieties of Attention*, R. Parasuraman and D. R. Davies, eds. London: Academic Press, 63–102.

Wickens, C. D., and C. Kessel. 1980. "The processing resource demands of failure in dynamic systems. *Journal of Experimental Psychology: Human Perception and Performance* 6:564–577.

Wickens, C. D., R. Braune, and A. Stokes. 1987. "Age differences in the speed and capacity of information processing I: A dual task." *Psychology and Aging* 2(2):70–78.

Wickens, C., A. Kramer, L. Vanasse, and E. Donchin. 1983. "Performance of concurrent tasks: A psychological analysis of the reciprocity of information-processing resources." *Science* 221:1080–1082.

Wood, C. C. 1982. "Application of dipole localization methods to source identification of human evoked potentials." *Annals of the New York Academy of Sciences* 388:113–135.

Wood, C. C., T. Allison, W. R. Goff, P. D. Williamson, and D. D. Spencer. 1980. "On the neural origin of P300 in man." *Progress in Brain Research* 54:51–56.

Wood, C. C., G. McCarthy, T. Allison, W. R. Goff, P. D. Wiliamson, and D. D. Spencer. 1982. "Endogenous event-related potentials following temporal lobe excisions in humans." *Society for Neuroscience Abstracts* 8:976.

Wood, C. C., G. McCarthy, N. K. Squires, H. G. Vaughan, D. L. Woods, and W. C. McCallum. 1984. "Anatomical and physiological substrates of event-related potentials: Two case studies," in *Brain and Information: Event-related Potentials*, R. Karrer, J. Cohen, and P. Tueting, eds. New York: New York Academy of Sciences, 681–721.

6

Improving Memory

William Hirst

If you listen to them, some people have worse memories than others, and anyone who has taught a course or tried to teach someone something new will agree. Some people remember all of the details and recall even days later what was said. For others, nothing seems to get in, and learning is slow at best.

This chapter is concerned with how research in cognitive psychology can be applied to helping those with "poor" memories learn better and more efficiently. It is concerned with just one form of memory—the kind of memory necessary to learn and master the demands of a new job. There are, of course, many different kinds of memory. Tulving (1972) for instance, has distinguished episodic memories from semantic memories. Episodic memories are those wrapped in the autobiographical context of a past event, for example, my memory of what I did last night or what I had for lunch today. The term "semantic memory" is a misnomer. It does not refer only to memory for words but to memories remembered without the context in which they were originally learned. I know that the square root of 2 is 1.414, but I cannot remember where I learned this fact. Such a memory would be semantic according to Tulving.

When people complain about their memory, they are often talking about their episodic memories. They cannot remember who said what to whom at a party or whether the purse snatcher had on a green or red shirt. But memory demands of a job rarely involve episodic memory. For many jobs one can rely on episodic memory to remember what the boss said you are supposed to do in a given situation, but if the job is truly mastered, one simply knows what to do. It is like my knowledge of the square root of 2. You do not have to know where or when you learned it; you just have to know it.

A study of memory techniques for a job should concentrate on mnemonics for semantic or at least well-learned memories, but even this focus may not be sharp enough. Any memory technique, no matter how generally it can be stated, must be tailored to the situa-

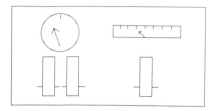

Figure 6.1
Illustrative control panel.

tion. The best way for actors to learn their lines may have nothing to do with the best way for nuclear reactor operators to learn how to use a complex control panel. One must first consider the task—"Memory for what?"—if one is going to design a method for improving students' memory.

This is not to say that there are no general principles for effective memorizing and remembering. There are. But the way these principles apply can vary quite radically from situation to situation (Hirst and Levine 1985). In this chapter I try to articulate some of the general principles of effective memory and try to show how these principles can be translated into specifics. In particular, I focus on ways to help people learn and remember a specific job skill, that is, the function of various levers and meters on a control panel (see figure 6.1). I am going to simplify matters in order to make the points that I develop clear. The control panel in figure 6.1 is relatively simple. Other control panels are not, and many panel operators—from nuclear technicians monitoring a reactor to the army recruit in a tank—must learn the functions of what at times seems like an overwhelming number of knobs, levers, and meters. To be sure, most people will learn the functions eventually. The question is, Is there a way to speed up the learning process? My discussion of the control panel will hopefully bear on this issue. I also want to emphasize that there is nothing unique about control panels. My discussion could apply to other types of information as well, a point that I reiterate at the end of this chapter. Again, I choose the control panel because it provides a straightforward medium in which to discuss the various topics in this chapter, and, second, it is the kind of thing that someone might have to learn in a job.

6.1   The Problem of Memory Capacity

It is common to say that people memorize and remember information poorly because they have a bad memory. Or to put it another way, their poor performance can be traced to a poor memory capacity. There are a variety of problems with this locution. First, there are different kinds of memory: short-term memory, long-term memory, procedural memory, declarative memory, episodic memory, semantic memory, etc. Memory capacity of one of these memories might be independent of other memories. Second, and more to the point, memory performance depends on what one does while memorizing or remembering, or, to use the jargon, encoding and retrieving. Difficulties arise because of the way information is encoded, the way one tries to retrieve the information, or both. Thus differences in memory performance are often a consequence of what people do when memorizing and remembering, not what their capacity is. The classic experiment on this issue was done with chess masters (Chase and Simon 1973; DeGroot 1965).

Chess masters and novices were shown a legal chess position for five seconds. They were then given a blank board and a full complement of chess pieces and were asked to reconstruct the position that they had just seen. Chess masters could accurately reproduce all or most of the original positions, whereas novices could place only seven or eight pieces accurately. This difference might arise because chess masters have a superior memory. A superior memory could possibly be a requisite ability if one is ever to become a chess master. Alternatively, chess masters' memory might be quite average. The difference between masters and novices may be in their knowledge of chess. Masters may see patterns in a legal position that novices do not. A pawn, knight, and bishop might seem unrelated to novices, but for masters they may form a unit, with the pawn protecting the knight from the bishop.

DeGroot (1965) and Chase and Simon (1973) showed that the better memory of chess masters cannot be attributed to superior memory capacity but to how masters use their knowledge of chess to relate the pieces on the board. When the masters and novices were exposed to an illegal position, the superiority of the masters disappeared. Indeed, in this instance, the masters actually performed worse than the novices.

The same principle—that superior memory can often be traced not to a larger capacity but to what we do with the material as a consequence of our superior knowledge—can be seen in a variety of situations. A cattle rancher will remember the price of cattle at past auctions better than someone only vaguely familiar with ranching (Bartlett 1932); a French cook will remember a recipe for French food better than one for Chinese food (Hirst 1980); and a person familiar with a city will remember directions better than a tourist (Levine

1980). However, it is not always the case. There are instances in which novices actually do better than experts. Wagner (1978), for instance, reported that college students at the University of Michigan remembered rug patterns better than the Moroccan rug dealers. This surprising result may reflect psychologists' lack of understanding about exactly what kind of expertise a Moroccan rug dealer has or it may underline the strength of the mnemonic skills that Westerners are taught in school. In either case the solution to the paradox probably relies on understanding what the individual does with the material rather than on looking for differences in memory capacity.

6.2   Strategies for Effective Memory

Memorizing can be thought of as an activity in which people transform and manipulate experience in order to make it more memorable. Experiences are not automatically committed to memory but in many cases must be digested and transformed, either intentionally or incidentally, into a form in which they are readily committed to memory. For example, people might find it difficult to learn the string of letters AREPOSNAEMTEMEHT as it is but would have no difficulty once they transformed it into the string THE MET MEANS OPERA, the reverse spelling of the original string.

In general, there are three not necessarily independent things one can do to promote effective memory. First, one can organize the material (Tulving and Donaldson 1972). One can relate an object to another or others to make an "effort after meaning" (Bartlett 1932). Second, one can form a visual image of the to-be-remembered material. There is substantial literature suggesting that imageable material is easier to memorize and remember than nonimageable material (Paivio 1971). Finally, one can memorize material so that one can have readily available retrieval cues to facilitate remembering (Tulving 1983). All memories do not simply come to mind once memorized. One must access them in a manner appropriate to how they were memorized. If you learned a string of words by attending to the meanings of the words, you no doubt would find it easier to retrieve the words with a semantic cue than if you studied the words by attending to their sounds. On the other hand, if the retrieval cue was a word that rhymed with the original word, then it probably would be better to have attended to the sound (Morris et al. 1977).

Voluntary versus Involuntary Memorizing
In discussing strategies of memory, it is important to separate voluntary memorizing from involuntary memorizing. The distinction

grows out of work on activity theory in Russian psychology [see Wertsch (1983)]. An activity is treated as a unit of behavior. An activity differs from a process because an activity is goal directed, whereas a process need not be. Thus in this terminology one can describe a process as a series of steps A, B, C, and D; the process becomes an activity only when these steps are carried out to achieve some goal. More important, the goal, not the steps, defines the activity. For a process the steps are all there is. An activity can be quite large in conception, as the activity of becoming a doctor, or fairly limited, as the activity of placing a coin in a slot.

When viewed in this way, the study of memory involves not only a characterization of the processes of memorization but also an examination of the interaction between processes and goals and motives. Any explanation of mnemonic behavior must take into account not only what people do when memorizing and remembering but also why they do the things they do. Memorizing and remembering becomes not just a sequence of processes but the outcome of problem solving, where the goal of the problem could be, for instance, to memorize the meaning of various dials and levers of a control panel. At the heart of such an investigation is the distinction between voluntary and involuntary memory (Smirnov 1973). Voluntary memorizing occurs when the goal is to memorize. A child who tries to learn a poem for school is voluntarily memorizing the poem; the goal that defines this activity is the memorization itself. Involuntary memorization occurs when memorization is a consequence of some unrelated activity. People watch a movie without any intention of memorizing its plot, but they can recall it even months later, often in great detail. The goal is to understand the movie, but, in realizing this goal, the movie viewer also memorizes the plot.

The activity of mastering a job, as when one learns the meaning of the levers and meters of a control panel, can involve either voluntary or involuntary memorizing. It depends on how the training proceeds. The trainer could explicitly tell people to memorize and remember the function of the levers and meters. On the other hand, the trainer could involve the trainees in a task that requires them to build on their understanding of the meaning of the levers and meters. In the first case the goal is to memorize the information, and as such it involves voluntary memorizing. In the second case the goal is to accomplish the task, which may involve treating the meters and levels meaningfully. This meaningful interaction may facilitate memory.

Little of what people remember is a function of voluntary memorization. Most memories are involuntarily memorized. Nevertheless, because voluntary memorization involves intentionally determined use of memory strategies, it is probably the best place to start looking if one is interested in what one can do to improve memory.

6.3   Strategies for Voluntary Memorization

Classical Mnemonics

The mnemonics taught in courses or books on memory improvement can be quite effective. Most of them can be traced back to the early Greeks, and the most effective take advantage of all three factors for good memory: (1) organization, (2) imagery, and (3) retrieval cues. Consider the method of loci. As Kosslyn points out (chapter 7 of this volume), this memory technique dates back to the ancient Greeks and the work of Simonides, the Greek orator. You can easily apply the method. Imagine a path that you often walk along. In order to re-member a long list of words, mentally walk along the path and place an image of each object described by the to-be-remembered words at different locations on the path. The number of objects that you can place is limited to the number of distinct locations. In order to remem-ber the list, start at the beginning of the path and, again, mentally walk along the path, examining each location for the object that was placed there. Most people can remember hundreds of words quite accurately using the method of loci.

In applying the method of loci, one relates the to-be-remembered object with a previously acquired object (the place on the path), forms an interactive image between the two, and then uses the walk to supply the retrieval cue (the path place). Although it quite powerfully and succinctly uses basic principles of good memory, its application is quite limited. Quintilian (1922), the Roman rhetorician, made this point about 2,000 years ago. It is still not fully appreciated today. The method of loci and many related mnemonics are good for memorizing discrete pieces of information that are easily imageable. But most things that we have to memorize do not come in discrete chunks, and in many instances they are not easily imageable.

Consider the control panel again. It is not clear how one would apply the method of loci or other related mnemonics to the task of memorizing the meaning of the levers and meters. What do you place in what location? What interactive image do you form? Can you really form an image of the function of a lever? To be sure, it may be possible to use some image or place mnemonic for the control panel, but it would be neither a straightforward nor even an effective application.

If the method of loci, or place mnemonics, are ineffective in many learning situations, can we turn to the more general principles and revise them to apply to the specific situation?

Organizing and Searching for Meaning
Bartlett (1932) argued that memorizing is an effort after meaning. If you want to memorize something, then understand it. This basic principle has been played out in psychology along three different lines: organization, elaboration, and discrimination.

Organization The role of organization in memory was intensely explored by psychologists in the late 1970s (Bower 1970; Tulving and Donaldson 1972). Substantial research clearly established that the more connections one can form between to-be-remembered information, the better one can remember the information. When shown a list of words such as "cat, carrot, dog, potato, squirrel, fish," many people organize the words into categories and subsequently recall the list as "cat, dog, squirrel, fish, pea, carrot, potato." Such reorganization can dramatically improve recall. Interestingly young children do not spontaneously reorganize categorizable lists (Moely et al. 1969), nor do some adults without a Western education, such as those in traditional cultures of Africa (Cole and Scribner 1974). Nevertheless, if forced to categorize, the children and traditional Africans show the same benefits as those who spontaneously categorize. Clearly categorization is not something that everyone does spontaneously, but it is effective if applied.

Skills of organization are not confined to categorization of word lists. Katona (1940), for example, offered numerous examples of the effect of organization on memory for more ecologically valid material. He used matchstick problems as his stimulus material. Subjects saw a configuration of matchsticks (as depicted in figure 6.2) and were asked to reduce the figure from five equal-size squares to four equal-

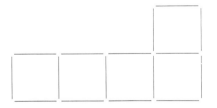

Figure 6.2
Matchstick problem from Katona (1940). The task is to make the five equal-size squares into four equal-size squares by moving only three matchsticks.

size squares by moving only three matches. They had to use all of the matches in their solution. Katona did one of three things: showed the subjects the solution, showed them the solution and explained the underlying principle, or let subjects discover the solution themselves. Katona reasoned that once the principles of solution were understood, the steps one must carry out would not seem unrelated but connected. Consequently subjects who discovered the solution themselves or were told the principles underlying it were better able to organize it than those who were simply told the sequence of steps necessary for solution. Even when Katona controlled for exposure time, he found that the solution was better recalled if it were better organized.

Organization imposes structure on what first appears to be unrelated or disorganized. The range of skills of organizing is quite large (Bower 1972b). Nonsense material can often be grouped in meaningful chunks, as when ICBMATTYMCA is restructured to ICBM ATT YMCA. Even when the material resists semantic grouping, it can still be grouped according to a rhythmic scheme, as is done in the singsong recitation of the alphabet: ABCD EFG HIJK LMNOP QRS TUV WX YZ. Surprisingly, even when there is no apparent way to group and structure a list of material, people seem to find a means. If people are asked to memorize and remember the same list over and over again, the order in which the words are remembered will remain constant across trials, even when the order of presentation differs from trial to trial. The degree of preserved order is called subjective organization, and several researchers have found a strong correlation between the degree of subjective organization and memory (Tulving 1962).

Although organization is usually discussed in the context of verbal stimuli, organizational effects can also be found for nonverbal material. Frost (1972) has shown organizational effects for a set of pictures. She designed material that could be organized along both semantic and visual dimensions. Some items could be organized along semantic dimensions alone; others along visual dimensions alone; and others along both visual and semantic dimensions, such as a picture of a belt and a picture of a shoestring. Frost examined free recall of the objects. When subjects were expecting a recognition test, they combined visual and semantic categories. Interestingly, when subjects were expecting a recall test, they only combined semantic categories.

Elaboration   Organization often refers to the discovery of relations between to-be-remembered items, but it also helps to relate to-be-remembered material to what is already known. The distinction between organization and what I call elaboration is not sharp. Indeed, organizing and elaborating often occur in tandem. The studies with chess masters dramatically demonstrate the importance of elaborating the to-be-remembered material on the basis of well-established knowledge, but the principle can be applied to almost any situation. In discussing this principle, researchers often invoke the concept of *schema* [for example, Bartlett (1932) and Rumelhart and Ortony (1977)]. A schema is a general term referring to the internal representation of an organized body of knowledge. There is no wide agreement on how this knowledge is represented. Schank and Abelson (1977) have suggested that schemata are best represented as scripts, procedural knowledge that is tied together by a small set of contingency relations. Scripts generally contain prescriptions for how to act in different contexts. Schank offers as an example of a script what adults know about ordering in a restaurant. Table 6.1 illustrates in the form of a database for a computer program the kind of information that Schank claims is in restaurant scripts. The information in a script is rather general. It does not specify what a person orders; rather it indicates the kinds of things one might do when ordering, depending on the situation.

The concepts of script and schema specify more exactly psychologists' long-held belief that knowledge is a set of associated concepts and that new material is learned by building associations to the extant network of associated concepts. Rumelhart and Ortony (1977) updated this idea in terms of schemata. They suggested that people represent an event in memory by recoding the schema with the details filled in. The schema, then, is like a format statement in a computer program, with general variables that can be filled in by the specifics of experiences. This process of filling in the details has a dual function. Not only is the incomplete schema completed, but also connections among disparate elements of the to-be-remembered event might be discovered in the schema. When a connection can be made, the material is more memorable than when a preexisting schema cannot supply the needed connections. For example, the sentence, "The check bounced because Sally forgot to go to the bank," is more memorable than, "The note was sour because the seam was split." People make the necessary connection in the first sentence based on their experience with banks, but nothing they know about music and sewing invites the appropriate inference in the second sentence. The second sentence becomes memorable once the connection can be made (Bransford and Johnson 1973). Only a little more information is needed—in this case, that the sentence was uttered at

Table 6.1
An example of a script: Going to a restaurant
_____

Open door
Enter
Give reservation name
Wait to be seated
Go to table

Be seated
Order drinks
Put napkins on lap

Look at menu
Discuss menu

Order meal
Talk
Drink water
Eat salad or soup
Meal arrives

Eat food
Finish meal
Order dessert
Eat dessert
Ask for bill
Bill arrives

Pay bill
Leave tip
Get coats

Leave
_____
Source: Schank and Abelson (1977).

a bagpipe contest. People will try to elaborate on what is given, but enough must be given in the first place. So much of what is hard to memorize and remember is simply incomprehensible. If the material can be made comprehensible, the memory difficulties disappear.

Unlike many organizational skills the ability to elaborate does not seem to depend crucially on either education or age. To be sure, the older you are or the more educated you are, the more complex and elaborate your schemata. Presumably these developed schemata will lead to more elaboration, but spontaneous elaboration seems to be a natural course of events. I discuss this in more detail in section 6.4. I simply note here that children appear to use schemata when they recall an event (Nelson 1986), as do people in more traditional cultures (Cole and Scribner 1974).

Figure 6.3
Discriminant chess positions.

Discrimination   Although people can memorize an event by integrating it into their generalized knowledge or schemata, forming connections that they might not have discovered without the guidance of the schemata, they can go too far. Although it helps to memorize a de Kooning painting by relating it to another well-known de Kooning, it is also possible that the two de Koonings might end up getting confused. Such confusions are at the heart of interference theories of memory.

In order to avoid confusions among memories, people can try to make separate memories discriminable. For instance, if the first word list consists of animal words and the second list consists of plant words, then interference between the two lists could be eliminated by discriminating the two lists along these lines.

Exactly how one discriminates similar events is also determined in part by one's generalized knowledge or schemata. Consider figure 6.3. If I ask you to study this array of chess positions and later ask you to reproduce only the positions on the right, the chances are that some of the positions on the left would end up in your recall protocol—that is, unless you are an expert chess player. If you are, you would notice that the positions on the right favor the black player, the positions on the left favor the white player.

Imagery

The importance of imagery in facilitating memory has been recognized since the early Greeks, and, except for a brief rebellion of a school of rhetoricians called the Ramists, imagery has always figured prominently in any course or book on improving memory. For example, the place system advanced by Simonides under the guise of the method of loci has always proved fashionable, although the details have changed frequently (Yates 1966). Metrodorus in A.D. 100, Romberch in 1520, and Bruno in 1580 used the zodiac to anchor the interactive images instead of a geographic path. Camillio and Fludd, both well-known Renaissance humanists, built their loci around theaters, Solomon's House of Wisdom and the Globe Theatre, respectively. Matteo Ricci (Spence 1984) went to China in the sixteenth century armed with the power of mnemonics and the place system. He felt that these "tricks" possessed a power that would prove decisive in his Christian conquest of the Orient.

Of course, we do not see such mystical qualities in mnemonics today. They are just tricks, but tricks that continue to fascinate. Bower (1972a) gives the place system a modern version when discussing the peg word system. A person first learns the peg words—one–bun, two–shoe, three–tree, etc. The subject then uses the second word in the pair as imaginal pegs on which to hook the to-be-remembered items. Thus the subject can easily learn a list of words, such as cigar, carrot, shoe, etc., by first imaging a bun smoking a cigar, a carrot in a shoe, and so on. On recall, the subject would repeat the poem, and for each object, such as bun, the subject would evoke the interactive image and hence the to-be-remembered object.

As I have already noted, the use of place systems may be limited to learning and remembering discrete lists. However, this limitation does not apply to imagery in general; the use of imagery as a mnemonic aid is not limited to such elaborate and deliberate systems. The church steeple, the cross, and the American flag are images that evoke strong associations and remembrances. They remind people of God, the death of Christ, and the sovereignty of the United States. They are intentionally introduced into the social structure to act as reminders. One reason for the differences in the Catholic and Protestant crucifixes—Jesus hangs from the Catholic crucifix; the Protestant cross is empty—is that the Catholic Church wants to remind her followers of the sacrifice of Jesus, whereas the Protestant Church wants to emphasize His resurrection. The use of these symbolic images is widespread and a hallmark of any advanced civilization.

The exact reason why imagery is so well remembered is unclear at present but clearly has something to do with its visual nature (Paivio

1971). People can accurately recognize literally thousands of pictures to which they were only briefly exposed (Standing et al. 1970). Their memory for concrete words is better than that for abstract words (Paivio 1971), presumably because they can image the concrete words and, more to the point, because they can remember words better if they visualize their referents during memorization (Paivio and Csapo 1973).

People, of course, vary in the "vividness" of their images (Betts 1909). Do vivid imagers show an advantage over bad imagers for, say, memory for concrete words? Several scales have been developed to group people into good and bad imagers (Betts 1909; Sheehan 1967). Using these scales, many researchers have shown that the difference between performance on a visual recognition test and a verbal recognition test is greater for strong imagers than for weak imagers (Stewart 1965), although some of these results have proved hard to replicate (Kosslyn, personal communication). This differential facilitation could be attributed directly to the vividness of the images of strong imagers, but other explanations are possible. Strong imagers may simply use imagery more often when memorizing. In addition, vividness of an image could be confounded with the organization inherent in it (Neisser 1967). By employing an image, a strong imager might be imputing more organization to the material than it would have had in its verbal form.

Building Retrieval Cues
As Tulving argued, memories can be available but not accessible (Tulving and Pearlstone 1966). That is, a trace may rest somewhere in memory but cannot be successfully retrieved. Clearly it is not enough to memorize something so that it is stored away. One must also memorize it so that one can effectively retrieve it. When trying to remember, one usually has various cues present. The cues may be supplied by the memory probe. A free recall probe—"Remember the list that you studied five minutes ago in this room?"—can supply spatiotemporal cues about to-be-remembered objects. Other retrieval cues tell the subject something about the semantic or physical nature of the to-be-remembered object. The subject might be told to recall the name of the animal that has stripes or the number of guns on a cruiser or the airplane manufacturer that rhymes with "going." In most cases semantic cues are more effective than rhyming cues or spatiotemporal cues. There are exceptions, however. These exceptions generally arise because the effectiveness of a cue depends in part on the way in which the to-be-remembered material was originally memorized.

In a series of experiments Tulving and Thomson (1973) demonstrated this "principle of encoding specificity" in the context of paired
associate learning. Subjects were asked to memorize pairs in which
the first item in the pair was weakly associated with the second item,
for example, cane–chair. They were then probed with a strong associate, for instance, table. The general finding was that this strong
associate was not an effective cue for the recall of the second item
when the second item was encoded in the context of the weak associate. The effectiveness of a cue, it seemed, depended on the nature
of the encoding.

If memories are to be accessible, then, one must study them with
the recall demands in mind. If one anticipates getting acoustic cues,
then one should concentrate on encoding the to-be-remembered material acoustically. Alternatively, if one anticipates weak associates as
cues, one should have these in mind when memorizing (Morris et al.
1977). Of course, one cannot always anticipate the exact circumstances in which one will be asked to recall the to-be-remembered
information. In these instances, it is probably best to encode the
material along as many dimensions as possible.

Applying These Principles
Clearly these more general principles can be easily applied to the task
of learning the function of the meters and levels of a control panel
than can mnemonics such as the method of loci, which are clever but
structured. For instance, instead of taking each lever and meter separately and learning its function, as if learning a paired associate, one
could try to relate each part to the others and the function of each to
the main function of the panel itself. One could, for instance, note
that two levers control the volume of water and one meter indicates
the present volume of water. Then by relating the levers with the
meter and organizing the three into a chunk, one could remember all
three as easily as one. Or one might note that one lever controls the
inflow of water into a tank and another controls the outflow and
relate these two levers. One might also note that the panel is designed to control the temperature of hot gas flowing through pipes in
the water tank, and consequently the level of water and its inflow and
outflow is important to this main function. Once realizing this, one
might want to relate the meter and the two levers to another meter
indicating the temperature of the gas in the pipe.

In addition to relating meters and levers on a functional level, one
can also try to relate function to the spatial location. One might note,
for instance, that the two water control levers are below the water
meter, or that the two water control levers are closer to each other

than they are to any other levers. In a similar fashion one might note the shape of the levers and meters to see if they can provide any clue to their function. And of course one would look for any labels.

In any complex control panel it is important to see not only how levers and meters relate to each other but also how to discriminate their functions. To some extent, paying attention to shape and physical location is as much of an attempt to discriminate functions as it is to relate function to physical attributes.

Finally, some investigators of learning would suggest that one can play on the visual quality of the control panel. One can imagine using the two water control levers together while looking at the meter with the mind's eye, thus forming an image of their functions. The success of such mental practice has never been convincingly demonstrated, however.

To some extent, many intelligent people intuitively try to memorize the function of the levers and meters in just the way described. So what is gained by knowing about general principles for improving memory? The advantage is that, once one understands how a good memorizer memorizes and remembers, one can then try to teach others. It may not be enough to tell learners what the meters and levers do. Rather, one might have the learners discover relations and note physical relations through various well-controlled exercises. At this point the task may no longer be to memorize but to discover relations, discriminate, and image. Nevertheless, the end result is the same—the functions of the meters and levers are learned.

Motivation and Strategies
One must be motivated to memorize something in order to do so voluntarily. The question arises, Does motivation per se contribute to successful learning, or does motivation affect memory only indirectly by affecting the extent to which a person applies mnemonic strategies? Loftus (1972) was able to dissociate these two factors in an experiment on picture memory. Subjects studied a complex picture while their eye movements were monitored. Different groups of subjects received different payoffs for successfully remembering the picture. Loftus found that successful memory for the picture was positively correlated with the number of eye fixations and that, the higher the payoff, the more eye fixations. Fortunately the number of fixations varied widely from individual to individual. Consequently Loftus was able to find subjects with the same number of eye fixations but different payoffs as well as subjects with the same payoffs but a different number of eye fixations. He found that payoff per se was not predictive of memory performance. The number of fixations was. The

payoff could increase the number of fixations, but it was the fixations, not the payoff, that were responsible for the better memory.

Thus it appears that motivation is an important factor in successful voluntary memorization, but only indirectly. What about people's beliefs about their ability to memorize and remember? Presumably people who believe that their memory capacity is small will try harder and apply more strategies, whereas people who believe that their memory capacity is superior will not make as great an effort. Issues concerning perceived memory abilities are of three kinds: (1) Are individuals' evaluations of their memory ability reliable? (2) Can individuals predict what kind of material is hard or easy for them to memorize and remember? (3) Do people know whether they can successfully recall something if they continually try to retrieve it, or is the feeling of knowing that you know unreliable?

First, beliefs about memory abilities are by and large not reliable. A number of memory questionnaires about memory beliefs have been developed. In them, subjects are asked to rate how frequently they forget different kinds of information and to respond to questions about their style of learning. For instance, Broadbent et al. (1982) in their Cognitive Failure Questionnaire asked subjects how often they forgot people's names or had things on the "tip of their tongue." In general, they assessed absentmindedness, memory for appointments, conversations, errands, and directions, tip-of-the-tongue experiences, and ability to learn. In another questionnaire Hermann and Neisser (1978) assessed the frequency of forgetting and clarity of remembering. For instance, they asked subjects to indicate how often they forgot a person's name after just meeting him or her or how well they remembered their childhood toys. [See Hermann (1982) for a review of other questionnaires probing beliefs about memory abilities.]

Although people had no trouble answering these questionnaires, their judgments by and large did not correlate with a range of standard tests of memory. Broadbent et al. (1982) examined the relation between Cognitive Failure Questionnaire scores and immediate memory for visually or acoustically presented items, size of acoustic suffix effect, size of articulatory suppression, ability to identify degraded words, long-term recall of categorized words, and delayed recall. No significant correlations were found. Schlechter and Hermann (1981) used a more ecologically valid measure of memory and sought a correlation between scores on a shortened version of the Hermann-Neisser Inventory of Memory Experience and memory for past events recorded in a diary without success. Interestingly both Hermann (Chaffin et al. 1980) and Broadbent et al. (1982) found that judgments about one's spouse's memory abilities correlated with the spouse's judgments, although Chaffin et al. found that the correlation was stronger for a wife's judgment of her husband's ability than the husband's judgment of his wife's ability.

These studies and others indicate that you cannot by and large trust people's judgments about their memories. People who say that they have a good memory do not necessarily have a good memory, whereas people who confess to a bad memory do not necessarily have a bad memory. Although people's beliefs about their memory abilities are not believable, they act as if they are. Both Broadbent and Hermann found that, whereas there was no correlation between the ratings people gave their memory ability in the two questionnaires and how well they did on a set of standard tests of memory, there was a strong correlation between their ratings and how much money they were willing to bet on their performance on the standard tests.

People's ability to predict what is easy or hard to remember is much more reliable. In an interview with young children Kreutzer et al. (1975) found that even 5- and 6-year-olds know that it is easier to remember the words embedded in story than the same words in a list without any structure, that it is easier to remember the gist of a story than to remember it verbatim, that it is easier to relearn something than to learn it, and that it is easier to remember a categorized list than an uncategorized list. Other interviewers have found that people can accurately state that pictures are easier to remember than words. Moreover, people can accurately predict what they find hard to remember, such as names. Thus, although people may not have a good assessment of their own memory ability, they know what is easy and hard for them to remember.

Finally, people can also accurately predict when they are going to remember something. People often experience tip-of-the-tongue phenomena. They know that they know it and can sometimes even tell you things about it but can nevertheless not quite access it. Their predictions about eventual success, if they continue to try, are better than chance. In experiments on "knowing that you know," people are taught new facts and then are asked to recall them. When they fail to recall the necessary information, they can nevertheless accurately predict whether they could recognize it (Hart 1967; Nelson and Narens 1980).

Thus to some extent our beliefs about what kinds of things we can remember are accurate. Although there are no studies on this, it is reasonable to think that these beliefs may govern the strategies that we apply. If we think something will be hard to remember, we may try harder when memorizing it. If we think it will be easy to remember, we may give it short shrift. The irony is that, even if we do compensate in this manner, our original beliefs still seem to obtain.

6.4   Involuntary Memory

Of course one does not have to make the memorization of the control panel a goal. Rather one could devise goals that involve an activity that inadvertently leads to memorization. Often there is no intent to remember, yet memorization occurs. The processing of reading forces a reader to understand text, and this meaningful processing reinforces memory (Bransford and Johnson 1973). A reader usually tries to relate and organize disparate elements in a text when reading. The reader does not undertake such actions in order to memorize the passage, although just such actions make it more memorable. Rather, the reader organizes the text because he or she wants to do a good job reading it. When voluntarily memorizing something, one tries to do something with the experience so that it becomes memorable. In involuntary memorization the overarching activity, such as reading or viewing a movie, is constituted so that the experience is changed into a more memorable form in the process of carrying out the activity.

Intention or Actions

Of course, if involuntary memorization is to be determined solely by the actions undertaken to achieve the non-memory-related goal, the intent to memorize must have little or no effect on the successful memory. Intent may be important in getting one to apply certain strategies designed to improve memory, but, the claim would be, if these same strategies are applied without the intent to memorize, presumably under another cover task, they should be equally effective.

The evidence suggests that memory is not a matter of intention but of action. First, consider the work on the levels-of-processing approach to memory (for example, Craik and Tulving 1975). Proponents of this approach argue that the extent to which an experience is retained depends on the depth at which it is processed; that is, memory is a matter of what one does when memorizing. Most experimental support of this claim involves orienting tasks. Subjects are asked to make judgments about stimuli, usually words. The judgments, or orienting tasks, require different levels of processing. For instance, subjects might be asked to count the number of e's in a word, indicate whether a word rhymes with "jat," or indicate whether the word is an example of an animal. The first task requires shallow processing, the second task deeper processing, the third task, even deeper processing. In some cases subjects are not told that their memory for the stimuli will be tested; rather, they are led to believe that the experiment revolves around the different orienting tasks. The experiment is usually designed so that the orienting task is first given to the subject, the stimulus is then flashed on a screen, subjects make their judgment, and then another orienting task is stated, another stimulus item flashed, etc. A surprise memory test follows this presentation phase. The interval between presentation and test varies across experiments, as does the form of the memory test.

The results of such experiments are quite robust. Subjects remember the items that were processed along the lines of the "deeper" orienting task better than those that were processed along the lines of the more shallow orienting tasks (Craik and Tulving 1975). It does not matter whether the stimuli are visual or verbal (Bower and Karlin 1974), whether the delay between presentation and test is one minute, an hour, or days (Craik and Tulving 1975), or whether the memory test involves recall or recognition (Craik and Tulving 1975).

It also does not matter whether or not subjects are told to remember the stimuli. For instance, Craik and Tulving (1975) contrasted intentional and incidental learning with fast presentation rates, thereby giving subjects little chance to do much more than what the orienting task demanded. They found that what subjects did to the words determined how well they recognized them. The subject's intentions during presentation had no effect.

Bower (1972a) reported an interesting nonverbal analogy to Craik and Tulving. It involves the use of interactive images, not the levels-of-processing effect. Subjects were presented with word pairs, told to form an interactive image based on each pair, and then asked to rate the vividness of their image. Half of the subjects were told that the experiment concerned imagery; the other half were told that they would be tested on their memory for the word pairs. In the test they were asked to recall the second item in the pair after being told the first. Subjects' memory did not depend on the instruction.

Involuntary Memorization and Memory for Levers and Meters
These experiments suggest that, if a trainer could get a person involved with a control panel in such a way that he or she related one lever to another and levers to meters, then memory might be as effective as if that person were given the explicit task of memorizing the function of the levers and meters. The trainer could, of course, just ask someone to use the control panel and continue to instruct the individual on its use until the learner could manipulate it easily. At

this point the function of the levers and meters would be memorized. Although some individuals may intentionally memorize the functions under these conditions, others will probably just continue to try to get the control panel to work and in the process notice relations that will facilitate their memory for the functions. Although this method would probably be more effective as a memory exercise than one involving strict memorization, the trainer could be more directive. A goal of any training procedure, for instance, could be to set subgoals involving the use of the control panel that also facilitates memory for the levers' and meters' functions.

As I have already mentioned, the trainer could explicitly ask learners or trainees to find relations among levers and meters, thereby making the goal the application of principles of organization, elaboration, and discrimination rather than memorization per se. However, it is better to have people discover the organization themselves. Katona (1940), in his experiments with matchstick problems, found that the solution was remembered best when subjects discovered it themselves. And recent experiments, under the label "the generation effect," have shown that elaboration of a word list is a more effective mnemonic if the elaboration is subject generated rather than provided by the experimenter (Slamecka and Graf 1978). The question then is, What cover tasks could the trainer give trainees so that they generate the elaboration, organization, and discrimination essential to the successful memorization of the functions of the levers and meters without pointing out the relations among levers and meters.

Most training procedures involve a series of progressive steps that allow a person to master one subskill after another until the whole can be put together out of well-practiced fragments. Anyone developing a training procedure must reverse the process and decide how to break the whole into fragments. This fragmentation could be done with memory in mind. For instance, the trainer could have trainees first learn to use the lever to govern the inflow of water, then the lever to govern the outflow, and finally to use both levers simultaneously, thereby regulating the level of water. The important point would be to make sure that trainees are aware of the function of the two levers and then, through the task of controlling the level of the water, become aware of the close proximity of the two levers. This progression, ideally done step by step, would be aimed at teaching trainees to control the level of water. Each part of the lesson would build on the next. More important, the relation between the two levers would not be obscured by other tasks. Consequently, the kind of organizational structure important to memory could be built up by the trainees' own observations.

The same point can be made when considering the water meter. It will surely help trainees to remember the function of the water meter if they note that it is above the levers that control the water level. This relation could be highlighted by asking trainees to note the numerical change in water level after adjusting it with the now-known water levers. Alternatively, the trainer could ask trainees to monitor the water meter and keep the water at a steady level. In both cases trainees will find themselves looking back and forth between levers and meters. The geographic relation between the two should become apparent.

6.5   Designing and Memory

The trainer does not have to wait helplessly for trainees to discover the relations among levers and meters that will facilitate memory. Barring actually telling them, the trainer or a human factors engineer can design the control panel, or any other stimulus material, so that the important relations are apparent. The trainer or human factors engineer can, for instance, group similar controls for similar functions together. I essentially did this in figure 6.1 when I placed the water levers and meters together as a group and physically separated them from other levers and meters. The trainer could also color-code items. The meters and levers concerning water could be aquamarine, and the meters concerning the temperature in the piped gas could be red. The advantage of coloring is, of course, twofold: First, the color heightens the functional grouping along a dimension that physical spacing does not; second, the color has mnemonic value—water is aquamarine and temperatures are often red hot.

Greater subtleties, however, are possible. Urban planners have thought intensely about the mnemonic implications of city planning, and the design principles that they have learned can be applied to other domains (Downs and Stea 1973). As any traveler knows, some cities are easier to learn than others. In some, one constantly gets lost; in others, one finds that one can navigate without a map within a few days. To a large extent the memorability of a city depends on the degree to which one can organize it and form an "image of the city," to use Lynch's (1960) phrase. This image can be better formed if there are landmarks that anchor a district and if the district has discrete boundaries. Landmarks can be important buildings or historical sites. Rockefeller Center acts as a landmark that anchors a good deal of midtown Manhattan. One's cognitive representation of the area seems to build on Rockefeller Center, and one locates other buildings and streets in relation to Rockefeller Center. It is much more difficult to form an image of the city without these landmarks.

These principles should apply to any spatial array, including a control panel. I have already emphasized the importance of grouping meters and levers with different functions into different physical locations. These groups, however, would be more memorable if there was a single landmark on which to anchor all the other meters and levers. The landmark could be a frequently used lever or an important one, for instance, a button that shuts down the water supply or perhaps just a large and distinctive lever or meter. The water meter, for instance, could be large, bright blue, and oddly shaped. Such design features should not only make it distinctive but could let it serve as the landmark for the rest of the "water group."

One caveat. Most of the discussion up to this point has assumed that the trainees have had little or no experience with the control panel or whatever it is they must memorize. When there is prior experience, the problems of designing both the material and the curriculum become much more difficult because the structure imposed by the curriculum or design may conflict with the internal structure of the to-be-remembered material built up by prior experience. To some extent, when the same past experience is shared by a large number of trainees, the past experience can be taken into account. In other instances, where past experience varies or is unknown, the choice of design and curriculum becomes more difficult and may require substantial pretesting.

6.6   Concluding Considerations

I have tried to emphasize that memory is an active process and that good, effective, and efficient memorizing and remembering involves the careful use of strategies. Yet I have also emphasized that people do not have to apply these strategies with the intention of memorizing the information. Rather a nonmnemonic task can be devised so that the strategies must be applied to meet its nonmnemonic goal.

As a consequence, mnemonic concerns must figure in all levels of design—both in curriculum and the actual design of the to-be-remembered material. In designing curricula, one usually breaks the main task, say, using a control panel, into subtasks. The way that these tasks are broken down usually reflects a componential analysis of the processes necessary to complete the task successfully. Although such considerations are paramount, the mnemonic demands of learning the task should also be factored into curriculum design. Too often the assumption is that people will somehow memorize the material. This assumption may be true, if you give the learners enough time and make it essential that they try to memorize the material. Nevertheless the artful design of instructions could make memorization a consequence of various exercises rather than an exercise itself.

The same warning can be offered in terms of designing job-related material, such as a control panel. Although memory demands occasionally figure in design—hot water faucets, after all, are always on the left—they are rarely a central design consideration. One could prevent many of the problems encountered in teaching someone how to use the panel and learning the function of the various levers and meters if one designed the panel so that it is easily remembered.

If you want to improve people's memories, then, don't just tell them to organize or image or do whatever is necessary to remember. Take the burden away from the individual and give it to the instructor and the designer. Get them to involve the individual with the to-be-remembered material in ways that facilitate memory but do not create memorization as a goal.

Although I have concentrated narrowly on learning the function of a relatively simple control panel, this conclusion has great generality. Consider, for instance, learning simple declarative facts. One way would be to present the facts over and over again until they are learned. Crawford and Hollan (1983) have developed the Computer-Based Memorization System (CBMS) in order to teach students of tactics a large body of tactical data about the Soviet navy. Although the computer system has the advantage of being quite modular, some of the "actual" games that the students are involved in are really just simple memory exercises. For instance, one game is oriented toward silhouette recognition. Students are required to recognize the silhouette presented on a screen. If they are unable, then hints, providing specific information about the silhouette, can be provided. The game is transparently a memory exercise.

Is this the best way to get someone to memorize a large body of data? When Smirnov and Zinchenko (1969) asked children to remember a list of grocery items, they found that they fared quite poorly. But when they asked them to go to the grocery store and read them a list of grocery items, they had no problem reproducing the list. Could the fact-learning exercise in the CBMS game be embedded in a larger activity that might be more engaging? Why not play a tactical game in which battles occur? Silhouette recognition would, of course, be essential to the successful play of the game. But the main goal and activity would not be to recognize the silhouette correctly. It would be to win the battle. Although the studies have not been done, I suspect that the silhouettes would be more efficiently learned in the tactical game than in the Crawford and Hollan silhouette recognition game.

Acknowledgments

I gratefully acknowledge the partial support of the National Institutes of Health under grant NS17776. I also thank Peter Garrard, Edward Levine, Jennifer Brunn, Steve Kosslyn, and Marta Kutas for their helpful comments.

References

Bartlett, F. C. 1932. *Remembering*. Cambridge: Cambridge University Press.

Betts, G. H. 1909. *The Distribution and Functions of Mental Imagery*. New York: Teacher's College, Columbia University.

Bower, G. H. 1970. "Organizational factors in memory." *Cognitive Psychology* 1:18–46.

Bower, G. H. 1972a. "Mental imagery and associative learning," in *Cognition in Learning and Memory*, L. W. Gregg, ed. New York: Wiley, 51–88.

Bower, G. H. 1972b. "Organizational processes and free recall," in *Organization of Memory*, E. Tulving and W. Donaldson, eds. New York: Academic Press, 93–145.

Bower, G. H., and M. B. Karlin. 1974. "Depth of processing pictures of faces and recognition memory." *Journal of Experimental Psychology* 103:751–757.

Bransford, J. D., and M. K. Johnson. 1973. "Consideration of some problems of comprehension," in *Visual Information Processing*, W. Chase, ed. New York: Academic Press, 383–438.

Broadbent, D. E., P. F. Cooper, P. Fitzgerald, and K. R. Parkes. 1982. "The Cognitive Failures Questionnaire (CFQ) and its correlates." *British Journal of Clinical Psychology* 21:1–16.

Chaffin, R., K. Deffenbacher, and D. J. Hermann. 1980. "Awareness and lack of awareness of memory function between spouses." Available from Roger Chaffin, Trenton State College, Trenton, New Jersey 08625.

Chase, W. G., and H. A. Simon. 1973. "The mind's eye in chess," in *Visual Information Processing*, W. G. Chase, ed. New York: Academic Press, 215–281.

Cole, M., and S. Scribner. 1974. *Culture and Thought*. New York: Wiley.

Craik, F. I. M., and E. Tulving. 1975. "Depth of processing and the retention of words in episodic memory." *Journal of Experimental Psychology: General* 104:268–294.

Crawford, A. M., and J. D. Hollan. 1983. *Development of a Computer-Based Training System*. Special Report NPRDC-SR-83-13. San Diego, Calif.: Navy Personnel Research and Development Center.

DeGroot, A. 1965. *Thought and Choice in Chess*. The Hague: Mouton.

Downs, R. M., and D. Stea, eds. 1973. *Image and Environment*. Chicago, Ill.: Aldine.

Frost, N. 1972. "Encoding and retrieval of visual memory tasks." *Journal of Experimental Psychology* 95:317–326.

Hart, J. T. 1967. "Memory and the memory-monitoring process." *Journal of Verbal Learning and Verbal Behavior* 6:685–691.

Hermann, D. J. 1982. "Know thy memory: The use of questionnaires to assess and study memory." *Psychological Bulletin* 92:434–452.

Hermann, D., and U. Neisser. 1978. "An inventory of everyday memory experiences," in *Practical Aspects of Memory*, M. M. Gruneberg, P. E. Morris, and R. N. Sykes, eds. New York: Academic Press.

Hirst, W. 1980. "Memory for recipes." Available from W. Hirst, Department of Psychology, 65 Fifth Ave., The New School for Social Research, New York, NY 10003.

Hirst, W., and E. Levine. 1985. "Ecological memory reconsidered." *Journal of Experimental Psychology: General* 114:269–271.

Katona, G. 1940. *Organizing and Memorizing.* New York: Columbia University Press.

Kreutzer, M. A., L. Leonard, and J. H. Flavell. 1975. *An Interview Study of Children's Knowledge about Memory.* Monographs for the Society of Child Development, ser. 159, 40(1).

Levine, E. 1980. "Cognitive maps, imagery, and memory for street directions." Ph.D. dissertation. Graduate Faculty of the New School for Social Research, New York.

Loftus, G. 1972. "Eye fixations and recognition memory for pictures." *Cognitive Psychology* 3:525–551.

Lynch, K. 1960. *Image of the City.* Cambridge, Mass.: MIT Press.

Moely, B. E., F. A. Olson, T. G. Halwes, and J. H. Flavell. 1969. "Production deficiency in young children's clustered recall." *Developmental Psychology* 1:26–34.

Morris, C. D., J. D. Bransford, and J. J. Franks. 1977. "Levels of processing versus transfer appropriate processing." *Journal of Verbal Learning and Verbal Behavior* 16: 519–533.

Neisser, U. 1967. *Cognitive Psychology.* New York: Appleton.

Nelson, K., ed. 1986. *Event Knowledge: Structure and Function in Development.* Hillsdale, N.J.: Erlbaum Associates.

Nelson, T. O., and L. Narens. 1980. "A new technique for investigating the feeling of knowing." *Acta Psychologia* 19:69–80.

Paivio, A. 1971. *Imagery and Verbal Processes.* New York: Holt, Rinehart, & Winston.

Paivio, A., and K. Csapo. 1973. "Picture superiority in free recall: Imaging or dual coding." *Cognitive Psychology* 5:176–206.

Quintilian, M. F. 1922. *Institutio Oratoria,* H. E. Butler, trans. New York: Putnam.

Rumelhart, D., and A. Ortony. 1977. "The representation of knowledge," in *Schooling and the Acquisition of Knowledge,* R. C. Anderson, R. J. Spiro, and W. E. Montague, eds. Hillsdale, N.J.: Erlbaum Associates, 99–136.

Schank, R., and R. Abelson. 1977. *Scripts, Plans, Goals, and Understanding.* New York: Wiley.

Schlechter, T. M., and D. J. Hermann. 1981. "Multimethod approach for investigating everyday memory." Paper presented at the meeting of the Eastern Psychological Association, April, New York.

Sheehan, P. W. 1967. "A shortened form of Betts' questionnaire upon mental imagery." *Journal of Clinical Psychology* 23:386–389.

Slamecka, N. J., and P. Graf. 1978. "The generation effect: Delineation of a phenomenon." *Journal of Experimental Psychology: Human Learning and Memory* 4:592–604.

Smirnov, A. A. 1973. *Problems in the Psychology of Memory.* New York: Plenum.

Smirnov, A. A., and P. I. Zinchenko. 1969. "Problems in the psychology of memory," in *A Handbook of Contemporary Soviet Psychology,* M. Cole and I. Maltzman, eds. New York: Basic Books, 452–502.

Spence, J. 1984. *The Memory Palace of Matteo Ricci.* New York: Viking.

Standing, L., J. Conezio, and R. N. Haber. 1970. "Perception and memory for pictures: Single-trial learning of 2560 visual stimuli." *Psychonomic Science* 18:89–90.

Stewart, J. C. 1965. "An experimental investigation of imagery." Ph.D. dissertation. Department of Psychology, University of Toronto.

Tulving, E. 1962. "Subjective organization in free recall of 'unrelated' words." *Psychological Review* 69:344–354.

Tulving, E. 1972. "Episodic and semantic memory," in *Organization of Memory,* E. Tulving and W. Donaldson, eds. New York: Academic Press, 381–403.

Tulving, E. 1983. *Elements of Episodic Memory.* New York: Oxford University Press.

Tulving, E., and W. Donaldson, eds. 1972. *Organization of Memory.* New York: Academic Press.

Tulving, E., and Z. Pearlstone. 1966. "Availability versus accessibility of information in memory for words." *Journal of Verbal Learning and Verbal Behavior* 5:381–391.

Tulving, E., and D. M. Thomson. 1973. "Encoding specificity and retrieval processes in episodic memory." *Psychological Review* 80:352–373.

Wagner, D. A. 1978. "Memories of Morocco: The influence of age, schooling, and environment on memory." *Cognitive Psychology* 10:1–28.

Wertsch, J. J. 1983. *The Concept of Activity in Soviet Psychology.* Chicago, Ill.: Sage.

Yates, F. A. 1966. *The Art of Memory.* Chicago, Ill.: University of Chicago Press.

7

Imagery in Learning

Stephen M. Kosslyn

There is a long history of the use of mental imagery in learning, which conveys one basic message: Imagery improves learning. Imagery can be used to help one remember a list, be it of objects (for example, a shopping list) or of abstract concepts (for example, points to make in a speech). Imagery can also help one learn to solve problems and to reason more effectively. These problems can be concrete (such as navigating a boat or assembling an engine) or abstract (say, reasoning about the relative amount of an abstract quantity).

Visual imagery was one of the first topics studied in scientific psychology, and the term initially referred to "seeing" with the mind's eye. More recently, the term has shifted to refer to a brain state that is accompanied by the experience of seeing in the absence of the appropriate sensory input. An image is taken to be a kind of mental "code" (often contrasted with a verbal code) that can be stored and manipulated in various ways.

The fact that imagery can be used to improve learning has been studied and applied in three waves of research. The first wave began with an accidental discovery by the ancient Greek bard Simonides, who stumbled on the use of imagery in memorizing lists. According to lore, Simonides was called away from a banquet right before the roof caved in, mangling all of the hapless dinner guests beyond recognition. Simonides discovered that he could remember who was present by forming an image of the table in his mind's eye, and mentally scanning around it, "seeing" who was seated in each chair. This insight led to the development of a technique the Greeks called the method of loci, which is a systematic way of improving one's memory by using imagery.

The method of loci requires one to learn a sequence of locations in a familiar place (for example, places in one's home seen as one walks along a particular route). After the locations are memorized, one can use them to fix in memory new information. In order to do so, when learning new material, one visualizes each to-be-remembered item sited at each of the memorized locations in turn. To remember the list, one later visualizes the locations and "mentally walks" from one place to another, "seeing" what is present at each location in the image. This technique is effective and improves memory at least twofold over many other methods [see Bower (1972), and Paivio (1971); for an extended discussion, see chapter 6 in this volume].

Many centuries later modern cognitive psychologists embarked on the second wave of research on imagery. These researchers studied the method of loci and related memory-improvement techniques and discovered a number of variables that affect how useful imagery is in learning (for example, that the degree of organization imposed among the items is critical). The focus of this work was on studying the ways in which different materials and instructions affect later memory.

In brief, the main discoveries were that imagery is useful in large part because it serves to integrate information into a single coherent structure. Thus the most effective images are those that serve to tie together two or more objects (having them interact in some way). In addition, it was found that imagery aids memory when it is used in conjunction with verbal coding, providing a second way to remember a fact. Furthermore, it was found that images are memorized more easily than words; indeed, if individual words are learned to the same degree as individual images (which requires more trials), they can be recalled as well as images [see Kosslyn (1980) for a review of this literature].

The second wave of research on imagery came to a peak in the early 1970s, primarily in the work of Allan Paivio, Gordon Bower, and their students. The result of much research was the development of dual code theory. The idea here is that imagery is one kind of internal code, language another. Memory is best when one can use both kinds of codes. The drawback of this work is that it addresses how one can memorize a set of information, which is not the same as how one can master a body of knowledge. When one has truly acquired knowledge, as opposed to simply memorizing a set of facts, one can use it effectively to help learn other information and can apply it effortlessly in the appropriate situations. Mastering a body of knowledge allows one to perform complex tasks that draw on that knowledge, as opposed to simply regurgitating a memorized list.

In addition, a striking drawback of the imagery memorization systems developed in the 1970s is that they require effort to use. Indeed, it has been my experience that, although most people can easily learn to use imagery in memorization and are impressed by the effectiveness of the technique, they do not then use it spontaneously in the future.

The third wave of research on imagery approaches the topic from a different angle, and it is this approach that will be my central concern here. This work focuses on imagery as a vehicle for reasoning, a kind of internal representation that is operated on within an information processing system. This approach can now be used to determine which individuals will learn to use imagery effectively to perform specific types of tasks. Thus the focus here is on using imagery to learn to perform complex tasks, such as navigation, and not on simple memorization. This approach has the promise of teaching us to exploit the virtues of imagery most fully and to do so in a way that most people will find easy and natural, encouraging them to benefit from new techniques in their day-to-day lives. This new research has been part and parcel of the birth of cognitive science, an interdisciplinary blend of cognitive psychology, artificial intelligence, and neuroscience.

7.1 Imagery Abilities

The central issue in cognitive science is a concern with the nature of internal representations and the processes that operate on them. This perspective leads researchers to attempt to characterize the mind in terms of a set of separate subsystems, each of which carries out a specific aspect of information processing (as will be illustrated shortly). Indeed, a major advance of the cognitive science approach to studying imagery is the discovery that "imagery" is not a single, undifferentiated event. Rather, imagery has an underlying structure and can be decomposed into a number of distinct subsystems.

These subsystems can be characterized functionally, although their characterization depends to some degree on an analysis of the underlying neural systems. At the functional level we can characterize subsystems that work together to carry out four main functions of imagery. First, most images are *generated* from information stored in long-term memory. The image itself is a transient short-term memory representation that is accompanied by an experience of "seeing with the mind's eye." We do not always have such images; they are generated from stored information when appropriate. Second, once one has an image, it often must be *maintained* over some period of time in order to be used. Third, imaged objects must be *inspected* in order for new information to be gleaned. One can inspect objects in images in much the same way that one inspects the actual object, except, of course, one cannot "see" anything that was not implicitly stored beforehand. Fourth, images often must be *transformed* in order to "see" what would happen if the corresponding transformations were performed on the actual object.

For example, imagery might be used in deciding how to load a set of crates in an irregularly shaped compartment, such as a helicopter cargo bay. In this case one would study the crates and then generate an image of a crate in a specific place in the bay. One would then image another crate and move it around in the image until it was in a good location, all the while maintaining the image of the first crate. Thus one would generate images, transform them, inspect the results, and maintain the entire scene. This process of "mentally packing" the crates would be repeated until one could "see" how to load the bay efficiently. Substituting mental transformations for physical ones saves much wear and tear both on the muscles and on the bay.

In this example one has mixed imagery with actual perceptual information, imposing one on the other. One can also use imagery in isolation. For example, one might be asked to navigate a truck through a heavily wooded, irregular terrain. In this case one might decide in advance which route to take by thinking about the terrain, mentally imagining the truck moving ahead, "seeing" where it would fit between boulders and trees. In order to do so, one would generate an image of the truck and the terrain and would transform the image of the truck in order to "see" how it would do if it took different routes.

For any given imagery task, some of these abilities are more important than others. For example, if one were asked to load ten crates into a bay, image maintenance ability would be more important than if one were asked to load only two crates. Similarly, if one were asked to imagine a trajectory of a moving object and to anticipate where it would strike another object, one's facility with image transformation and inspection would be of paramount importance.

Thus practical uses of imagery require two steps: First, we must be able to analyze a task, understanding which subsystems of imagery are required (or can be used) to perform it. Second, we must be able to diagnose how effective those subsystems are in a particular person. This procedure would allow us to match the person to the job. Alternatively we might attempt to train a person for a given job, selectively enhancing his or her ability to use the requisite subsystems.

7.2   Characteristics of Imagery Processing

An enormous amount has been learned about imagery over the past two decades. Before being able to analyze the processing used to perform a given task, we must first consider some of the characteristics of imagery that will be more or less relevant for any given task. What follows is a brief review of some of the characteristics of these abilities.

Image Inspection
Images are patterns of activity like those that are evoked during perception (Finke 1980; Finke and Shepard 1986; Kosslyn 1983; Segal 1971; Segal and Fusella 1970; Shepard and Cooper 1982). As such, they can be interpreted as depicting some object, part, or property. Because image interpretation is at the heart of the role of imagery in cognition (if one cannot inspect imaged patterns, they are useless), it has received the most attention in the literature. The interpretation process has a number of characteristics.

Image Scanning   When asked to decide from memory whether a given airplane has a sharp nose, most people will try to visualize the plane and shift their attention to mentally "look" at its nose. The time to make this decision will be shortest if one is mentally focusing on the nose when the question is posed. More time will be required if one is focused on the body when the question is delivered, and even more time will be required if one is focused on the tail when the question is delivered. The time required for a person to make a decision about a property at one location of an imaged object increases with the distance necessary to scan to that location. This increase is typically linear, and the correlation between time and distance is very high [as high as 0.97; see Kosslyn et al. (1978)]. This increase in time with distance occurs when one scans images of pictures or of three-dimensional scenes; in three-dimensional scenes time typically increases with distance in three dimensions (Pinker 1980).

Perhaps the most interesting implication of the finding that images can be scanned is the idea that images "depict"; that is, imaged objects seem to extend in some kind of "functional space" in the brain. Although images are not real pictures, they mimic the spatial characteristics of real pictures. [As discussed in detail by Kosslyn (1980), a useful metaphor is an array in a computer, which is not physically spatial but can function spatially; some locations are adjacent, some diagonal from each other, and so on.] This inference has met some resistance, particularly in the artificial intelligence community; some of these researchers object on principle to anything but the kind of languagelike representations that are easy to program in a conventional computer, and a debate has centered on this issue for years [see Pylyshyn (1973, 1981) and also Kosslyn (1980, ch. 2)]. I do not attempt to review the debate here, for it has become increasingly technical and methodologically oriented and is not directly relevant to present concerns.

Grain Effects   If you had started out with an image of a tiny airplane, more time would have been required to judge the shape of its nose than if you had started out with the plane imaged at a normal size. Subjects in experiments in which image size is manipulated report that they have to "zoom in" in order to "see" parts of objects imaged at small sizes (Kosslyn 1975; Kosslyn 1980, chs. 3 and 7). This result makes sense if mental images occur in parts of the brain also used to represent perceptual input. The eyes have a limited resolution, and hence the brain needs to encompass only that level of resolution. Thus, even if the image arises from previously stored information (mental imagery) rather than from incoming information (perception), resolution limits will still be evident. It is as if there is only a limited number of pixels available on which to display an object on a screen and all images are subject to the "grain" of the screen, whatever their origin.

Now consider another task: Try to imagine an umpire wearing a striped shirt. Pretend you are seeing the umpire from a distance of 4 feet and are slowly backing away from him. Is there a point at which the shirt stripes are no longer distinguishable, when they meld into an undifferentiated gray? (This is a difficult task to perform, partly because the capacity limits of imagery make it difficult to "see" many stripes at once.) When this task is done formally, showing subjects striped gratings and having them learn them in advance, we find that the thicker and wider apart the stripes, the farther away people can imagine "seeing" them as distinct in an image (Kosslyn et al. 1984). However, possibly more interesting is the fact that there are great individual differences in image acuity. People with sharp images report acuity (in tasks such as estimating the apparent distance at which individual stripes are not distinguishable) that rivals that of perception, but most people have substantially worse acuity in their imagery (Finke and Kosslyn 1980). Also of interest, the degree of acuity in mental imagery is not related to the acuity of corrected vision.

Maximal Size   If you imagine fixating on the side of a large truck standing one foot away, you would not be able to "see" all of the truck at once (Kosslyn 1980). The truck would have "overflowed" the available "space." This observation has been verified experimentally in a number of ways. In one experiment people were asked to image walking toward an object until all of it was not "visible" in the image and then were asked to estimate the apparent distance of the object. The larger the object, the farther away it seemed at the point of overflow. Furthermore, similar effects were found when the objects were actually present. Apparently the "size" of the "mental screen" used in imagery and perception is about the same. This result makes perfect sense if images occur in parts of the brain also used in perception, and the size limitation is a consequence of the capacity of these structures.

Image Construction
One of the most obvious facts about mental images is that they are not always present. Images come to mind and then fade from consciousness. Furthermore, when images are evoked, they are not simply turned on (in the way one turns on a slide); rather, images are actively constructed.

Not only can one combine previously viewed objects in novel ways but one can also image objects with new parts or image altogether new objects. Although it is not obvious to introspection, the time to form an image increases for every additional part included in the image. For example, imaging the letter *C* is faster than imaging *P*, which is faster than imaging *G* (Kosslyn et al., in press).

An important discovery about image generation is that the way one organizes a pattern has dramatic effects on the time to image it: The more parts one imposes on a pattern, the more time later required to form an image of it (Kosslyn et al. 1983). For example, if one sees a Star of David as two overlapping triangles, the image can later be generated more quickly than if one sees it as a hexagon with six small triangles along the rim. This is important because the amount of material that can be held in an image is determined largely by the number of parts that can be maintained. Thus the way one organizes a pattern has important consequences for how easily one can use images of it in thinking.

Image Transformation
Once one has an image, it can be manipulated in a variety of ways. For example, one can mentally rotate an uppercase version of the letter *n* 90 degrees clockwise, and then "see" if it would be another letter (*Z*). The further one rotates an imaged pattern , the more time is required. Shepard and Metzler (1971; see also Shepard and Cooper (1982)] were the first to report this relationship between the amount of rotation and time and also found that the time to rotate was the same in the picture plane and in depth. This finding suggests that people rotate imaged objects along a trajectory, passing through the

intermediate points as they go. This result is remarkable because mental images are not real pictures and hence are not constrained by the laws of physics to rotate along a trajectory. There is a mystery here, which will be addressed briefly in section 7.5.

Another image transformation that has been studied in some detail is image size scaling. Subjects are asked either to prepare to evaluate a stimulus by adjusting an image to a certain size or to compare two stimuli of different sizes [Bundesen and Larsen 1975; Larsen and Bundesen 1978; Sekular and Nash 1972; for reviews, see Kosslyn (1980) and Shepard and Cooper (1982)]. The results parallel those in the mental rotation literature: The larger the transformation, the more time required.

Image Maintenance
Try to image a brick floating in space. And now add a second brick, floating slightly apart from the first. And now another brick, and another, and so on. At some point (probably after about six bricks are floating) you will not be able to keep all of the images in mind at once. Imagery has a limited capacity. It requires effort to maintain objects in images. This is true both in terms of the number of items that can be maintained and in terms of how long images can be maintained. Visual mental images often have been likened to objects seen in a brief flash, which then can be maintained only in a degraded form and only for a brief period of time (Kosslyn et al. 1984; Weber and Harnish 1974). People differ dramatically in how well they can maintain objects in images (Kosslyn et al. 1984). Indeed, some people can maintain only about two simple line segments in an image at the same time.

Although we can discuss separately these four imagery abilities— generation, inspection, transformation, and maintenance—it is an error to assume that each of these abilities is subserved by a separate subsystem. The idea of a direct correspondence between ability and subsystem is attractive and seduced the Phrenologists into believing that specific brain areas were used for specific tasks. However, there apparently are more than four imagery subsystems, and the subsystems are best understood at an "information processing" level, akin to subroutines in a large computer program. These subsystems appear to crosscut the abilities, with some subsystems being used in numerous different contexts. For example, when we first attempted to program a computer to mimic imagery (Kosslyn and Shwartz 1977), we discovered that the subsystems used to "inspect" imaged patterns were also required in image transformation (to determine when to stop the imaged transformation) and in image generation (to "see" where additional parts should be placed in an image). Thus one set of subsystems cut across three imagery abilities. Some subsystems do seem limited to a specific context, but this is not necessarily the case.

7.3 The Imagery Processing System: Foundations of the Theory

The component subsystems of imagery are reasonably well understood at a relatively coarse level of analysis. A subsystem is functionally characterized; it describes what a group of neurons accomplishes in carrying out some information processing task. A subsystem typically can be subdivided into more detailed subsystems, and specifies only *what* is done, not *how* it is actually accomplished [confer Marr (1982)].

A theory of imagery is best built on three sets of foundations. Before launching into a characterization of the imagery subsystems, the basic rationale behind the present formulation will be considered briefly; a more detailed treatment of the motivation for this theory is provided by Kosslyn (1987) and a more detailed description of the subsystems and computer simulation model is provided in Kosslyn et al. (1988).

First, a fundamental claim about visual mental imagery is that it invokes some of the same mechanisms used in visual perception. This claim receives support from behavioral studies [for an exhaustive review, see Finke and Shepard (1986)] and from neuropsychological studies (Farah 1984; Kosslyn 1987). For example, if one forms a visual image, this will interfere more with simultaneous visual perception than with auditory perception, but vice versa if one forms an auditory image. Furthermore, brain damage can disrupt both imagery and perception, although the two abilities can be selectively damaged (indicating that they are not identical). The observation that imagery is to a large degree parasitic on perceptual mechanisms is of critical importance because perception is easier to understand than imagery (in part because the stimuli and responses are more easily observed). If we can understand the "mental" (high-level) aspects of perception, we will be able to induce a remarkable amount about imagery [see Kosslyn (1987)].

A second source of motivation for a theory of imagery is information about the neurology of high-level vision. Given the inference that mechanisms of visual perception also are used in imagery (Farah, in press; Kosslyn 1987), we can learn something about imagery by examining the neurology of these mechanisms. These mechanisms are used in high-level vision, which begins with the organized perceptual units that are produced by the low-level mechanisms responsible for figure-ground segregation and the like (Kosslyn 1987). The high-level mechanisms are extrastriate and appear to exist primarily in the inferior temporal lobe and in the parietal lobe. That is, it is now believed that there are two cortical visual systems (Ungerleider and Mishkin 1982; Van Essen 1985). The "ventral" pathway, running from the occipital lobe down the inferior temporal lobe, apparently deals with shape. Experiments with animals have shown that damaging this area of the brain disrupts perception of pattern but leaves perception of location intact (Ungerleider and Mishkin 1982). Furthermore, cells in this area tend to be responsive to shape and do not register position information [for a review, see Kosslyn 1987)].

In contrast, the "dorsal" pathway, running from the occipital lobe to the parietal lobe, apparently deals with location. Experiments with animals have demonstrated that damaging the parietal lobe disrupts perception of location but leaves perception of pattern intact. Cells in this area are not responsive to shape, and at least some of them are sensitive to location (Anderson et al. 1985). Clinical findings with humans have demonstrated similar dysfunctions following accidental injury to the two systems. Indeed, corresponding findings have been reported in both imagery and perception (Levine et al. 1985). The two pathways are illustrated in figure 7.1.

A third source of motivation for a theory of imagery information processing is an analysis of what problems must be solved in order to build a system that mimics human performance, producing the observed behavior and being consistent with the underlying neurology. The separation of shape and location information is important when we consider it in conjunction with a closer analysis of what problems must be solved by the visual system. Consider what the visual system must do in order to recognize an object. Recognition requires that we represent the input in such a way that it makes contact with the

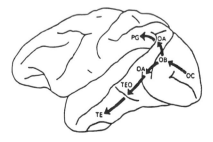

Figure 7.1
The dorsal and ventral cortical visual systems. Adapted from Mishkin et al. (1983).

appropriate stored representations. This task requires picking out the characteristic properties of the object and ignoring irrelevant stimulus variations. That is, many objects vary from instance to instance, especially flexible ones; a human form, for example, can be configured in any number of ways from moment to moment. We have to pick out the important aspects of shape and ignore the rest.

The kind of representation of shape that will be most useful for recognition depends in part on characteristics of the object. Although some objects are subject to a near infinite number of transformations and so may not look the same from instance to instance, other objects (for example, a given face) vary little. For flexible objects it is useful to have a representation that will be stable across a wide range of transformations. Two kinds of attributes remain constant under such transformations. First, the characteristic parts remain the same; although some may be hidden depending on the configuration, none are added or deleted from the object. Second, at one level of abstraction relations among parts remain constant under all transformations. For example, the "connectivity" relation between the arm and shoulder remains constant under all the different positions the arm can take. General categories of relations, such as "top and bottom," "side of," and "connected to at the end," can be used to describe relations that remain constant under a wide range of transformations.

Given that imagery shares high-level mechanisms with perception, we may best understand the mechanisms of imagery in the context of how they function in perception proper. Thus I develop these mechanisms by first describing their apparent role in perception.

7.4   Mechanisms of High-Level Visual Processing

These considerations put one in a position to hypothesize a number of subsystems, which are illustrated in figure 7.2. Because of space limitations, only the briefest summary of the theory can be presented here. This summary will be sufficient to consider in subsequent sections the possible roles of imagery in complex learning. For a detailed description of the theory and its motivation, see Kosslyn, Flynn, and Amsterdam (1988).

Subsystems of the Ventral System

At the extreme right of figure 7.2 is the "visual buffer." This structure corresponds to numerous topographically mapped visual areas of the cortex (Van Essen 1985) and is roughly equivalent to Marr's (1982) "2½-D sketch." This structure contains parsed scenes, which are divided into separate objects, and parsed objects, which are divided

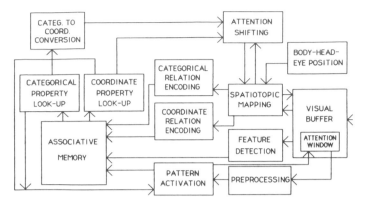

Figure 7.2
The high-level visual subsystems.

into separate parts. The outputs from this structure (to the ventral and dorsal systems) are used to recognize the object or part. First, we consider three subsystems hypothesized to operate in the ventral system.

Preprocessing   The first subsystem is used to extract relatively invariant properties of input [see Biederman (1987) and Lowe (1987)]. We see objects at different distances and from different angles. A relatively early system must be used to extract features that are independent of the size and angle before proceeding.

Pattern Activation   Once the input is preprocessed, it becomes feasible to attempt to categorize shape. The pattern activation subsystem stores visual patterns, which can be activated by input from the preprocessor. The shape categorization process begins by assigning input to a visual category. The pattern activation subsystem does not assign a name to a shape, it simply maps the input into a stored pattern. The same stored pattern can be activated by a range of similar inputs. We must group the shape into a class so that we can generalize to novel instances, examples never before seen. This operation is necessary if we are to be able to use names of categories (such as "chair"), which cover classes of objects. Following this grouping process, one can then enter associative memory and attempt to access the corresponding name.

The pattern activation subsystem also plays a key role in visual mental imagery. Imagery requires that a stored pattern be activated to produce an image proper. This sort of information is stored in the pattern activation subsystem. If this information is activated from the top down and fed back through the system, one can "paint" an image in the visual buffer. This image can then be recycled, reinspected just as an actual object. In the Kosslyn, Flynn, and Amsterdam (1988) computer simulation model the imaged shape is produced at the location being attended. Thus the mechanisms that shift attention in perception can also be used to direct the placement of parts as an image is constructed. These mechanisms will be discussed shortly.

Feature Detection   In addition, color, texture, and other nonshape visual features can be extracted from input. A multipart subsystem is posited to perform this sort of processing.

Subsystems of the Dorsal System
As one is attending to a shape, the location of the shape is processed in a separate dorsal system while the form of the shape is processed in the ventral system. The dorsal system is hypothesized to have at least three main subsystems.

Spatiotopic Mapping   In the first subsystem the location must be represented relative to space, not to the retina. The output from early visual processing (the contents of the visual buffer) is in terms of location on the retina, and these coordinates must be transformed into a representation that is more useful for the organism. That is, the location of the object on the eye is not very useful; knowledge of the location in space is necessary for reaching, coordinating separate objects together in a single frame of reference, and so on. Thus eye position, head position, and body position all must be taken into account to locate an object or part of an object in space.

Following this, one needs to derive spatial relationships among objects or parts. The theory posits that two additional subsystems are used here, each computing a different type of spatial relationship; evidence for these subsystems is presented by Kosslyn (1987).

Categorical Relations Encoding   One subsystem must be able to derive a description of relations that will remain constant when objects are contorted. These descriptions themselves cannot be images; images are representations of specific stimulus configurations. Instead, the dorsal system must be able to make use of more abstract, *categorical* representations. Such representations capture general properties of a relationship without specifying the details (for example, "next to" without specifying how much or exactly at what angle). These sorts of representations are particularly useful for specifying the relations among adjacent parts, with each relation being relative to a specific pair of parts. This kind of "local coordinate system" is useful for building complex descriptive structures of flexible, multipart objects [see Marr (1982)]. Thus we can posit a subsystem that computes a categorical relation among perceptual units (parts or objects).

Kosslyn (1987) provides evidence that these sorts of representations of spatial relations are carried out more effectively in the left cerebral hemisphere (of right-handed people).

Coordinate Relations Encoding   In contrast, there are other types of objects that would not be usefully represented for recognition using categorical relations. These objects do not vary much from instance to instance and have spatial relations among parts that differ only subtly from those of similar objects. For example, knowing that a person's eyes are next to each other, above the nose, which is above the mouth, will not allow one to recognize that particular face. Rather, one needs to know the actual metric spatial relationships among the parts. For this sort of recognition problem it is useful to have a subsystem that derives a representation of the locations of parts in a coordinate space (which uses metric distances, as does a standard xy Cartesian coordinate space). This sort of representation specifies the coordinates of objects or parts relative to an origin, which could be centered on an object or place (allocentric coordinates) or on one's body (egocentric coordinates). This representation provides information needed to compute second-order metric relations, such as ratios of distances among pairs of parts, which may be useful for recognizing faces and the like [see Diamond and Carey (1986)].

A coordinate representation of this kind is also useful for navigation. In navigation one needs to know precisely where an obstacle is located, not just that it is against a wall or next to some object. In climbing a rocky path, one wants to know whether the gap between two rocks is large enough to accommodate one's foot, not just that the rocks are next to each other.

Kosslyn (1987) presents evidence that this sort of spatial representation is carried out most effectively in the right cerebral hemisphere (of right-handed people). The finding that the two kinds of representations are most effective in opposite hemispheres is in itself evidence for the distinction and is evidence that separate subsystems are in fact used for the separate kinds of representations.

Associative Memory
When we are looking at a stimulus, the output from the dorsal and ventral systems must come together. Afterall, the relations among parts is an important aspect of shape. Furthermore, given the simple

fact that we can recall where parts belong on objects, there must be an associative memory in which parts are associated with locations. A possible locus of this juncture is the association cortex near Wernicke's area (in the posterior superior temporal lobe); this area appears to be involved in semantic processing.

Active Searching

So far we have discussed two "bottom-up" processing pathways, one for shape and one for position. In addition, the theory posits a third pathway, a "top-down" search system. That is, we are not passive, waiting to see what is outside. Rather, once we have some idea of what is in front of us, we actively generate a hypothesis and look for parts or characteristics that should be present if we are right (Gregory 1970; Neisser 1967, 1976). This sort of activity is critical in imagery, as will become clear shortly. In order to perform this kind of active search to test a hypothesis, we need at least three more subsystems.

Categorical Lookup   First, we must be able to look up in associative memory the properties an object should have. This subsystem is most efficient if it begins by looking up the most distinctive properties. That is, if you want to tell a cat from a dog, looking for four legs won't help you much. But looking for a particularly shaped head is helpful, as is looking for vertical slits on the eyes. The categorical lookup subsystem should access not only the names of distinctive properties but also their categorical locations.

This subsystem can also be used in imagery to determine which part to activate next and where it belongs. In imaging a new part, one directs attention to the appropriate position (in relation to a part of the object already in the image) and then activates the appropriate pattern at the appropriate size [for evidence that this occurs, see Kosslyn (1980, ch. 6)]. Thus images can be built up from separately stored components. Once an image is formed, the pattern can be "inspected" using the ventral and dorsal systems just as they are used in perception.

Coordinate Lookup   Similarly, one can look up stored coordinate information, using it to direct attention. Such information is useful when one is recognizing objects that have precisely placed parts or that do not vary from instance to instance.

Category-to-Coordinate Conversion   Another problem must be solved if we look up a categorical description of a part's location. If so, then, before we can use the information to position attention, we must convert the categorical relation to a coordinate. We must specify where to look in space, given that relation. Depending on the size of the example and its distance from us, we will have to move our attention to different locations. This problem must be solved if we are to use a categorical relation to direct our attention to a place where a part should be.

Attention Shifting   Finally, we need a subsystem that actually shifts attention. This system probably includes at least the three subsystems hypothesized by Posner et al. (1984, 1985), namely, one that shifts attention to a position, one that engages attention at that position, and finally one that disengages attention when appropriate. Posner and his colleagues present evidence that each of these subsystems can be disrupted independently of the others following brain damage in different regions.

Additional Imagery Subsystems
According to the present theory, the previously discussed subsystems are invoked when one generates and inspects objects in images. In generating an image, one activates stored information and composes multipart images by shifting attention to the appropriate locations and activating parts one at a time. One inspects objects in images using the subsystems used to inspect actual objects, encoding both shape and position information separately (Levine et al. 1985). In addition, the mechanism that generates imagery can regenerate an image, keeping it refreshed over time. These mechanisms are also used in image transformation, but in conjunction with other subsystems.

Pattern Shifting   In order to rotate or otherwise manipulate an imaged object, one must alter the position representations of the parts. These representations are in the spatiotopic map. The location of each part is shifted, and the part's location in the visual buffer is then shifted accordingly. That is, in perception one maps the contents of the visual buffer into the spatiotopic map; this transformation is accomplished in part by knowing how far away the object is (allowing one to represent actual, not retinal, size in the spatiotopic map). The reverse transformation occurs here; when one manipulates a location in the spatiotopic map, the corresponding part is moved the correct amount in the visual buffer by using the inverse of the original mapping function.

Dedicated Transformation Operations   Although we can manipulate images in a variety of ways and hence presumably have a general-purpose pattern shift operation, some transformations may be implemented as special-purpose "macros." For example, size scaling may be accomplished by a special piece of hardware (as indeed might rotation). The necessary empirical work has not been done to examine whether skill at one image transformation transfers to another.

7.5   Accounting for the Data

The theory outlined allows us to explain the various phenomena reviewed in section 7.4. To get a sense of the usefulness of the theory, let us briefly consider an account for each phenomenon here.

Image Inspection

Three characteristics of image inspection were reviewed. First, the present theory suggests that there are two mechanisms for image scanning. One mechanism involves shifting attention, so that one attends to different portions of an imaged object. This mechanism is good for "fine tuning," but has a fundamental limitation: It will "bump into the edge" if shifted too far; that is, the parts of the visual cortex used in imagery apparently are also used in visual perception (Farah, in press; Finke and Shepard 1986). These mechanisms evolved to represent only a limited visual angle, namely, that subtended by the eyes. Thus there are spatial limits to these representations. However, in imagery one can scan around the walls of a room, never bumping into an edge. This phenomenon suggests that scanning can also be accomplished by shifting the imaged object under a fixed field of attention, filling in new portions along the leading edge. By analogy, it is like the display on a TV screen as a camera sweeps along.

Second, grain effects presumably also reflect a limitation of the parts of cortex used to support image representations. Spatial summation results in similar effects in perception, and the same mechanisms may also be at work in imagery. However, it is an open question whether this mechanism explains individual differences in image resolution.

Third, the maximum size (apparent visual angle) of images is also a consequence of the visual role of the relevant parts of the cortex. As noted, these mechanisms need only represent input from the eyes and hence need only have a limited scope. Given the striking similarity in the maximum scope of visual attention in perception and imagery (Finke and Kosslyn 1980; Kosslyn 1978, 1980, 1983), it is plausible that the same underlying mechanism is at work in both cases.

Image Construction
The finding that more time is required to form images of objects containing more parts is easily explained. For each additional part one must look up the relation, adjust attention to the appropriate location, and activate an image of the part. These processes require time. In addition, because categorical relations can be used to juxtapose objects or parts in an image, the theory accounts for our abilities to generate images of described scenes (for example, the president riding a surfboard down a giant wave).

Image Transformations
The major finding in the literature on mental rotation is that more time is required to rotate objects greater amounts in images. The reason for this incremental rotation is not clear. The laws of physics require that real objects move through a trajectory when rotated (because instantaneous movement is impossible), but images are not real objects and hence in principle need not necessarily be transformed through a trajectory. One reason why we transform images gradually may be that the categorical encoding subsystem is used to monitor image transformations, if for no other reason than to allow one to cease rotation when the shape is properly aligned. Thus it behooves one to rotate in relatively small increments so that one does not overshoot the correct orientation. Similarly the operation that scales images would be monitored and hence would also operate incrementally. Kosslyn (1987) offers additional possible reasons why transformations are performed in small increments.

Image Maintenance
I have argued that images occur in a visual buffer that is also used in perception, which leads to the properties of the buffer evident in perception also being evident in imagery. If so, then our inability to maintain information in images for long periods may be another consequence of this common mechanism. That is, in perception one does not want an image to linger; one wants to clear the buffer every time the eyes move. Indeed, if images did not fade rapidly, one would overlay them. Any animal that did this probably would not survive long enough to have many descendants. Thus representations in the visual buffer fade and require effort to maintain. I hypothesize that the pattern activation subsystem can be used to maintain images for brief periods of time. If this operation works on one perceptual unit at a time, then imagery may be like a juggling act: As each part is being reactivated, others are fading. Thus the speed of the fading process, the speed of the reactivation process, and the speed of shifting from

one part to another would define the amount of information one could maintain in an image.

7.6   Individual Differences in Imagery

Perhaps the most dramatic demonstration of the utility of the cognitive science approach to imagery has been in the understanding of individual differences in imagery. It once was believed that a person is good, intermediate, or poor at imagery. Imagery was treated as a single trait, which a person had to one degree or another. The analysis of imagery into subsystems led Kosslyn et al. (1984) to ask the following question: Do people differ in terms of a general imagery ability, or do they differ in terms of a set of separate abilities?

In order to investigate this issue, Kosslyn et al. (1984) tested fifty subjects on thirteen imagery tasks. The tasks ranged from ones requiring image generation to ones requiring image rotation, maintenance, and various ways of scanning. If imagery is a single undifferentiated general ability, then, if a person is good at any imagery task, he or she should be good at all of the others; if a person is poor at any imagery task, he or she should be poor at the others. If imagery is not a single ability, then differences in task performance will depend on (1) the kinds of processing required in the tasks and (2) a person's ability to perform the specific processes required. Thus the first result of interest was evident in the correlations among the scores on these tasks. High intertask correlations were not found. Rather, the observed correlations ranged from $r = -.44$ to $r = .79$. Thus people do not have a general imagery ability on which they differ.

The next question Kosslyn et al. (1984) asked was whether their theory of imagery subsystems could account for the observed pattern of variation in performance over the tasks. This theory was an earlier version of the one described in section 7.4. The theory was used to generate a model for each task. These models specified the processing subsystems and the flow of information processing among them. The models were used to calculate the similarity of processing between each pair of tasks; the more shared subsystems two tasks had, the more similar they were (the actual way of computing similarity was more complicated than this and involved "weighting" the more important subsystems, but this notion serves to illustrate the basic idea).

Kosslyn et al. (1984) then compared the similarity matrix for the models with the observed correlations among the tasks. They reasoned that, if the theory approximates reality, then the similarity matrix should reflect how similar the tasks are. If so, then the correlations in task performance should resemble the patterns of similarity. That is, Kosslyn et al. expected that the more similar two tasks are, the more likely it is that a person would perform similarly on them. This did indeed prove to be the case. The correlation between the observed and predicted matrices was highly significant and was far higher than that obtained using a commonsense theory of individual differences. This commonsense theory was used to compute task similarity based on the importance of image vividness, imagery control, and other such commonsense dimensions that had previously been offered to explain individual differences in imagery. That is, tasks were scored in terms of how important each variable should be, and similarity was assessed by examining the number of important variables in common between each pair of tasks. The processing theory was still far superior even when the number of parameters was pared down so that the two theories were equally simple.

Kosslyn et al. (1984) used an older version of the theory discussed here to generate their predictions. This theory was not grounded in facts about the anatomy and physiology of the brain but was motivated primarily by computational considerations. Kosslyn, Van Kleeck, and Kirby (in press) reanalyzed the old data using the new theory and discovered that it did slightly better than the earlier theory in predicting the patterns of variation. Whereas the correlation between predicted and observed similarity was $r = .56$ before, it was $r = .63$ now. Furthermore, the present theory posits two fewer subsystems (which were used as parameters in fitting the data) than the earlier theory.

This discovery—that individual differences in imagery break down into components—has important implications for learning.

7.7   Using Imagery

Imagery is used in a variety of situations. We can understand these situations by beginning with the parallels between the purposes of vision and imagery. Vision is used in part to allow us to recognize objects and thereby to know more about them than is evident in the sensory input. These mechanisms presumably are used in imagery in the service of memory retrieval. For example, if one is asked to decide how many windows are in a room, one images the room and "inspects" it, "seeing" the locations of the windows, which were not explicitly described before. The recognition mechanisms can be used in imagery as a way of accessing stored information.

A second purpose of vision is to allow us to navigate and to track moving objects. The problem to be solved here requires updating metric spatial relations as one or more objects move. In imagery these mechanisms presumably are used for visual reasoning. That is, one can perform imagery simulations to anticipate what would happen if one performed some act. For example, one can mentally project an object through an opening, "seeing" if it would fit. This use of imagery has applications in navigation, packing objects into defined spaces, and a wide variety of similar spatial tasks.

These two basic uses of imagery can be used as the foundation for accomplishing additional ends. As discussed earlier, one can not only inspect an imaged object but also remember the image itself, thereby improving memory for the object. In addition, one can mentally practice an act, and, so long as actual pratice is intermixed with mental practice, one will improve actual performance. Here imagery simulations apparently invoke the motor system and the visual system. In addition, imagery can be used symbolically to help one to reason. For example, one can imagine a line with dots staggered along it, where the line indicates some abstract dimension (for example, "dangerousness") and the dots indicate relative amounts of that dimension for three things (for example, types of weapons). This technique greatly aids reasoning about the entities. For example, if one is told, "an x is more dangerous than a y, but a z is less dangerous than a y, and a p is not more dangerous than an x," it is easy to decide which is most dangerous if one uses this technique.

As noted at the beginning of this chapter, from a practical point of view the importance of the cognitive science approach to imagery hinges on two procedures. First, we must be able to use theories to perform task analyses. These task analyses specify which processing subsystems are used to perform any given task. For example, Kosslyn et al. (1984) used the general theory of imagery to formulate flow charts for specific tasks, indicating the constituent subsystems and their order of use (Kosslyn et al., in press). Second, we must be able to measure the efficacy of each subsystem in a given person. This work is under way but is only preliminary (Kosslyn, Berndt, and Doyle 1985). Only after performing both procedures will we be in a position to know which tasks a given person will find easy or difficult.

Thus the first part of this section briefly reviews how one uses the theory to formulate a model for any given imagery task [see Kosslyn et al. (in press) for a more detailed treatment]. The second part of this section reviews possible methods of training imagery.

Formulating Models
The theory described in this chapter can be used to formulate models of specific imagery tasks. These models indicate which subsystems

must be used in order to accomplish a task. One way to do this is to adjust a computer simulation model so that it performs the task. One of the discoveries that emerges from this exercise is that there is more than one way to accomplish any given task. This observation opens the door for avoiding one's weaknesses by formulating a strategy—a method for performing the task—that does not depend on an ineffective subsystem.

Although it is often difficult to determine the precise order in which subsystems are used (in part because many may be used either fully or partially in parallel), it is relatively easy to identify the subsystems used in a given task according to the following rules.

1. Whenever an image is formed, the pattern activation processing subsystem must be used.

2. The preprocessing subsystem and pattern activation subsystem are used whenever one "inspects" the image for a shape.

3. The categorical relations encoding subsystem is used whenever one "inspects" an imaged object for a spatial relation, except when precise metric distances are necessary, in which case the coordinate encoding system is used.

4. Whenever the imaged object includes more than one part, one of the two lookup subsystems is used and the attention shifting mechanisms are used to generate an image of it. If the precise metric positions of the parts of the object are important for recognizing it, then the coordinate property lookup subsystem is used; otherwise, the categorical property lookup subsystem is used.

5. Whenever the categorical property lookup subsystem is used, the category-to-coordinate conversion subsystem is also used.

6. Whenever parts are placed on an image, the preprocessing and pattern activation subsystems are used, as is the categorical relations encoding subsystem, unless the image is of an object whose parts must be placed precisely, in which case the coordinate encoder is used instead.

7. The pattern activation subsystem must be used if the image must be maintained more than one second or so; in practice this translates into the subsystem's being used in this way if more than one shape or relation is being encoded.

8. The categorical or coordinate encoding subsystem must be utilized to monitor the progress of any image transformation.

9. If the imaged object must be transformed in some way, the pattern shifting subsystem is used.

10. If attention must be shifted over part of the imaged object, either the attention shifting mechanisms are used or the scanning (image shifting) pattern shifting subsystem is used.

More detailed rules, with examples of their application, are presented by Kosslyn et al. (in press).

Perhaps not surprisingly, much of the entire system is used whenever one performs an imagery task. However, not all subsystems are drawn on to an equal degree in any given task, which results in important differences among tasks. That is, some subsystems are "weighted" as more important than others in a given task, and Kosslyn et al. (1984) found that it was the differences in these weighted subsystems that were most important for predicting which tasks a person would find easy or difficult.

Weighting the Subsystems
It is unavoidable that not all processing subsystems are of equal importance in performing a task. This is true because the criterion of what constitutes "performing a task well" varies for different tasks, depending on different factors, such as the time, speed, or accuracy with which one accomplishes the task. Different measures of performance are sensitive to the efficacy of different processing subsystems. Thus we need to identify the relative contributions of the processing subsystems to a given performance measure.

Kosslyn et al. (1984) developed a method for determining which subsystems should be weighted as particularly important for a given task (using binary weights, reflecting relative importance or unimportance). This method received a strong measure of validation, as discussed later. The method is as follows. For each task Kosslyn et al. began by selecting the relevant subsystems and hand-simulated how the model would operate. The rules help one to posit a model, selecting the appropriate subsystems. Working through the process step by step ensures that one has selected a sufficient set. Kosslyn et al. then considered how variations in the efficacy of each processing subsystem used in the model would affect the measure of task performance. They assumed that, if a person can perform the task to any degree of proficiency, then all of the relevant processing subsystems must be operating at some minimal level of efficacy. The question is, For which subsystems will increased efficacy improve the score on the dependent measure? For some subsystems there is nothing gained—on a specific dependent measure—by performance above the bare minimum. For other subsystems increased speed, capacity, sensitivity, or accuracy directly affect the performance measure. It was these processing subsystems that were weighted (categorized as relatively important).

In addition, as a convergent method Kosslyn et al. (1984) reasoned that the processing subsystems that are increasingly taxed when stimulus factors are varied—and the task becomes more difficult, according to the dependent measure—would have disproportionate influence in the converse situation, when the task difficulty is constant but the component varies in efficacy. Thus Kosslyn et al. considered which stimulus factors had been already shown to affect the dependent measure in group data (the tasks used were similar to those already studied, so this information was usually available) and then considered which processing subsystems were taxed by variations in these stimulus factors.

Kosslyn et al. (1984) validated these methods of assigning weights empirically. In a regression analysis they obtained beta weights for the different subsystems used in the various tasks, which reflected how important each was. These beta weights were then correlated with the degree to which the subsystems were theoretically weighted. This correlation was quite substantial (.7 and higher, depending on the precise method of correlation). Thus there is some reason to be confident that the subsystems need to be given different weights, depending on the task and performance measure, and that the simple procedure described earlier is a reasonable method for categorizing a subsystem as relatively important or unimportant.

In short, if one has difficulty in performing a task, it is likely that the difficulty is due to ineffective weighted subsystems. If so, then varying the stimuli in selected ways should affect how easy the task is. For example, one can observe how much difficulty a person has when asked to rotate stimuli by a large amount versus a small amount; this variation taxes the pattern shifting and categorical relations encoding subsystems, increasing amounts.

If a person can rotate a little bit or can rotate something simple but not something complex, the problem is not in other subsystems used in the task. If this occurs, two options are available: First, one can try some other strategy, either using imagery or not. For example, one can try discontinuous transformations, which can be done by letting one image fade and then generating a new image of the object transformed in some way; for most people this is a difficult strategy, but for some it may be easier than incremental transformations. Second, one can attempt to train the relevant subsystems, as is described in what follows.

Training
Theory-based training programs to improve imagery skills have not yet been developed. However, there is good reason to believe that they are possible but highly constrained: In my laboratory we typically observe large practice effects. That is, even in the space of an

hour, most subjects dramatically improve their performance of imagery tasks.

The issue, however, is whether such training is transferable across tasks. Depending on how the subsystems are actually implemented in the brain, such generalization may be highly task specific. That is, if the subsystems are implemented in neural networks, then different patterns in the network will correspond to different states. Practice presumably affects just the part of the network involved in performing a task. If so, then one would not expect wide generalization following practice. And, in fact, in my laboratory we have found that practice improves activating a given imaged object but does not transfer very much to other imaged objects.

The bottom line here is that the best training may involve simply practicing the tasks at hand. If one wants to become adept at using imagery as a mnemonic, one should use imagery as a mnemonic frequently. If one wants to become efficient at using imagery as a "mental simulator," practicing some skill, one should use it that way often. The trick here, however, is to discover which subsystems are the weak links in a person's ability to perform a task and then to work on variations of the task that progressively tax that subsystem. Standardized tests are now being developed that will diagnose a person's relative strengths and weaknesses in using imagery.

For example, say that you want to use imagery to learn the names of parts of a machine. You could use a modified version of the method of loci. You would first memorize the appearance of the machine, forming a set of loci. Next, you would label each part by imagining an object corresponding to the name of the part as if it were interacting with the part. For instance, a "carburetor" sounds like a "car berater," and hence you could image a cartoon car standing on its rear tires bawling out a carburetor held in its hand (tire, bent over to cup the part). The car image would be placed in miniature on the correct place on the engine. In order to perform this task, you must first encode the images of the parts. If you have difficulty doing this, training might consist of looking at an object, shutting your eyes, trying to "see" the afterimage, and then opening your eyes and comparing the image to the object. This procedure could be repeated over the course of about two weeks, gradually lengthening the time the eyes are closed and the image retained. In order to perform the task, you also must activate the images. If you have difficulty in activating images, you would repeat the learning process just described but would first practice retaining images (by looking at objects and shutting your eyes, maintaining the image) and then generating them a second or two after looking at something else. Although the task

requires maintaining images and inspecting them, these requirements are rather minimal (only one part need be imaged at a time); if
you can image at all (and by far the majority of people can), the
bottlenecks should be in encoding the parts and activating them into
images.

Similar training can be used for any task, emphasizing any of the
subsystems. The general procedure, then, is to start with a simple
example of the task and repeat it over the course of weeks, gradually
increasing the complexity of the task. Although this procedure has
never been formally tested, an informal study with a single subject
yielded encouraging results.

However, a major caveat must be kept in mind: Training may serve
to improve the subsystems used in a task only in the precise way they
are being used. If the option is available, it is better to select a person
with the right skills for a task than to try to train a person for the task.
That is, if it is possible, I recommend first analyzing the task requirements and then finding a person who is adept at using the relevant
subsystems.

7.8   Conclusions

Imagery provides a powerful way of learning information. However,
the effectiveness of a specific imagery technique depends on the nature of the problem being solved and on the effectiveness of the
various imagery subsystems for a given person. In order to use imagery effectively in a given task, one first needs an analysis of the
underlying component subsystems evoked in performing the task.
Next, one needs to know which subsystems are most important for
that task. If one is not adept at using that particular subsystem, one
can adopt an alternative strategy or can try to exercise the subsystem.
However, such training is apt to be limited and specific to a particular
task; if possible, people with the requisite abilities should be selected
for the task at hand.

7.9   Summary

Mental imagery is an effective way of performing rote memorizing,
such as remembering the names of parts of a machine. In addition, it
is an effective means of reasoning about objects under transformation
and about abstract qualities.

Mental imagery is not a single, undifferentiated ability. Rather,
imagery can be decomposed into a number of distinct subsystems.
Any given imagery task requires some combination of these subsystems. For example, mentally projecting the trajectory of a truck's path

through rough terrain requires subsystems used in image generation (visualizing the truck and terrain from stored information), transformation (imagining the truck moving), and inspection ("seeing" the results of the transformation), whereas mentally loading crates into an irregularly shaped bay requires these abilities plus image maintenance (keeping in mind previously placed crates while new ones are being considered).

People differ in how effectively they can use specific imagery subsystems. They are not generally "good" or "bad" at imagery. Thus, to select the right person for a specific imagery task, one must first understand which abilities are critical for performing the task and then must determine whether a given person is effective in those ways.

This chapter provides guidelines for determining which processing subsystems are used to perform specific tasks and for assessing whether a person is adept at that sort of processing. Tentative guidelines for training are also provided, but with the major caveat that training is likely to be task specific and of uncertain effectiveness.

References

Anderson, R. A., G. K. Essick, and R. M. Siegal. 1985. "Encoding of spatial location by posterior parietal neurons." *Science* 230:456–458.

Biederman, I. 1987. "Recognition by components: A theory of human image understanding." *Psychological Review* 94:115–147.

Bower, G. H. 1972. "Mental imagery and associative learning," in *Cognition in Learning and Memory*, L. Gregg, ed. New York: Wiley, 51–88.

Bundesen, C., and A. Larson. 1975. "Visual transformation of size." *Journal of Experimental Psychology: Human Perception and Performance* 1:214–220.

Diamond, R., and S. Carey. 1986. "Why faces are and are not special: An effect of expertise." *Journal of Experimental Psychology: General* 115(2):107–117.

Ehrlichman, H., and J. Barrett. 1983. "Right hemisphere specialization for mental imagery: A review of the evidence." *Brain and Cognition* 2:55–76.

Farah, M. J. 1984. "The neurological basis of mental imagery: A componential analysis." *Cognition* 18:245–272.

Farah, M. J. In press. "Is visual imagery really visual? Overlooked evidence from neuropsychology." *Psychological Review*.

Finke, R. A. 1980. "Levels of equivalence in imagery and perception." *Psychological Review* 86:113–132.

Finke, R. A., and S. M. Kosslyn. 1980. "Mental imagery acuity in the peripheral visual field." *Journal of Experimental Psychology: Human Perception and Performance* 6:126–139.

Finke, R. A., and R. N. Shepard. 1986. "Visual functions of mental imagery," in *Handbook of Perception and Human Performance*, K. R. Boff, L. Kaufman, and J. P. Thomas, eds. New York: Wiley-Interscience, 37-1–37-55.

Gregory, R. L. 1970. *The Intelligent Eye*. London: Weidenfeld and Nicholson.

Kosslyn, S. M. 1975. "Information representation in visual images." *Cognitive Psychology* 7:341–370.

Kosslyn, S. M. 1978. "Measuring the visual angle of the mind's eye." *Cognitive Psychology* 10:356–389.

Kosslyn, S. M. 1980. *Image and Mind*. Cambridge, Mass.: Harvard University Press.

Kosslyn, S. M. 1983. *Ghosts in the Mind's Machine*. New York: Norton.

Kosslyn, S. M. 1987. "Seeing and imaging in the cerebral hemispheres: A computational approach." *Psychological Review* 94:148–175.

Kosslyn, S. M., and J. Feldman. 1987. "Image generation and the cerebral hemispheres: Alternative strategies." Harvard University.

Kosslyn, S. M., and P. Jolicoeur. 1980. "A theory-based approach to the study of individual differences in mental imagery," in *Aptitude, Learning, and Instruction: Cognitive Processes Analyses of Aptitude*, R. E. Snow, P. A. Federico, and W. E. Montague, eds. Hillsdale, N.J.: Erlbaum, vol. 2, 139–175.

Kosslyn, S. M., and S. P. Shwartz. 1977. "A simulation of visual imagery." *Cognitive Science* 1:265–295.

Kosslyn, S. M., T. M. Ball, and B. J. Reiser. 1978. "Visual images preserve metric spatial information: Evidence from studies of image scanning." *Journal of Experimental Psychology: Human Perception and Performance* 4:47–60.

Kosslyn, S. M., R. S. Berndt, and T. J. Doyle. 1985. "Imagery and language: A neuropsychological approach," in *Attention and Performance*, M. I. Posner and O. S. Marin, eds. Hillsdale, N.J.: Erlbaum, vol. II, 319–334.

Kosslyn, S. M., R. A. Flynn, and J. B. Amsterdam. 1988. "Components of high-level vision: A cognitive neuroscience analysis." Cambridge, Mass.: Harvard University.

Kosslyn, S. M., M. Van Kleeck and K. N. Kirby. In press. "A neurologically plausible model of individual differences in visual mental imagery," in *Imagery: Current Developments*, J. T. E. Richardson, P. Hampson and D. Marks, eds. Hillsdale, N.J.: Erlbaum Associates.

Kosslyn, S. M., A. Barrett, C. B. Cave, and J. Tang. 1987. "Evidence for two types of spatial representations: Hemispheric specialization for categorical and coordinate relations." Harvard University.

Kosslyn, S. M., J. L. Brunn, K. R. Cave, and R. W. Wallach. 1984. "Individual differences in mental imagery ability: A computational analysis." *Cognition* 18:195–244.

Kosslyn, S. M., C. B. Cave, D. A. Provost, and S. M. von Gierke. In press. "Sequential processes in image generation: Evidence from an objective measure." *Cognitive Psychology*.

Kosslyn, S. M., J. D. Holtzman, M. J. Farah, and M. S. Gazzaniga. 1985. "A computational analysis of mental image generation: Evidence from functional dissociations in split-brain patients." *Journal of Experimental Psychology: General* 114:311–341.

Kosslyn, S. M., B. J. Reiser, M. J. Farah, and S. L. Fliegel. 1983. "Generating visual images: Units and relations." *Journal of Experimental Psychology: General* 112:278–303.

Larsen, A., and C. Bundesen. 1978. "Size scaling in visual pattern recognition." *Journal of Experimental Psychology: Human Perception and Performance* 4:1–20.

Levine, D. N., J. Warach, and M. J. Farah. 1985. "Two visual systems in mental imagery: Dissociation of 'what' and 'where' in imagery disorders due to bilateral posterior cerebral lesions." *Neurology* 35:1010–1018.

Lowe, D. 1987. "Three-dimensional object recognition from single two-dimensional images." *Artificial Intelligence* 31:355–395.

Marr, D. 1982. *Vision*. San Francisco, Calif.: Freeman.

Mishkin, M., L. G. Ungerleider, and K. A. Macko. 1983. "Object vision and spatial vision: Two cortical pathways." *Trends in Neurosciences* 6:414–417.

Moran, J., and R. Desimone. 1985. "Selective attention gates visual processing in the extrastriate cortex." *Science* 229:782–784.

Neisser, U. 1967. *Cognitive Psychology.* New York: Appleton-Century-Crofts.

Neisser, U. 1976. *Cognition and Reality.* San Francisco, Calif.: Freeman.

Paivio, A. 1971. *Imagery and Verbal Processes.* New York: Holt, Rinehart & Winston.

Pinker, S. 1980. "Mental imagery and the third dimension." *Journal of Experimental Psychology: General* 109:354–371.

Posner, M. I., A. W. Inhoff, F. J. Friedrich, and A. Cohen. 1985. "Isolating attentional systems: A cognitive-anatomical analysis." Paper presented at the meetings of the Psychonomics Society, Boston, Mass.

Posner, M. I., J. A. Walker, F. J. Friedrich, and R. D. Rafal. 1984. "Effects of parietal lobe injury on covert orienting of visual attention." *Journal of Neuroscience* 4:1863–1974.

Pylyshyn, Z. W. 1973. "What the mind's eye tells the mind's brain: A critique of mental imagery." *Psychological Bulletin* 80:1–24.

Pylyshyn, Z. W. 1981 "The imagery debate: Analogue media versus tacit knowledge." *Psychological Review* 87:16–45.

Segal, S. J. 1971. "Processing of the stimulus in imagery and perception," in *Imagery: Current Cognitive Approaches,* S. J. Segal, ed. New York: Academic Press, 69–100.

Segal, S. J., and V. Fusella. 1970. "Influence of imaged pictures and sounds on detection of visual and auditory signals." *Journal of Experimental Psychology* 83:458–464.

Sekular, R., and D. Wash. 1972. "Speed of size scaling in human vision." *Psychonomic Science* 27:93–94.

Shepard, R. N., and L. A. Cooper. 1982. *Mental Images and Their Transformations.* Cambridge, Mass.: MIT Press.

Shepard, R. N., and J. Metzler. 1971. "Mental rotation of three-dimensional objects." *Science* 171:701–703.

Ungerleider, L. G., and M. Mishkin. 1982. "Two cortical visual systems," in *Analysis of Visual Behavior,* D. J. Ingle, M. A. Goodale, and R. J. W. Mansfield, eds. Cambridge, Mass.: MIT Press, 549–586.

Van Essen, D. 1985. "Functional organization of primate visual cortex," in *Cerebral Cortex,* A. Peters and E. G. Jones, eds. New York: Plenum Press, vol. 3, 259–329.

Weber, R. J., and R. Harnish. 1974. "Visual imagery for words: The Hebb test." *Journal of Experimental Psychology* 102:409–414.

III

Present and Future of Memory Research and Its Applications

William Hirst and
Michael S. Gazzaniga

Anyone with even a passing professional interest in memory has been faced with the smiling face of a relative probing, "So, you study memory, do you? Well, I have a terrible memory. Can't remember names. How can you help me?" Most students of memory return the smile, mumble something about things being complex, and scan the room for a more pleasant conversationalist, for the truth is that despite many years of study little is known about how to improve memory. Students of memory might caution that improvement and application is not their goal; rather, they want to understand how memory works. We often reply to our inquisitive relatives that their memory is quite fine, at least as good as one can expect. This assurance might be true for many, but for the elderly sinking into dementia, for students unable to keep up with the rest of the class, for employees who have trouble mastering their jobs in a timely fashion, memory is clearly not working as well as expected. For these people application, not understanding, is important.

In this part we summarize the lessons learned from the previous chapters. The book was motivated by the question, Does present and forseeable biological and psychological knowledge about the structure and function of memory hold hope for people with memory problems? Each contributor was asked to push his or her current understanding about either the neuroscience or psychology of memory beyond the current state of knowledge. They were asked to see if any insights into the functions or structure of memory could be applied to a variety of educational, medical, and vocational settings. Thus much of the book is speculative. Black et al. offer a model of neuronal change with long-term persistence; Lynch and Baudry infer psychological function of brain structures from lesion work and the route of connections; Shepherd investigates commonalities among neural circuitries; Sejnowski and Rosenberg explore the implication that recent advances in neuronal modeling have for memory; Kutas pushes event-related potential (ERP) data toward questions of psychological relevance; Hirst examines how psychological principles of memory might be applied to the job environment; Kosslyn develops a model of imagery based on neurological and psychological data.

We began our review of these chapters with a prejudice about what is meant by the term "memory." At some level, even a spring can be said to have a memory, in that it bounces back to its original position every time it is squeezed. Clearly, if we are interested in human memory, as we must be if our concern is application, then a broad-ranging definition of memory will not do. Accompanying any human memory is the belief that the information was acquired in the remem-berer's personal past. People may not remember the incident in which a remembered event or fact occurred, but nevertheless they must believe that they either experienced the remembered event or learned the remembered fact. This concept of belief is a bit woolly, and clearly with a better understanding of memory a less subjective term may be possible. But something along these lines is necessary if memory "images" are ever to be differentiated from images as prod-ucts of pure imagination. From this perspective cells cannot be said to have "memories." They may show persistent structural changes, but this structural change is quite removed from the human experience of memorizing and remembering. This persistence may indeed serve as a basis for memory, in the sense that we will use it, but work must be done to establish the connection. It cannot be taken for granted.

The Present State of Knowledge

None of the authors here is ready to offer a strong solution for peo-ple's memory difficulties. Hirst argued that curriculum and the to-be-remembered material itself should be designed with the demands and principles of memory in mind. He actually shows some exam-ples of how this designing might be done. But even his chapter is programmatic in nature because it points in the right direction rather than maps out an easily applicable algorithm. The real ques-tion, however, is not whether the chapters offer solutions for memory problems but whether they suggest ways in which research might progress so that solutions are eventually found.

We discuss first the work on the neuroscience of memory and then the chapters written from a psychological perspective.

Neuroscience
The neuroscience of memory has made much progress since Hebb (1949) first sketched a theory of memory and learning, but Hebb's thoughts on the matter still guide much of the work. Hebb argued

that any experience leads to the transmission of nervous impulses through a neuronal circuit. Repeated exposure facilitates transmission. The resulting cell assembly, with the rapid transmission of impulses, constitutes a biological trace of the experience.

Hebb supplied a framework for understanding memory in biological terms. He left a host of questions, however. How are nerve impulses transmitted? What changes occur in the neuron to facilitate transmission? How long is this change in effect? How are the circuits structured? Are there similarities among circuits? And so on. In other words, one needed to fill in the Hebbian framework with details about anatomy, biochemistry, physiology, and computational power.

The contributors to the neuroscience part of this book summarize recent attempts to fill in these details. It is probably worthwhile to pause to see how far each of them goes in developing a biological theory of memory.

The Biochemistry of Memory   In their chapter, Black et al. are interested in the biochemistry of "information storage in the nervous system." As they note, the transmission of nerve impulses across a synapse depends crucially on the neurotransmitters present. On average, a neuron uses three different neurotransmitters, and, if we accept Black et al.'s assumption that these transmitters come in five different concentrations, then each neuron can be in 1 of 244 different neurotransmitter-defined states. When it is considered that there are 100 billion neurons, the potential that neurotransmitters have for defining unique brain states is transparent. For Black et al. these unique brain states can be said to represent information, and, as a consequence, neurotransmitters can be treated as "communicative symbols."

If these communicative symbols are to have anything to do with the storage of information, as opposed to the expression of information, then the time course of any change is important. If environmental stimulation causes a change in the production and concentration of neurotransmitters, then the change must be maintained for a long time if it is to represent the storage of information. The effort for Black et al. then, is to find changes in neurotransmitter concentrations that have a long-term presence.

Black et al. use as their model the sympathetic nervous system, which is involved in fight-or-flight responses, and examine the role of norepinephrine (NE) and substance P. Consider the discussion of NE. The biosynthesis of NE depends on the conversion of circulating tyrosine to L-DOPA. The key enzyme for this conversion is tyrosine hydroxylase (TH), and the thrust of Black et al.'s argument is that TH is a communicative symbol important to the storage of information. Black and his co-workers show that stressful stimuli resulting in sympathetic activation elicit a two- to threefold elevation of TH in sympathetic neurons within two days, and that the enzyme remains elevated for at least three days. Moreover, the elevated level of TH will depend on the extent of the initial stimulation and the number of stimulations, reflecting well-known properties of memory. TH clearly acts as if it plays a role in information storage.

One, of course, must face the question of whether this mechanism, defined on the periphery, has anything to do with memory, which after all involves the central nervous system. Black et al. raise this question and argue that the same properties of TH found in the sympathetic nervous system can also be found in the nucleus locus ceruleus. Indeed, enzyme activity following stimulation is significantly elevated after twelve days and in the frontal cortex can last up to three weeks. But this argument does not directly confront the relevance of the TH model to a theory of memory. Therein lies the limitations of Black et al.'s theory.

Black and his co-workers' energies are focused on the actions of neurotransmitters and related enzymes. They present evidence for various neuronal changes with stimulation that have long-lasting effects. How these long-lasting effects influence memory have yet to be determined. So far, the duration of any observable change is no more than three or four weeks; yet some memories last for years. Clearly the mechanisms sketched by Black et al. cannot be the complete story.

A Neural Model of Memory Function   Lynch and Baudry try to map some of the functions of memory onto neurophysiological structures and processes. Olfactory memory is considered for two main reasons: first, because it is simple (the sensory epithelium is only two synapses away from the cortex) and, second, because there is little interspecies variation. Lynch and Baudry trace the flow of information from the olfactory bulb through the pyriform cortex to the dorsomedial thalamic nucleus or the hippocampus, and from the thalamic structure to the frontal cortex. Each of these structures is linked to an aspect of olfactory memory on the basis of lesion work. The pyriform cortex is associated with representational memory because of the quasi-random nature of the connections between the lateral olfactory tract and the pyriform cortex. The distribution ensures that any combination of cell firing in the tract causes excitation in a small area of the pyriform cortex. The dorsomedial thalamus is associated with either the mapping of appropriate response patterns to particular olfactory cues or the categorization of odors. As support for this claim, Lynch and Baudry point to the highly convergent nature of the projections from the pyriform cortex, where individual odors are represented, to the thalamus. Finally, the hippocampus is associated with consolidation of representational but not procedural memory by means of encoding of contextual information, in part because the hippocampus receives equal-size inputs of olfactory and nonolfactory (contextual) information. Lynch and Baudry also note that the hippocampus is capable of long-term potentiation (LTP), that is, a persistent potentiation of hippocampal synapses following brief periods of high-frequency synaptic stimulation. This LTP may be the mechanism by which memories are consolidated in the hippocampus, a proposal that Lynch and Baudry explore in detail.

It is interesting that Lynch and Baudry propose a context theory of memory on the basis of the functional neuroanatomy of the olfactory memory system and the hippocampus. That is, they assign to the hippocampus the role of integrating olfactory and contextual or nonolfactory information rather than the traditional role of memory consolidation per se. This thesis conforms with some work on temporal lobe amnesia in humans. Several investigators have suggested that damage to the hippocampus disrupts the encoding of information about the context in which the target occurred, not the encoding of the target itself (Hirst 1982; Hirst and Volpe 1984a; Mayes et al. 1985). The resulting mnemonic representation is impoverished, with targets connected semantically but not contextually. This proposal is supported by several lines of evidence. First, amnesiacs can show retention of the to-be-remembered material if properly cued. Thus amnesiacs' responsiveness to a recognition probe (Hirst et al. 1986) and strong semantic cues is better than one might expect from their poor free recall (Hirst et al. 1987; Warrington and Weiskrantz 1971). Second, although there is some controversy over the contribution of the frontal lobe (Schacter 1987b), amnesiacs' memory for the spatial location of to-be-remembered objects (Hirst and Volpe 1984b; Smith and Milner 1981), the temporal order of events (Hirst and Volpe 1982; Mayes et al. 1985), and the source of the to-be-remembered material (Schacter et al. 1984) is much worse than one would expect from their target recognition scores. Third, work with normal subjects indicates that the encoding of contextual information is qualitatively different from the encoding of target information. Finally, again in normal subjects, the ability to discriminate to-be-remembered events on the basis of contextual information is more important for successful recall than it is for successful recognition.

Thus Lynch and Baudry's functional analysis, their review of the lesion work with rats, the recent work on amnesia in humans, and the studies of contextual encoding in normal subjects converge to underline the importance of contextual information for successful encoding of information. But this progress should not obscure some of the problems inherent in Lynch and Baudry's model. First, to make a point similar to one raised in the discussion of Black et al.'s work, there is at this point no direct evidence that LTP is related to psychological memory. LTP is essentially a neuronal change that can last for weeks. The causal link between this change and memory must still be established. Second, the assignment of psychological functioning to various structures on the basis of their connections to other structures is at best conjectural. Again, the necessary behavioral work has not yet been done. Finally, it is unclear how the role assigned to the hippocampus for odors will generalize to other stimuli, despite Lynch and Baudry's assurances.

The Circuitry of Memory   Shepherd is concerned with microcircuitry, the structure that links an input to a neuron with its output. Shepherd shows that nature is conservative and the structure present in the more primitive paleocortex holds, with variations, for the archicortex and even the neocortex. Consequently the genetic mechanism governing cortical growth may be much simpler than might be expected, inasmuch as the genetic mechanism does not have to be sensitive to the cortical area in which the growth is taking place.

Shepherd organizes his discussion of the extant research around the synaptic triad: principal output neuron, input fiber, and interneurons. For the paleocortex, the hippocampus, the submammalian general cortex, and the mammalian neocortex, Shepherd identifies the three elements and characterizes their organization in terms of input processing and output control. Some of the similarities that he finds between the basic circuitry of these cortical structures are as follows. First, each cortex has as its principal output neuron a pyramidal type of cell, with apical and basal dendritic compartments. Second, specific inputs to the three types of simple cortex are made onto the apical dendrites of the pyramidal neurons. For all cortices the input fibers make excitatory synapses onto spines of the distal apical branches. Feed-forward inhibitory pathways are also found in several of the cortical structures.

Moreover, the input processing in each cortex is remarkably similar. The process of integrating different inputs begins at the individual spines of the apical dendrite and continues as spines and branches interact. Integrative interactions are governed by several factors, including spatial distribution of excitatory and inhibitory inputs and the distribution of voltage-gated membrane channels. Output control is mediated in each cortex by inhibitory interneurons, which can either feed forward or feed back. Reexcitation within a circuit is mediated by axon collaterals.

The challenge of Shepherd's research is to go from the detailed microcircuitry to a discussion of memory. Shepherd is claiming that the structures are similar across the cortex, but memory functioning is not uniformly distributed across cortices. Nevertheless, Shepherd does suggest that the reexcitation provided by axon collaterals can account for short-term memory. He further suggests that, whatever the mechanism of long-term memory, it probably rests at the connection between input fibers and the spines on the apical dendrites.

It is unfair to Shepherd's aims to demand a model of memory from his work. His chapter is more a discussion of constraints rather than a framework for understanding memory and learning. If memories are to be represented in the weighted connections of a network, as many researchers have claimed since Hebb—the contribution of Sejnowski and Rosenberg in this book fits into this school—then Shepherd places firm constraints on the architecture of these networks. It is often difficult to see what the implications of these constraints are for psychological functioning. The virtue of building them into a network model such as Sejnowski and Rosenberg's is that one can then compare the functioning of the model with and without the constraints. Such a comparison should provide some hint about the implications of the constraints mentioned by Shepherd. We return to this point when discussing Sejnowski and Rosenberg's chapter.

Summary Most biological models of memory assume that memories are laid down through changes in neuronal connections, either through neuronal growth or through changes at the level of the synapse, or, to follow Shepherd, at dendritic spines. Most of the models presented here involve changes that occur rather quickly following stimulation but last for at most four weeks. Thus they can nicely account for the rapid acquisition of memories, especially short-term memories. Their difficulties arise when trying to describe changes that would account for memories that last years if not decades. Moreover, even if any of the accounts could be extended to cover lasting memories, the necessary behavioral research clearly establishing a link between the posited mechanism and memory needs to be pursued.

Thus in the chapters here we see several proposals for a biological theory of memory. They would be more accurately described as sketches of a theory. Their chief virtue is that they raise many empirically addressable questions; their chief vice is that they are more data impoverished, especially in terms of behavioral results, than a theory should be.

Cognitive Science
In considering the psychology of memory, one is tempted to forgo any theoretical development and just use one's intuitions. Ancient Greeks did just that, with some success, but this intuitive method has its limits. The Greeks, for instance, disagreed over the effectiveness of mnemonics like the method of loci for memorizing material such as prose. This issue can clearly be resolved empirically using the methodology of psychology. The same point can be made for several other deeper issues. To what extent can training improve memory? To what extent does mnemonic capacity differ across individuals? What are the biological constraints on memory, and are they susceptible to psychological manipulation? These questions are raised in several of the chapters, and empirical research, not intuitions, form the basis of the tentative answers offered by the authors. All of the research described in part II on the psychology of memory involves humans as research subjects. We consider each chapter separately.

Using Biological Measures to Constrain Theories of Mind   Kutas reviews recent evidence from the event-related potential literature that bears on cognitive psychological modeling. In doing so, she underlines the close relation between mind and brain. Her discussion focuses on three issues. First, she argues that one should examine the function of latency of P300 plotted against memory set size when considering the Sternberg search experiment. In particular, she argues that the slope of this function is a more accurate measure of speed of serial comparison than the standard reaction time (RT) slope because the RT measure includes the time it takes to encode a stimulus and the time it takes to respond, whereas the P300 measure directly assesses serial comparison speed. The need for alternative interpretations of P3 latencies and RT is dramatically illustrated in work on memory scanning in the aged. The slope of the standard function plotting RT against set size increases with age, whereas the slope of the function plotting P3 against set size does not. If P3 is a more accurate measure of speed of serial comparison, then memory scanning may slow in the elderly not because their speed of serial comparison slows but because the speed with which stimuli are encoded or responses are made decreases.

Second, Kutas reviews research on P3 in verbal learning experiments. She adopts the viewpoint that large P3's can be found whenever an item in working memory must be updated. To the extent that this updating will lead to a strong memory trace, a large P3 in encoding should predict subsequent recall. In a variety of experiments this prediction seems to be verified. There are some interesting twists. For instance, Karis et al. (1984) examined the von Restorff effect and presented subjects with lists of words in which all of the words but one were typed in small letters. The "isolate" was typed in capital letters. Karis et al. found that P3 measured during encoding best predicted recall for the isolate for those subjects who seemed most sensitive to the von Restorff effect. Thus some subjects recalled the list quite well but did not remember the isolate any better than the other words in the list. These subjects presumably used associational and other semantic strategies when memorizing. The updating of the isolate in working memory had little bearing on the outcome of these strategies. Consequently P3 was not very predictive of recall for this group. Other subjects recalled the list poorly but remembered the isolates quite well. Clearly the oddness of the word was important to their memorization strategy. For this group P3 was predictive of subsequent recall. In this experiment P3 appears to be a sensitive measure of cognitive strategies.

Third, Kutas reviews work investigating whether ERPs can serve as a measure of depth of processing, a measure that has eluded traditional cognitive psychologists. Unfortunately, at present there does not seem to be any difference in the ERPs found when subjects process a word superficially or meaningfully. However, the nature of the response—for instance, a "yes" versus a "no" response—does elicit differentiable ERPs.

Much research has built on this observation. The N400 wave is relevant here. It is produced by semantic incongruity, for instance, an unexpected ending to a sentence. Semantically incongruous words, that is, words with strong N400's, are not remembered well. Interestingly Kutas is able to predict that incongruous words related to a possible congruous word (for example, "The game was called when it started to umbrella") would be remembered better than incongruous words unrelated to a possible congruous word (for example, "George was fired but he could not tell his fog") purely on the basis of the N400's that she observed with these sentences. Other work had shown that words with small N400's were better remembered than words with large N400's and that related incongruous words produced smaller N400's than the unrelated incongruous words. Thus Kutas accurately predicts that the related incongruous words would be better remembered than the unrelated incongruous words. N400 and P300 appear to probe mental processing sensitively enough that detailed predictions about the consequences of this processing can be made.

Theories of Imagery and Implications about Biological Constraints   Kosslyn is mainly concerned with imagery, not memory, but the principles that he expounds are central to any cognitive theory of memory. In his chapter he notes that cognitive scientists attempt to characterize the mind in terms of separate subsystems. Imagery, for instance, is not a single undifferentiated event or ability; rather, it can be divided into subsystems that carry out four separate functions: the generation of images from information stored in long-term memory, the retention of an image, the inspection of an image, and the transformation of an image, such as rotation. A chief claim of Kosslyn's is that the different subsystems are neurologically real; that is, various neuroscientific probes will alter behavior in ways consistent with the disruption of normal functioning of a subsystem. Kosslyn has developed a model of imagery detailed enough to permit successful computer simulation. The computer program's subsystems include a normalizer, a shape categorizer, a position calculator, associative memory, and so on. Kosslyn maps these subsystems onto two well-known visual tracts. This effort is important because the tracts serve two quite different perceptual functions. The ventral system is involved with the perception of shape, whereas the dorsal system is involved with the perception of location. Thus subsystems important to the analysis of shape, such as the shape categorizer and the normalizer, are treated as parts of the ventral system, whereas subsystems important in placing an image in a mental coordinate plan, such as the categorical relations encoder and the coordinate relations encoder, are treated as parts of the dorsal system.

This modularity is important when considering training for imaging or other cognitive tasks. As Kosslyn notes, people do not differ in their ability to image; they differ in their ability to transform, create, or maintain an image. That is, differences exist in the subsystems and not the overall process. Consequently, when devising a training curriculum, one must concentrate on improving the individual subsystems. It may help to teach someone to image, but it would be better to teach him or her to normalize an image or to categorize a shape. For Kosslyn a fuller understanding of the components of imaging is a necessary prerequisite for any training program because these components indicate what skills must be taught. The same point can be made for memory training. Of course, Kosslyn is not as concerned about memory as he is with imaging, but a componential analysis of memory may guide the development of memory training just as it should guide the development of imaging training.

At the end of his chapter Kosslyn asserts that "training probably will improve only the subsystems used in a task and only in the precise way they are being used. If the option is available, it is better to select a person with the right skills for a task than to try to train a person for the task." Two claims are embedded in this proposal. First, training is usually quite task specific and often does not transfer from one situation to another, even if the same subsystem is used. Second, basic abilities, representing what Kosslyn claims are neurologically real subsystems, may be individual traits not easily altered with training.

Application   Most of the chapters in this book are concerned with development of theory. In his chapter Hirst tries to apply what theory exists to practical problems. He offers a brief review of the literature on improving memory and emphasizes that memory is to a great extent what people do with stimuli, not what their intentions or motivations are. He articulates several well-known principles to a better memory. People, for instance, can organize material and search for its meaning, see connections between the material itself (organizing), establish relations between the material and other knowledge (elaborating), and draw distinctions between different to-be-remembered material and general world knowledge (discriminating). They can also image material or build retrieval cues in order to aid memorizing and remembering. Almost all courses on memory aids and all the well-known mnemonic techniques taught in them involve one or more of these general strategies. Hirst shows how these strategies could be applied to practical settings, illustrating his discussion with an example in which trainees have to learn the function of meters and levers on a control panel. Hirst argues that, although these strategies could be applied intentionally by memorizers in order to facilitate their memory, it is probably more worthwhile for the material to be structured and tasks be given so that learners must organize, elaborate, discriminate, image, and build retrieval cues regardless of their intentions or motivations. Thus cover tasks could force individuals to memorize and remember in effective ways, even though the learner may not conceive of the task as involving memory. Hirst argues that the careful design of such cover tasks should lead to as effective memorization as any intentional memorization would yield, but without the need for motivation or even good strategic thinking.

Hirst confronts many of the issues raised by Kosslyn, but he is not as pessimistic about the possibilities of training as Kosslyn is. First, consider the problem of task specificity. Hirst readily admits that, whatever the nature of any training, it must be designed for the task at hand. For Kosslyn this constraint creates severe limitations, in that Kosslyn probably in the end wants training to make a more intelligent person or a better imager or a better memorizer. Hirst would agree with Kosslyn that the prognosis for such drastic changes is not encouraging [but see Herrnstein et al. (1986)]. But if you are concerned with designing a curriculum to teach someone how to use a piece of equipment on the job or the attributes of a set of boats, you do not have to make a more intelligent person or a better memorizer. You just have to teach the material at hand. From this perspective both Kosslyn and Hirst would agree that training can be designed to be more effective.

Hirst outlines several things that should be considered when planning a training procedure or developing equipment. They are a direct outcome of theories of memory that stress organization, discrimination, and elaboration as central to the encoding process. But Hirst admits that applying these principles is an art and probably requires a better than average person. His point is that the training should be devised so that the processes important to memorization occur outside the trainees' own volition.

As noted, the heart of his proposal is that what matters in memory is what you do, not what your capacity is. On the surface this contention also seems to contradict Kosslyn, who argues for individual differences in the capacity of the subsystems of imaging; however, once Kosslyn's argument is carefully stated, the apparent contradiction disappears. For Kosslyn individual differences are traceable to the subsystems of imaging and not imaging per se. This same point can be mapped onto memory. Memory is not a unified process any more than imaging is. It also involves a host of systems and processes, any one of which could be better or worse than the average. So to speak of someone as having a good or bad memory makes no more sense than to speak of someone as being a good or bad imager. One may have trouble classifying or elaborating on a list of equipment terms, and these difficulties may lead to poor recall or recognition. This statement, however, is different from saying that a person has a bad memory.

Thus, although Hirst may be right that the ability of someone to memorize and remember may not be limited by a general memory capacity, a far more subtle limitation on the components or modules underlying memorizing and remembering may exist. Kosslyn has systematically studied individual differences in imaging with an emphasis on the subsystems, not overall performance. As far as we know, a similar program has not been carried out in the area of memory. Such a program of research may provide a better understanding of how to assess students or trainees and what kind of instruction they should receive.

Uniting Mind and Brain
The background research reports from which this summary has been made possible is divided into two parts: the first concerned with neuroscience research and the second concerned with psychological research. Although both areas are concerned with memory, their vocabulary and methodology are quite different. It would be nice if there was some way to unite the two. The one chapter that we have not discussed so far offers a possible means of filling the gap. The parallel distributed processing (PDP) discussed by Sejnowski and Rosenberg offers a powerful tool for modeling psychological function in physiological terms. The model that they discuss consists of a network of nodes with weighted connections. The network is capable of learning through changes in the weighting of the connections. Such changes are accomplished by an algorithmic process known as backward propagation, which reassigns weight values in parallel across the network. Consequently the resulting representation of the learned material is distributed across the network. Early network models consisted of only two layers: a set of input nodes connected to a set of output nodes. The current generation of PDPs contain a third layer, the hidden layer, in which nodes mediate between input and output.

Sejnowski and Rosenberg focus on a particular PDP model, called NETtalk. Here the input is a set of orthographic features of words and the output is the phonological features of the words. As Sejnowski and Rosenberg show, NETtalk can learn to "read" text and in other learning contexts demonstrate such well-known psychological effects as spacing.

Clearly a network consisting of connected nodes can show quite impressive learning if the weights of the connections are allowed to change with experience. From a neuroscience perspective there is an easy analogy between massive parallel networks and neuronal circuitry, at least on an abstract level. Nodes and connections can be thought of as neurons and synapses, respectively. Changes in neuronal structure occurring with experience can be thought of as changes in the weights of the connections between nodes. From a psychological perspective massively parallel networks can not only learn but seem to learn in psychologically real ways, as Sejnowski and

Rosenberg imply when discussing the spacing effect. So at one level we have a plausible psychological model; at another level, a plausible physiological model.

Yet it may be premature to cast an unreserved vote for PDP models. First, it is not known whether PDP models, as currently conceived, should elegantly capture all sorts of processing. As any cognitive psychologist knows, some processing is done serially, whereas other processing is done in parallel. For instance, there is much evidence that search through short-term memory is done serially and that search through a large array of trigrams is parallel. Should both forms of search be modeled as parallel processing? In the early days of information processing psychology, when the von Neumann computers dominated theorizing, many investigators were tempted to model every process as serial. Now, many workers on PDP try to model every process as parallel. Clearly some thought must be given to the best medium for modeling a particular process.

Moreover, although NETtalk mimics the spacing effect, there is more to memory than the spacing effect. For instance, NETtalk learns things more quickly than the psychological study of reading would suggest. Moreover, it learns to read in a qualitatively different way from the way a child learns to read. NETtalk heard the same passage over and over again. Children may hear the same story over and over again, and they do not generalize from this one story and begin reading words in new contexts. Indeed, a child learns by working with simple text first and then slowly building up to complex task. NETtalk jumps right into the complex texts. The situation here may be similar to that in early work on transformational grammar, when it was pointed out that transformational grammar as a formal mechanism was much too powerful (Peters and Richie 1973). It could describe not only natural language but also a much larger class of languages—natural and unnatural language if you like. The PDP models currently being considered may also be too powerful. They may not only model human processing and human representation of information; at the extreme they may also be able to capture a much larger class of processing, human and nonhuman alike.

A related problem is that, as a biological model of brain processing, the current crop of PDP models do not fully capture the complexity of biological phenomena. As already noted, there are limits on the extent of nonstructural LTP and time constraints on neuronal growth. These time parameters are presumably important in the formation of memories; yet there is nothing in the general conception of PDP that takes into account these limitations. Similarly, as several of the chapters make clear, the workings of the synapse are quite complex and presumably have implications for learning. Again, the PDP models do not capture this complexity. Finally, Shepherd pointed out several principles governing the structure of neural microcircuitry. These same principles should presumably be built into the microcircuitry of PDP networks.

It would seem, then, that if the PDP models are to bear more than a superficial similarity to biological models of memory, they must be constrained in both biological and psychological terms. And there is no reason why they cannot be. As currently conceived, the models are indeed general, but there is nothing inherent in their formulation that forces this generality. Indeed, one of the promises of PDP modeling is that it may provide a good language in which to test formally the consequences of many observable biological constraints.

Moving from Present Research to Future Research: Implications for Training and Instruction

So far we have summarized chapters from this book on the state of both neuroscience and psychology of memory. Research has to date proved quite fruitful, and each area reviewed shows promise for future growth. But at some point one must move beyond the specifics of current research efforts and address what motivated this collection in the first place. One wants to know whether any of these specifics can translate into possible application. Particularly, three questions should be addressed: (1) How can the current state of the art of memory research be expanded so that it can bear on issues of instruction and training? (2) What aspects of training and instruction might be affected by current research and the proposed research? (3) How close is current and future research to actual application?

Let us say at the outset that at some level these are impossible questions to answer. Both neuroscience and the cognitive science of memory are in their infancy. They certainly have not developed to the point that applications fall out willy-nilly. There is still much art in going from the tentative findings of these fields to applications in learning and training. To some extent the difficulty has to do with the way information is presented in the field of memory. Neuroscientists and cognitive scientists are not driven by the need for application. They simply want to know how memory works. As a consequence, they are more likely to structure their information around questions central to a full understanding of the functioning of memory than around questions central to its improvement. To be sure, a full understanding of how memory works would probably tell us how to improve memory, but the field is far from such a complete story. Until it is available, applications of research findings might seem like glib translations of complex work to many working scientists.

Embedded in the three questions concerning application is a deeper issue. Even if there is agreement that application is not around the corner, how can the long-term goals of the neuroscientists and cognitive scientists be structured so that applications will seem more apparent or at least be closer to fruition? Could either the neuroscience or psychology of memory benefit by tying theory development and experimental research to practical concerns?

Neuroscience

Let us first consider neuroscience. When discussing neuroscience, we often reduce practical applications to pharmacological aids. The chapters in this volume did not address issues of pharmacology directly. They emphasized the development of theory about the biological foundations of memory. Although the theories chart rapid progress, theory development has not reached the stage at which it is possible to predict what drugs will improve memory. For that to happen, there must be a theory of how information is encoded, stored, and retrieved. Such a theory does not presently exist.

Should the research goal of developing a theory of the biology of memory be changed so that research focuses on finding a pharmacological aid to memory rather than a theory of how memory works? The emphasis on theory has led to simulations such as Sejnowski and Rosenberg's, studies of synaptic organization, as typified by Shepherd's work, and research on neurotransmitters, as in Black's work. A goal of discovering a memory drug might narrow the scope of discussion, with an emphasis on neurotransmitters.

But beyond narrowing the focus of discussion, emphasis on finding a drug for memory improvement might not be as productive as one might hope. The pharmacology of memory has not been terribly successful and has only revealed immense complications. It is worth reviewing briefly.

The Quick Fix   Those researchers concerned foremost with the discovery of a memory drug are guided by the work on L-DOPA and Parkinson's disease. For many years, investigators of Parkinson's knew that an impoverished level of the neurotransmitter dopamine was associated with the disease, and consequently they tried to use dopaminergic drugs to cure the disease. The problem was finding the right drug and the right dosage. For years they tried without success. It was only when Cotzias administered L-DOPA at what appeared to be a senselessly high dosage that the "cure" was found. Similar serendipity is prayed for in the work with so-called memory drugs. But an examination of the literature suggests that this trial and error approach has little chance of succeeding.

First, many different neurotransmitters appear to be involved in memorial processes. In a recent review of the literature on drugs and memory, Squire and Davis (1981) cautioned that they were limiting the range of their discussion but then discussed an incredibly large number of different neurotransmitter systems, reviewing drugs that affect the cortical level of neurotransmitters and related substances, including acetylcholine, norepinephrine, dopamine, ACTH, vasopressin, endorphins, and the opioid peptides. Clearly, unlike investigators of Parkinson's who were able to limit themselves to the dopaminergic system, memory researchers must investigate many more neurotransmitter systems.

But even if the number of systems is small, there are still problems and complications. Many drugs with an apparent effect on memory performance may act indirectly (by increasing attention, for instance) rather than directly on the mechanisms underlying memory.

Consider the work with vasopressin. Work with animals suggests that vasopressin is important for successful memory. For instance, administration of vasopressin such as lysine-8-vasopressin (LVP) to rats facilitates long-term retention of passive avoidance training (Ader and de Wied 1972; Bohus et al. 1978; Krejci and Kepkova 1978; Leshner and Roche 1977; Gold and van Bushkirk 1976) and sexually motivated learning (Bohus 1977). But this positive effect with animals does not easily transfer to humans. To be sure, positive effects of vasopressin on memory can be found. Four depressed patients treated with a long-acting analogue of vasopressin showed improved memory scores on a range of tests (Gold et al. 1979), and a group of normal adults aged 50 to 65 showed similar improvement when given a daily regimen of 16 IU of vasopressin nasal spray (Legros et al. 1978). In both cases, however, the observable memory improvement was also accompanied by improvement in other cognitive activities that could indirectly affect memory. The depressed patients showed improved affect, and the normal adults performed better on tests of perceptual-motor speed and attention. Thus apparent effects on memory may often have little to do with changes in the actual biological mechanism of memory.

Of course, careful research can separate the indirect effects on memory from the direct effects. And again, even if the effort were made and putative direct effects could be found, the right drug would probably still not be at hand. Consider acetylcholine (ACh). The brains of Alzheimer's patients with severe memory problems have an abnormally low level of ACh (Davies and Maloney 1976). Inasmuch as ACh facilitates transmission of nerve impulses across synapses, this abnormality is thought to bear on the Alzheimer's memory problems [see Baddeley (1976) for a discussion]. If the ACh level could be increased in these patients, the reasoning goes, then, like the work with L-DOPA, memory problems should be alleviated.

Unfortunately the scenario proved much more complicated than this. First, although nerve transmission will not occur if there is too little ACh, it also will not occur if there is too much ACh. For example, administration of an anticholinesterase, such as physostigmine or diisopropyl fluorophosphate (DFP), will inhibit the breakdown of ACh at the synapse and thereby increase the amount of ACh present for nerve impulse transmission. As the dosage of anticholinesterase increases, memory performance will first improve and then decline, reflecting the level of ACh (Deutsch et al. 1966).

But matters become even more complex, because the natural production of ACh appears to follow a complicated path when a nerve is stimulated. According to Deutsch (1971), the level of ACh declines between 30 minutes and 1 day after training and then gradually increases. This production schedule is not as counterintuitive as it may seem at first. When rats' maze learning was studied, their memory performance paralleled this putative production schedule, with performance dipping when tested between 30 minutes and 1 day after training and then gradually improving (Huppert and Deutsch 1969).

This ACh production schedule makes detailed and confirmed predictions about the effect of DFP a heartening prospect for anyone interested in empirical science. Thus DFP administered 30 minutes after training will facilitate memory performance because the level of ACh is low and the DFP increases it. However, by day 5, administration of DFP will actually hinder memory performance. At this point in time the level of ACh at the synapse has increased so much that any addition supplied through the mechanisms of DFP would raise the quantity to harmful levels.

The level of ACh cannot increase unendingly. At some point it must gradually decline, as the memory itself weakens. Indeed, Deutsch et al. (1966) found that, if DFP is administered late enough after training, it will once again have a facilitatory effect. In one study administrations after 14 and 28 days were compared. An inhibitory effect was observed after 14 days, but a facilitative effect was found after 28 days. This and other studies suggest that the effect of DFP depends on the strength of the trace and on the amount of time after training. Along the same lines it has been found that slow learners respond to physostigmine differently from fast learners.

Thus one simply cannot administer a cholinergic drug and expect a general improvement in memory performance. The success of the drug depends on the abilities of the learner, the age of the memory, and how well the memory was learned in the first place. This complicated picture must be viewed within a larger perspective to see how disastrous it is. As noted, the work on cholinergic drugs began because some patients with Alzheimer's disease have an impoverished level of ACh. What ACh has to do with memory is unclear. To be sure, under the right circumstances it enhances the transmission of nerve impulses, but does enhanced nerve transmission have anything to do with memory? No one knows. It could equally have an effect on task speed. In other words, ACh, even given its complexity, is investigated simply because people with memory problems have an impoverished level in the brain, not because it is known to have anything to do with memory.

Given this complicated and tenuous set of findings and connections, it is not surprising that work with cholinergic drugs in the clinic has met with little success. Researchers administer either anticholinesterases, which raise ACh level by preventing its breakdown, or choline and lecithin, which raise ACh level by aiding in the manufacture of ACh. Either set of drugs yields small but positive effects in some studies and no effects in others (Pearce 1984). Little order can be given to these studies, except that any positive effects that can be found depend on the severity of the amnesia.

Recently, more encouraging results have been reported using 1,2,3,4-tetrahydro-9-amniocridine (THA), a potent centrally acting anticholinesterase (Summers et al. 1986). When Alzheimer's patients of varying severity are placed on a daily regimen of THA, dramatic positive effects were seen for patients with mild dementia. Patients who had been forced to retire returned to their jobs, and others who could not manage daily tasks were once again responsible enough to govern their own affairs. Like so many drugs, however, THA improved not only memory but also a host of other cognitive activities. Whether it is a "memory" drug or a general cognitive enhancer is not known. Of course, from a clinical viewpoint, this distinction might not matter, and THA and other drugs, such as the cognitive enhancers being developed by Ayerst and Squibb, should be further explored. But will THA or any other cognitive enhancer help the subpopulation of people with memory problems, but without the more general cognitive deficits found in dementia?

Back to Theory   Thus the pharmacology of memory has not fulfilled its promise. The few success stories, such as that with THA, may not even involve a memory drug but a general cognitive enhancer. The serendipity and trial and error quality that characterizes the search for a memory drug will probably continue so long as it is not guided by a theory of biology of memory. For that reason we would encourage future research on neuroscience to continue to be directed by theoretical concerns rather than applications. Advances in neuroscience have been swift, and the necessary theoretical framework for application may lie in the foreseeable future. We should, however, emphasize that, by turning away from the "quick fix" of pharmacology, we are not saying that such research should be avoided. It has its place, in small doses. But the main thrust of future research on the neuroscience of memory should continue to be driven by theory.

Cognitive Science

Discovering Subsystems   Although the neuroscience of memory might not benefit from a strong focus on application, the cognitive science of memory may. In examining Hirst's and Kosslyn's chapters, a common theme emerges. To a large extent the folk psychology terms for talking about memory and imagery may not be the correct ones. Any cognitive system, be it the memory system or the imagery system, consists of separate subsystems. Cognitive science and cognitive neuroscience have focused energies on discovering the exact nature of these subsystems. Indeed, one of the major findings in cognitive science is that skills and abilities that had been viewed as unitary and undifferentiated, especially in folk psychology, have in fact a rich and complex underlying structure.

Kosslyn is particularly clear about this point when discussing work on imagery. Rather than being a single ability or trait, imagery appears to be a host of abilities. In his review Kosslyn mentions several abilities, including image retention, image generation, and image transformation. Individuals do not differ in their ability to image but in their ability to retain, generate, and transform images. Each of these processes is a separate unit of the cognitive system. The processes are called on when people image. The resulting phenomenological experience of imaging is in reality a complex combination of these processes.

This work on imagery illustrates the kind of research we think should be encouraged in cognitive science, especially memory research. Cognitive scientists must be encouraged to discover the subsystems of memory. Almost all researchers in the area of memory agree that memory is not a unitary faculty but consists of subsystems. The list of possible subsystems is quite long. People have differentiated separate storehouses in which memory can be stored. There are short-term and long-term memories (Atkinson and Shiffrin 1968), episodic and semantic memories (Tulving 1983), procedural and declarative memories (Cohen 1984; Squire 1982), and memories with and without awareness (Jacoby and Whiterspoon 1982). Researchers have also distinguished qualitatively different kinds of encoding. For instance, information about the spatial location, temporal order, and frequency of occurrence of an event may be encoded automatically, whereas information about the content of an event must be encoded effortfully (Hasher and Zacks 1979). Several distinctions have also been made in discussions of retrieval. Investigators, for instance, distinguish direct access to an item, as observed in a recognition task, from the retrieval of an item, as observed in a recall test [see Kintsch (1970)]. Others separate the processes on which familiarity judgments are based from the processes that guide retrieval (Mandler 1980). These storage, encoding, and retrieval distinctions are only beginning to be assembled into a coherent model of the subsystems of memory. Clearly more research must be done.

Methodology for Further Research   Of course, before a model can be proposed, one must know which of the subsystems proposed by various researchers truly reflects the architecture of human memory. The subsystems mentioned in the preceding paragraph have already received some attention, especially the difference between short-term memory and long-term memory and between episodic memory and semantic memory. The distinctions between procedural and declarative memories and between direct and indirect memories are less well-understood (Hirst 1987; Schacter 1987a). As for the encoding and retrieval distinctions, these are only now beginning to receive extensive research interest. Furthermore, as far as we know, each of the distinctions tends to be treated without regard to its relation to the other distinctions. In other words, no one has taken the putative subsystems and fitted them into a single model of memory. For instance, no one has explored the relation between the formation of episodic memories and the automatic encoding of spatiotemporal information.

To a large extent the discovery of subsystems depends on discovering dissociations. But it is often easy to supply alternative interpretations for any putative dissociation. For that reason a single piece of evidence is rarely conclusive. Converging evidence based on a wide variety of techniques is necessary.

Psychologists argue for separate subsystems when performance in a task that requires subsystem A but not subsystem B is stochastically independent of performance in a task that requires subsystem B but not subsystem A. Thus short- and long-term memories are assumed to be separate components of memory because 15 seconds of distraction will obliterate a short-term memory but will have little or no effect on a long-term memory.

Such dissociations can be found in experiments using normal subjects when two tasks have differential effects on memory performance. One can also look at individual differences. Two tasks tap different subsystems if individual variation in performance in one task is stochastically independent of individual variation in performance in the second task. The study of brain-damaged patients is also important in the discovering of memory subsystems. For instance, the distinction between procedural and declarative memories is based to an overwhelming extent on the discovery that amnesiacs can learn perceptual-motor skills at the same rate as normal subjects, even though they cannot remember the fact of learning the skill. Kutas illustrates how the use of evoked potentials can support putative dissociations by showing that behavior in one task elicits different ERPs from those elicited in other tasks. Other imaging techniques, such as positron emission tomography (PET), magnoencephalography, and magnetic resonance imagery (MRI), can also provide support for dissociation between varying subsystems.

Thus it is possible to show that two subsystems exist because people behave differently when they perform tasks that require the two subsystems and because their brains also behave differently when different parts of the brain mediate different subsystems. Taken together, a compelling story can usually be assembled in favor of the distinct subsystems. The search for subsystems must take a multidisciplinary approach. Research on subsystems must search for interactions between memory tasks done by normal individuals, for stochastically independent variation among individuals on memory tasks, for dissociations among patients with varying degrees of brain damage, and for differences in brain activity for different memory tasks, as imaged by techniques such as ERPs, PET scans, MRI, and magnoencephalography.

A Distinction in Search of Articulation   What putative subsystems of memory appear to be most deserving of continued research effort? One of the more interesting distinctions in the literature and one of the most poorly understood is the one that variously goes under the labels "procedural" versus "declarative" memories, "explicit" versus "implicit" memories, "semantic" versus "episodic" memories, and memory "with awareness" or "without awareness." This distinction may reflect the difference between skill learning and fact learning, or it may reflect the difference between verbalizable and nonverbalizable knowledge, or there may be an alternative way to phrase the distinction.

To a large extent this set of distinctions has been introduced in the context of the study of amnesia. In order to appreciate what phenomenon researchers are trying to explain and why there are so many different versions, we review briefly the relevant work.

Although amnesia is often thought of as a failure to remember events shortly after they occur, the memory failure is rarely, if ever, complete. Insights into the subsystems of memory can be garnered from a full understanding of what aspects of memory are preserved and disrupted with amnesia. Initial studies of amnesia by Milner et al. (1968) supported the distinction between long-term memory and short-term memory. They found that amnesiacs could retain information for a short period without rehearsal but would quickly forget new information if distracted. That is, their short-term memory was intact and their long-term memory was disrupted. Although the distinction between short-term memory and long-term memory may account for this dissociation, it cannot explain more recent findings. Cohen and Squire (1980) reported that amnesiacs learn to read mirror images of words at the same rate as normal subjects, even though they do not remember learning the task. Clearly some kinds of long-term memories are preserved, whereas other kinds are disrupted. Cohen and Squire suggest the distinction between procedural and declarative memories, which, although intuitively appealing, cannot readily account for work on priming in amnesiacs.

If exposed to the word "garbage" and then later asked to say the first word that comes to mind that completes the stem "gar," amnesiacs are as likely to say "garbage" as are normal subjects. However, if asked instead to complete "gar" with a studied word, amnesiacs are much less likely to say "garbage" than are normal subjects [see Schacter (1987a) for a review of the relevant literature]. Cermak et al. (1985) have used such results to argue that declarative memory is subdivided into semantic and episodic memories and that the amnesiac's deficit rests with episodic memory. According to this model the memory system would be a three-tier hierarchy, with the memory system first divided into long-term memory and short-term memory, long-term memory then divided into declarative memory and procedural memory, and declarative memory finally divided into episodic and semantic memory.

Graf and Schacter (1985) have argued that this account cannot explain normal associate priming in amnesiacs. That is, when subjects study the paired associate "tulip–garbage" and are later asked to complete the stem "gar," they are more likely to complete it with "garbage" if the stem is given in the same context in which it was learned ("tulip") than if given in a novel context. This effect is as robust for amnesiacs as it is for normal subjects. Inasmuch as the context is semantically unrelated to the target, the improved priming in amnesiacs cannot be accounted for by simple spreading activation in an intact semantic memory. Graf and Schacter offer a discriptive dichotomy—between explicit memory and implicit memory. Amnesiacs have trouble with tasks involving the explicit use of memory but not with those involving the implicit use of memory.

Hirst et al. (1986) have argued that even this descriptive dichotomy cannot fully account for what is preserved with amnesia. They showed that amnesiacs can recognize information better than one might expect given their poor recall. Moreover, this relatively preserved recognition cannot be attributed to their intact priming. Hirst argued that the amnesiac deficit is best described in terms of a breakdown in one kind of processing over another rather than in a disruption of particular storehouses of memory. Some of the mnemonic processes that supply the glue that holds individual events together and creates a unified representation are lost with amnesia. Without this glue memories would consist of a collection of individual traces of past events unconnected to one another. An amnesiac might be able to obtain direct access to these memories if provided with the appropriate probe (as in a priming or recognition task) but would not be able to search through memory in a systematic fashion. Hirst (1982) specifically builds on the distinction between the automatic encoding of context and the effortful encoding of content to suggest that amnesiacs do not encode the context of to-be-remembered events. As a consequence, events are not connected to each other along spatiotemporal dimensions.

Although each proposal—declarative versus procedural memories, explicit versus implicit learning, episodic versus semantic memories, encoding context versus encoding content—has been debated, the basic data has not. Research should be directed toward explaining these data. Each proposed distinction appears to be focusing on something that is as central to any theory of memory as the distinction between short-term and long-term memory. A full understanding of the implications of these distinctions is essential for the building of a model of memory. Research that would aggressively determine the empirical basis for such distinctions as procedural versus declarative memory should be encouraged. As noted, Hirst et al.'s (1986) results suggest that some aspect of declarative memory may be intact with amnesia. Thus the amnesia syndrome does not place a clear cleavage between declarative and procedural memory. Hirst et al. (1986) suggest that it may be wrong to argue for qualitatively different forms of memory. Rather, they propose that emphasis should be placed on understanding qualitative differences in the way normal subjects and amnesiacs encode, retrieve, and represent information. Amnesiacs may be able to learn perceptual-motor skills and not a list of words because learning of the latter requires them to store the context in which the words were learned and to form associations between them, whereas the encoding of context and the formation of interlist associations is less important for the learning of perceptual-motor skills or the learning involved in priming or recognition. Research that goes beyond the discovery of dissociations and the establishment of different memory systems should be encouraged. A better understanding of the way amnesiacs encode, retrieve, and represent information is now needed.

A fuller understanding of amnesiac encoding, retrieval, and representation will permit a finer discussion of qualitatively different structures and processes in the memory system. The simple distinction between procedural and declarative memory is interesting, but it does not provide the kind of foothold needed by someone interested in training. If a person has difficulty learning declarative memories and not procedural memories, it does not help to know that these two might be qualitatively different when developing a training strategy. It would be better if one knew what about the way a person encoded, retrieved, and represented information made it difficult for them to learn declarative memories. For instance, if the problem is with the use of contextual information to aid retrieval, then training could be focused on ameliorating this deficit, either by overcoming it or by finding ways to circumvent it. Thus a fuller understanding of the amnesia syndrome may not only clarify the distinction between procedural and declarative memory but may also provide more refined categories on which a more sophisticated training strategy may be developed.

Implications for a Subsystem Approach for Training and Instruction   Careful articulation of the subsystems of memory has implications for training and instruction. Any training and instructional program should consist of two phases: evaluation and training. In the evaluation phase tests should be given to determine individuals' strengths and weaknesses. These evaluations can then be used to assign trainees to the second phase: the instruction per se. The trainer could use the evaluation to assign trainees to an instructional program that stresses their strengths. People with good quantitative ability might be assigned to a program that teaches them to program computers. When there is no job or training program that fits a person's strengths, the evaluation can be used to target weaknesses and the trainee can be placed in a program that works with the weaknesses.

The success of this two-phase procedure will depend on the degree to which the evaluation procedure actually taps distinct abilities and the degree to which one can relate the distinct abilities to the tasks taught in the training. If the evaluations are not based on a componential analysis but on categories from folk psychology, it might not effectively measure individuals' strengths and weaknesses. Again, Kosslyn illustrates the point. Consider a test that examines subjects' ability to image rather than their ability to transform, preserve, or generate an image. The test might indicate that a particular trainee has poor imaging abilities, and, as a consequence, that trainee might not be put into a training program that requires good image generation. But this person might be quite good at generating images. He or she might have difficulty with image retention. The evaluation would fail to pick this up, and a good trainee would be lost. Similarly a trainee with putatively poor imaging skills might be put into a training program that focuses on building general imaging skills. This assignment would also be a mistake, inasmuch as the trainee does not need training on image generation.

The same procedure can be followed for the evaluation of memory strengths and weaknesses. For an effective evaluation strategy one must determine the subsystems underlying memory abilities and then use this information to construct evaluation procedures that assess each subsystem. Of course, one does not have to worry about the relevance of the discovery of mnemonic systems to training and instruction in order to do research on this issue. Simply wanting to know about the architecture of memory is motivation enough. So, as far as the discovery of subsystems goes, such discoveries may have implications for evaluation and hence training and instruction, but scientists doing the work do not have to worry about applications in order to produce useful knowledge. It is probably best to leave cognitive scientists to their own devices.

Determining the Subsystems Used When Completing a Task   Tying research goals to practical concerns and applications becomes important when trying to determine the circumstances under which various subsystems are used. It is not enough to simply know what the subsystems are; one must also know how and when they are used. Processing subsystems probably do not mimic the overt behavior internally. Two tasks that seem quite similar on the surface may involve quite different subsystems. Alternatively two quite different tasks may draw on many of the same processing subsystems. Ice and water may seem quite different on the surface, but their underlying structure is quite similar. For example, to build on Kosslyn's chapter once again, image transformation and image generation may share a subsystem, even though on the surface they seem quite different. Transforming an object in an image (for example, imaging an object rotating) may be a noisy process, and hence a subsystem that realigns scrambled parts may be used. This subsystem in turn may draw on another subsystem that looks up in memory the proper alignment of the parts [see Kosslyn (this volume) for further details]. Image generation involves the process of forming a short-term-memory visual representation on the basis of information stored in long-term memory. Thus both image generation and image transformation require a person to look up in memory the spatial relations among parts of an object. Kosslyn has argued that much progress has been made in understanding what imagery tasks call on what subsystems, although clearly much research still needs to be done.

Schacter (personal communication) makes a similar point when he discusses a patient with a severe memory deficit following a stroke. The company the patient worked for decided to transfer her to the mailroom. They thought that a mail clerk performed menial tasks, and hence the patient could easily handle the job. She could not. It turned out that she performed well as a keypunch operator. Mail clerks use their memory constantly—in sorting the mail, in deciphering telegraphic addresses, and in plotting out their delivery route. A keypunch operator, however, places few demands on memory. Thus it is not enough to classify a job as menial or "higher level." A job that may be higher on the pay scale may make fewer demands on memory than a lesser paying job. Only a detailed task analysis can determine the demand characteristics of the job.

Cognitive scientists are task analyzers par excellence. They specialize in reducing a task to its components, and they have the requisite skills for determining which subsystems are involved in a particular task. But this analysis is not straightforward and requires careful experimentation and model building, often involving computer simulation. Thus, if there are tasks that need examination, it pays to emphasize them.

At present, such contact does not exist. If a trainee must learn to identify different ships, then there is no reason why ships cannot serve as the stimulus material for an experiment instead of nonsense shapes, pictures of faces, or words. If one starts with understanding the circumstances under which various subsystems of memory are used to memorize faces, one must still study whether the principles learned in the face study generalize to ships. This extra step could be avoided if the aim of the study was made clear from the start.

Designing Instruction Programs   We have suggested that cognitive scientists be urged to continue to discover the subsystems of memory. A careful articulation of these subsystems should include a means of evaluating individual differences. Moreover, it should involve the articulation of circumstances under which these subsystems are used, particularly in tasks relevant to the aims of an instructional institution. Such knowledge can be gathered by asking cognitive scientists to keep these aims in mind while designing research tasks. The research program that we have in mind, then, has several stages. For instance, cognitive scientists might be told that trainees must learn the procedure for repairing complex equipment. The scientists first determine what subsystems are needed for such learning and then develop a means of evaluating strengths and weaknesses of these subsystems in individuals. The training institution can then evaluate recruits and assign them to training programs emphasizing their strengths. If people with the requisite strengths cannot be found, then the weaknesses of the potential trainees should be assessed and instruction should be targeted to overcome these weaknesses. This research program has practical consequences—effective evaluation—but is based on research squarely focused on the discovery of the architecture of memory. Such close interaction between the development of evaluative instruments and work on the mental architecture has heretofore been missing and should serve as a major aim for future research.

We still have not said a great deal about instruction. We have emphasized that instruction should be geared to trainees' strengths or weaknesses. That is, if the trainees are bad at image generation and the task you want them to learn involves image generation, then instruction should focus on improving their ability to generate images. How this is done will, of course, depend on what has to be taught. There is, of course, a vast research enterprise concerned with education and instruction, and we will not comment on this line of research. Hirst makes the suggestion that memorization conducted involuntarily is as effective as memorization conducted voluntarily. He illustrates his points with a number of experiments from cognitive psychology but admits that more research needs to be done. We concur. He also suggests that the to-be-learned task be structured so that it is easily memorable. Hirst is arguing that human factors engineers consider memory and training demands and performance demands when designing equipment. Again, we concur.

In making these points, Hirst in essence is claiming that the expectation of a memory test has little bearing on subsequent memory for past events. Hirst asserts that, in teaching people to identify different ships, it does not matter whether you explicitly teach them to identify the features of the ship or embed the feature-learning task in a game that requires feature detection for success. But clearly there must be an interaction between the way something is taught and the way it is tested. For instance, a person who explicitly learns the features of ships may more easily be able to verbalize what these features are than a person who learns the features in the context of a game. Thus, in designing instruction, one must first decide not only what knowledge trainees must acquire but also how they must produce this knowledge.

This distinction between knowing and manifesting this knowledge is similar to the one that we argued was deserving of further research, that is, the one between explicit and implicit knowledge or between procedural and declarative knowledge. Many of the relevant theoretical questions are also similar. In particular, we must determine whether verbalizable knowledge is stored in different locations, processed differently, or represented differently from nonverbalizable knowledge. Information is usually taught explicitly in the classroom, and subsequently testing usually requires verbalization. But it is rarely the case that this knowledge must be verbalized on the job. It just has to be used. For this reason it is important to determine whether explicit instruction aids, interferes, or has no effect on the actual conduct of the job for which the employee is trained. Does verbalizable knowledge help when learning a skill? Will it help people to learn to identify ships if they first learn explicative features of the ships? Or does such verbalizable knowledge function independently of the knowledge that governs the actual identification? Moreover, are there certain conditions under which verbalizable knowledge does interact with the knowledge governing skills? And in drawing the distinction between these two forms of knowledge is it best to draw the line by considering verbalizations or by considering the degree to which the information is explicitly recalled? As far as we know, these questions still await an answer.

Final Considerations and Specific Recommendations

Although lists are usually dangerous affairs, because they are so naked and explicit, several themes do emerge from our present discussion and the chapters themselves. Consequently we conclude this discussion with a brief statement of each of the themes. They essentially point to the direction present research on memory is taking or should take.

1. *There should be a continued development of a theory of the biological basis of memory.* The neuroscience of memory has progressed rapidly in the past few years, and research along the same lines, with the same priorities, should continue to prove fruitful.

2. *To a limited extent, research directed toward finding a drug to improve memory should be done. Emphasis, however, should be given to so-called cognitive enhancers as opposed to specific "memory drugs."* Although it has proven difficult to develop drugs that are specifically targeted to improving memory, drugs that have a more general effect on cognition may prove useful as a memory aid. The relevance of the new cognitive enhancers currently being developed at Squibb and Ayerst should be investigated.

3. *A close tie between the neuroscience of memory and the cognitive science of memory should be developed.* Research should be done to establish whether the various biochemical and physiological models of memory do indeed have anything to do with memory. This research should include behavioral work investigating conditioning and simple learning in vertebrates and should examine more complex aspects of memory, especially what psychologists concerned with human memory call free recall. The research on long-term potentiation should be encouraged. But more important, the connection between long-term potentiation and memory must be better mapped out. Of course, before this mapping can be done convincingly, there must be some general understanding about what memory is or should include. To this end, emphasis should be placed on interdisciplinary work between cognitive scientists and neuroscientists that focuses on essential definitional issues. As far as a unified theory of memory goes, it is probably premature to expect a theory of memory that accounts for both biological and psychological data. Nevertheless, there is enough interest among neuroscientists and cognitive scientists in the goal of a unified theory that discussions among them, no matter how preliminary, should be encouraged. Currently the fields are in the tunnel together, and some workers can see the light at the end of the tunnel. Nevertheless, there is still a great distance to travel, and the light is still quite dim.

4. *The development of connectionist models that have a strong tie to research in neuroscience should be encouraged.* As a better under-

standing develops of the cognitive science and neuroscience of memory, research should be done to study the means by which various anatomical and physiological constraints on the nervous system can be incorporated into parallel distributed networks. Along the same lines, PDP models should be used to study the function of these anatomical and physiological constraints. At present, PDP models do not have the tight connection with the work of neuroscience that their structure suggests. More must be done to make neuroscience computational and to make computational cognitive science constrained by neuroscience.

5. *Research on the subsystems of memory, especially the subsystems that underlie procedural and declarative memories and implicit and explicit learning, should be encouraged.* As we have argued, it is necessary for both instruction and evaluation to know what the subsystems of memory are. Although much work has been done already, the distinction between procedural and declarative memory (and related distinctions) still needs a strong theoretical foundation if it is to prove useful. Research on the architecture of memory should include standard cognitive psychological experiments, neuropsychological experiments with brain-damaged patients, and experiments using various brain imaging techniques. Model building may involve computer simulations.

6. *Work on the subsystems of imagery should be continued.* Work on imagery has guided much of the research program we have outlined for memory. For this reason imagery research should be vigorously extended. It has reached the stage at which knowledge about the architecture of imagery can now be applied to practical problems, such as the use of imagery in navigation.

7. *Evaluative instruments should be designed in accordance with new knowledge about the architecture of the memory system.* Much of the current means of evaluation is based on outdated knowledge about what the memory system is like. These means should be assessed on the basis of new information in cognitive science, and, where they no longer provide the kind of fine-grained assessment dictated by a subsystems approach, the instruments should be redesigned.

8. *Researchers should be made aware of the kinds of tasks used by the work force. Research should then be directed toward understanding what subsystems are involved in successful performance of these tasks.* It is not enough to discover what the subsystems are. One must also understand how and when they are used. Here it pays to tailor the experimental task to the practical concerns of the relevant funding agency.

9. *The relation between implicit and explicit learning or verbalizable and nonverbalizable knowledge should be understood, and the impact of the research results on instruction should be investigated.* Instruction often involves teaching trainees to verbalize knowledge that is relevant to some task. The ability to verbalize knowledge may have little to do with the actual performance of the task. Research must determine if and when explicit knowledge bears on the performance of a task.

References

Ader, R., and D. de Wied. 1972. "Effects of lysine vasopressin on passive avoidance learning." *Psychonomic Science* 29:46–48.

Atkinson, R. C., and R. M. Shiffrin. 1968. "Human memory: A proposed system and its control processes," in *The Psychology of Learning and Motivation: Advances in Research and Theory,* K. W. Spence and J. T. Spence, eds. New York: Academic Press, vol. 2, 89–195.

Baddeley, A. D. 1976. *The Psychology of Memory.* New York: Basic Books.

Baddeley, A. D. 1982. "Domains of recollection." *Psychological Review* 89:708–729.

Bohus, B. 1977. "Effect of desglycinamide-lysine vasopressin (DG-LVP) on sexually motivated T-maze behavior of the male rat." *Hormones and Behavior* 8:509–517.

Bohus, B., G. Kovacs, and D. de Wied. 1978. "Oxytocin, vasopressin and memory: Opposite effects on consolidation and retrieval processes." *Brain Research* 157:414–417.

Cermak, L. S., N. Talbot, K. Chandler, and L. R. Wolbarst. 1985. "The perceptual priming phenomenon in amnesia." *Neuropsychologia* 23:615–622.

Cohen, N. J. 1984. "Amnesia and the distinction between procedural and declarative knowledge," in *The Neuropsychology of Memory,* N. Butters and L. R. Squire, eds. New York: Guilford Press, 83–103.

Cohen, N. J., and L. R. Squire. 1980. "Preserved learning and retention of pattern-analyzing skill in amnesia: Dissociation between 'knowing how' and 'knowing that.'" *Science* 210:207–209.

Davies, P., and A. J. F. Maloney. 1976. "Selective loss of central cholinergic neurons in Alzheimer's disease." *Lancet* 2:1403.

Deutsch, J. A. 1971. "The cholinergic synapse and the site of memory." *Science* 174:788–794.

Deutsch, J. A., M. D. Hamburg, and H. Dahl. 1966. "Anticholinesterase-induced amnesia and its temporal aspects." *Science* 151:211–223.

Eich, E. 1985. "Context, memory, and integrated item/context imagery." *Journal of Experimental Psychology: Learning, Memory, and Cognition* 11:764–770.

Gold, P. E., and R. van Bushkirk. 1976. "Effects of posttrial hormone injections on memory processes." *Hormones and Behavior* 7:509–517.

Gold, P. W., H. Wiengartner, J. C. Ballenger, F. K. Goddwin, and R. M. Post. 1979. "Effects of 1-desamo-8-*d*-arginine vasopressin on behavior and cognition in primary affective disorder." *Lancet* 2:992–994.

Graf, P., and D. L. Schacter. 1985. "Implicit and explicit memory for new associations in normal and amnesia subjects." *Journal of Experimental Psychology: Learning, Memory, and Cognition* 11:508–518.

Hasher, L., and R. Zacks. 1979. "Automatic and effortful processes in memory." *Journal of Experimental Psychology: General* 108:356–368.

Hebb, D. O. 1949. *The Organization of Behavior*. New York: Wiley.

Herrnstein, R. J., R. S. Nickerson, M. de Sanchez, and J. A. Swets. 1986. "Teaching thinking skills." *American Psychologist* 41:1279–1289.

Hirst, W. 1982. "The amnesic syndrome: Descriptions and explanations." *Psychological Bulletin* 91:435–460.

Hirst, W. 1987. "Cognitive psychologists become interested in neuroscience," in *The Making of Cognitive Science*, W. Hirst, ed. New York: Cambridge University Press.

Hirst, W., and B. T. Volpe. 1982. "Temporal order judgments with amnesia." *Brain and Cognition* 1:294–306.

Hirst, W., and B. T. Volpe. 1984a. "Automatic and effortful encoding in amnesia," in *The Handbook of Cognitive Neuroscience*, M. S. Gazzaniga, ed. New York: Plenum, 369–386.

Hirst, W., and B. T. Volpe. 1984b. "Encoding of spatial relations with amnesia." *Neuropsychologia* 22:631–634.

Hirst, W., E. A. Phelps, M. K. Johnson, and B. T. Volpe. 1987. "The effectiveness of different retrieval cues in amnesics."

Hirst, W., M. K. Johnson, J. K. Kim, E. A. Phelps, G. Risse, and B. T. Volpe. 1986. "Recognition and recall in amnesics." *Journal of Experimental Psychology: Learning, Memory, and Cognition* 12:445–451.

Huppert, F., and J. A. Deutsch. 1969. "Improvement in memory with time." *Quarterly Journal of Experimental Psychology* 21:267–271.

Jacoby, L. L., and D. Whiterspoon. 1982. "Remembering without awareness." *Canadian Journal of Psychology* 36:300–324.

Karis, D., M. Fabiani, and E. Donchin. 1984. "P300 and memory: Individual differences in the von Restorff effect." *Cognitive Psychology* 16:177–216.

Kintsch, W. 1970. *Learning, Memory and Conceptual Processes*. New York: Wiley.

Krejci, I., and B. Kepkova. 1978. "Effects of vasopressin analogues on passive avoidance behavior." *Activitas Nervosa Superior* 20:11–12.

Legros, J. J., P. Gilot, X. Seron, J. Claessens, A. Adams, J. M. Moeglen, A. Audibert, and P. Bercheir. 1978. "Influence of vasopressin on learning and memory." *Lancet* 1:41–42.

Leshner, A. I., and K. E. Roche. 1977. "Comparisons of the effects of ACTH and lysine vasopressin on avoidance of attack in mice." *Physiology and Behavior* 18:879–883.

Mandler, G. 1980. "Recognizing: The judgment of previous occurrence." *Psychological Review* 87:252–271.

Mayes, A. R., P. R. Meudell, and A. Pickering. 1985. "Is organic amnesia caused by a selective deficit in remembering contextual information?" *Cortex* 21:167–202.

Milner, B., S. Corkin, and H. L. Teuber. 1968. "Further analysis of the hippocampal amnesic syndrome. Fourteen year follow-up study of H.M." *Neuropsychologia* 6:215–234.

Pearce, J. M. S., ed. 1984. *Dementia: A Clinical Approach*. Oxford: Blackwell Scientific.

Peters, S., and R. Richie. 1973. "On the generative power of transformational grammars." *Information Sciences* 6:49–83.

Schacter, D. L. 1987a. "Implicit and explicit learning" *Journal of Experimental Psychology: Learning, Memory, and Cognition* 13:501–518.

Schacter, D. 1987b. "Memory, amnesia, and frontal lobe dysfunction." *Psychobiology* 15:21–36.

Schacter, D. L., J. Harbluck, and D. R. McLachlan. 1984. "Retrieval without recollection: An experimental analysis of source amnesia." *Journal of Verbal Learning and Verbal Behavior* 23:593–611.

Smith, M. L., and B. Milner. 1981. "The role of the right hippocampus in the recall of spatial location." *Neuropsychologia* 19:781–794.

Smith, S. M. 1979. "Remembering in and out of context." *Journal of Experimental Psychology: Human Learning and Memory* 5:460–471.

Squire, L. R. 1982. "The neuropsychology of human memory." *Annual Review of Neuroscience* 5:241–273.

Squire, L. R., and H. P. Davis. 1981. "The pharmacology of memory: A neurobiological perspective." *Annual Review of Pharmacology and Toxicology* 21:323–356.

Summers, W. K., L. V. Majovski, G. M. Marsch, K. Tachiki, and A. Kling. 1986. "Tetrahydroaminoacridine in long-term treatment of senile dementia, Alzheimer-type." *New England Journal of Medicine* 315:1241–1245.

Tulving, E. 1983. *Elements of Episodic Memory.* New York: Oxford University Press.

Warrington, E., and L. Weiskrantz. 1971. "Amnesic syndrome: Consolidation or retrieval?" *Nature* 228:628–630.

Index